THE **COMPLETE** **IDIOT**'S **GUIDE**®

D0807530

Learning German

Fourth Edition

Revisions by Lisa Graham

by Alicia Müller and Stephan Müller

ALPHA

A member of Penguin Group (USA) Inc.

ALPHA BOOKS

Published by Penguin Group (USA) Inc.

Penguin Group (USA) Inc., 375 Hudson Street, New York, New York 10014, USA • Penguin Group (Canada), 90 Eglinton Avenue East, Suite 700, Toronto, Ontario M4P 2Y3, Canada (a division of Pearson Penguin Canada Inc.) • Penguin Books Ltd., 80 Strand, London WC2R 0RL, England • Penguin Ireland, 25 St. Stephen's Green, Dublin 2, Ireland (a division of Penguin Books Ltd.) • Penguin Group (Australia), 250 Camberwell Road, Camberwell, Victoria 3124, Australia (a division of Pearson Australia Group Pty. Ltd.) • Penguin Books India Pvt. Ltd., 11 Community Centre, Panchsheel Park, New Delhi—110 017, India • Penguin Group (NZ), 67 Apollo Drive, Rosedale, North Shore, Auckland 1311, New Zealand (a division of Pearson New Zealand Ltd.) • Penguin Books (South Africa) (Pty.) Ltd., 24 Sturdee Avenue, Rosebank, Johannesburg 2196, South Africa • Penguin Books Ltd., Registered Offices: 80 Strand, London WC2R 0RL, England

Copyright © 2013 by Amaranth

International Standard Book Number: 978-1-61564-314-1
Library of Congress Catalog Card Number: Available upon request

15   14   8 7 6 5 4 3 2

Interpretation of the printing code: The rightmost number of the first series of numbers is the year of the book's printing; the rightmost number of the second series of numbers is the number of the book's printing. For example, a printing code of 13-1 shows that the first printing occurred in 2013.

Printed in the United States of America

Note: This publication contains the opinions and ideas of its authors. It is intended to provide helpful and informative material on the subject matter covered. It is sold with the understanding that the authors, book producer, and publisher are not engaged in rendering professional services in the book. If the reader requires personal assistance or advice, a competent professional should be consulted.

The authors, book producer, and publisher specifically disclaim any responsibility for any liability, loss, or risk, personal or otherwise, which is incurred as a consequence, directly or indirectly, of the use and application of any of the contents of this book.

Most Alpha books are available at special quantity discounts for bulk purchases for sales promotions, premiums, fund-raising, or educational use. Special books, or book excerpts, can also be created to fit specific needs. For details, write: Special Markets, Alpha Books, 375 Hudson Street, New York, NY 10014.

Publisher: *Mike Sanders*	**Production Editor:** *Jana M. Stefanciosa*
Executive Managing Editor: *Billy Fields*	**Copy Editor:** *Louise Lund*
Acquisitions Editor: *Tom Stevens*	**Cover Designer:** *William Thomas*
Book Producer: *Lee Ann Chearneyi/ Amaranth@LuminAreStudio*	**Book Designers:** *William Thomas, Rebecca Batchelor*
	Indexer: *Brad Herriman*
Senior Development Editor: *Christy Wagner*	**Layout:** *Brian Massey, Ayanna Lacey*
Development Editor: *Nancy Lewis*	**Proofreader:** *Gene Redding*

Contents

Introduction

In the last hundred years, parts of the world that we would have had to travel months by boat to reach are now just a few hours away. There are, however, many other ways of traveling. We travel in books, in movies, and on the internet, through video chatting online, and—don't forget—we travel also in our imaginations.

Some people believe that the soul of a culture resides in the grammatical patterns, in the linguistic intricacies, and in the phonetics of its language. The authors of this book share this view. If bank robberies aren't your thing, learning German may be the next most satisfying and effective way of enriching yourself fast.

The German language reveals German books, people, and customs in ways that are lost in translation. If you plan a trip to a German-speaking country, even before you get on a plane, you should have the basic tools with which to decipher the code of the culture you're about to enter. Many chapters in this book are held together thematically as if you were off on an imaginary journey to a German-speaking land. In Chapter 11 you'll learn vocabulary related to air travel and airports. In Chapter 12 you'll learn how to tell your bus or taxi driver where you're going. By the end of Chapter 13 you'll be able to ask the desk clerk for the kind of room you want.

Each chapter builds on the one that preceded it, expanding on what you have learned. Learning a new language is, after all, a bit like evolving rapidly from neophyte to expert. First you learn to familiarize yourself with the new sounds of the German language, and then you learn to progress proudly through basic grammar and vocabulary. When you can keep your balance with everything you've learned, you're well on your way to enjoying conversations with patient Berliners or the Viennese.

The Sum of Its Parts

Part 1, Learning German Basics, starts by outlining why German is a tremendously important language and how it will be of use to you as a student, businessperson, or tourist. Not only will you learn all about the advantages of reading German texts in the original, but you'll find out how much you already know (before you've even started learning anything). You'll also learn German consonant and vowel sounds.

Part 2, Ready, Set, Go! introduces you to a selection of common German idioms (expressions in which the meaning is not predictable from the usual meaning of the words that make it up) and slang. You'll get your first taste of German grammar, and you'll be able to use what you know of German through cognates. By the end of this part, you'll be engaging in and understanding simple conversations.

Part 3, Up, Up, and Away, introduces you to the vocabulary and grammar you'll need to plan and take a trip to a German-speaking country. You'll use the real greetings Germans use with each other; you'll introduce yourself and give elementary descriptions. You'll ask basic questions. A chapter at a time, you'll arrive at an airport, catch a taxi or a bus, and make your way to the hotel of your choice. Most important, you'll be able to get the room you want furnished with all those indispensable things (cable television, extra blankets, hair dryers, and so on) that many of us cannot do without when we travel. Then you'll be able to go out and search for addresses, address a postcard, decipher a phone number, or exchange your dollars for euros and francs.

Part 4, Out and About in Germany, furnishes you with the vocabulary you'll need to do practically anything fun, from playing tennis to going to the opera to night-clubbing. You'll also learn how to make sense out of the weather report, whether it's in the newspaper, on TV, or revealed to you via the aches and pains in the bones of the local baker. The chapter on food will help you understand where to buy all kinds of food in Germany and how to interpret a German menu. Finally, you'll be introduced to the phrases and vocabulary words you'll need to go on a shopping spree for chocolates, silk shirts, and Rolexes while the exchange rate is still high.

Part 5, Angst: Solving Problems on the Go, prepares you for the inevitable difficulties that crop up when you travel. You'll learn how to make local and long-distance phone calls from a German phone and how to explain yourself to the operator if you have problems getting through. Is your watch broken? Do you need film for your camera? Did some food stain your new shirt? You'll be ready to take care of anything, to ask for help, and to explain what happened to your German friends or colleagues when your angst-ridden moments are (hopefully) distant memories.

Part 6, When in Germany, Do as the Germans Do, instructs you in the terminology you'll need for an extended stay in Deutschland. By the end of this part, you should be able to buy or rent a house, an apartment, or even a castle (if extravagance appeals to you). You'll also be able to express your needs in the future tense.

In the appendixes, the **Answer Key** gives you the answers to the exercises you perform in this book. The **Lexicon: English to German, German to English** translates essential vocabulary and lists the pronunciation of each.

Bonus Audio CD

The Complete Idiot's Guide to Learning German, Fourth Edition, includes an audio CD specifically developed to accompany the book. The object of listening to the audio is to engage your senses and give you a chance to work on your pronunciation skills for certain words and phrases in the book. Track 1 leads you in to the many pronunciation exercises.

Extras

Besides the idiomatic expressions, helpful phrases, lists of vocabulary words, and down-to-earth grammar, this book has useful information that is provided in sidebars throughout the text. These elements are distinguished by the following icons.

DEFINITION

These sidebars give you definitions of grammatical terms. Many foreign words have been adopted by the German language and still retain their foreign pronunciation. These words do not follow the German pronunciation guide included in this book.

GERMAN CULTURE

These sidebars provide facts about interesting facets of life in Germany and other German-speaking cultures. They offer you quick glimpses into the German culture.

WE ARE FAMILY

These sidebars tell you all about the linguistic connections between German and our own language, English.

AS A RULE

These sidebars highlight or expand on some aspect of German grammar that has been touched on in the text, usually summing it up in a rule so that it's easier to remember.

ACHTUNG

These sidebars warn you of mistakes that are commonly made by those who are learning the German language and offer advice about how to avoid these mistakes yourself.

Trademarks

All terms mentioned in this book that are known to be or are suspected of being trademarks or service marks have been appropriately capitalized. Alpha Books and Penguin Group (USA) Inc. cannot attest to the accuracy of this information. Use of a term in this book should not be regarded as affecting the validity of any trademark or service mark.

Learning German Basics

Here is your first introduction to the building blocks of the German language: pronouncing vowels and consonants—and dipthongs, too. You'll learn about cognates and how to use quinessentially German idiomatic expressions. You might be surprised to learn that German is the most spoken language in the European Union and is one of the 10 most spoken languages on Earth. No matter your reason for being irresistably drawn to the German language, this part will help you take the plunge and pronounce. You already know more than you think.

Learning German

In This Chapter

- Advantages of learning German
- Using a bilingual dictionary
- Why German and English are similar

If you think that you'll only need to know German if you travel to or communicate with people in Germany, Austria, or Switzerland, think again. German is the most frequently spoken mother tongue in the European Union and one of the 10 most widely spoken languages in the world. While learning German can connect you to 120 million native speakers around the globe, consider the fact that millions of people also learn German as a second language. It is the third most popular language taught worldwide and the second most popular language taught in Europe and Japan after English. Furthermore, your chances of encountering a German speaker in the United States, or wherever you make your home, may be greater than you think. Germans rank number one in the world in travel.

Why Learn German?

German culture has shaped certain disciplines to such a degree that, in many schools and universities, you can't get away with not taking a basic German language course if you're studying art history, psychology, chemistry, or philosophy. After all, about 1 in 10 books published throughout the world has been written in German. The German book-publishing industry as a whole ranks third in the world behind England and China, traditionally producing over a third more new titles each year than the United States. If technology is your thing, bear in mind that German is one of the most frequently used languages on the internet, and ".de" (an abbreviation for *Deutsch*, "German") is the world's most widely used country-specific domain. While Silicon Valley might be the first location that comes to mind when you think about innovation in technology, the Munich area forms the world's fourth largest concentration of hardware and software producers.

Knowledge of German will give you access not only to rich literary, philosophical, and artistic traditions, but also to many other kinds of contemporary cultural, economic, political, and scientific developments.

Business Benefits of German

In addition, many businesses, industries, and specialties such as medicine and science use German terms, particularly those with international markets or affiliations. Germany has the largest economy in the European Union and the fourth largest in the world. An attractive center for investors, there are 45,000 foreign companies representing the world's 500 largest firms. Many German industrial enterprises are known throughout the world and have branches or research facilities overseas.

A leading exporter of machinery, vehicles, chemicals, and household equipment, Germany's economy is inexorably linked to the United States. It is one of Germany's most important trading partners and is the second largest market for German products. So get way ahead of your colleagues and learn German. Not only will you find it interesting and enriching, but it'll lead you to a greater appreciation of a foreign culture and enhance your global understanding.

Getting Serious About German

Having a clear sense of why you're learning German can help you maximize your efforts. Take a moment to consider your motives:

- If you're learning German to be able chat at *Oktoberfest*, you may not need to spend a lot of time on cases and grammatical paradigms beyond basic sentence structure. Instead you'll want to focus on vocabulary and phrases that'll help you get around Germany and get to know its people.

- If music is your thing, you'll have a head start with German musical terms such as *die Lieder* and *das Leitmotif* that pop up in music from Mozart to Lady Gaga. And you'll be able to fine-tune your pronunciation so that even the last row will be able to understand your rendering of *die Walküren*.

- If your goal is to be able to read German, you may want to focus on the cognate section of this book—that is, the noun and verb sections. Additionally, figuring out how German structures its sentences will help you decipher who is doing what to whom and to develop the patience to wait for the verb. Never fear! All this German grammar jargon will make perfect sense to you as you pursue your studies with this book as your guide.

If you determine what you want to achieve with your knowledge of the German language, you can easily tailor this book to your needs and use it to your advantage.

Look It Up

Whatever your particular needs are, a bilingual dictionary is essential to your learning. In addition to providing an accurate translation, a good German-English/English-German dictionary supplies grammatical information, field labels that differentiate various meanings of the word, and style labels that mark words and phrases that are not neutral in style level or that are no longer current in the language. What do you need to know to use a bilingual dictionary? Be forewarned: using a bilingual dictionary is a little more involved than using an English dictionary. After finding the German translation for an English word in the English section, take a moment to look up the German word in the German section. It may not have the meaning you were intending—in English, we can "spend time and money," but German has two different words for "to spend": *verbringen* (*feR-bRin-guhn*), with time, and *ausgeben* (*ous-gey-buhn*), with money.

If an electronic device is a natural extension of your hand, online bilingual dictionaries such as WordReference.com supply similar information. After finding the German word you're looking for, be sure to take a moment to look up and confirm the German word in the German section to make sure you've secured the right word.

In order to make sense of dictionaries, you'll need to be familiar with the grammatical abbreviations used in the entries. Here are a few of them:

adj.	Adjective
adv.	Adverb
f.	Feminine noun
m.	Masculine noun
n.	Noun
nt.	Neuter noun

pl.   Plural noun

prep.   Preposition. Prepositions are words such as *above, along, beyond, before, through, in, to,* and *for* that are placed—or pre-positioned—before nouns to indicate a relationship to other words in a sentence. Or, think of them in terms of "anywhere a cat can go." We discuss prepositions further in Chapter 11.

v.i.   Intransitive verb. An intransitive verb can stand alone, without a direct object, as *travel* does in the sentence "I travel."

v.r.   Reflexive verb. The object of a reflexive verb refers back to the subject itself, as in "I kicked myself."

v.t.   Transitive verb. A transitive verb must be followed by a direct object, as in "I saw a cat." Unlike intransitive verbs, transitive verbs cannot stand on their own.

In addition to labeling the parts of speech, dictionary entries often contain "field labels," which identify various subject areas that an entry may refer to and give the reader a better "sense" of the word. These may include *comput.* (computer), *mech.* (mechanical), *sport, med.* (medical), and *chem.* (chemistry). Words not used freely as part of the standard vocabulary are given "style labels" so that the reader can make useful judgments about the setting in which a term might be appropriate. Here are some possible style labels to guide actual language usage:

dated   This indicates that the word now sounds somewhat old-fashioned, although it is still occasionally used.

fig.   Figurative refers to nonliteral, metaphorical uses of words, as in figures of speech.

form.   Formal. Formal language is used on official forms, for official communications, and in formal speeches.

inf./coll. Informal or colloquial. Informal language is colloquial, typically used in an informal conversational context or in email. It is inappropriate in more formal speech or writing.

old/obs   Old or obsolete refers to words that are no longer in current use and that the reader will normally only find in classical literature.

sl.   Slang. Slang words and phrases are highly informal and are appropriate only in very restricted contexts.

Using a Bilingual Dictionary

If you look up the verb "change" in an English/German dictionary, you will see something like this:

> **change**   1. *transitives Verb* a. (switch) wechseln; **change one's clothes,** sich umziehen; **change one's address/name**, seine Anschrift/seinen Namen ändern; **change trains/buses**, umsteigen; b. (*transform*) verwandeln (**into** in + Akk.); (*alter*) ändern; c. (*exchange*) eintauschen (**for** für); wechseln [Geld]
>
> 2. *intransitives Verb* a. (alter) sich ändern; **person, land;** sich verändern; b. **(into something else)** sich verwandeln; c. **(put on other clothes)** sich umziehen; d. **(change trains, buses, etc.)** umsteigen

Whoa! What's so complicated about *change*? It all depends on what kind of changing you're doing. But German is specific about *change*, and this specificity is revealed in the dictionary entry. If you recall the difference between two types of verbs—transitive and intransitive—you'll be able to deduce that the first entry describes *change* that involves someone or something else (a direct object). The second entry contains *change* variations that do not involve something other than the subject to enact *change*. That is to say, German intransitive verbs of *change* are reflexive.

Time to Change

Using the dictionary entry of *change* just given, figure out which verb meaning "change" you would use in the following situations. Check your answers in Appendix A.

1. You're *changing* locations, moving to a larger house.

2. A caterpillar *changes* into a butterfly.

3. You need to *change* your clothes.

4. You need to *change* money.

5. You're traveling and need to *change* your modes of transportation.

Compounding Your German Vocabulary

You're likely to come across German compound words in everything you read from popular fiction and magazines to political essays, to blogs and websites. Because the possible combinations of nouns are practically unlimited, you can actually create your own compound words pretty much as you please by linking nouns together.

The ability to create words at will in German is one reason that this language has been so instrumental to many great thinkers. They have been able to express new concepts and ideas by *coining*, or making up, new words. The flip side to this flexibility is that these compound words are not easily translatable. To express the meaning of the single word *Zeitgeist* in English, for example, you have to use the cumbersome and rather spiritless phrase "spirit of the times." And this morphological process is not limited to combining two nouns to form a compound word. As in English, it's possible to combine adjectives such as *bittersweet* or verbs such as *sleepwalk* to form new words. There's even some mixing of the two languages, coupling the German preposition *über-* (*üh-buhR*), meaning "above," "beyond," and "super," with an English noun or adjective, as in *übertough* or *überstar*.

AS A RULE

Many German words in academic texts are compound words, and some of these compound words are not in the dictionary. A knowledge of basic German vocabulary will enable you to take apart those big, compound words and look up their components one by one in a bilingual dictionary. The more you rely on and trust your powers of deduction, the easier learning a foreign language becomes!

The Genetic Relationship Between German and English

Even the casual student soon becomes aware of many similarities between German and English. Although vocabulary correspondences are perhaps the most obvious, the two languages also share structural secrets—consider the way they form the comparative and superlative (*blond, blonder, blondest*) or the striking parallels in the verbal systems (*sing, sang, gesungen*). These similarities exist because English and German belong to the same language family, the Germanic family of languages, a relationship also shared by Danish, Icelandic, Norwegian, Swedish, and Dutch.

So what happened to cause the rift between English and German? An actual shift. No, not of Earth, but of consonants, which occurred in the southernmost reaches of the German-speaking lands some time around the fifth century. "Aha!" you exclaim triumphantly. That explains why it's *child* and *Kind, ship* and *Schiff, salt* and *Salz*.

The Least You Need to Know

- Whether you're a student, a businessperson, or someone in the arts field, learning the German language will give you a head start in understanding and assimilating German terms and phrases.

- A bilingual dictionary can help you tremendously in your study of German.

- Similarities between English and German will become more apparent to you as you continue your study of German. You truly do know more than you think you do!

Pronounce It Properly: Vowels

In This Chapter

- Oh, the stress of it all
- Peculiarities of the German language
- Untie your tongue

You think you have it bad with German pronunciation? Consider the English *rain*, *reign*, and *rein*—three words with different spellings and meanings but with identical pronunciations. You're going to have a much easier time learning German pronunciation because what you see is what you hear. German is what is called a phonetic language; German words are pronounced exactly as they are spelled. You don't ever have to wonder whether the *e* at the end of a word is silent, which it sometimes is and sometimes isn't in English. In German, it is always pronounced. This rule makes it easy to spell as well. You need simply to learn what sounds are represented by the letters in German.

Before you can pronounce German words correctly, however, you'll have to learn how to say the vowels, because the sounds of vowels in German are significantly different from the sounds of the same letters in English. Also, you should get comfortable enunciating every letter in a word. This chapter helps you figure out how to pronounce German vowels.

Vowels That May Mutate

Three German *vowels—a*, *o*, and *u*—may be written as such and pronounced similar to these sounds in English, or they may be written with two dots above them. These two dots are called an *umlaut* and signal a change in the sound and meaning of a

German word. The sounds represented by *ö* and *o* are just as different as the English *a* and *o* in "hat" and "hot." Here's just one example of how significant this difference in sound is: *schon* means "already"; *schön* means "beautiful" or "nice." The vowel tables in this chapter provide hints, English examples, and the letters used as symbols to represent the sounds of vowels in German words.

DEFINITION

Vowel sounds—*a, e, i, o,* and *u*—are produced without significant constriction of air.

Umlaut is the term for the two dots (diacritics—additional markings on written symbols) that can be placed over the vowels *a, o,* and *u*.

Linguistic Stress

No, linguistic *stress* isn't what happens to you when your Mercedes breaks down on the *Autobahn*. Stress is the emphasis placed on one or more syllables of a word when you pronounce it. A general rule for determining the stressed syllable in German is that the emphasis is usually placed on the first syllable, as in the words *Bleistift* (pencil), *Schönheit* (beauty), and *Kaugummi* (chewing gum), thanks to the accenting established in early Germanic.

DEFINITION

Stress is the emphasis placed on one or more syllables of a word when you pronounce it.

Foreign words such as *Hotel* and *Musik* have been assimilated into the German language. They do not follow German rules of stress although they do acquire German pronunciation of vowels. Such words maintain the lender language's stress patterns. Hence, *Hotel* and *Musik* retain their second syllable main stress, as in English.

Assuming an Accent

To pronounce words correctly in a new language, you must retrain your tongue. Those intuitive skills you used to *acquire* your first language will enable you to *learn* a foreign language. Don't worry if you can't make the exact German sound—chances are, what you're trying to communicate will be understood.

A Few Peculiarities of the German Language

The relationship between German pronunciation and spelling is much closer than the relationship between English pronunciation and spelling—no Great Vowel Shift or Norman Invasion to affect sound/symbol correspondences in German. After you learn how to pronounce German words correctly, reading them will be a breeze. You'll also be glad to hear that the German alphabet consists of the same 26 letters as the English alphabet, so you won't have to learn an entirely new alphabet as you would if you were studying Russian or Greek. Additionally, this same alphabet represents consistent sounds in German. There are, however, a few distinctly German language phenomena that you just can't do without.

The Umlaut

Remember those versatile two dots we spoke about earlier? In German, those two dots are known as an umlaut—literally, *um* ("around") + *Laut* ("sound"). The umlaut, really just a writing device to indicate another vowel sound, alters the sound of a vowel and results in a meaning change—it changes the sound. Sometimes the change is grammatical, as in a plural form and in the comparison of an adjective, but most of the time the change is lexical—that is, it produces an entirely different word. English has vestiges of the umlaut, observable in irregular forms such as *old/elder, mouse/ mice*, and *foot/feet*. When you say *foot/feet*, you should be able to feel your tongue slide forward; that slide is vowel mutation!

ACHTUNG

An umlaut can be added only to *a, o,* or *u*. It can never be added to the front vowels, *e* or *i*.

Capitalizing on Nouns

When you see half a dozen capital letters in the middle of a German sentence, they're not typos. One of the differences between written English and written German is that German nouns are always capitalized. This convention goes back to the Reformation when Martin Luther opted to capitalize those nouns he deemed significant, such as *Glaube (glou-buh)*, "faith" or "belief," and *Gott (got)*, "God"—perhaps the e. e. cummings of his time!

Compare this English sentence with the translated German sentence. Can you identify the nouns in this German proverb that is the equivalent of "Talk is cheap, silence is golden"?

Reden ist Silber, Schweigen ist Gold.
Talk is silver, silence is gold.

The unwavering capitalization of German nouns helps learners of German focus on content words and readily identify people, places, and things.

Classification of Vowel Sounds

When it comes to the pronunciation of vowels, keep in mind that vowel sounds are organized into three principal types. These three types of vowel sounds are referred to throughout this book as vowels, modified vowels, and diphthongs. We've already discussed vowels and modified vowels. In German, both of these groups can have long vowel sounds, which, as their name suggests, have a drawn-out vowel sound (like the *o* sound in *snow*) or shorter vowel sounds, which have a shorter sound (like the *o* sound in *both*). *Diphthongs* are combinations of vowels that are treated as a single vowel. They begin with one vowel sound and end with a glide, a vowel-like *y* or *w* sound in the same syllable, as in the words *dine* and *cow*. Diphthongs represent a sliding together of two vowel sounds.

Track 2 In the following pronunciation guide, each vowel appears in its own section. We try to give you an idea of how vowel sounds are pronounced by providing an English equivalent. Obviously, we cannot account for regional differences in either the German or English pronunciations of vowels and words. As you read this guide, remember that in English we have a tendency to glide, elongate, or "dipthongize" vowels, whereas in German vowels are "pure"—that is, they have a single sound. It may help to read the English pronunciation example first and then repeat each German word out loud for practice. You can also listen to Track 2 on the CD included with this book to get an idea of the proper pronunciation.

Say *a* as in *Spa*

For the short *a*, assume a British accent and make the sound of the vowel in the back of your throat. Say: *cast, fast*. Now read the following German words out loud:

Mann	Stadt	Rand	lachen	Matsch
mAn	*shtAt*	*rAnt*	*lA-CHuhn*	*mAtsh*
man, husband	city	frame	to laugh	mush

The long *a* is a prolongation of the short *a*. Pretend you're at the dentist's office and say: *ahhhhhhh*.

Wagen	haben	Staat	Mahl	lahm
vah-guhn	*hah-buhn*	*shtaht*	*mahl*	*lahm*
car	to have	state	meal	lame

German Letter	Symbol	Pronunciation Guide
a (short)	*A*	Close to *a* in *spa*
a, aa, ah (long)	*ah*	Say *a* as in *father*

Say e as in *Bed*

Smile while making the sound of the short stressed *e*, and your pronunciation will improve. This vowel is always flanked by double consonants in German.

Bett	Dreck	Fleck	nett
bet	*dRek*	*flek*	*net*
bed	dirt	spot	nice

When the *e* is unstressed, as it will be at the end of a word, it is pronounced like the *o* in *mother*.

Bitte	alle	bekommen	Dame	Hose
bi-tuh	*A-luh*	*buh-ko-muhn*	*dah-muh*	*hoh-zuh*
request	all	to receive	lady	trousers

There is no exact equivalent of the German long *e* sound in English, but you can approximate it by trying to make the sound of the stressed *e* and *ay* at the same time (be careful not to produce a diphthong—to add a *y* sound). Try saying these words:

Weg	Meer	Beet	Mehl	mehr
veyk	*meyR*	*beyt*	*meyl*	*meyR*
way	see	beet	flour	more

German Letter	Symbol	Pronunciation Guide
e (short, stressed)	*e*	Say *e* as in *bed*
e (short, unstressed)	*uh*	Say *uh* as in *ago*
e, ee, eh (long)	*ey*	Close to the *ey* in *hey*

Say *i* as in *Wind*

The short *i* is easy. It sounds like the *i* in the English words *wind* or *winter.* Try saying the following words:

Wind	Kind	schlimm	Himmel	hinter
vint	*kint*	*shlim*	*hi-muhl*	*hin-tuhR*
wind	child	bad	heaven	behind

For the long *i*, try saying *cheeeeeeese* and widening your mouth!

Liter	Tiger	ihr	Fliege	schieben
lee-tuhR	*tee-guhR*	*eeR*	*flee-guh*	*shee-buhn*
liter	tiger	her; you	fly	to push

German Letter	Symbol	Pronunciation Guide
i (short)	*i*	Say *i* as in *wind*
i, ie, ih (long)	*ee*	Say *i* as in *magazine*

Say *o* as in *Lord*

In German, the sound of the short *o* should resonate slightly farther back in your mouth than the *o* sound in English.

Mord	Loch	kochen	Ort
moRt	*loCH*	*ko-CHuhn*	*oRt*
murder	hole	to cook	town

English does not have an exact equivalent of the German long *o*, but if you drop the *oow* sound at the end of *snow* and hold your jaw in place as the vibrations of the *o* sound come up your throat from your vocal chords, you'll be pretty darn close.

hoch	Boot	Ohr	loben
hohCH	*boht*	*ohR*	*loh-buhn*
high	boat	ear	to praise

German Letter	Symbol	Pronunciation Guide
o (short)	*o*	Say *o* as in *lord*
o, oo, oh (long)	*oh*	Say *o* as in *no*

Say *u* as in *Shook*

The sound of the short *u* has just a touch of the sound of the long *u* in it. If you can add a little *moon* to the sound of the short *o*, you'll be on the right track.

Mutter	Luft	Schuld	bunt	Geduld
moo-tuhR	*looft*	*shoolt*	*boont*	*guh-doolt*
mother	air	guild	bright	patience

Imitate your favorite cow (*Kuh*) for this long *u* sound: *mooo*.

zu	tun	Schuh	Uhr	Fuß
tsew	*tewn*	*shew*	*ewR*	*fews*
to	to do	shoe	clock	foot

German Letter	Symbol	Pronunciation Guide
u (short)	*oo*	Close to *oo* in *shook*
u, uh (long)	*ew*	Say *ew* as in *stew*

Be careful not to run the two u's together when pronouncing uu in words like Vakuum (va-koo-oom) and Individuum (in-dee-vee-doo-oom). In most cases, the two letters are read as short u's and are given equal stress (treated as separate syllables). Don't treat other vowels this way, however; this rule applies only to side-by-side u's, not to the a, e, or o.

Modified Vowels

Track 2 In German, an umlaut changes the way a vowel is pronounced. Many German words are consistently spelled with umlauts, but other words take an umlaut when they undergo some change in grammar—as with some nouns in the plural and monosyllabic adjectives in the comparative and superlative: *lang*, long; *länger*, longer; (*am*) *längsten*, longest. This guide treats each modified vowel separately, giving you hints to help you make the correct sounds. Focus on getting the sounds right one sound at a time. To hear modified vowels, check out Track 2 on the CD included with the book.

Say *ä* as in *Fair*

The short *ä* is pronounced like the short *e* in German.

Stärke	Männer	hängen	standing
shtäR-kuh	*mä-nuhR*	*hän-guhn*	*shtän-diH*
strength	men	to hang	constantly

The long *ä* is the same sound as the short *ä*, only with the sound prolonged—a quantitative rather than qualitative alteration.

ähnlich	Mähne	Bär	prägen
ähn-liH	*mäh-nuh*	*bähR*	*pRäh-guhn*
similar	mane	bear	to coin

German Letter	Symbol	Pronunciation Guide
ä (short)	*ä*	Say *e* as in *bed*
ä, äh (long)	*äh*	Say *a* as in *fair*

Say *ö* as in *Fur*

This sound does not have an exact English equivalent. Round your lips and say *ey* while tightening the muscles at the back of your throat and then round your lips as if you were pronouncing *o*.

Öffnung	möchten	Hölle	Löffel
öf-noong	*möH-tuhn*	*hö-luh*	*lö-fuhl*
opening	would like to	hell	spoon

AS A RULE

If you've read through this pronunciation guide thoroughly, you may have already noticed a certain correlation between the spellings of words and their pronunciations. For example, a vowel is short when followed by two consonants. When a vowel is followed by an *h* and another consonant, or even by a single consonant, the vowel is long.

Keep the long *ö* sound going for twice as long, just as you did the short *ö* sound.

hören	schön	fröhlich	Störung
höh-Ruhn	*shöhn*	*fRöh-liH*	*shtöh-Roong*
to hear	pretty	happy	disturbance

German Letter	Symbol	Pronunciation Guide
ö (short)	*ö*	Close to *u* in *fur*
ö, öh (long)	*öh*	Close to *u* in *hurt*

Say *ü* as in the French Word *Sûr*

This *ü* sound does not have an English equivalent. If you speak French, though, you're in luck: the *ü* is very close to the *u* sound in the French word *sûr*. Another way to accomplish this is to say *ee*, hold your jaw and tongue in this position, and then round your lips as if you were pronouncing *u*.

Glück	Mücke	Rücken	Rhythmus
glük	*mük-uh*	*Rü-kuhn*	*Rüt-moos*
luck	mosquito	back	rhythm

The long *ü* or *y* is the same sound, just held for a longer interval of time.

rühren	führen	Lüge	Pseudonym
Rüh-Ruhn	*füh-Ruhn*	*lüh-guh*	*psoy-doh-nühm*
to stir	to lead	lie	pseudonym

German Letter	Symbol	Pronunciation Guide
ü, y (short)	*ü*	Close to *i* in *sir*
ü, üh, y (long)	*üh*	Close to *i* in *sir*

Diphthongs

Track 2 Diphthongs are made up of two different vowel sounds that glide in the same syllable. In English, we tend to dipthongize vowels in words like *sky*, where the *y* is pronounced *ah-ee*, and *go*, where the *o* is pronounced *oh-oo*. You've also seen diphthongs in vowels positioned back to back, as the *o* and the *e* are in the word *Noel*. In German, diphthongs are vowels that travel in pairs. Here are the diphthongs most frequently used in German. For other diphthongs, each vowel should be pronounced the same way it would be if pronounced separately: *Kollision (ko-lee-zeeohn)*, *Familie (fah-mee-leeuh)*. You can hear examples of diphthongs on Track 2 of the CD included with this book.

The Diphthongs *ei* and *ai*

To make the sound of these two diphthongs, start with your mouth halfway open and end with your mouth almost—but not quite—closed. Practice with these words:

Bleistift	Mai	vielleicht	klein	fein
blay-shtift	*may*	*fee-layHt*	*klayn*	*fayn*
pencil	May	maybe	small	fine

German Letter(s)	Symbol	Pronunciation Guide
ei, ai	*ay*	Say *ay* as in *cry*

ACHTUNG

Don't confuse your pronunciation of the diphthongs *ei* and *ie*. *ie* is pronounced like *ee* in *feet*, whereas *ei* is pronounced like the English word *eye*. Think *Bier* (*beeR*) versus *Wein* (*vayn*).

The Diphthong *au*

Let's suppose that you've been trying so hard to pronounce these new sounds correctly that you bite your own tongue by mistake: Ow! That's precisely the sound of this next diphthong. Try making this *ow* sound as you say these words:

Haut	Braut	schauen	verdauen	Sauerkraut
hout	*bRout*	*shou-uhn*	*feR-dou-uhn*	*sou-eR-kRout*
skin	bride	to look	to digest	sauerkraut

German Letter(s)	Symbol	Pronunciation Guide
au	*ou*	Say *ou* as in *couch, mouse*

The Diphthongs *eu* and *äu*

Try saying this: "Boy oh boy oh boy oh boy oh boy." If you managed that without too much trouble, chances are, you have the sound of this diphthong down.

heute	Euro	neu	Schläuche	Häute
hoy-tuh	*oy-Roh*	*noy*	*shloy-Huh*	*hoy-tuh*
today	euro	new	hoses	skins

German Letter(s)	Symbol	Pronunciation Guide
eu, äu	*oy*	Say *oy* as in *boy*

We're finished with vowels. You might need a little time to get used to making sounds you've never made before. Talking with German-speaking friends, watching subtitled movies in German, or visiting online German resources would come in handy now. You should try to listen to native German speakers, particularly because many of the modified vowel sounds do not have English equivalents. At this point, concentrate on getting the sounds right.

The Least You Need to Know

- Untie your tongue. Before you know it, you'll be pronouncing words like *Bratwurst* and *Fahrvergnügen* correctly.

- After you learn the basic pronunciation of German vowels, you will be able to read some German aloud without too much difficulty.

- Umlauted vowels are only slightly different from pure vowels, but this difference significantly alters the meanings of words. Practice making the umlauted vowel sounds, just as you would any new sound.

Pronounce It Properly: Consonants

In This Chapter

- Consonants that sound the same
- Consonants to clear your throat
- Worthwhile combos
- Hissing and grrrring in German

By now you should be able to make the correct sounds of vowels in German. But what good are all the vowel sounds you learned in Chapter 2 without consonants? The good news is the sounds of German consonants will not be as unfamiliar as many of the sounds you tried in the previous chapter. German consonants either are pronounced like their English counterparts or are pronounced like other consonants in English. The only German consonant sounds you won't encounter in English are the two sounds represented in this book by the symbol *H* (the *ch* in *ich*) and the symbol *CH* (the *ch* in *Loch* [*loCH*]).

In written German, you'll also come across a new letter: the consonant *ß*; this symbol is called an *es-tset* and is pronounced like an *s*. When people can't figure out how to make an es-tset on their keyboard, they often write the es-tset as a double *s* (*ss*). The es-tset is used only after long vowels (a concept introduced in the last chapter).

Conquering Consonants

Before you start stuttering out *consonants*, we should probably tell you a little about how this section works. The consonants in the following tables are not given in alphabetical order. They are grouped according to pronunciation type. For each letter, we provide English examples of how German consonants are pronounced, along with the symbols used throughout this book to represent the sounds. We've tried to

Track 3 & 4 choose symbols that correspond closely to the sounds they represent and are easy for English speakers to recognize at a glance. If you'd like to hear some pronunciation examples, listen to Track 3 for consonants and Track 4 for combinations of consonants on the CD included with this book.

> **ACHTUNG**
>
> The German *l* is not articulated in precisely the same place in the mouth as the English *l*. The English *l* is dark, formed with the tongue more relaxed. The German *l*—light, nearly as vibrant as the German *r*—is formed with the tip of the tongue just behind the upper front teeth.

Same Letters, Same Sounds

Many consonants are pronounced the same way in German and in English. When you see these letters, just go ahead and pronounce them the way you do in English words.

German Letter(s)	Symbol	Pronunciation Guide
f, h, k, l, m, n, p, t	The same as English letters	Pronounced the same as in English

Plosives: *b*, *d*, and *g*

Let's take a look at the letters *b*, *d*, and *g*. They are called *plosives* because of the way their sounds are articulated: with small explosions of air. At the beginning of a word (word initial) or when followed by a vowel, these sounds involving a stoppage of air utilize the vocal cords. Utter a *b* sound with a hand on your throat (where your vocal box is). You should feel vibrations because it is a *voiced* sound.

> **DEFINITION**
>
> **Voicing** is the production of audible vibration—a buzzing sound—caused by air from the lungs passing through the vocal cords when they are partly closed.

Its corresponding sound articulated at exactly the same place in the mouth, in exactly the same way but not involving the vocal cords, is a *p*, a voiceless sound. Whisper, and you will not feel the vibrations in your vocal cords. This voiceless sound is heard in German at the end of a word but is orthographically represented (spelled) with a *b*. For example, at the beginning of a syllable, *b* is pronounced the same way as it is in English: *Bleistift* (*blay-shtift*), "pencil"; *braun* (*bRoun*), "brown"; and *aber* (*ah-buhR*), "but." When *b* occurs at the end of a syllable, however, it is pronounced like a *p* (without the use of the vocal cords): *Laub* (*loup*), "foliage"; or *Korb* (*koRp*), "basket."

German Letter	Symbol	Pronunciation Guide
b	*b*	Say *b* as in *big*
b at the end of a syllable	*p*	Say *p* as in *pipe*

At the beginning of a syllable, the *d* is voiced and pronounced like an English *d: denken* (*den-kuhn*), "to think"; or like the first *d* in *Deutschland* (*doytch-lAnt*), "Germany." At the end of a syllable, the *d*, like its friend the *b*, loses its voicing and is pronounced like a *t: Leid* (*layt*), "sorrow," or like the last *d* in *Deutschland* (*doytch-lAnt*).

German Letter	Symbol	Pronunciation Guide
d	*d*	Say *d* as in *dog*
d at the end of a syllable	*t*	Say *t* as in *tail*

At the beginning of a syllable, *g* is voiced and pronounced the same as it is in English: *Gott* (*got*), God. At the end of a syllable, *g* becomes voiceless and is pronounced like *k: Weg* (*veyk*), "way." But you already deduced that, didn't you? The consonant *g* has yet another pronunciation, thanks to foreign infiltration. In certain words, usually ones that have been assimilated into the German language from other languages—namely, French—*g* sounds like the *g* as in the English pronunciation of *Massage* (*mA-sah-juh*).

German Letter	Symbol	Pronunciation Guide
g	*g*	Say *g* as in *God*
g at the end of a syllable	*k*	Say *k* as in *kitchen*
g in foreign language words	*j*	Say *j* as in *massage*

Fricatives

Fricatives are consonants articulated when the air stream coming up the throat and out of the mouth meets an obstacle, causing—you guessed it—friction.

Got a Frog in Your Throat? *ch, chs, h, j*

There's no exact English equivalent to the *ch* sound in German, but when you say words like *hubris* and *human*, the sound you make when you pronounce the *h* at the very beginning of the word is very close to the correct pronunciation of the German *ch* in *ich*. If you can draw out this *h* sound longer than you do in these two English words and somewhat imitate a cat's hiss, you should have very little trouble pronouncing the following words accurately: *ich* (*iH*), "I"; *manchmal* (*mAnH-mahl*), "sometimes"; *vielleicht* (*fee-layHt*), "maybe."

The second *ch* sound is articulated at the same place in the back of the throat as *k*, but the tongue is lowered to allow air to come through. To approximate this sound (represented in this book by the symbol *CH*), make the altered *h* sound you just learned farther back in your throat—a little like gargling. Can you pronounce Johann Sebastian Bach's name correctly? Give this a shot: *Yoh-hAn zey-bAs-tee-ahn bahhhh* (gargle and hiss like a cat simultaneously at the end). Once you can do this, you have mastered this second *ch* sound. Practice by reading the following words aloud: *Buch* (*bewCH*), "book"; *hoch* (*hohCH*), "high"; *Rache* (*RA-CHuh*), "revenge." Take heart, however, because you don't have to be conscious of the variation between *H* and *CH*; you will automatically produce the one prompted by the preceding vowel. That is to say, if the vowel coming before the *ch* sound is produced in the front part of the oral cavity (linguistic term for "mouth") as in *ich*, the *ch* will come out less guttural than the *ch* after a back vowel, like the *a* in *Bach*.

In general, when *ch* occurs at the beginning of a word, it is pronounced like a *k*: *Chaos* (*kA-os*), *Charisma* (*kah-ris-mah*). Exceptions occur, however, as in *China* or *Chemie*, where the *ch* may be pronounced like a *k* or the way it is in *ich*.

The *ch* can also be pronounced as *sh*. This pronunciation is usually used only for foreign words that have been assimilated into the German language: *Chef* (*shef*), "boss"; *Chance* (*shahn-suh*).

German Letter(s)	Symbol	Pronunciation Guide
ch	*H*	Close to *h* in *human*
	CH	No English equivalent
	k	Say *k* as in *character*
	sh	Say *sh* as in *shape*

You won't have any trouble with the *chs* sound. Say *Fuchs* (*foox*), "fox"; *Büchse* (*büh-xuh*), "box." You've simply combined a *k* with an *s*, like you do every time you say "box," "sox," or "fox."

German Letter(s)	Symbol	Pronunciation Guide
chs	*x*	Say *x* as in *fox*

The *h* is silent when it follows a vowel, to indicate that the vowel is long: *Stahl* (*shtahl*), "steel." The *h* is silent when it follows a *t*, as in *Theater* (*tey-ah-tuhR*). Otherwise, the *h* is pronounced very much like the English *h*—just a little breathier, as in both the English "hello" and its German equivalent, *hallo* (*hA-loh*).

German Letter	Symbol	Pronunciation Guide
h	*h*	Say *h* as in *house*

AS A RULE

The English *th* sound does not exist in German. Either the *h* is silent or both *t* and *h* are pronounced separately, as in the compound words *Stadthalle* (*shtAt-hA-luh*), "town hall"; and *Misthaufen* (*mist-hou-fuhn*), "dung heap," both of which are "divided" by a glottal stop between the syllables. You produce glottal stops all the time, believe it or not, whenever you disagree, shake your head, and utter *uh-uh*. That tiny pause between the syllables is referred to as a glottal stop!

Whenever you see a *j* in German, pronounce it like an English *y*: *Ja* (*yah*), "yes"; *Jaguar* (*yah-gwahR*).

German Letter	Symbol	Pronunciation Guide
j	*y*	Say *y* as in *yes*

Familiar Sound, Different Position: *z* and *c*

The *z* sound is made by combining the consonant sounds *t* and *s* into one sound: *zu* (*tsew*), "to"; *Zeug* (*tsoyk*), "thing"; *Kreuz* (*kRoyts*), "cross." Although this sound may *seem* new to you, English has the exact same sound—merely in a different position—word final, as in *cats*.

German Letter	Symbol	Pronunciation Guide
z	*ts*	Say *ts* as in *cats*

In German, you will rarely run into a *c* that isn't followed by an *h*, but when you do, that *c* should be pronounced *ts* whenever it occurs before *ä*, *e*, *i*, or *ö*: *Cäsar* (*tsäh-zahR*), or like the first *c* in *circa* (*tseeR-kah*). Otherwise, it should be pronounced like a *k*: *Creme* (*kReym*), "cream"; *Computer* (*kom-pew-tuhR*); or the last *c* in *circa* (*tseeR-kah*).

German Letter	Symbol	Pronunciation Guide
c	*ts*	Say *ts* as in *nuts*
	k	Say *k* as in *killer*

Double or Nothing: *kn*, *ps*, *qu*

The combinations of consonants in this section are pronounced together—that is, one after another.

In English, the *k* is silent in words like *knight* and *knot*. In German, however, both *k* and *n* are pronounced: *Kneipe* (*knay-puh*), "pub"; *Knie* (*knee*), "knee."

German Letter(s)	Symbol	Pronunciation Guide
kn	*kn*	Say *k* as in *kitchen* and *n* as in *now*

As in English, the consonants *ph* are pronounced *f*: *Photograph* (*foh-toh-gRahf*), *Physik* (*füh-zik*).

Both letters are pronounced in the consonant combinations in the following chart: *Pfeife* (*pfay-fuh*), "whistle"; *Pferd* (*pfeRt*), "horse"; *Pseudonym* (*psoy-doh-nühm*).

German Letter(s)	Symbol	Pronunciation Guide
pf	*pf*	No English equivalent
ph	*f*	Say *ph* as in *photo*
ps	*ps*	Say *ps* as in *psst*

The *qu* sound in German is a combination of the consonant sounds *k* and *v*: *Quantität* (*kvAn-tee-täht*); *Qual* (*kvahl*), "torment"; *Quatsch* (*kvAtsh*), "nonsense."

German Letter(s)	Symbol	Pronunciation Guide
qu	*kv*	No English equivalent

The German *r*

Mastering the German *r* will help you sound less American and more Germanlike. Whereas the American *r* is a hard *r*—that is to say, it is produced strongly near the front of the oral cavity—the German *r* is less strident and produced farther back.

To produce the German *r*, position your lips as if you are about to make the *r* sound, but then make the gargling sound you made for the German sound represented in this book by the symbol *CH*. The sound should come from somewhere in the back of your throat. The *r* sound can be soft, as in the words *Vater* (*fah-tuhR*), "father," and *Wasser* (*vA-suhR*), "water," or harder, as in the word *Reich* (*RayCH*), "kingdom." The distinction between these sounds is a subtle one. This book uses the same symbol (*R*) for both sounds.

German Letter	Symbol	Pronunciation Guide
r	*R*	No English equivalent

In southern Germany, in cities such as München and Stuttgart, the *R* is rolled on the tip of the tongue, whereas in the north, in Hamburg and Berlin, the *R* is pronounced deep at the back of the throat. This "uvular" pronunciation of the *R* is the most frequently used, but if you can't master it, try rolling your *R*'s (if someone asks about your accent, say you studied German in Stuttgart). Speaking of Hamburg, that accent is remarkably recognizable by its "sharp" *s*—instead of *Spitze* (*shpit-suh*), "point," you'll hear *spit-suh*.

s, ß, sch, st, tsch

The *s* is similar to the English *z* when followed by a vowel or surrounded by vowels: *Sohn (zohn)*, "son"; *Seife (zay-fuh)*, "soap"; *rose (Roh-zuh)*, "pink." At the end of a word, however, *s* is pronounced like the English *s: Maus (mous)*, *Glas (glahs)*—note that there's no vowel following these *s*'s!

German Letter	Symbol	Pronunciation Guide
s	*z*	Say *z* as in *zero*
	s	Say *s* as in *house*

The letter *ß* (es-tset) and the letters *ss* are both pronounced like an *s: nass (nAs)*, "wet"; *dass (dAs)*, "that"; *Straße (shtRah-suh)*, "street"; *Klasse (klA-suh)*, "class"; *müssen (müs-uhn)*, "to have to." According to the recently instated spelling reforms in German, the double *s* is used instead of *ß* after or between two short vowels.

German Letter	Symbol	Pronunciation Guide
ß, ss	*s*	Say *s* as in *salt*

The consonants *sch* are pronounced *sh: schreiben (shRay-buhn)*, "to write"; *Schatten (shA-tuhn)*, "shadow."

German Letter(s)	Symbol	Pronunciation Guide
sch	*sh*	Say *sh* as in *shape*

In German, *sp* is a combination of the *sh* sound in *shake* and the *p* sound in *pat*. Try saying *ship* without the *i*. Now practice with these words: *Spiel (shpeel)*, "game"; *Spanien (shpah-nee-uhn)*, "Spain."

The word-initial *st* sound is a combination of the *sh* sound in *shake* and the *t* sound in *take*. Try saying *shot* without the *o* sound. Practice by saying the following words out loud: *steigen (shtay-guhn)*, "to climb"; *stolz (shtolts)*, "proud"; *Stuhl (shtewl)*, "chair."

The *st* sound is pronounced the same way as it is in English when it occurs within a word or word-final in German: *Meister (may-stuhR)*, "master"; *Nest (nest)*, "nest."

German Letter(s)	Symbol	Pronunciation Guide
sp	*shp*	Say *ship* without the *i*
st	*sht*	Say *shot* without the *o*
	st	Say *st* as in *state*

Four consonants in a row! Don't panic. It's easier to read than it appears. *Tsch* is pronounced *tch*, as in the word *witch*. See? A breeze, right? Remember *Quatsch* (*kvAtsh*), "nonsense," from your *qu* practice? Also try out *lutschen* (*loo-tchuhn*), "to suckle"; and *deutsch* (*doytch*), "German."

German Letter(s)	Symbol	Pronunciation Guide
tsch	**tch**	**Say** *tch* **as in** *witch*

Herbie the Love Bug: The Classic *vw*

In most cases, the *v* is pronounced like an *f*: *Vater* (*fah-tuhR*), "father"; *Verkehr* (*feR-keyR*), "traffic"; *viel* (*feel*), "many." In some cases, though, particularly with words that have been assimilated into the German language from Latin-based languages such as French, the *v* is pronounced *v*: *Vampir* (*vAm-peeR*), *Vase* (*vah-zuh*). You will readily recognize these because English has borrowed them from French as well!

German Letter	Symbol	Pronunciation Guide
v	*f*	Pronounced as the *f* in *father*
	v	Sometimes as the *v* in *voice*

The *w* is pronounced like a *v*: *wichtig* (*viH-tiH*), "important"; *Wasser* (*vA-suhR*), "water"; *Wurst* (*vuRst*) "sausage."

German Letter	Symbol	Pronunciation Guide
w	*v*	Say *v* as in *vast*

Pronunciation Guide

When you are further along in this book, you may not have time to flip through page after page looking for the letter or the symbol you want to pronounce. The following table is an abbreviated pronunciation guide of vowels, modified vowels, diphthongs, and consonants that differ in pronunciation from English consonants.

Abbreviated Pronunciation Guide

Letter(s)	Symbol	English Example	German Example
Vowels			
a (short)	*A*	Close to m*o*dern	M*a*nn
a (long)	*ah*	f*a*ther	W*a*gen
e (short, stressed)	*e*	b*e*d	B*e*tt
e (short, unstressed)	*uh*	*a*go	Bitt*e*
e (long)	*ey*	Close to h*ey*	W*e*g
i (short)	*i*	w*i*nd	W*i*nd
i (long)	*ee*	s*ee*	w*i*r
o (short)	*o*	l*o*rd	*O*rt
o (long)	*oh*	Close to sn*ow*	h*o*ch
u (short)	*oo*	sh*oo*k	M*u*tter
u (long)	*ew*	st*ew*	F*u*ß
Modified Vowels			
ä (short)	*ä*	f*ai*r	St*ä*rke
ä (long)	*äh*	Close to f*a*te	B*ä*r
ö (short)	*ö*	Close to f*u*r	L*ö*ffel
ö (long)	*öh*	Close to h*u*rt	sch*ö*n
ü (short)	*ü*	Close to s*i*r	Gl*ü*ck
ü (long)	*üh*	Close to s*i*r	L*ü*ge
Diphthongs			
ai, ei	*ay*	*I*	Bl*ei*stift
au	*ou*	c*ou*ch	H*au*t
äu, eu	*oy*	t*oy*	h*eu*te
Consonants That Differ from English			
b	*b*	*b*ig	*B*leistift
	p	*p*ipe	Kor*b*

Letter(s)	Symbol	English Example	German Example
c	*ts*	ba*ts*	*C*äsar
	k	*k*iller	*C*omputer
ch	*H*	Close to *h*uman	i*ch*
	CH	No equivalent	Bu*ch*
	k	*ch*aracter	*Ch*aracter
	sh	*sh*ape	*Ch*ef
chs	*x*	fo*x*	Fu*chs*
d	*d*	*d*og	*d*eutsch
	t	*t*ime	Lan*d*
g	*g*	*g*ood	*G*ott
	k	*k*itten	We*g*
	j	mas*s*age	Mas*s*age
h	*h*	*h*ouse	*H*aus
j	*y*	*y*es	*J*a
kn	*kn*	No equivalent	*Kn*eipe
pf	*pf*	No equivalent	*Pf*eife
ph	*f*	*ph*oto	*Ph*oto
ps	*ps*	*ps*st!	*Ps*eudonym
ng	*ng*	si*ng*	Si*ng*en
qu	*kv*	No equivalent	*Qu*atsch
r	*R*	No equivalent	*R*eich
s	*z*	*z*ero	*S*uppe
	s	mou*s*e	Gla*s*
ß, ss	*s*	*s*alt	Stra*ß*e, Kla*ss*e
sch	*sh*	*sh*ape	*Sch*atten
sp	*shp*	No equivalent	*sp*ielen
st	*sht*	No equivalent	*St*uhl
	st	*st*ate	Ne*st*
tsch	*tch*	sni*tch*	deu*tsch*
v	*f*	*f*ather	*V*ater
	v	*v*oice	*V*ase
w	*v*	*v*ast	*w*ichtig
x	*x*	ta*x*i	Ta*x*i
z	*ts*	ca*ts*	*Z*eug

Practicing Pronunciation

Have you practiced all these new sounds? If you have, we are willing to bet that you have succeeded in making most, if not all, of the sounds you will need to pronounce German words correctly. Now practice some more by reading the following sentences out loud.

German	English
Guten Tag, mein Name ist ….	Good day, my name is ….
Ich komme aus den Vereinigten Staaten.	I'm from the United States.
Ich spreche Englisch.	I speak English.
Ich habe gerade begonnen, Deutsch zu lernen.	I just started to learn German.
Die Aussprache ist nicht so schwer.	The pronunciation isn't so difficult.
Deutsch ist eine schöne Sprache.	German is a beautiful language.

The Least You Need to Know

- With some exceptions, German consonants are pronounced like their English equivalents.

- German is a phonetic language, in that every letter represented in orthography will be heard in its pronunciation. So once you link a letter with a sound, you can pronounce a word 18 syllables long!

- Read, watch, and listen to whatever German you can get your hands on; any website ending with a ".de" (including Google) will supply endless exposure to German, as well as podcasts and apps you can download. Don't forget to access YouTube for more practice opportunities! What seems peculiar in written or spoken German will quickly become familiar to you, and soon—particularly if you listen to the German being spoken by a native speaker—you will begin to associate letters with their corresponding sounds.

- Speaking of the internet, numerous websites offer pronunciation guides using breakthrough software. Just click on a sound or word and hear it produced.

You Know More Than You Think

Chances are, you've been speaking German for years without even knowing it! *Kindergarten, Wind, Mensch, Angst, Arm, blond, irrational*—the list of German words you already know is longer than you think. The reason you know so much German is that many words in German are similar to or exactly like their English counterparts. These words are called *cognates*. Many German words have been used so much by English speakers that they have been swallowed whole, so to speak, into the English language to become a part of our vocabulary. Many other German words are so similar to English words that you can master their meanings and pronunciations with little effort. By the end of this chapter, you should be able to put together simple but meaningful sentences in German.

Cognates: What You Already Know Can Help You

Imagine that you've been invited to an art opening of a German artist. When the day of the show arrives, you go to the address on the invitation. You listen to the conversations of other people—*auf Deutsch* (*ouf doytch*). What surprises you most is how well you understand what is being said, having as little knowledge of it as you do. You are able to pick up on certain words: *interessantes Object, gute Familie, phantastische Party, modern, blau, braun.* Clearly, a new language—a hybrid, perhaps, of German and English—is being spoken, possibly even invented by this sophisticated crowd. How else would you be able to make sense of so many words?

The fact is, German and English are not just kissing cousins—they're sisters. Both languages like to borrow words from the same places—namely, Greek, Latin, and other Romance languages. Because both English and German are members of the Germanic family of languages, they share a lot of "genetic material"—*cognates,* for one thing. Another readily visible similarity is their word-building strategies—that is, add a little something to a noun or verb to make it an adjective: *child + ish = childish* in English; likewise, *Kind + isch = kindisch* auf Deutsch!

But back to words that have the same meaning and similar form—the really great part about cognates is that they have the same meanings in German and in English. Pronunciation does vary, of course, but most of the time, these words are familiar to us. And don't forget the American influence on Germany. Since the late 1940s, thanks to postwar reconstruction and increasing globalization, the German language has taken many words from English without changing them at all, aside from capitalizing the nouns. Consider, for example, *team, fitness center, make-up, style, cool, email, fair,* and *camping.*

Perfect Cognates

The following table lists by article *perfect cognates*—words that are exactly the same in English and German. If you really want to get ahead of the game, use the pronunciation guide in Chapter 3 to pronounce these words the way a German would.

> **DEFINITION**
>
> **Cognates** are words that are historically derived from the same source. They may be similar to (near cognates) or exactly like (perfect cognates) counterparts in another language.

Perfect Cognates

Adjectives	Nouns (*der*)	Adjectives (*die*)	Nouns (*das*)
aktiv	Alligator	Adaptation	Auto
Ak-teef	*A-li-gah-toR*	*A-dAp-tA-tsion*	*ou-to*
blond	Arm	Bank	Chaos
blont	*ARm*	*bAnk*	*kah-os*
elegant	Bandit	Basis	Element
e-le-gAnt	*bAn-deet*	*bAh-zis*	*eh-leh-ment*
formal	Bus	Hand	Volk
foR-mahl	*boos*	*hAnt*	*folk*

Adjectives	Nouns (*der*)	Adjectives (*die*)	Nouns (*das*)
international *in-teR-nA-tsio-nahl*	Café *kah-fe*	Inspiration *in-spee-rA-tsion*	Hotel *hoh-tel*
irrational *ee-RA-tsio-nahl*	Defekt *dey-fekt*	Isolation *ee-zo-lA-tsion*	Museum *mew-zey-oom*
irrelevant *ee-Re-le-vAnt*	Film *film*	Negation *ney-gA-tsion*	Nest *nest*
modern *moh-deRn*	Hamburger *hAm-boor-guhR*	Olive *oh-lee-vuh*	Optimum *op-tee-moom*
nonstop *non-shtop*	Jaguar *yah-gwahR*	Pause *pou-suh*	Organ *oR-gahn*
parallel *pA-rA-lehl*	Moment *moh-ment*	Religion *rey-lee-geeohn*	Panorama *pA-no-Rah-mA*
permanent *peR-mA-nent*	Motor *moh-tohr*	Situation *zee-too-A-tseeohn*	Photo *foh-to*
total *toh-tahl*	Name *nah-muh*	Taxi *ta-xee*	Pseudonym *psoy-doh-nühm*
warm *vahRm*	Tiger *tee-guhR*		Radio *rA-dee-o*
wild *vilt*	Wind *vint*		System *süs-teym*
			Tennis *te-nis*

AS A RULE

In English, we have only one definite article, the, which indicates specificity—a certain something is familiar and recognized in the referred-to situation. German has three definite articles: *der* (*deyR*), for masculine singular nouns; *die* (*dee*), for feminine singular nouns; and *das* (*dAs*), for neuter singular nouns.

We call this *grammatical gender,* as opposed to *biological gender,* because the noun following the article doesn't have to represent something male, female, or sexless. *Mädchen* (*mäht-Huhn*), for example, which means "girl," takes the neuter article *das.* Grammatical gender is arbitrary—unpredictable, in fact!

Remember, in German, all nouns are capitalized. Nouns and their definite articles are explained in greater detail in Chapter 6.

How Much Do You Understand Already?

Now you could probably go back to your friend's art opening, or to some other gathering of Germans, and carry on a simple conversation in German. How do we recommend that you practice pronouncing these new words? If you haven't already developed the habit of talking to yourself, start talking now. Utilizing the following German noun and adjective cognates, build sentences by inserting the appropriate definite article before the noun (*der, die,* or *das*), the verb *ist* (expressing "is" in German), and the adjective. Check your sentences in Appendix A.

Example: You might say of a painting of a tiger in a jungle …

Tiger/wild: *Der Tiger ist wild.*

1. You might say of a painting of a cowboy in the Wild West

   Bandit/blond:

2. You might say of a painting of a futuristic bank

   Bank/modern:

3. You might say of an abstract painting of an olive

   Olive/parallel:

4. You might say of the breeze coming in through the open window of the art gallery

   Wind/warm:

5. You might say of an abstract-expressionistic piece of art hung upside down

   Chaos/irrational:

Did you remember to lead your noun with the grammatically correct form of "the" (der, die, das)?

Near Cognates

The following table lists *near cognates,* words that are spelled almost—but not quite—the same in English and German. Although their spellings differ, their meanings are the same. While German and English were once one and the same, a consonant shift led to the separation and distinction of English from German. We can use awareness of this to our advantage with digging deeper for near cognates. Consider, for example, the correspondence between the German *t* and English *d*. There's *taub* for "deaf," *tief* for "deep," *die Flut* for "flood," *das Bett* for "bed," and *hart* for "hard."

If you vocalize both sounds, you will realize that both *t* and *d* are made in the same location in the mouth, in the same manner—the only difference is the utilization of the vocal cords. Practice pronouncing the German words correctly. Don't forget to gargle those *CH*'s and *R*'s!

Near Cognates

Adjectives	Nouns		
	der	*die*	*das*
akademisch *Ak-A-dey-mish*	Aspekt *As-pekt*	Adresse *A-dRe-suh*	Adjektiv *Ad-yek-teef*
akustisch *A-koos-tish*	Autor *ou-tohR*	Realität *Rey-ah-lee-tät*	Ballett *bA-let*
amerikanisch *A-mey-Ree-kah-nish*	Bruder *bRew-duhR*	Bluse *blew-zuh*	Blut *blewt*
äquivalent *eh-kvi-vah-lent*	Charakter *kA-Rak-tuhR*	Energie *eh-neR-gee*	Buch *bewH*
attraktiv *A-tRAk-teef*	Detektiv *dey-tek-teef*	Existenz *egz-is-tents*	Ding *Ding*
blau *blou*	Disput *dis-pewt*	Familie *fA-mee-lee-uh*	Ende *en-duh*
direct *dee-Rekt*	Doktor *dok-tohr*	Gitarre *gee-tA-Ruh*	Glas *glahs*
dumm *doom*	Elefant *ey-ley-fAnt*	Jacke *yA-kuh*	Gras *gRahs*
durstig *dooR-stiH*	Fuß *fews*	Kassette *kA-se-tuh*	Haus *Hous*
frei *fRay*	Kaffee *kA-fey*	Lampe *lAm-puh*	Herz *heRts*
freundlich *fRoynt-liH*	Markt *mARkt*	Liste *lis-tuh*	Licht *liHt*
gut *gewt*	Muskel *moos-kuhl*	Logik *loh-gik*	Medikament *meh-dee-kah-ment*
interessant *in-tuh-Re-sAnt*	Onkel *on-kuhl*	Medizin *meh-dee-tseen*	Objekt *ob-yekt*
jung *yoong*	Organismus *oR-gah-nis-moos*	Methode *me-toh-duh*	Papier *pah-peeR*

continues

Near Cognates (continued)

Adjectives	Nouns		
	der	*die*	*das*
kalt *kAlt*	Ozean *oh-tse-ahn*	Musik *mew-zeek*	Paradies *pA-RA-dees*
kompetent *koom-pe-tent*	Pfennig *pfe-niH*	Nationalität *nA-tseeo-nA-lee-tät*	Parfüm *pAR-füm*
lang *lAng*	Präsident *pRey-zee-dent*	Natur *nA-tooR*	Phänomen *fäh-noh-men*
mystisch *mühs-tish*	Preis *pRays*	Nudel *new-dulh*	Prinzip *pRin-tseep*
nervös *neR-vöhs*	Salat *zA-laht*	Nummer *Noo-muh*	Produkt *pRoh-dookt*
passiv *pA-seef*	Schock *shok*	Oper *Ooh-puhR*	Programm *pRo-gRAm*
perfekt *peR-fekt*	Schuh *schew*	Optik *op-tik*	Resultat *Reh-zool-taht*
platonisch *plah-toh-nish*	Skrupel *skRew-puhl*	Qualität *kvah-lee-tät*	Salz *zAlts*
popular *poh-pew-lähr*	Stamm *shtAm*	Rhetorik *Reh-toh-Rik*	Schiff *Shif*
primitiv *pRi-mee-teef*	Strom *shtRom*	Skulptur *skoolp-tewR*	Skelett *skeh-let*
sozial *zoh-tsee-ahl*	Supermarkt *zew-peR-maRkt*	Socke *so-kuh*	Telefon *tey-ley-fohn*
sportlich *shpoRt-liH*	Wein *vayn*	Theorie *te-oh-Ree*	Wetter *Ve-tuhR*
tropisch *tRo-pish*	Wille *vi-luh*	Tomate *toh-mah-tuh*	Zentrum *tsen-tRoom*
typisch *tüh-pish*	Vater *fah-tuhR*	Universität *Ew-nee-veR-zee-tät*	
weiß *vays*	Zickzack *tsik-tsAk*	Walnuss *wAl-noos*	
		Warnung *VaR-noong*	

Cognate Conversation

Now imagine that you have just boarded a sleeper train from Köln to München. Only one other person is sharing your compartment. Use the adjective and noun cognates you have learned to engage your neighbor in conversation. Check your translations in Appendix A.

1. The weather is good.

2. Is the book interesting?

3. The author is popular.

4. The perfume is attractive.

5. The wind is warm.

6. The character is primitive.

7. The heart is wild.

8. *The salt is white.

*You think to yourself, "Did I really mean to say that?"

Verb Cognates

It's time now to take a look at verb cognates in their infinitive forms. The *infinitive form* of a verb in German usually ends with an *-en*, as in the words *helfen* (*hel-fuhn*), "to help"; *lernen* (*leR-nuhn*), "to learn"; and *machen* (*mA-CHuhn*), "to do." However, sometimes an infinitive ends in a simple *-n*, as in *sammeln* (*zam-muhln*), "to collect." The following table is a list of verbs that are near cognates in their infinitive form.

DEFINITION

Infinitive form is the unconjugated form of a verb. In German, the infinitive form of verbs end in *-en* or, in some cases, simply *-n*. Verbs are listed in the dictionary in the infinitive form. The English equivalent is *to* + verb.

Verb Cognates

German	Pronunciation	English
backen	*bA-kuhn*	to bake
baden	*bah-duhn*	to bathe
beginnen	*buh-gi-nuhn*	to begin
binden	*bin-duhn*	to bind
brechen	*bRe-Huhn*	to break
bringen	*bRin-guhn*	to bring
finden	*fin-duhn*	to find
fühlen	*füh-luhn*	to feel
haben	*hah-buhn*	to have
halten	*hAl-tuhn*	to hold
helfen	*hel-fuhn*	to help
kochen	*kO-CHuhn*	to cook
kommen	*ko-muhn*	to come
können	*kö-nuhn*	can/to be able to
kosten	*kos-tuhn*	to cost
machen	*mA-Huhn*	to make
müssen	*mü-suhn*	must/to have to
öffnen	*öf-nuhn*	to open
packen	*pA-kuhn*	to pack
parken	*pAR-kuhn*	to park
planen	*plah-nuhn*	to plan
reservieren	*Rey-zeR-vee-Ruhn*	to reserve
rollen	*Ro-luhn*	to roll
sagen	*zah-guhn*	to say
schwimmen	*shvi-muhn*	to swim
senden	*zen-duhn*	to send
singen	*zin-guhn*	to sing
sinken	*zin-kuhn*	to sink
stinken	*shtin-kuhn*	to stink
sitzen	*zi-tsuhn*	to sit
spinnen	*shpi-nuhn*	to spin
telefonieren	*tey-ley-foh-nee-Ruhn*	to telephone
trinken	*tRin-kuhn*	to drink

Putting It All Together

This isn't so bad, is it? You can probably already read and understand the following German sentences. Don't get waylaid by a verb ending with a *–t*. The verb doesn't change meaning, just number. That is to say, the *–t* marks a verb singular instead of plural. Check your interpretations with the answers in Appendix A:

1. Der Präsident und der Bandit backen Tomaten.
   deyR pRä-zee-dent oont deyR bAn-deet bA-kuhn toh-mah-tuhn

2. Der Onkel trinkt Wein.
   deyR on-kuhl tRinkt vayn

3. Der Tiger und der Elefant schwimmen im Ozean.
   deyR tee-guhR oont deyR ey-ley-fahnt shvi-muhn im oh-tse-ahn

4. Der Film beginnt im Supermarkt.
   deyR film buh-gint im zew-peR-mArkt

5. "Religion und Chaos? Ein modernes Problem," sagt der junge, intelligente Autor.
   Rey-lee-geeohn oont kah-os? ayn moh-deR-nuhs pRo-bleym, zAkt deyR yoon-guh, in-te-lee-gen-tuh ou-tohR

6. Der Doktor und der Detektiv finden die Lampe interessant.
   deyR dok-tohr oont deyR dey-tek-teef fin-duhn dee lAm-puh in-tuh-Re-sAnt

7. Mein Bruder und mein Vater haben eine Gitarre.
   mayn bRew-duhR oont mayn fah-tuhR hA-buhn ay-nuh gee-tA-Ruh

8. Der Aligator kostet $10,000.
   deyR ah-lee-gah-toR kos-tet $10,000

False Friends

No shortcut is without its pitfalls. Now that you've mastered the art of using words you already know to figure out words in German you didn't know you knew, we must warn you about false friends, or *falsche Freunde* (*fAl-shuh fRoyn-duh*). In language as in life, false friends are misleading. What are linguistic false friends? They are words spelled the same or almost the same in two languages that have different meanings. While *hell* is self-explanatory in English, it's an innocuous adjective meaning "bright" in German. As you can see, these two words, which are spelled exactly the same, have totally different meanings. A word of caution: cognates can be of help to you in learning German, but false friends can trip you up. Don't assume that you already know the meaning of *every* German word that looks like an English word. It's not always that simple. The following table lists some common false friends.

ACHTUNG

When you look up a verb in a dictionary, it's important that you look it up under its *infinitive* form—that is, under its unconjugated form—just as you would if you were looking up a verb in English. Otherwise, you'll have trouble finding the verb because many German verbs change significantly (as do many English verbs) after they are conjugated. They're changed to reflect logical (grammatical) agreement with the subject, as in *I am* and *she is*.

False Friends

English	Part of Speech	German	Part of Speech	Meaning
after	adverb	der After *Af-tuhR*	noun	anus
also	adverb	also *Al-zoh*	conjunction	so, therefore
art	noun	die Art *ARt*	noun	type, sort
bald	adjective	bald *bAlt*	adverb	soon
blaze, blase	noun	die Blase *blah-zuh*	noun	bladder, blister, or bubble
brief	adjective	der Brief *bReef*	noun	letter, official document
chef	noun	der Chef *shef*	noun	boss
closet	noun	das Klosett *kloh-zet*	noun	toilet bowl
fast	adjective	fast *fAst*	adverb	almost
gift	noun	das Gift *gift*	noun	poison
kind	adjective	das Kind *kint*	noun	child

English	Part of Speech	German	Part of Speech	Meaning
knack	noun	der Knacker *knA-kuhR*	noun	old fogy
lusty	adjective	lustig *loos-tiH*	adjective	funny
most	adjective	der Most *most*	noun	young wine
note	noun, verb	die Note *noh-tuh*	noun	grade, musical note
rock	noun	der Rock *Rok*	noun	skirt
see	verb	der See *zey*	noun	lake
sin	noun	der Sinn *zin*	noun	sense
sympathetic	adjective	sympathisch *züm-pah-tish*	adjective	likeable

The Least You Need to Know

- By using cognates, you can express yourself in German with very little effort.
- Many German words and expressions are in use every day in English.
- Beware of false friends. Don't let them trick you into saying things you don't mean.

Idiomatic Expressions: Quintessentially German

In This Chapter

- How idioms are used in language
- Expressions of time, location, and direction
- Expressions you can use to get your opinion across
- German sayings

It's raining cats and dogs, and you're bored to tears, so you sit down to hit the books and study a little German. Today you're going to focus on common expressions in German, many of which are idioms. What are idioms? They are the peculiarities of a given language whose meaning cannot be derived literally from the words.

Let's say you fall in love with a German politician and have a hasty wedding. He's anxious for you to meet his mother, and the two of you fly to Köln after your honeymoon. Unfortunately, he's called away suddenly on a top-secret mission. He arranges for you to have breakfast at the hotel with his mother the following morning. That night you're so worried about your *Mann* (*mAn*) that you are unable to sleep. You read a few children's stories to yourself, something that has always soothed and relaxed you, and soon you fall asleep. The following morning at breakfast your mother-in-law asks you how you managed to get through the night without her son. You have a working knowledge of German, and you know that *Bett* (*bet*) means "bed" and that *Geschichte* (*guh-shiH-tuh*) means "story," so you say, "*Mit einer Bettgeschichte.*" Your mother-in-law goes pale, rises from her chair, and stumbles from the room. Without realizing it, you have used the German idiom for having a one-night stand.

Using Idioms

The German expression for being lucky is *Schwein haben* (*shvayn hah-buhn*), which, literally translated, means "to have pig." Don't be too quick to take offense at something that sounds like an insult; it may be an idiomatic expression. *Idiomatic expressions* are groups of words of words always used together as a phrase, where the meaning of the phrase isn't clear from the meaning of the words. They cannot be understood by literal translation—they must be learned and memorized along with their meanings. While most German idioms differ greatly from their English counterparts in meaning as well as in construction, a respectable number differ only slightly. In English you say, "I'm going home." In German you say, "*Ich gehe nach Hause*," or "I'm going *to* home." Because prepositions in general are idiomatic, it helps to learn them with certain expressions.

> **DEFINITION**
>
> **Idioms** are fixed phrases whose meaning cannot be inferred from the meanings of the individual words. They tend to be frozen in form and thus do not readily enter into other combinations or allow the word order to change.

Idioms make a language colorful. Most idioms originate as metaphorical expressions that establish themselves in the language and become frozen in their form and meaning. Idiomatic expressions tend to be culturally specific because the lexical items that a certain language relies on to express nonliteral meanings generally have significance in that culture. For example, the German expression *seinen Senf dazugeben* (*zain-uhn zenft dA-tsew-gey-buhn*) literally means "to give his mustard to something." Huh? Well, mustard *does* play a rather prominent culinary role in German, so take a guess. Exactly—it means to give one's opinion—adding one's *two cents*. After all, would you rather have some mustard to go along with your *Wurst*, or two pennies?

To help you get a clearer idea of what idiomatic expressions are, here are a few in English:

sell down the river	haul over the coals
let one's hair down	put one's foot in one's mouth
snap out of it	bite your tongue
hit it off	eat your heart out

How?

Let's say you live in Wisconsin and you're going away for the weekend to your parents' farm in Vancouver, Canada. One of your new German friends (who doesn't speak any English) asks you how you're getting there. You are at a loss for words. The truth is that you'll be traveling by plane to Vancouver, then going by car from the airport to the lake on the other side of your parents' house, and then traveling by boat across the lake to the dock where a horse will be waiting for you, which you will then ride to the house, where you will go for a walk—but how in the world are you going to start explaining this? What you need are some expressions for travel and transportation. Look at the following table for some suggestions.

Expressions for Travel and Transportation

Expression	Pronunciation	Meaning
mit dem Bus	*mit deym boos*	by bus
mit dem Fahrrad	*mit deym fah-Rat*	by bicycle
mit dem Flugzeug	*mit deym flewk-tsoyk*	by plane
mit dem Motorrad	*mit deym moh-toh-RAt*	by motorcycle
mit dem Schiff	*mit deym shif*	by boat
mit der Straßenbahn	*mit deyR shtrah-suhn-bahn*	by streetcar
mit dem Zug	*mit deym tsewk*	by train
mit Rollerblades	*mit deyn Rol-luhR-bleydz*	by rollerblades
mit der U-Bahn	*mit deyR ew-bahn*	by subway
mit einem Auto	*mit ay-nuhm ou-toh*	by car
mit einem Pferd/zu Pferd	*mit ay-nuhm pfeRt/tsew pfeRt*	on a horse
zu Fuß	*tsew fews*	by foot

Describing Travel

Now it's time to practice what you've learned. Use the preceding table to fill in the blanks of the following sentences with the correct German expressions. Check your answers in Appendix A.

    1. Ich fliege _____ von Wisconsin nach Vancouver.
       (I travel <u>by plane</u> from Wisconsin to Vancouver.)

2. Ich fahre _____ vom Flughafen zum See.
(I travel <u>by car</u> from the airport to the lake.)

3. Ich fahre _____ über den See. (I go <u>by boat</u> over the lake.)

4. Ich reiter _____ nach zum Haus. (I travel <u>by horse</u> to the house.)

5. Dann gehe ich _____. (Then I go <u>by foot/walk</u>.)

When?

Many times expressions have a wide range of interpretations based on the perception of the speakers, whereas others are more grounded and specific. The following table has a few idiomatic time expressions you will find useful.

Time Expressions

Expression	Pronunciation	Meaning
am Ende von	*Am en-duh fon*	at the end of
auf Wiedersehen	*ouf vee-deR-zey-uhn*	good-bye
bis bald	*bis bAlt*	see you soon
bis heute Abend	*bis hoy-tuh ah-buhnt*	see you this evening
bis Morgen	*bis moR-guhn*	see you tomorrow
bis später	*bis shpäh-tuhR*	see you later
(zu) früh	*(tsew) fRüh*	(too) early
früher	*fRüh-uhR*	earlier
gleichzeitig	*glayH-tsay-tiH*	simultaneously
guten Tag/Abend	*gew-tuhn tahk/ah-buhnt*	good day/evening
hallo	*hA-loh*	hello
heute	*hoy-tuh*	today
in einer Weile	*in ay-nuhR vay-luh*	in a while
jeden Tag	*yey-duhn tAk*	every day
jetzt	*yetst*	now
monatlich	*moh-nAt-liH*	monthly
plötzlich	*plöts-liH*	suddenly

Expression	Pronunciation	Meaning
pünktlich	*pünkt-liH*	punctually
regelmäßig	*rey-guhl-mäh-siH*	regularly
sofort	*zoh-foRt*	immediately
(zu) spät	*(tsew) shpäht*	(too) late
später	*shpäh-tuhR*	later
täglich	*Tähk-liH*	daily
von morgens bis abends	*fon moR-guhnz bis ah-buhnts*	from morning till night
von Tag zu Tag	*fon tahk tsew tahk*	from day to day
von Zeit zu Zeit	*fon tsayt tsew tsayt*	from time to time
wöchentlich	*vö-Hent-liH*	weekly
zur gleichen Zeit	*tsewR glay-Huhn tsayt*	at the same time

Expressing Time

What German idioms of time would you use in the following situations? Check your mastery of time in Appendix A.

1. When your partner leaves on a business trip for the weekend, you say: _____

2. When you say good-bye to a friend you will be seeing later that evening, you say: _____

3. If the movie begins at 5 P.M. and you arrive at 5 P.M., you arrive: _____

4. If the movie begins at 5 P.M. and you arrive at 7 P.M., you arrive: _____

5. If the movie begins at 5 P.M. and you arrive at 4 P.M., you arrive: _____

6. If you watch TV every now and then, you watch it: _____

7. You should brush your teeth: _____

8. If you follow a ritual every Friday: _____

Where?

Some of the most useful vocabulary you can learn, particularly if you plan to travel in German-speaking countries, are the words for expressing location and direction. To use many of these expressions, you need to know about cases in German (see Chapter 7). The following table focuses on simple terms to help you get to wherever you're going.

Expressions Showing Location and Direction

Expression	Pronunciation	Meaning
draußen	*dRou-suhn*	outdoors
entlang	*ent-lAng*	along
gegenüber	*ge-gen-üh-buhR*	opposite, facing
geradeaus	*ge-Rah-duh-ous*	straight ahead
hinter	*hin-tuhR*	behind
(nach) links	(*nACH*) *links*	(to the) left
neben	*ney-buhn*	beside
(nach) rechts	(*nACH*) *ReHts*	(to the) right
S\esitlich	*zayt-liH*	at the side
Ü\uber	*üh-buhR*	over, across
unter	*oon-tuhR*	beneath, below, under
vor	*fohr*	in front of

Stating Location

Now you can find anything, right? Here's a simplified map of a city street. Referring to the following map, see if you can fill in the blanks correctly by following the directions in German. Check your directional knowledge in Appendix A.

Example: Rechts neben dem Café ist die Bäckerei.

1. Gegenüber der Post ist _____.

2. Vor dem Museum ist _____.

3. Links neben dem Hotel ist _____.

4. Hinter dem Café ist _____.

5. Neben der Bäckerei ist _____.

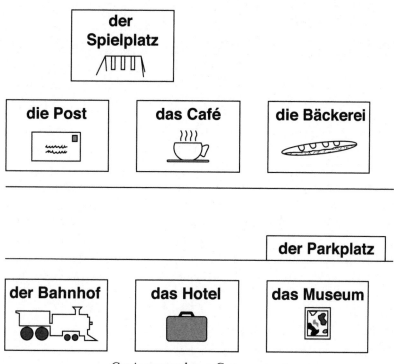

Getting around on a German street.

So What Do You Think?

Opinions—who doesn't have them? And who doesn't like to express them? People tell you how the food tastes, whether they liked the movie, and what they think of politics and religion. Now it's your turn: Express yourself in German—*auf Deutsch, bitte* (*ouf doytch, bi-tuh*). (See the following table.)

Expressing Your Opinions

Expression	Pronunciation	Meaning
Mir geht es ähnlich.	*meer geyt es ähn-liH*	I feel similarly.
bestimmt	*buh-shtimt*	certainly
klar	*klahR*	clearly
Das ist mir egal.	*dAs ist meeR ey-gahl*	That's all the same to me.
Das macht nichts.	*dAs mACHt niHts*	It doesn't matter.

continues

Expressing Your Opinions (continued)

Expression	Pronunciation	Meaning
genau	*guh-nou*	exactly
Ich habe keine Ahnung.	*iH hA-buh kay-nuh ah-noong*	I have no idea.
Ich weiß nicht.	*iH vays niHt*	I don't know.
natürlich	*nah-tüR-liH*	of course
offensichtlich/klar/ einleuchtend	*o-fen-ziHt-liH/klAR/ayn-loyH-tend*	obviously
ohne Zweifel/zweifellos	*oh-nuh tsvay-fuhl/ tsvay-fuhl-lohs*	without a doubt; doubtless
Du hast Recht.	*dew hAst Reht*	You are right. (inf.)
Sie haben Recht.	*zee hah-buhn ReHt*	You are right. (form.)
selbstverständlich	*zelpst-feR-shtänt-liH*	self-evident
Das ist falsch.	*dAs ist fAlsh*	That is wrong.
Das ist viel besser.	*dAs ist feel be-suhR*	That's much better.
Das ist völlig richtig.	*dAs ist fö-liH riH-tiH*	That's entirely correct.
Das finde ich gut/schlecht.	*dAs fin-duh iH gewt/shleHt*	That's good/bad.
Das ist eine tolle/schlechte Idee.	*dAs ist aynuh to-luh/shleH-tuh ee-dey*	That's a good/bad idea.
danke	*dAn-kuh*	thanks
keine Ursache	*kay-nuh ooR-zah-CHuh*	no need (no problem)

What's Your Opinion?

Imagine this: You're spending the weekend with a friend. Your friend suggests ways for the two of you to spend the afternoon. Use the clues suggested in your responses to fill in the blanks with the appropriate German responses with their English meanings. Check your responses in Appendix A.

1. **Your friend:** Heute scheint die Sonne. Denkst du, dass es warm ist? (Today the sun is shining. Do you think that it is warm?)

   You: _____. Es ist schwer zu sagen. (<u>I don't know</u>. It is difficult/ hard to say.)

2. **Your friend:** Hast du Lust, heute Nachmittag schwimmen zu gehen? (Do you feel like going swimming this afternoon?)

   You: _____. Ich schwimme sehr gern! (That's a good idea. I love swimming!)

3. **Your friend:** Vielleicht sollten wir zunächst den Wetterbericht lesen. Das Wetter könnte sich ändern. (Maybe we should read the weather forecast first. The weather may change.)

   You: _____. Das Wetter ist nie stabil. (You're right. The weather is never stable.)

4. **Your friend:** Welche Webseite sollen wir besuchen? (Which website should we visit?)

   You: _____. Alle Wetterwebseiten haben einen guten Wetterbericht. (It's all the same to me. All weather websites have a good weather report.)

5. **Your friend:** Ach, es wird regnen. Gehen wir ins Kino? (Oh, it's going to rain. Should we go to a movie?)

   You: _____. Ich will den neusten Arnold Schwarzenegger Film sehen! (Clearly. I want to see the latest Arnold Schwarzenegger movie!)

How Do You Feel?

Many physical and emotional conditions in German can be expressed with the verb *sein* (*zayn*), which means "to be," just as they would be in English: "I am sad," "I am happy," and so on. To express many other conditions, however, you must use the verb *haben* (*hA-buhn*), "to have." For example, in German you would say *Ich habe Angst* (*iH hah-buh Ankst*), literally, "I have fear." To express certain physical conditions, you can use both *sein* and *haben*. It's important to memorize the German expressions that clearly deviate from the English ones because you might create an embarrassing misunderstanding otherwise. Feelings that are expressed with the verb *haben* are followed by a noun. Feelings that are expressed with the verb *sein* are followed by an adjective. Chapters 9 and 10 discuss these verbs and how their form changes to *agree* with the subject. For now, concentrate on expressing how *you* feel: *ich bin* (*iH bin*) for expressions with *sein*, and *ich habe* (*iH hah-buh*) for expressions with *haben*. (See the following table.)

ACHTUNG

If you say, "I am hot" in German, you are certain to be misunderstood. *Ich bin heiß (iH bin hays)* expresses the speaker's level of sexual arousal. To express that you are hot physically, you would say, *"Mir ist heiß" (meeR ist hays)*—literally, "It's hot to me."

Physical Conditions

Expression	Pronunciation	Meaning
… Jahre alt sein	… yah-Ruh Alt zayn	to be … years old
Angst haben (vor)	Ankst hah-buhn (foR)	to be afraid (of)
beleidigt sein	buh-lay-diHt zayn	to be offended
beschämt sein	buh-shämt zayn	to be ashamed (of)
besorgt sein/Sorgen haben	buh-zoRkt zayn/zoR-guhn hah-buhn	to be worried/to have worries
durstig sein/Durst haben	dooR-stiH zayn/dooRst hah-buhn	to be thirsty
fertig sein	feR-tiH zayn	to be finished, done
fit sein	fit zayn	to be in shape
froh sein	froh zayn	to be happy
gut/schlecht gelaunt sein	gewt/shleHt guh-lount zayn	to be in a good/foul mood
hässlich sein	häs-liH zayn	to be ugly
hungrig sein/Hunger haben	hun-gRiH zayn/hun-guhRh A-buhn	to be hungry
Mir ist kalt.	meeR ist kAlt	I am cold.
Mir ist heiß.	meeR ist hays	I am hot.
müde sein	müh-duh zany	to be tired
schlapp sein	schlAp zany	to be worn out
Schmerzen haben	shmeR-tsuhn hah-buhn	to have an ache, to be in pain
schön sein	shöhn zayn	to be beautiful
traurig sein	tRou-RiH zayn	to be sad
verliebt sein	feR-leept zayn	to be in love

How Are You?

Express how you feel using the expressions in the preceding table. Check your accuracy in Appendix A.

1. Ich bin _____. (I am <u>tired</u>.)

2. Mir ist _____. (I am <u>cold</u>.)

3. Sie weint. Sie ist _____. (She cries. She is <u>sad</u>.)

4. Ich bin _____, dass das Wetter gut ist. (I'm <u>happy</u> that the weather is good.)

5. Mein Magen knurrt. Ich bin _____. (My stomach is growling. I'm <u>hungry</u>.)

6. Ich bin _____. (I'm <u>in love</u>.)

7. Ich kann nicht mehr! Ich bin_____. (I just can't do any more! I'm <u>finished</u>.)

8. Ich trainiere jeden Tag und mache Bodybuilding. Ich bin _____. (I train every day and do bodybuilding. I am <u>in shape</u>.)

9. Ich esse jetzt mein Lieblingseis. Ich bin _____. (I'm eating my favorite ice cream. I'm <u>in a good mood</u>.)

You know the saying "The early bird gets the worm"? Sayings are everywhere in language, embodying familiar truths and generally accepted beliefs in colorful, expressive language. Here are a few German sayings and their English counterparts.

Sayings

German Saying	Pronunciation	English Equivalent
Wer zuerst kommt, mahlt zuerst.	*veyR tsew-eRst komt, mahlt tsew-eRst*	The early bird gets the worm.
Was ich nicht weiß, macht mich nicht heiß.	*vas iH niHt vays, mACHt miH niHt hays*	What I don't know can't hurt me.
Wer zuletzt lacht, lacht am Besten.	*veyR tsew-letst lACHt, lACHt Am bes-tuhn*	He who laughs last, laughs best.
Wer lügt, der stiehlt.	*veyR lühkt, deyR shteelt*	He who lies, steals.

continues

Sayings (continued)

German Saying	Pronunciation	English Equivalent
Iss, was gar ist, trink, was klar ist, sprich, was wahr ist.	*is, vAs gahR ist, tRink, vAs klahR ist, shpriH, vAs vahR ist*	Eat what is cooked, drink what is clear, speak what is true.
Ein Unglück kommt selten allein.	*ain oon-glük kOmt zel-tuhn uh-layn*	It never rains, but it pours.
Wer wagt, gewinnt.	*veyR vAkt, guh-vint*	Nothing ventured, nothing gained.
Kommt Zeit, kommt Rat.	*komt tsayt, komt Rat*	Time will tell.
Andere Länder, andere Sitten.	*An-duh-ruh län-duhR, An-duh-ruh zi-tuhn*	When in Rome, do as the Romans do.

The Least You Need to Know

- Every language has idiomatic expressions that are specific to it. Such colorful expressions reveal a culture's history and habits.

- Certain terms, phrases, and expressions in German will be useful when you want to express location or direction.

- The verbs with the highest frequency in both English and German are "to have" and "to be." Start learning them and express your opinions and feelings.

- When you use popular sayings, don't translate from English to German. Although the sense may be the same in both languages, they use different words. Your best bet is to learn these sayings by rote and sound multicultural.

Ready, Set, Go!

Now that you can pronounce German, it's time for some more vocabulary and a little structure. Even if you're not a glutton for grammar, a little reintroduction to some grammatical principles will take you a long way toward speaking and reading in German. In this part of the book, you'll acquire not only the basics—nouns, verbs, sentence structure—but you'll also learn how to express yourself more colorfully.

Gender: More Than Male or Female

In This Chapter

* How to determine the gender of nouns
* Changing gender
* Plural formation

Think a girl is female (*das Mädchen*)? Think your female babysitter is female (*der Babysitter*)? Think your infant girl is female (*der Säugling*)? Not in the German language. In this chapter, you'll learn everything you need to know about the gender of German nouns.

Determining Gender

If you have taken any French or Spanish, you have already dealt with nouns that have two genders. In German, it's more complex: German nouns have *three* distinct genders. If you've been reading this book carefully, you've probably already noticed that German nouns are preceded by three distinct *definite articles:* the masculine article *der* (*deyR*), the feminine article *die* (*dee*), or the neuter article *das* (*dAs*). All plural nouns are preceded by the plural article *die* (*dee*).

Although the natural, or biological, gender of the noun and the grammatical gender of the definite article may work the way you'd expect them to—*Herr* (*heR*), for example, the noun for "man," takes the masculine article *der* (*deyR*)—determining linguistic gender can be tricky. Gender is divided into three linguistic classes that don't correspond to the real world. The fact of the matter is that grammatical gender is arbitrary and unpredictable—basically, a matter of rote memorization. Consider this: why is the meat you eat at dinner neuter (*das Fleisch*), the potato feminine (*die Kartoffel*), and the cauliflower masculine (*der Blumenkohl*)?

The only fail-safe way of ensuring that you are about to use the correct gender of a German noun is to learn the gender and plural of a noun along with the noun itself. Without committing a noun's gender to memory, you'll need to constantly rely on looking up the noun in a dictionary; masculine nouns are followed by *m.*, feminine nouns by *f.*, and neuter nouns by *n.* Bear in mind that the gender of a noun affects its relationship to other words in a sentence, and if you learn the definite articles along with the nouns, it will be easier for you to form sentences correctly later. Nevertheless, a few tricks can help you determine the gender of certain nouns as well as alter the gender of certain other nouns, as in English when you change the word *waiter* to *waitress.* We'll share them with you later in this chapter. Keep reading!

Definite Articles

Before you get into German nouns, you must take into account one little diversion: the *noun marker* that precedes most singular nouns. We use the term noun marker to refer to an article or adjective—something that indicates the gender of the noun— whether it is masculine (m.), feminine (f.), neuter (n.), singular (s.), or plural (p.) The most common noun markers, shown in the following table, are definite articles expressing "the" and indefinite articles expressing "a," "an," or "one."

Singular Noun Markers

Noun Marker	Masculine	Feminine	Neuter
the	der	die	das
one, a, an	ein	eine	ein

Singular Nouns

 Track 5 The nouns in the following table are easy to remember. An obvious correspondence exists between the grammatical gender of the noun marker and the natural, biological gender of the noun. Even the different types of mothers remain predictably feminine, while the different types of fathers are masculine in gender. Later in this chapter, you'll learn how to predict the gender of compound nouns. But for now, become acquainted with family terms. If you'd like to hear the pronunciation of some of these examples, check out Track 5 on the CD included with this book.

Gender-Obvious Nouns

Masculine Noun	Pronunciation	English
der Bruder	*deyR bRew-duhR*	the brother
der Cousin	*deyR koo-zin*	the cousin
der Freund	*deyR fRoynt*	the friend
der Onkel	*deyR on-kuhl*	the uncle
der Opa/Großvater	*deyR oh-pah/gRohs-fah-tuhR*	the grandfather
der Vater	*deyR fah-tuhR*	the father
der Schwieger-vater	*deyR shvee-guhR-fah-tuhR*	the father-in-law
der Stiefvater	*deyR steef-fah-tuhR*	the step-father
der Mann	*deyR mAn*	the husband
der Sohn	*deyR zohn*	the son
die Schwester	*dee shves-tuhR*	the sister
die Cousine/Kusine	*dee koo-zee-nuh*	the cousin
die Freundin	*dee froyn-din*	the friend
die Tante	*dee tAn-tuh*	the aunt
die Oma/Großmutter	*dee oh-mah/gRohs-moo-tuhR*	the grandmother
die Mutter	*dee moo-tuhR*	the mother
die Schwieger-mutter	*dee shvee-guhR- moo-tuhR*	the mother-in-law
die Stiefmutter	*dee shteef-moo-tuhR*	the step-mother
die Frau	*dee fRou*	the wife
die Tochter	*dee toCH-tuhR*	the daughter

Even in a world where hardly anything is what it seems, you can still determine the gender of certain kinds of nouns even if you haven't memorized their definite articles. For example, nouns referring to male persons (*der Mann, der Sohn*); nouns of professions ending in -*er*, -*or*, -*ler*, or -*ner* (*der Pastor, der Bäcker*); and most nouns referring to male animals of a species (*der Tiger, der Elefant*) take the article *der*. But don't worry about gender equality, because you'll soon learn a sure-fire way to effeminate masculine persons and animals! The following tables group endings that will help you to identify the gender of nouns.

Masculine Nouns

Masculine Endings	Example	Pronunciation	English Meaning
-ich	der Strich	*deyR shtRiH*	the line
-ig	der Honig	*deyR hoh-niH*	the honey
-ing	der Ring	*deyR Ring*	the ring
-ling	der Sträfling	*deyR shtRähf-ling*	the prisoner

Exception: das Ding (dAs ding), "the thing"

Even if you aren't a botanist, it may be helpful to keep in mind that most trees and flowers take the feminine article: *die Tulpe (dee tool-puh), die Rose (dee Roh-zuh), die Eiche (dee ay-Huh)*. Generally, two-syllable nouns ending in -*e*, such as *Sonne (zo-nuh)* and *Blume (blew-muh)*, take the feminine article *die*.

Feminine Nouns

Feminine Endings	Example	Pronunciation	English Meaning
-ei	die Malerei	*dee mah-luh-Ray*	the painting
-heit	die Gesundheit	*dee guh-zoont-hayt*	the health
-keit	die Möglichkeit	*dee mök-liH-kayt*	the possibility
-schaft	die Gesellschaft	*dee guh-zel-shAft*	the society
-ung	die Wanderung	*dee vAn-duh-Rung*	the walking tour

Das Berlin, das Deutschland, das Paris—most countries, towns, and cities all take the neuter article *das,* as do the letters of the alphabet: *das A, das B, das C, das D,* and so on. So will *most* words borrowed directly into German from other languages: *das Hotel, das Poster,* and so on.

AS A RULE

When added to a noun, the suffix *–lein* (*layn*) or *–chen* (*Huhn*) alters the meaning of the noun, changing it to a diminutive. These nouns are always neuter: *die Stadt* (*dee shtAt*), "the city," becomes *das Städtchen* (*dAs shtät-Huhn*), "the little city." Monosyllabic nouns with *o, u,* or *a* incur an umlaut in this linguistic process of making a noun refer to something smaller.

Neuter Nouns

Neuter Endings	Example	Pronunciation	English Meaning
-chen	das Kätzchen	*dAs käts-Huhn*	the kitty
-lein	das Büchlein	*dAs büH-layn*	the little book
-nis	das Ergebnis	*dAs eR-gep-nis*	the result
-tel	das Drittel	*dAs dRi-tuhl*	the third
-tum	das Eigentum	*dAs ay-guhn-tewm*	the property

Exceptions: *der Irrtum* (*deyR iR-tewm*), "the error"; *der Reichtum* (*deyR RayH-tewm*), "the wealth"; *die Erlaubnis* (*dee eR-loup-nis*), "the permission"; and *die Erkenntnis* (*dee eR-kent-nis*), "the knowledge."

Certain German nouns never change gender, regardless of whether they refer to a male or a female person or animal. Here are a few of them.

German	Pronunciation	English
das Genie	*dAs jey-nee*	the genius
das Individuum	*dAs in-dee-vee-doo-oom*	the individual
das Kind	*dAs kint*	the child
das Model	*dAs moh-del*	the model
das Opfer	*dAs op-feR*	the victim
der Flüchtling	*deyR flüHt-ling*	the refugee
die Person	*dee peR-zohn*	the person

In most cases, making nouns feminine is as easy as changing the definite article from *der* to *die*, dropping the vowel (if the noun ends in a vowel), adding *-in* to the masculine noun, and, if the noun contains an *a*, an *o*, or a *u*, modifying this vowel: *der Koch* (*deyR koCH*), for example, becomes *die Köchin* (*dee kö-Hin*). The following table lists some common nouns that can undergo sex changes.

AS A RULE

Compound nouns combine two or more nouns into one. They are written as one word in German and take the gender of the last noun in the compound. Likewise, compound nouns, being governed by the right end of things, take the plural form of the last noun. *Der Zahnarzt* (*deyR tsahn-ARtst*), for example, is made up of the two words *der Zahn* and *der Arzt* (*deyR ARtst*). Because *Arzt* comes last, it is the only part of the compound noun that can become plural.

Sex Changes

Masculine Ending	Pronunciation	Feminine Ending	Pronunciation	Meaning
der Anwalt	*deyR An-vAlt*	die Anwältin	*dee An-väl-tin*	the attorney
der Arzt	*deyR ARtst*	die Ärztin	*dee äRts-tin*	the doctor
der Bauer	*deyR bou-uhr*	die Bäuerin	*dee boy-uhR-in*	the farmer
der Lehrer	*deyR ley-Ruhr*	die Lehrerin	*dee ley-Ruh-Rin*	the teacher
der Löwe	*deyR löh-wuh*	die Löwin	*dee löh-vin*	the lion
der Schüler	*deyR shüh-luhR*	die Schülerin	*dee shüh-luh-Rin*	the school boy/girl

Compound Nouns

Meeresgrundforschungslaborauswertungsbericht—pronounced *mey-Ruhs-gRoont-foR-shoongz-lah-bohR-ous-veR-toongz-buh-RiHt*—what in the world, you may ask, is that? Believe it or not, *that* is a word—a compound noun, to be exact. It means "sea-floor research lab evaluation report." While English joins words together to form new, compound words such as *bittersweet, homework,* or *spoonfeed,* compound nouns of the cargo-train variety are a German phenomenon. Don't let these words frighten you. If you can recognize the individual nouns, adjectives, or verbs within the longer word, you should have no trouble figuring out the meaning. In the first table of this section, you learned that *die Mutter* means "the mother" and *der Vater* means "the father." It didn't take you long to figure out that the particle *Stief* adds a layer of meaning—"step"—and that *Schwieger* adds "in-law." You also noticed that *all* forms of mothers were feminine—that is to say, they took the feminine marker, *die*. Hmmm …. Is a pattern emerging here? Why, yes! German looks to the right end of a noun to determine its gender. Another way to think of it is that the (directional) right end governs the entire noun. And after all, government likes to tell us how to do things, and nouns must abide by these very same rules!

See whether you can put the following words together to form compound nouns and consult Appendix A to verify your new nouns:

Example:

die Zeit ("time") + der Geist ("spirit") = der Zeitgeist

1. das Hotel ("hotel") + die Kette ("chain") =
   _____

2. die Musik ("music") + das Geschäft ("store") =
   _____

3. das Geschenk ("gift") + das Papier ("paper") =
   _____

4. das Telefon ("telephone") + die Nummer ("number") =
   _____

5. der Brief ("letter") + der Kasten ("box") = _____

6. schwer ("heavy") + die Kraft ("power") = *_____

7. treff (from "to meet") + der Punkt ("point") =
   *_____

Don't forget to capitalize the newly formed compound noun!

Did you figure out what the compound noun in number 6 means? Consult Appendix A!

An *n* or an *s* is sometimes used between nouns to connect them:

die Tomate ("tomato") + der Saft ("juice") = der Tomatensaft

die Liebe ("love") + die Erklärung ("declarations") = die Liebeserklärung

More Than One

In English, talking about more than one thing is relatively easy—usually, you just add an *-s* to a word. But there are plurals that stump learners of our language. How many *childs* do you have—or, rather, *children?* Are they silly little *gooses,* uh, *geese?* German plurals seem to be confusing, too, but there is a method to the madness. The German language has rules about forming plurals, yet nonetheless, when a noun becomes plural in German, the noun marker becomes plural with it, and the articles *der, die,* and *das* all become *die* in their plural forms.

Pluralities

Every English speaker knows that if you have more than one cat, you have cats. In German, however, it's a little trickier. When nouns become plural in German, the noun may remain unchanged (*Mädchen,* for example, remains *Mädchen* in the plural); may take an ending such as *-e, -er, -n, -en,* or *-s;* and/or may undergo a vowel modification. Rest assured, there are rules for forming plurals in German, and with enough attention and devotion, you will develop a linguistic feel for them, a type of *Sprachgefühl.* For now, the best way to be sure that you are forming the plural of a noun correctly is to memorize it along with the noun and the article. The following tables give you some basic rules on how to form plurals.

When the nouns in the following two tables become plural, they take either *-n* or *-en.* A majority of German nouns fall into this group, including most feminine nouns. The nouns in this group never take an umlaut in the plural, but if they already have one in the singular, it is retained.

When the nouns ending in *-e, -el,* and *-er* in the following table become plural, they take *-n.*

Plural Nouns Group I: Add an *-n*

German Noun Singular	Pronunciation	German Noun Plural	Pronunciation	English Meaning
das Auge	*dAs ou-guh*	die Augen	*dee ou-guhn*	eye(s)
der Bauer	*deyR bou-uhR*	die Bauern	*dee bou-uhRn*	farmer(s)
der Junge	*deyR yoon-guh*	die Jungen	*dee yoon-guhn*	boy(s)
der Name	*deyR nah-muh*	die Namen	*dee nah-muhn*	name(s)
die Gruppe	*dee gRoo-puh*	die Gruppen	*dee gRoo-puhn*	group(s)
die Kartoffel	*dee kAR-to-fuhl*	die Kartoffeln	*dee kAR-to-fuhln*	potato(es)

German Noun Singular	Pronunciation	German Noun Plural	Pronunciation	English Meaning
die Schüssel	*dee shü-suhl*	die Schüsseln	*dee shü-suhln*	bowl(s)
die Steuer	*dee shtoy-uhR*	die Steuern	*dee shtoy-uhRn*	tax(es)

Most of the nouns in the following table that take the ending -*en* in the plural are feminine nouns ending in -*ung*, -*ion*, -*keit*, -*heit*, -*schaft*, and -*tät*. All nouns referring to female persons or animals ending in -*in* double the *n* in the plural form before adding the plural -*en*. This convention keeps the *i* sound short.

Plural Nouns Group II: Add an *-en* (*-nen*)

German Noun Singular	Pronunciation	German Noun Plural	Pronunciation	English Meaning
das Herz	*dAs heRts*	die Herzen	*dee heR-tsuhn*	heart(s)
das Ohr	*dAs ohR*	die Ohren	*dee oh-Ruhn*	ear(s)
der Mensch	*deyR mensh*	die Menschen	*dee men-shuhn*	human being(s)
die Freiheit	*dee fRay-hayt*	die Freiheiten	*dee fRay-hay-tuhn*	liberty(ies)
die Königin	*dee köh-ni-gin*	die Königinnen	*dee köh-ni-gi-nuhn*	the queens(s)
die Löwin	*dee löh-vin*	die Löwinnen	*dee löh-vi-nuhn*	the lioness(es)
die Mannschaft	*dee mAn-shAft*	die Mannschaften	*dee mAn-shAf-tuhn*	crew(s), team(s)
die Möglichkeit	*dee mö-kliH-kayt*	die Möglich-keiten	*dee mö-kliH-kay-tuhn*	possibilities
die Qualität	*dee kvah-lee-täht*	die Qualitäten	*dee kvah-lee-täh-tuhn*	quality(ies)
die Religion	*dee Rey-lee-gee-ohn*	die Religionen	*dee Rey-lee-gee-oh-*	religion(s)
die Zeitung	*dee tsay-toong*	die Zeitungen	*dee tsay-toon-guhn*	newspaper(s)

The nouns in the following table take no ending in their plural form. Some of the masculine nouns in the group undergo a vowel modification, as do the only two feminine nouns in this group. The neuter nouns don't change.

Plural Nouns Group III: Add Nothing (Except Possibly an Umlaut)

German Noun Singular	Pronunciation	German Noun Plural	Pronunciation	English Meaning
das Fenster	*dAs fen-stuhR*	die Fenster	*dee fen-stuhR*	the window(s)
das Mittel	*dAs mi-tuhl*	die Mittel	*dee mi-tuhl*	the mean(s)
das Zimmer	*dAs tsi-muhR*	die Zimmer	*dee tsi-muhR*	the room(s)
der Garten	*deyR gAR-tuhn*	die Gärten	*dee gäR-tuhn*	the garden(s)
der Lehrer	*deyR ley-RuhR*	die Lehrer	*dee ley-RuhR*	the teacher(s)
der Vater	*deyR fah-tuhR*	die Väter	*dee fäh-tuhR*	the father(s)
die Mutter	*dee moo-tuhR*	die Mütter	*dee mü-tuhR*	the mother(s)
die Tochter	*dee toCH-tuhR*	die Töchter	*dee töH-tuhR*	the daughter(s)

When the nouns in the following table become plural, they take the ending *-e*. All neuter and feminine nouns that end in *-nis* double the *s* in the plural form before adding *-e*, again ensuring that the *i* sound remains short. Take note that some monosyllabic nouns incur a vowel modification along with assuming the *-e* plural ending.

Plural Nouns Group IV: Add an *–e* (and Possibly an Umlaut)

German Noun Singular	Pronunciation	German Noun Plural	Pronunciation	English Meaning
das Ereignis	*dAs eR-ayk-nis*	die Ereignisse	*dee eR-ayk-ni-suh*	the event(s)
das Gedicht	*dAs guh-diHt*	die Gedichte	*dee guh-diH-tuh*	the poem(s)
das Jahr	*dAs yahR*	die Jahre	*dee yah-Ruh*	the year(s)
das Pferd	*dAs pfeRt*	die Pferde	*dee pfeR-duh*	the horse(s)
der Baum	*deyR boum*	die Bäume	*dee boy-muh*	the tree(s)
der Brief	*deyR bReef*	die Briefe	*dee bRee-fuh*	the letter(s)
die Kenntnis	*dee kent-nis*	die Kenntnisse	*dee kent-ni-suh*	the knowledge
die Kunst	*dee koonst*	die Künste	*dee küns-tuh*	the art(s)
die Wand	*dee vAnt*	die Wände	*dee vän-duh*	the wall(s)

The plurals of the nouns in the following table end in *-er*. Wherever possible, vowels are modified. When they cannot be modified, as in the noun *das Bild* (the vowels *e* and *i* never take an umlaut in German), the word takes the *-er* ending. Note that all the words that follow have only one syllable.

Plural Nouns Group V: Add an *-er* and an Umlaut

German Noun Singular	Pronunciation	German Noun Plural	Pronunciation	English Meaning
das Bild	*dAs bilt*	die Bilder	*dee bil-duhR*	the painting(s)
das Buch	*dAs bewCH*	die Bücher	*dee bü-HuhR*	the book(s)
das Land	*dAs lAnt*	die Länder	*dee län-duhR*	the country(ies)
der Geist	*deyR gayst*	die Geister	*dee gay-stuhr*	the ghost(s)
der Mann	*deyR mAn*	die Männer	*dee mä-nuhR*	the man (men)

Practice Those Plurals

Here is a list of singular items found around the house. Rewrite the list, changing the nouns into their appropriate plural form (all preceded by *die!*). Check Appendix A to verify your plural forms:

> Ex. das Haus die Häuser

1. das Zimmer
2. der Garten
3. die Wand
4. das Bild
5. das Buch
6. die Schüssel
7. der Brief
8. die Zeitung

Noteworthy Plurals

Track 5 As in English, some nouns in German are used only in their plural forms. These are worth noting, particularly because you don't have to worry about whether the articles preceding them are masculine, feminine, or neuter. They always take the plural article *die*. One exception worth mentioning is the English plural noun for spectacles, "glasses," which is singular in German: *die Brille* (*dee bri-luh*). If you'd like to hear the pronunciation of some of the following examples, check out Track 5 on the CD included with this book.

German	Pronunciation	English
die Ferien	*dee fey-Ree-uhn*	vacation
die Geschwister	*dee guh-shvis-tuhr*	siblings
die Leute	*dee loy-tuh*	people
die Eltern	*dee el-tuhrn*	parents

A few nouns in German (usually words ending in *a*, *i*, or *o*) take an *-s* to form the plural, as in *das Lotto* (*die Lottos*), "the national lottery(ies)." In addition, add *-s* in the plural for nouns of foreign origin, such as *die Kamera* (*die Kameras*), *das Café* (*die Cafés*), and *das Auto* (*die Autos*). German abbreviated nouns also add an *-s* in the plural: *der/die Azubi* (*die Azubis*), being an abbreviation for *der/die Auszubildende*, a type of student undertaking further education.

The Least You Need to Know

- The only sure-fire way to know a noun's gender is to memorize the definite article with the noun.
- Most nouns referring to male persons and animals become feminine nouns when *-in* is added.
- Compound nouns in German are easy to formulate and instantly increase your vocabulary power. Figuring out their gender or their plural form won't be a problem because gender and plural forms of even the longest compound words are always determined by the rightmost constituents.
- There are many exceptions to rules about forming plurals. Plural forms of nouns should be learned along with the noun and the definite article. If you think of nouns in terms of a triangle—one point being the noun; the second, its gender; and the third, its plural form—you'll be learning three parcels of information for the price of one!

Guiding Grammar: Fitting Form with Function

In This Chapter

- Cases in German
- Definite and indefinite articles
- An introduction to subject pronouns
- Formality issues

Now that you have familiarized yourself with nouns, it's time to start forming sentences. In English, once you have the subject, the verb, and the direct object, forming a sentence is easy enough; you put the words in the right order and start talking. It doesn't work this way in German, however. Word order—the position of words in a sentence—isn't as crucial in German as it is in English because German has retained many of the inflections that English dropped along the way. German nouns, pronouns, articles, adjectives, and pronouns are inflected—that is to say, they have overt markings showing their grammatical relations and functions in sentences.

The Four Cases in German

You don't have to be Sherlock Holmes to figure out *cases* in German. Cases are the forms that articles, adjectives, pronouns, and a few nouns take in a sentence, depending on their function. When we speak of cases and nouns, we are speaking of their articles, because the article that precedes a noun is the primary indicator of its gender, number, and—you guessed it—case. German uses four cases to express grammatical relations between sentence parts: nominative, accusative, dative, and genitive. By altering the form of *the*, *a*, or an adjective, you can figure out what's happening to whom, no matter where the nouns are in the sentence. In a nutshell, the nominative case indicates the subject of a sentence, the accusative case indicates the direct object of a sentence, and the dative case indicates the indirect object of a sentence. The genitive case shows possession.

> **DEFINITION**
>
> A **case** is the form that articles, adjectives, pronouns, and a few nouns in German take, depending on their grammatical function in a sentence. Cases make it clear whether a noun phrase is functioning as a subject of a verb or an object of a verb or preposition.

Subject	Verb	Indirect Object	Direct Object
The girl	buys	the cat	a fish
Das Mädchen	*kauft*	*der Katze*	*einen Fisch*

In German, cases enable you to vary the order of nouns and pronouns without changing the overall meaning of the sentence, allowing you to place focus on whatever element of the sentence you like!

Das Mädchen kauft den Fisch.

Den Fisch kauft das Mädchen.

Although the second sentence might make you think that the fish is buying the girl, it isn't, thanks to the cases taken by the nouns *das Mädchen* (nom.) and *den Fisch* (acc.). Despite the position of the nouns, the noun markers remain the same in both sentences, clearly indicating that the fish is being bought by the girl, not that the girl is being bought by the fish.

Naming the Nominative Case

Nominative is the case of the *subject* of a sentence—that is, of the noun or pronoun performing the action (or undergoing the state of being) of the verb. Think of the nominative case as "naming" who or what is performing the action in the sentence.

Nominative (Subject)	Verb
Ich (I)	denke (think)

What Gets the Action: The Accusative Case

The accusative case is used with the direct object. The *direct object* tells you to whom or what the action of the verb is being directed. You also use the accusative case with time and in measuring data that specifies how short, how soon, how often, how much, and how old and after certain prepositions. Some varieties in English still express the accusative case (in English it's called the *objective* case) by using the alternative form of who: *whom*. Think of the accusative case as expressing whom or what is being "accused" by the verb.

Nominative (Subject)	Verb	Accusative (Direct Object)
Ich (I)	schicke (send)	ein Paket (a package)

Indirectly: The Dative Case

The dative case can be used instead of a possessive adjective with parts of the body and after certain verbs, prepositions, and adjectives. It is used primarily to indicate the indirect object, however. The *indirect object* is the object for whose benefit or in whose interest the action of the verb is being performed. Think of giving, helping, pleasing, and such—an animate object is receiving the action and usually something else (the direct object), to boot! English has lost most of its inflectional endings reflecting this case, so it relies on *word order* and prepositions, such as *to* and *for*, to express the dative function.

DEFINITION

Word order is the order of the basic sentence elements—subject, object, and verb—that contributes to the meaning or sense of a sentence.

Nominative (Subject)	Verb	Dative (Indirect Object)	Accusative (Direct Object)
Er (he)	schickt (sends)	seinem Bruder (his brother)	ein Paket (a package)

Possessing the Genitive Case

The genitive case indicates possession. Whereas English uses an -*s*, as in "the neighbor's yard," or the preposition *of* in "the yard *of* the neighbor" to express possession, German can use either an -*s* (without an apostrophe) after a person's name or the German prepositional equivalent—in this case, *von*. Most of the time, however, German marks possession on both the noun marker (the article or adjective preceding the noun) and, with neuter and masculine nouns, after the noun with -(*e*)*s*. Although this construction might seem confusing at first, think of it in terms of the word *possessive*; look at all of those -*s* additions. Why not latch on to that idea in German?

Nominative	Verb	Dative (Indirect Object)	Genitive (Possessive)	Accusative (Direct Object)
Er (he)	Schickt (sends)	der Frau (the wife)	seines Bruders (of his brother)	ein Paket (a package)

Marking Who's Doing What to Whom

If you've been exposed to Latin or a Slavic language such as Polish or Russian, you might have heard about *declension*, the term used to talk about the changes occurring in a noun or pronoun to indicate different cases.

> **DEFINITION**
>
> **Declension** is the pattern of inflectional markings that occurs in articles, adjectives, pronouns, and a few nouns in each of the four cases in German.

Declension refers to the patterns of change followed by different groups of words in each case. Declension in German is pretty much limited to articles, adjectives, and a few instances of nouns. In addition, pronouns change form according to their function, but this change is very similar to English: *he* versus *him* and such. Be sure that when you are looking up a noun, you look for it under its base form, not its plural or possessive form. The nominative singular is the form under which nouns appear in the dictionary, just as the infinitive is the form under which verbs appear.

The Case of the Definite Article

German has four possible declensions for each definite article (remember, definite articles are used when you are speaking about a particular person or thing). In addition, the plurals of *der*, *die*, and *das* have separate declensions. Commit this chart to memory, rewrite it on a card, use a different color for each case—do anything and everything to help yourself conceptualize the case system. This system is your springboard, and you won't be able to dive in if you don't learn this *paradigm*. In addition, you will be able to plug in new information as you go along.

> **DEFINITION**
>
> **Paradigm** is a grammatical chart, organized in a regular way so that new information may be plugged in and easily assimilated.

Case	Masculine	Feminine	Neuter	Plural
Nom.	der	die	das	die
	deyR	*dee*	*dAs*	*dee*
Acc.	den	die	das	die
	deyn	*dee*	*dAs*	*dee*
Dat.	dem	der	dem	den
	deym	*deyR*	*deym*	*deyn*
Gen.	des	der	des	der
	des	*deyR*	*des*	*deyR*

Masculine Nouns

Using the same paradigm—the same setup of cases in descending order of nominative, accusative, dative, genitive—we can plug in actual masculine nouns. Notice the noun endings in the genitive case. You'll observe that a monosyllabic noun gets an *-e* before its genitive *-s*. A masculine noun of more than one syllable in the genitive case requires a mere *–s*.

Case	Noun	Pronunciation	Noun	Pronunciation
Nom.	der Sohn	*deyR zohn*	der Vater	*deyR fah-tuhR*
Acc.	den Sohn	*deyn zohn*	den Vater	*deyn fah-tuhR*
Dat.	dem Sohn	*deym zohn*	dem Vater	*deym fah-tuhR*
Gen.	des Sohnes	*des zohn-uhs*	des Vaters	*des fah-tuhRs*

A few masculine nouns take an -(e)n ending in all cases except the nominative. Because they get an -(e)n in the genitive, you don't need to add that usual -(e)s. This group includes many nouns of foreign origin that are accented on the last syllable, such as *der Assistent, der Demokrat, der Polizist, der Präsident, der Tourist*; Germanic masculine nouns that end in an unstressed -e, such as *der Löwe* ("lion"), *der Kunde* ("customer"), and *der Junge* ("boy"); and in a few monosyllabic nouns, such as *der Mensch* ("human being"), *der Held* ("hero"), and *der Herr* ("man").

AS A RULE

An easy way to remember the definite article, or *der*-word, paradigm is with the mnemonic device reflecting the last sound of each of the genders, numbers, and cases represented left to right, top to bottom: RESE (*Ree-see*), NESE (*nee-see*), MRMN (*muhR-muhN*), SRSR (*suhR-suhR*).

Case	Noun	Pronunciation	Noun	Pronunciation
Nom.	der Student	*deyR shtew-dent*	der Junge	*deyR yoon-guh*
Acc.	den Studenten	*deyn shtew-den-tuhn*	den Jungen	*deyn yoon-guhn*
Dat.	dem Studenten	*deym shtew-den-tuhn*	dem Jungen	*deym yoon-guhn*
Gen.	des Studenten	*des shtew-den-tuhn*	des Jungen	*des yoon-guhn*

Feminine Nouns

Fair's fair, so here are a few feminine nouns plugged into our paradigm. Notice that, unlike the masculine nouns, feminine nouns do not need endings. They remain unchanged.

Case	Noun	Pronunciation	Noun	Pronunciation
Nom.	die Kunst	*dee koonst*	die Blume	*dee blew-muh*
Acc.	die Kunst	*dee koonst*	die Blume	*dee blew-muh*
Dat.	der Kunst	*deyR koonst*	der Blume	*deyR blew-muh*
Gen.	der Kunst	*deyR koonst*	der Blume	*deyR blew-muh*

Neuter Nouns

And now for the neuter nouns. Just like the masculine nouns, neuter nouns take an -(e)s in the genitive case.

Case	Noun	Pronunciation	Noun	Pronunciation
Nom.	das Jahr	*dAs yahR*	das Fenster	*dAs fen-stuhR*
Acc.	das Jahr	*dAs yahR*	das Fenster	*dAs fen-stuhR*
Dat.	dem Jahr	*deym yahR*	dem Fenster	*deym fen-stuhR*
Gen.	des Jahres	*des yah-Ruhs*	des Fensters	*des fen-stuhRz*

Plurals

Coming now to the right side of the original paradigm, we can plug in the plural nouns for *father* and *child*, only augmenting them with an *-n* in the dative case. If the plural form already ends in an *-n*, as in *Katzen* ("cats"), you have nothing to worry about. All plurals in the dative case take an additional *-n*, if possible.

Case	Plural	Pronunciation	Plural	Pronunciation
Nom.	die Väter	*dee fäh-tuhR*	die Kinder	*dee kin-duhR*
Acc.	die Väter	*dee fäh-tuhR*	die Kinder	*dee kin-duhR*
Dat.	den Vätern	*deyn fäh-tuhRn*	den Kindern	*deyn kin-duhRn*
Gen.	der Väter	*deyR fäh-tuhR*	der Kinder	*deyR kin-duhR*

Identifying Function

Now it's time to apply form to function. Underline the subject (in the nominative case) and put parentheses around the direct object (accusative case) and brackets around the indirect object (dative case) in the following sentences. Not all sentences have both an indirect and a direct object! Check your analyses in Appendix A.

1. Den Studenten findet der Detektiv intelligent.

2. Dem Vater schicken die Kinder den Kaffee.

3. Die Menschen helfen den Kindern.

4. Das Paket packt der Lehrer.

5. Die Mütter bringen den Vätern die Blumen.

Indefinite Articles

The English equivalent of the indefinite article is *a* or *an*. *Indefinite articles* are used when you are speaking about a noun in general, not about a specific noun. Only three declensions are possible for the indefinite article because indefinite articles do not occur in the plural. Just as in English, it's not possible or logical to talk about *a books*. Again, we're using that original paradigm and plugging in this *new* information that really isn't all that *new*. If you compare this chart of indefinite articles (the *ein*-word paradigm) with the definite article chart (the *der*-word paradigm), you'll see that all the feminine endings exactly resemble the ends of the feminine definite articles: *die, eine; die, eine; der, einer; der, einer.* Now look for correspondences in the masculine and neuter. Sure enough, only three new bits of information are actually on this chart, provided that you've done your homework and learned the other paradigm: masculine and neuter nominative and neuter accusative indefinite articles (*ein*) don't take an ending. See? German *is* simple, after all!

> **DEFINITION**
>
> An **indefinite article** is an article used when you are speaking about a noun in general, not about a specific noun. The indefinite article is used to introduce a topic into discourse.

Case	Masculine	Feminine	Neuter	Plural
Nom.	ein	eine	ein	none
	ayn	*ay-nuh*	*ayn*	
Acc.	einen	eine	ein	none
	ay-nuhn	*ay-nuh*	*ayn*	
Dat.	einem	einer	einem	none
	ay-nuhm	*ay-nuhR*	*ay-nuhm*	
Gen.	eines	einer	eines	none
	ay-nuhs	*ay-nuhR*	*ay-nuhs*	

Subject Pronouns

Before you can form sentences with verbs in German, you have to know something about subject pronouns. A subject pronoun is, as its name suggests, the subject of a sentence—the who or what that performs the action. The verb must agree with the subject pronoun (grammatically speaking, that is, in person and number—we all know verbs don't have opinions of their own). You can link this bit of information to what you already know about cases. The case of the subject is nominative, so you can also think about these pronouns as nominative personal pronouns. The German subject pronouns in the following table have a person (first person is *I*, second person is *you*, and third person is *he*, *she*, or *it*), just as subject pronouns do in English, and a number (singular or plural). If you've ever studied literature, you may recall discussing narrators' perspectives: first person omniscient or limited was told by the narrator using *I*; third person objective had the narrators talking about the story and characters using *he* and *she*. So what is second person all about? It involves directly addressing someone—talking to someone.

Subject Pronouns

Person	Singular	English	Plural	English
First	ich *iH*	I	wir *veer*	we
Second	du *dew*	you	ihr *eer*	you
Third	er, sie, es *eR, zee, es*	he, she, it	sie *zee*	they
Formal Second	Sie *zee*	you	Sie *zee*	you

Du and *Ihr* Versus *Sie:* Informal Versus Formal

While English has just one form of "you," German has three different forms, depending on the level of formality and number (singular or plural). *Sie* is a polite form implying a certain formality between people and takes into account social considerations. *Sie* is used when talking to people you'd address as *Herr* (*heR*), "Mr.," *Frau* (*frou*), "Miss, Mrs.," and with other titles. It should also be used with people you don't know or to indicate respect. *Du*, the informal "you," is used more casually—with a single peer, a family member, a close friend, a pet, or God, whereas *ihr* is the informal plural used with more than one of your peers or with those you know well.

WE ARE FAMILY

Stepping back into the not-so-mythical linguistic past, both English and German used to decline nouns. Our English possessive *-s* is a remnant. All nouns in German and English used to take an ending. You may thank your lucky stars that in present day German, only trace vestiges of this complex system remain. In the fifth century, neuter and masculine monosyllabic nouns were members of the same class of nouns; reflective of this history, an *-e* ending remains with neuter and masculine monosyllabic nouns in the dative case. This practice of declension is gradually falling by the wayside yet is *fossilized* in such fixed expressions as *im Jahre* and *zu Hause*.

Du, Ihr, or *Sie*?

How would you address the following people? Formally or informally? If informally, in the singular (*du*) or in the plural (*ihr*)? Check your pronoun mastery in Appendix A.

1. Ein Tourist aus Amerika:

   Wie ("how") finden _____ Amerika?

2. Frau und Herr Dallman:

   Was ("what") machen _____?

3. 4 Kinder:

   Was bringt _____ zum Park?

4. Ein Student:

   Was trinkst _____?

5. Eine Katze:

   Warum ("why") stinkst _____?

6. Der Präsident:

   Was planen _____?

ACHTUNG

Don't confuse the singular *sie* ("she") with the plural *sie* ("they"). The verb form that you will encounter in the next chapter indicates whether the pronoun *sie* is being used as third person singular or third person plural. The formal *Sie* (pronoun) is always capitalized and further designated by its verb form.

Pronouns, items that can substitute for a noun (Klaus) or a noun phrase (the very handsome man), streamline your speech. You'll note from the following examples that the gender of the pronoun must correspond to the gender of the noun. As in English, the same "they" (*sie*) is used to refer to more than one person, be they of mixed company, all feminine, or all masculine.

Noun(s)	Pronouns
Klaus	er
Bettina	sie
Kerstin und Frank	sie
Tania und Anne	sie
Julia und Klaus	sie

You can also use pronouns to replace the name of a common noun referring to a place, thing, or idea. Whereas in English we use the blanket pronoun "it" to refer to anything inanimate, the gender of the pronoun in German must correspond to the gender of the noun that you have so diligently memorized.

Noun	Pronunciation	Pronoun	Meaning
das Café oder das Kino	*dAs kah-fey oh-duhR dAs kee-noh*	es	the café or the movie theater
der Hafen oder das Schiff	*deyR hah-fuhn oh-duhR dAs shif*	er	the harbor or the ship
die Schuhe	*dee shew-uh*	sie	the shoes
die Straße oder die Kirche	*dee ShtRah-suh oh-duhR dee KeeR-Huh*	sie	the street or the church

Er, Sie, or *Es*?

Try your hand at rewriting the following sentences comprised of words you should recognize (they were in the charts!). Replace the noun phrase with the appropriate pronoun. Remember that the gender of the pronoun must correspond to the gender of the noun!

Check your choices with those in Appendix A, where you'll also find a translation of the original sentence.

Example: Die populäre Musik ist gut.

Answer: <u>Sie</u> ist gut.

1. Das perfekte Haus ist blau.

2. Der freundliche Onkel telefoniert regelmäßig.

3. Die rote Wand ist modern.

4. Der elegante Brief ist lang.

5. Das blonde Kind singt oft.

The Least You Need to Know

- The function of German nouns and pronouns in a sentence is indicated by their case, which can be nominative, accusative, dative, or genitive.

- The declension of articles and some nouns is the pattern of changes a word undergoes to express various grammatical functions, as represented by the four cases.

- Subject (nominative) pronouns streamline your speech. The gender of the pronoun must correspond to the gender of the noun.

- Because you're probably accustomed to the largely uninflected English language, these concepts might take a little getting used to. Refer to this chapter—or to the cards reflecting paradigms you've artistically created—as you work through this book and try to assimilate the basic concepts of cases and declensions gradually.

Nuts and Bolts of German Sentences

In This Chapter

- Understanding subject pronouns
- Conjugating weak and strong verbs
- Using common weak and strong verbs
- Learning how to ask questions

In the preceding chapter, you learned about determining the gender, number, and case of nouns, and you were introduced to German pronouns. Now it's time to move on to verbs, the building blocks in language that convey action in a sentence. To communicate, you must have a basic understanding of verbs. In this chapter, you're introduced to weak and strong verbs, thereby acquiring the tools to set the world in motion!

What's the Subject?

Just as people all around the world share similar fundamental characteristics, so do languages. All languages form sentences with two fundamental components: a subject and a verb.

To express action, occurrence, or states of being (what people do and are), you need *verbs*—and verbs, of course, require a *subject* to set the course in action:

> *The world traveler* <u>visits</u> important landmarks.

Subjects can be either nouns or pronouns that replace nouns:

> *The artist* <u>painted</u> a picture. *He/she* <u>painted</u> a picture.

When a sentence takes the *imperative form*, the form of a command, the subject (*you*) is understood: paint!

> **DEFINITION**
>
> The **imperative form** is the form a verb takes to express a command, request, or directive. This form is easily deduced from the conjugated second person verb. In the imperative form, the expressed or understood subject is always *you*.

Verb Basics

It's easier to understand how a plane takes off if you know something about its parts. The same is true of verbs. Here are some basic things you should know about verbs before you start using them.

The *stem* of a verb refers to what you get when you remove the ending *-en* from the German infinitive. The *stem vowel* refers to the vowel within this stem. In English, for example, when you conjugate the verb *run* (I run, you run, she runs), it retains the same stem vowel throughout the conjugation, marking the third person singular (he/she/it runs) with the addition of the inflectional suffix *-s*. *Conjugation* refers to the changes the verb undergoes, internally and externally (by the addition of inflectional endings), that keep the verb in agreement with the subject.

> **DEFINITION**
>
> **Conjugation** refers to the changes of the verb, the inflection attached to a verb, that occur to indicate who or what is performing the action (or undergoing the state of being) of the verb and when the action (or state of being) of the verb is occurring: in the present, the past, or the future.

Verbs in Motion

We need verbs to express action, motion, or states of being. When you acquired English, you very readily discerned the difference between being able to add a little something to a verb to express yesterday, as in *pushed* and *pulled*, and changing the verb internally: *sing, sang, sung*. Little did you know it then, but you were differentiating between two classes of verbs: *weak* and *strong*. Perhaps you learned to refer to them in school as *regular* and *irregular*. In German, as well, the most common way of grouping verbs is weak (*schwach*), strong (*stark*), or mixed (*schwark*). When verbs are conjugated to indicate that an action has already occurred, a relatively predictable pattern of endings is attached to the stem of weak verbs, as occurs in English (*-ed* in the past tense). Strong verbs have a relatively predictable pattern of endings when they are conjugated in the *present tense* (the form a verb takes to indicate that action is occurring in the present), but the stem undergoes a sound change in the past tense (think *sing, sang, sung*). Mixed verbs have features of both weak and strong verbs, hence the innovative term *schwark*—a blend of *schw*ach and st*ark*. The rest of this chapter examines *schwach* and *stark* verbs in the present tense. Mixed (*schwark*) verbs are discussed in Chapter 22.

Weak Verbs

In Chapter 4 you learned about the infinitive, the unconjugated building block base form of verbs. *Weak verbs* are verbs that, when conjugated, follow a set pattern of rules and retain the same stem vowel throughout. Think of them as being too weak to alter the sound patterns they've already established. Let's follow the weak English verb *kiss* through its full conjugation.

> **DEFINITION**
>
> **Weak verbs** are verbs (*schwach*) that follow a set pattern of rules and retain the same stem vowel throughout their conjugation. Compare this pattern with the English verbs that form their past tense with the addition of *-ed*.

Person	Singular	Plural
First	I kiss	we kiss
Second	you kiss	you kiss
Third	he/she/it kisses	they kiss

Your first step is to determine the stem of the verb. That's right, lop off the *-en* of the infinitive. Second, add a little something to this stem, just as you add an *-s* in the English third person singular. Looking at the *schwach* verb "to live," you can observe just how the verb endings differ with each subject pronoun.

Weak Verb Conjugation: *leben*

Person	Singular	English	Plural	English
First	ich leb**e** *iH ley-buh*	I live	wir leb**en** *veeR ley-buhn*	we live
Second	du leb**st** *dew leypst*	you live	ihr lebt *eeR leypt*	you live
Third	er, sie, es lebt *eR, zee, es leypt*	he, she, it lives	sie leb**en** *zee ley-buhn*	they live
Formal	Sie leb**en** *zee ley-buhn*	you live	Sie leb**en** *zee ley-buhn*	you live

Verbs with stems ending in *-d or -t*, such as *finden* or *kosten*, add an *-e* before the *-st* (*du*) or *-t* (*er/sie/es* and *ihr*) endings. Why add the *-e*? A simple matter of lingual practicality—without it, your tongue would get tangled and you'd end up tripping. The verb endings are exactly the same as for those verbs that don't end in a *d* or *t*, with the tiny addition of that *-e* to facilitate pronunciation. The following table spells out the conjugation of *finden*, a verb stem that ends in *d*. But this time, just one third person singular pronoun, *er*, is used.

Weak Verb Conjugation: *finden*

Person	Singular	English	Plural	English
First	ich find**e** *iH fin-duh*	I find	wir find**en** *veeR fin-duhn*	we find
Second	du find**est** *dew fin-duhst*	you find	ihr find**et** *eeR fin-duht*	you find
Third	er ... find**et** *eR fin-duht*	he ... finds	sie find**en** *zee fin-duhn*	they find
Formal	Sie find**en** *zee fin-duhn*	you find	Sie find**en** *zee fin-duhn*	you find

Verb Endings

Think of weak verbs as timid, law-abiding creatures that would never cross the street when the light is red. The easy thing about weak verbs is that they obey grammar laws and follow a predictable pattern of conjugation, even in the past tense. Once you've learned this pattern (and the few exceptions to stems ending in *d*, *t*, *ß*, *s*, and *z*), you can conjugate present tense verbs in German without too much difficulty: drop the -*en* from the infinitive and then add the endings shown in the following table. Here's your verb paradigm to be *memorized* and written out on a card!

Person	Singular	Ending	Plural	Ending
First	ich	**-e**	wir	**-en**
Second	du	**-(e)st**	ihr	**-(e)t**
Third	er, sie, es	**-(e)t**	sie	**-en**
Formal	Sie	**-en**	Sie	**-en**

Painless Conjugation

Now it's time to practice a little of what you've learned. See whether you can drop the –*en* from the infinitive and add the appropriate verb ending to create the correct form of the verbs in the following sentences. Remember, the verb must agree with the subject, and you can check your verbs in Appendix A.

1. (suchen) Ich _____ das Museum.

2. (reservieren) Klaus _____ ein Hotelzimmer.

3. (warten) Sie (Anne und Otto) _____ auf den Bus.

4. (mieten) Ihr _____ ein Auto.

5. (fragen) Wir _____ nach der Adresse.

6. (lernen) Ich _____ Deutsch.

7. (reisen) Ich _____ nach Hamburg.

8. (brauchen) Er _____ ein Taxi.

9. (besuchen) Du _____ deine Mutter.

10. (bestellen) Tina _____ ein Glas Wein.

11. (tanzen) Christoph, du _____ gut!

12. (arbeiten) Der Professor _____ jeden Tag.

13. (öffnen) Die Professorin _____ das Fenster.

14. (kosten) Die Pizza _____ nur 10 Euro.

In the following table, you will find some of the most commonly used weak verbs in German. Read the list a few times, make your own simple example sentences, and try to commit these verbs to memory.

Common Weak Verbs

Verb	Pronunciation	Meaning
antworten	*Ant-voR-tuhn*	to answer
arbeiten	*AR-bay-tuhn*	to work
bestellen	*buh-shte-luhn*	to order
blicken	*bli-kuhn*	to look, glance
brauchen	*bRou-CHuhn*	to need
danken	*dAn-kuhn*	to thank
fragen	*fRah-guhn*	to ask
glauben	*glou-buhn*	to believe
kochen	*ko-CHuhn*	to cook
kosten	*ko-stuhn*	to cost, to taste, to try
heiraten	*hay-rA-tuhn*	to marry
lernen	*leR-nuhn*	to learn, to study
lieben	*lee-buhn*	to love
machen	*mA-CHuhn*	to make, to do
mieten	*mee-tuhn*	to rent
öffnen	*öf-nuhn*	to open
rauchen	*Rou-CHuhn*	to smoke
regnen	*reyk-nuhn*	to rain
reisen	*ray-zuhn*	to travel
reservieren	*ruh-zeR-vee-Ruhn*	to reserve
sagen	*zah-guhn*	to say, to tell
schicken	*shi-kuhn*	to send
schwänzen	*shvän-tsuhn*	to skip class
sehen	*zey-uhn*	to see
spielen	*shpee-luhn*	to play
studieren	*shtew-dee-Ruhn*	to look over, to be enrolled
suchen	*zew-CHuhn*	to look for
tanzen	*tAn-tsuhn*	to dance
telefonieren	*tey-ley-foh-nee-Ruhn*	to telephone

Verb	Pronunciation	Meaning
warten	*vAR-tuhn*	to wait
weinen	*vay-nuhn*	to cry
wohnen	*voh-nuhn*	to reside
zeichnen	*tsayCH-nuhn*	to draw
zeigen	*tsay-guhn*	to show, to indicate

Strong Verbs

Of course, verbs don't lift weights or have muscles. You can't tell the difference between *strong verbs* and weak verbs just by looking at them. The only way you can distinguish between them is to memorize them as such. Of course, as an English speaker, you will have the advantage of already being familiar with strong verbs, and those strong verbs in English are just as *stark* in German.

DEFINITION

A **strong verb** is a verb whose stem vowel undergoes a change or a modification when conjugated in the past tense. Only some strong (*stark*) verbs undergo a vowel modification in the present tense (*sehr stark*).

Strong Verbs Exhibit Their Strength

Strong verbs can be deemed "strong" because they are strong enough to sustain a stem vowel change in the past tense, unlike weak verbs. This pattern becomes readily evident in the past tense (recall *pushed* versus *sang*). Some strong verbs change their stem vowel in the present tense—they are "very strong," *sehr stark*. Present tense endings, however, are the same for both weak and strong verbs. With the *sehr stark* verbs, vowel alterations occur only in the second and third persons (*du* and *er/sie/es*) in the stem vowel. Although *everything* in German might seem to be an exception, take heart; vowel changes follow a limited number of patterns. As far as present tense stem changes, the only permutations are these:

a(u), o, u may become *ä(u), ö,* or *ü. e* may become *i* or *ie.*

The following tables illustrate the stem changing of some *sehr stark* verbs. Note that the stem -*e* changes to -*ie* only in the second and third person singular! Other verbs that incur this stem change (because their stem vowel is the long *ey*) include *lesen, befehlen, empfehlen,* and *geschehen.* Very strong verbs that modify their stem vowel from *e* to *i* (without the subsequent *e*) include *essen, nehmen, geben,* and *sprechen* (again, an *ey* sound in the stem).

Very Strong Verb Conjugation: *sehen* (e → ie)

Person	Singular	English	Plural	English
First	ich sehe *iH zey-uh*	I see	wir sehen *veeR zey-uhn*	we see
Second	du sie**h**st *dew zeest*	you see	ihr seht *eeR zeyt*	you see
Third	er ... sie**h**t *eR zeet*	he ... sees	sie sehen *zee zey-uhn*	they see
Formal	Sie sehen *zee zey-uhn*	you see	Sie sehen *zee zay-uhn*	you see

Again, note that in the following table, *a* changes to *ä* only in the second and third person singular! Other verbs that incur this stem change include *fahren, fangen, halten, laden, lassen, laufen, schlafen, tragen, wachsen,* and *waschen.*

The Other Very Strong Verb Conjugation: *fallen* (a → ä)

Person	Singular	English	Plural	English
First	ich falle *iH fA-luh*	I fall	wir fallen *veeR fA-luhn*	we fall
Second	du fä**ll**st *dew fälst*	you fall	ihr fallt *eeR fAlt*	you fall
Third	er ... fä**ll**t *eR fält*	he ... falls	sie fallen *zee fA-luhn*	they fall
Formal	Sie fallen *zee fA-luhn*	you fall	Sie fallen *zee fA-luhn*	you fall

Bear the Sound Change and Conjugate

Although most *stark* verbs do not incur a sound change in the present tense, you might as well become well versed in the handful that do. See whether you can conjugate these *very* strong verbs in the following sentences and check your answers in Appendix A.

1. (essen) Hans _____ gern Bratwurst.

2. (geben) Er _____ mir einen guten Tip.

3. (sehen) Christoph _____ einen Biergarten.

4. (treffen) Petra _____ ihre deutsche Brieffreundin.

5. (sprechen) Du _____ sehr gut Englisch.

6. (lesen) Karl _____ die Süddeutsche Zeitung.

7. (fahren) Almut _____ nach Köln.

8. (halten) Der Bus _____ vor der Kirche.

9. (blasen) Der Bayer _____ das Horn.

10. (empfehlen) Meine Freundin _____ das Restaurant.

11. (schlafen) Du _____ lange.

12. (waschen) Du _____ jede Woche die Wäsche.

13. (laufen) Paul _____ sehr schnell und oft.

14. (schlagen) Er _____ den Tennisball.

15. (tragen) Die Professorin _____ einen Mini-rock.

The following table lists some commonly used strong verbs. Read through them a few times, as you did with the weak verbs. The very strong-verb vowel changes are indicated in parentheses after the infinitive. You shouldn't have too much trouble memorizing them—many are near cognates. Don't forget to learn the present tense stem change, if there is one!

Common Strong Verbs

Verb	Pronunciation	Meaning
befehlen (ie)	*buh-fey-luhn*	to command
beginnen	*buh-gi-nuhn*	to begin
besitzen	*buh-zi-tsuhn*	to possess
beweisen	*buh-vay-zuhn*	to prove
bieten	*bee-tuhn*	to offer
blasen (ä)	*blah-zuhn*	to blow

continues

Common Strong Verbs (continued)

Verb	Pronunciation	Meaning
bleiben	*blay-buhn*	to remain
empfangen (ä)	*em-pfAn-guhn*	to receive
empfehlen (ie)	*em-pfey-luhn*	to recommend
essen (i)	*es-uhn*	to eat
fahren (ä)	*fah-Ruhn*	to drive
fallen (ä)	*fA-luhn*	to fall
fangen (ä)	*fAn-guhn*	to catch
finden	*fin-duhn*	to find
fliegen	*flee-guhn*	to fly
geben (i)	*gey-buhn*	to give
gehen	*gey-uhn*	to go
genießen	*guh-nee-suhn*	to enjoy
geschehen (ie)	*guh-shey-uhn*	to happen
halten (ä)*	*hAl-tuhn*	to hold, to stop
hängen	*hän-guhn*	to hang
helfen (i)	*hel-fuhn*	to help
laden (ä)	*lah-duhn*	to load
lassen (ä)	*lA-suhn*	to leave, to let
laufen (ä)	*lou-fuhn*	to run
leiden	*lay-duhn*	to suffer
leihen	*lay-uhn*	to lend, to borrow
lesen (ie)	*ley-zuhn*	to read
liegen	*lee-guhn*	to lie, to be situated
nehmen (i)*	*ney-muhn*	to take
raten (ä)	*Rah-tuhn*	to advise
reißen	*Ray-suhn*	to tear
reiten	*Ray-tuhn*	to ride
rufen	*ewR-fuhn*	to call
scheinen	*shay-nuhn*	to shine, to seem
schießen	*shee-suhn*	to shoot
schlafen (ä)	*shlah-fuhn*	to sleep
schlagen (ä)	*schlah-guhn*	to hit

Verb	Pronunciation	Meaning
schreiben	*shray-buhn*	to write
schweigen	*shvay-guhn*	to be silent
schwimmen	*shvi-muhn*	to swim
sehen	*zey-uhn*	to see
singen	*zin-guhn*	to sing
sitzen	*zi-tsuhn*	to sit
sprechen (i)	*shpRe-Huhn*	to speak
stehen	*shtey-uhn*	to stand
stinken	*shtin-kuhn*	to stink
tragen (ä)	*trah-guhn*	to wear, to carry
treffen (i)	*tRe-fuhn*	to meet
trinken	*tRin-kuhn*	to drink
tun	*tewn*	to do
vergessen	*feR-ge-suhn*	to forget
versprechen (i)	*feR-shpRe-Huhn*	to promise
wachsen (ä)	*vACH-suhn*	to grow
waschen (ä)	*va-shuhn*	to wash
ziehen	*tsee-uhn*	to pull

*halten → er/sie/es hält (no additional -(e)t); nehmen → du ni**mm**st and er/sie/es ni**mm**t. (doubling of "m")*

WE ARE FAMILY

English and German share many features when it comes to strong verbs. The irregular forms—such as *take, took, taken*, or *drink, drank, drunk*—date back more than 6,000 years! They are examples of original Indo-European verbs and haven't changed too much since.

Ask Me Anything

Imagine that you're planning a trip to a German-speaking country. You'll probably want to ask a lot of questions when you get to your destination. Stick to the easy questions, the ones that can be answered with a simple yes or no. You'll deal with more complicated questions in Chapter 9.

There are other ways, besides the confused look on your face, to show that you're asking a yes/no question: through intonation, the addition of the tag *nicht wahr*, and inversion.

Intonation

One of the easiest ways to indicate that you're asking a question is by simply raising your voice slightly at the end of the sentence. To do so, speak with a rising *inflection*.

> Du denkst an die Reise?
> *Dew denkst An dee Ray-zuh*
> Are you thinking about the trip?

Nicht Wahr?

Another easy way of forming questions in German is by adding the tag *nicht wahr* (*niHt vahR*) to your statements. *Nicht wahr* means "Right?" or "Isn't this true?"

> Du denkst an die Reise, nicht wahr?
> *Dew denkst An dee Ray-zuh, niHt vahR*
> You think about the trip, don't you?

Inversion

The final way of forming a yes/no question is by *inversion*. Inversion is what you do when you reverse the word order of the subject and the conjugated verb. We use inversion all the time in English with the addition of *do* as a helper to the verb. Statement: He eats pie. Question: Does he eat pie?

- The following examples will give you a feel for how inversion works:

Du gehst nach Hause.	Gehst du nach Hause?
Er spricht Deutsch.	Spricht er Deutsch?
Wir reisen nach Cottbus.	Reisen wir nach Cottbus?
Ihr esst Sauerkraut.	Esst ihr Sauerkraut?
Sie trinken Bier.	Trinken sie Bier?
Du fährst mit dem Zug.	Fährst du mit dem Zug?

• Avoid inverting with *ich*. It's awkward and rarely done.

DEFINITION

Inversion is reversing the word order of the subject noun or pronoun and the conjugated form of the verb to make a statement a question.

Remember that whether you are using intonation, *nicht wahr*, or inversion, you are asking for exactly the same information: a yes or no (*ja oder nein*) answer.

Ask Me If You Can

Now it's time to put what you've learned about inversion to use. You're in an airport, and you need information. After waiting in line at the information counter, it's finally your turn. See whether you can use inversion (flipping around the subject and the verb) to provide the questions for the following statements. Check your word order in Appendix A.

Example: Das Flugzeug <u>fliegt</u> um 10 Uhr. (The plane leaves at 10.)

Answer: <u>Fliegt</u> das Flugzeug um 10 Uhr?

1. Das Ticket kostet 400 Euro. (The ticket costs 400 euros.)

2. Das ist das Terminal für internationale Flüge. (This is the terminal for international flights.)

3. Die Flugnummer steht auf dem Ticket. (The flight number is indicated on the ticket.)

4. Es gibt Toiletten auf dieser Etage. (There are bathrooms on this floor.)

5. Der Flug dauert zwei Stunden. (The flight is two hours long.)

6. Das Abendessen ist nicht inklusiv. (The evening meal is not included.)

And the Answer Is ...

If you generally look on the bright side of things, you'll probably want to know how to say "yes." To answer in the affirmative, use *ja* (*yah*) and then give your statement.

Sprichst du Deutsch?　　　Ja, ich spreche Deutsch.
shpRiHst dew doytch　　　*yah, iH shpRe-Huh doytch*

Or, if your time is valuable and you are constantly being harangued to do things you have no interest in doing, you should probably learn to say "no." To answer negatively, use *nein* (*nayn*) at the beginning of the statement and then add *nicht* (*niHt*) at the end of the statement.

Rauchen Sie?	Nein, ich rauche nicht.
Rou-CHuhn zee	*nayn, iH Rou-CHuh niHt*

You can vary the forms of your negative answers by putting the following negative phrases after the conjugated verb.

… nie(mals) *nee(mahlz)*	never
Ich rauche nie(mals). *iH Rou-CHuh nee(mahlz)*	I never smoke.
… nicht mehr *niHt meyR*	no longer
Ich rauche nicht mehr. *iH Rou-CHuh niHt meyR*	I no longer smoke.
… gar nicht (*gAR*)*niHts*	(absolutely) nothing
Ich rauche nichts. *iH Rou-CHuh niHts*	I'm not smoking anything.

If you want to form simple sentences in the present tense, you'll need to have as many verbs as possible at the tip of your tongue. Refer to the lists of verbs earlier in the chapter for help.

The Least You Need to Know

- All verbs take the same endings in the present tense.
- Weak verbs never incur a sound mutation and follow a set pattern of rules.
- Strong verbs always undergo a stem-vowel change in the past tense, and some also undergo a vowel change in the present tense.
- To formulate a yes/no question to elicit information, invert the subject and the verb so that the verb begins the question.
- You can ask questions by using intonation, inversion, or the tag *nicht wahr*.

Up, Up, and Away!

After you learn the basics, the next step is to start to converse (don't worry about being left behind—we'll be taking baby steps throughout this part). One of the first things you'll acquire is a working knowledge of common introductory phrases that German speakers use in various situations. You can use these phrases to start conversations and to expand your vocabulary.

Making Introductions and Small Talk

In This Chapter

- Common greetings
- The verb *sein*
- Professions
- Finding out about people

In Chapter 8, you learned how to create simple German sentences (using subject nouns, pronouns, and verbs) and how to ask basic yes or no questions. Now you're going to put some of what you learned to work. It's time to start engaging in conversation.

Conversation Openers

Track 6 Let's face it: you can listen to a thousand podcasts or online audio clips, and you can read every language book in the bookstore—the moment of truth arrives only when you are face to face with someone who is speaking to you in German. Each and every German speaker you meet will give you the chance to practice what you've learned so far. You may find the following conversation openers useful. And if you'd like to hear pronunciations of some of the examples in this section, check out Track 6 on the CD included with this book.

Formal Greetings and Salutations

Using the *du* form of address with someone who isn't a friend or relative is considered rude. Because you don't know the person you're speaking to, you'll probably want to take the formal approach. It is worth noting, however, that younger generations are tending to use the informal *du* form more extensively.

German	Pronunciation	Meaning
Guten Tag.	*gew-tuhn tahk*	Hello.
Guten Abend.	*gew-tuhn ah-bent*	Good evening.
mein Herr	*Mayn heR*	Sir
meine Dame	*may-nuh dah-muh*	Miss, Mrs.
Ich heiße …	*iH hay-suh*	My name is …
Wie heißen Sie?	*vee hay-suhn zee*	What is your name?
Wie geht es Ihnen?	*vee geyt es ee-nuhn*	How are you?
Danke, sehr gut.	*dAn-kuh, zeyR gewt*	Thank you, very well.
Danke, nicht schlecht.	*dAn-kuh, niHt shleHt*	Thank you, not bad.
Danke, es geht so.	*dAn-kuh, es geyt zo*	Thank you, so so.

Informal Greetings and Salutations

You hit it off with your plane buddy right away, and he says, "*Dutzen Sie mich, bitte* (*dew-tsuhn zee miH, bi-tuh*)," which means, "Please, use *du* with me." His request means that you've earned the right to a certain degree of linguistic intimacy with this person. You can now use the following phrases:

German	Pronunciation	Meaning
Hallo!	*hA-lo*	Hi!
Ich heiße …	*iH hay-suh*	My name is …
Wie heißt du?	*vee hayst dew*	What is your name?
Wie geht's dir?	*vee geyts deeR*	How are you?
Was machst du so?	*vAs mACHst dew zo*	What's up?
Ganz gut.	*gAns gewt*	Okay.
Ich kann nicht klagen.	*iH kAn niHt klah-guhn*	I can't complain.
Es geht.	*es geyt*	So so.
Nicht schlecht.	*niHt shleCHt*	All right.

GERMAN CULTURE

Hallo is informal for "hello" practically everywhere, but in southern Germany and Austria, the term *Grüß Gott* (*gRüs got*), literally, "God greets you," is used formally instead of *Guten Tag* (*gew-tuhn tAhk*).

Where Are You From?

To continue this conversation, you will need to familiarize yourself with the strong verb *kommen* (*ko-muhn*). Take out your verb-ending chart, lop the *-en* off the infinitive to produce the stem (*komm-*), and try to come up with a match to the following table.

The Verb: *kommen*

Person	Singular	English	Plural	English
First	ich komm**e** *iH ko-muh*	I come	wir komm**en** *veeR ko-muhn*	we come
Second	du komm**st** *dew komst*	you come	ihr komm**t** *eeR komt*	you come
Third	er, sie, es komm**t** *eR, zee, es komt*	he, she, it comes	sie komm**en** *zee ko-muhn*	they come
(Formal)	Sie komm**en** *zee ko-muhn*	you come	Sie komm**en** *zee ko-muhn*	you come

To question someone about his or her origins, try the following:

Formal:	**Informal**	**Response:**
Woher kommen Sie?	Woher kommst du?	Ich komme aus …
voh-heR ko-muhn zee	*voh-heR komst dew*	*iH ko-muh ous …*
Where are you from?	Where are you from?	I come from …

> **ACHTUNG**
>
> Using informal language to address someone with whom you have not established a friendship or bond is generally considered quite rude. To *duzen* (*dew-tsuhn*) someone—in other words, to use the informal *du* form of address with a person—may alienate the stranger, neighbor, or business acquaintance you are addressing. Generally, you have to earn the privilege to use the informal *du* with people you don't know.

You might recall from Chapter 6 that most countries, towns, and cities are neuter nouns and take the article *das*. *Die USA* (*dee ew-es-ah*) and *die Vereinigten Staaten* (*dee feR-ay-nik-tuhn shtah-tuhn*), "The United States," are exceptions; because they are plural, they take the plural article *die*. Some other countries that don't take *das* are *die Schweiz* (*dee shvayts*), "Switzerland"; *die Türkei* (*dee tüR-kay*), "Turkey"; *der Irak* (*deyR ee-Rahk*), "Iraq"; *der Iran* (*deyR ee-Rahn*), "Iran"; *der Libanon* (*deyR lee-bah-non*), "Lebanon," and *der Kongo* (*deyR kon-go*), "The Congo."

When you use countries, cities, or towns with the neuter article, drop the article *das:*

Ich komme aus New York.	Ich komme aus Amerika.
iH ko-muh ous new yoRk	*iH ko-muh ous ah-mey-Ree-kah*

To Be or Not to Be?

After you've established where someone is from, you will probably want to find out more about what that person does. To do so, you should learn the conjugation of the irregular verb *sein* (*zayn*), or "to be," and learn some professions. The following table illustrates the conjugation of *sein*, "to be."

> **DEFINITION**
>
> **Sein** is one of the four irregular verbs in German. These verbs vary from strong verbs, which follow a regular sound-shift pattern in stem vowels, because consonants as well as vowels change in the truly unpredictable irregular verbs.

The Verb: *sein*

Person	Singular	English	Plural	English
First	ich bin *iH bin*	I am	wir sind *veeR zint*	we are
Second	Du bist *dew bist*	you are	ihr seid *eeR zayt*	you are
Third	Er, sie, es ist *eR, zee, es ist*	he, she, it is	sie sind *zee zint*	they are
(Formal)	Sie sind *zee zint*	you are		

The following phrase may help you elicit information about someone and tell about yourself. Note the forms of *sein* that agree with the subject pronoun.

Formal:

Was sind Sie von Beruf?

VAs sint zee fon buh-Rewf

What is your profession?

Informal:

Was bist du von Beruf?

vAs bist dew fon buh-Rewf

What is your profession?

Was machst du?

vAs maCHst dew

What do you do?

Response:

Ich bin …

iH bin …

I am …

The following table lists a few professions with the feminine form in parentheses.

Professions

Profession	Pronunciation	English
der Architekt (die Architektin)	*deyR AR-Hi-tekt* *(dee Ar-Hi-tek-tin)*	architect
der Arzt (die Ärztin)	*deyR ARtst* *(dee äRts-tin)*	doctor
der Bäcker (die Bäckerin)	*deyR bäh-kuhR* *(dee bäh-kuh-Rin)*	baker

continues

Professions (continued)

Profession	Pronunciation	English
der Beamte (die Beamtin)	*deyR buh-Am-tuh* (*dee buh-Am-tin*)	government employee
der Bibliothekar (die Bibliothekarin)	*deyR bib-lee-oh-tay-kAhR* (*dee bib-lee-oh-tay-kA-Rin*)	librarian
der Chemiker (die Chemikerin)	*deyR He-mee-kuhR* (*dee He-mee-kuh-Rin*)	chemist
der Elektriker (die Elektrikerin)	*deyR ey-lek-tRi-kuhR* (*dee ey-lek-tRi-kuh-Rin*)	electrician
der Flugbegleiter (die Flugbegleiterin)	*deyR flook-buh-glay-tuhR* (*dee flook-buh-glay-tuh-Rin*)	flight attendant
der Friseur (die Friseuse)	*deyR fRee-zühR* (*dee fRee-züh-zuh*)	hairdresser
der Geschäftsführer (die Geschäftsführerin)	*deyR guh-shäfts-füh-RuhR* (*dee guh-shäfts-füh-Ruh-Rin*)	business manager
der Informatiker (die Informatikerin)	*deyR in-foR-mah-tee-kuhR* (*dee in-foR-mah-tee-kuh-Rin*)	computer scientist
der Kaufmann (die Kauffrau)	*deyR kouf-mAn* (*dee kou-frou*)	merchant, shopkeeper
der Kellner (die Kellnerin)	*deyR kel-nuhR* (*dee kel-nuh-Rin*)	waiter, waitress
der Krankenpfleger (die Krankenschwester)	*deyR kRAn-kuhn-pfley-guhR* (*dee kRAn-kuhn-shves-tuhR*)	nurse
der Künstler (die Künstlerin)	*deyR kün-stluhR* (*dee kün-stluh-Rin*)	artist
der Mechaniker (die Mechanikerin)	*deyR mey-Hah-ni-kuhR* (*dee mey-Hah-ni-kuh-Rin*)	mechanic
der Musiker (die Musikerin)	*deyR mew-zee-kuhR* (*dee mew-zee-kuh-Rin*)	musician
der Politiker (die Politikerin)	deyR poh-lee-tee-kuhR (dee poh-lee-tee-kuh-Rin)	politician
der Polizist (die Polizistin)	*deyR poh-lee-tsist* (*dee poh-lee-tsis-tin*)	police officer
der Professor (die Professorin)	*deyR proh-fe-soR* (*dee proh-fe-soh-Rin*)	professor

Profession	Pronunciation	English
der Rechtsanwalt (die Rechtsanwältin)	*deyR ReHts-An-vAlt* (*dee ReHts-An-väl-tin*)	lawyer
der Schauspieler (die Schauspielerin)	*deyR shou-shpee-luhR* (*dee shou-shpee-luh-Rin*)	actor, actress
der Schriftsteller (die Schriftstellerin)	*deyR shrift-shte-luhR* (*dee shrift-shte-luh-Rin*)	writer
der Sekretär (die Sekretärin)	*deyR sek-Re-tähR* (*dee sek-Re-täRin*)	secretary
der Student (die Studentin)	*deyR shtew-dent* (*dee shtew-den-tin*)	student

AS A RULE

In German, the indefinite article *ein(e)* is generally not used when a person states his profession, unless the profession is qualified by an adjective. To say, "I'm a policeman," you would say, "*Ich bin Polizist (ich bin poh-lee-tsist).*" To say "I'm a good policeman," however, you would say, "*Ich bin ein guter Polizist (iH bin ayn gew-tuhR poh-lee-tsist).*"

You've been introduced to the verb *sein* and to some of the most common professions. But what's the use of all this newly acquired information if you can't use it? Put what you've learned to use by translating the following sentences into German. Pay attention to the gender of the pronoun and check your translations in Appendix A.

1. I am a waiter.
2. He is a nurse.
3. She is a doctor.
4. I am a lawyer.
5. You are a student.
6. He is a police officer.
7. She is a business manager.
8. You are a writer.

Finding Things Out

When you learn a new language, you often revert to what feels like a somewhat infantile state of existence. You have a limited vocabulary and, at best, a somewhat sketchy understanding of grammar. You point to things a lot and ask, "What is that?," "*Was ist das? (vAs ist dAs)*"; or "What does that mean?," "*Was bedeutet das? (vAs buh-doy-tuht dAs).*" Yet even someone with a limited knowledge of a language can convey a broad range of meaning.

> **WE ARE FAMILY**
>
> Have you noticed how the endings for professions in both English and German are often *-er*? Both languages share the same lexical morphology for forming agentive suffixes. That is to say, an additional *-er* suffix turns the verb into a doer of the verb: One who sings is a singer, or a *Sänger*. Note that there is no plural suffix added to the German masculine form: one or a room full of *Sänger*.

Track 6 One advantage of learning a new language is that you can indulge your curiosity all in the name of language acquisition. So start learning by asking about everything. Following are some interrogative helpers. If you'd like to hear pronunciations of some of these examples, check out Track 6 on the CD included with this book.

Information Question Expressions

German	Pronunciation	English
mit wem	*mit veym*	with whom
um wie viel Uhr	*ewm vee-feel ooR*	at what time
von wem	*fon veym*	of, about, from whom
wann	*vAn*	when
warum/wieso/weshalb	*va-Rum/vee-zoh/ves-hAlp*	why
was	*vAs*	what
wer	*veR*	who
wie	*vee*	how
wie lange	*vee lAn-guh*	how long
wie viel/viele	*vee feel*	how much, many
wo	*voh*	where
woher	*voh-heR*	from where

German	Pronunciation	English
wohin	*voh-hin*	where (to)
womit/mit was	*voh-mit/mit vAs*	with what
worüber	*voh-Rüh-buhR*	what about
wovon/von was	*voh-fon/fon vAs*	of, about, from what
zu wem	*tsew veym*	to whom

Gleaning Information

Here are other ways to break the ice.

Formal	Informal	English
Mit wem reisen Sie? *mit veym Ray-zuhn zee*	Mit wem reist du? *mit veym Rayst dew*	With whom are you traveling?
Warum reisen Sie? *vah-Room Ray-zuhn zee*	Warum reist du? *vah-Room Rayst dew*	Why are you traveling?
Wie lange reisen Sie? *vee lAn-guh Ray-zuhn zee*	Wie lange reist du? *vee lAn-guh Rayst dew*	How long are you traveling for?
Wohin reisen Sie? *voh-hin Ray-zuhn zee*	Wohin reist du? *voh-hin Rayst dew*	Where are you traveling?
Wie finden Sie das Land? *vee fin-duhn zee dAs lAnt*	Wie findest du das Land? *vee fin-duhst dew dAs lAnt*	How do you like the country?
Wo wohnen Sie? *voh voh-nuhn zee*	Wo wohnst du? *voh vohnst dew*	Where do you live?
Woher kommen Sie? *vo-heR ko-muhn zee*	Woher kommst du? *vo-her komst dew*	Where are you (coming) from?
Wovon sprechen Sie? *voh-fon shpRe-chuhn zee*	Wovon sprichst du? *voh-fon shpriHst dew*	What are you speaking about?
Wie viele Kinder haben Sie? *vee-fee-luh kin-duhR hah-buhn zee*	*Wie viele Kinder hast du?* *vee-fee-luh kin-duhR hAst dew*	How many children do you have?
Wann reisen Sie zurück? *vAn Ray-zuhn zee tsu-Rük?*	Wann reist du zurück? *vAn Rayst dew tsü-Rük*	When are you traveling home?

Ask Away

Each of the following statements is an answer to a question. Try to ask the questions that elicit these statements. In the first example, use the informal *du* to pose questions to Klaus. In the second example, use the formal *Sie* to pose questions to Frau Sahlmann. Don't forget what you learned about inversion in Chapter 8. Your questions may be simple or conjoined by "and"—*und.* Verify your questions in Appendix A.

> **AS A RULE**
>
> To express directions of motion, the adverb particles *her-* and *hin-* may be used with the interrogative *wo* to suggest motion toward the speaker (*woher,* "where from") or motion away from the speaker (*wohin,* "where to"). In spoken German, the question words *wohin* and *woher* are often separated: *wo* is placed at the start of the question; *hin* and *her* appear at the end: *Wohin geht Christine*? or *Wo geht Christine hin?* In a statement, *hin* and *her* occupy the last position in the sentence.

> **Example:** Ich heiße Klaus. **Question:** Wie heißt du?

A. Ich heiße Klaus und ich komme aus Köln. Ich reise mit meiner Schwester nach München. Ich trinke Bier auf der Wiese (at Oktoberfest) für zwei Wochen (for two weeks) in München.

B. Ich bin Frau Sahlmann und komme aus Kiel. Ich reise einen Monat lang (for a month) in der Schweiz. Ich finde die Schweiz sehr schön. Ich reise bald zurück (back).

The Least You Need to Know

- Don't use *du* with strangers or with your superiors! The greetings you use depend on your familiarity with a person.
- The verb *kommen* with the question word *woher* is used to ask people where they're from.
- For most professions, simply add an *-in* to speak about a female and don't precede the profession with *ein(e).*
- You can get information by learning and asking a few key questions, so learn those question words, most of which begin with a "w."

Getting to Know Family and Friends

Chapter 10

In This Chapter

- Introducing your relatives
- Expressing possession two ways
- Introducing and talking about yourself
- The irregular verb *haben* and adjectives

By now you should be well on your way to making small talk on your own. But what if your mother, father, uncle, and in-laws are all hanging out with you, peering over your shoulder every time you strike up a conversation? Perhaps the best thing to do is to find people to introduce them to. Introducing your relatives is the first thing you'll learn to do in this chapter.

The next thing you'll learn is how to find out about other people. One approach is to ask the objects of your curiosity what they think about themselves: Do they consider themselves to be creative, intelligent, sensitive, or adventurous? To ask these kinds of questions, you're going to need adjectives. And to use adjectives correctly, you must attach the appropriate ending to them so that they agree in gender and case with the noun they are modifying. This process is similar to changing the definite (*der*) and indefinite (*ein*) articles according to their gender and grammatical function, as you did in Chapter 7.

Family Matters

Start practicing now with the words for family members in the following table, some of which you were exposed to in Chapter 6.

Family Members

Male	Pronunciation	English	Female	Pronunciation	English
das Kind	*dAs kint*	child	das Kind	*dAs kint*	child
der (Ehe) Mann	*deyR (ey-yuh) mAn*	husband	die (Ehe) Frau	*dee (ey-yuh) fRou*	wife
der Bruder	*deyR brew-duhR*	brother	die Schwester	*dee shves-tuhR*	sister
der Cousin	*deyR kew-zahN*	cousin	die Cousine	*dee kew-see-nuh*	cousin
der Enkel	*deyR en-kuhl*	grandson	die Enkelin	*dee en-kuh-lin*	granddaughter
der Freund	*deyR fRoynt*	boyfriend	die Freundin	*dee fRoyn-din*	girlfriend
der Neffe	*deyR ne-fuh*	nephew	die Nichte	*dee niH-tuh*	niece
der Onkel	*deyR on-kuhl*	uncle	die Tante	*dee tAn-tuh*	aunt
der Opa/ Großvater	*deyR oh-pah/ gRohs-fah-tuhR*	grandfather	die Oma/ Großmutter	*dee oh-mah/ gRohs-moo-tuhR*	grandmother
der Schwiegersohn	*deyR shvee-guhR-zohn*	son-in-law	die Schwiegertochter	*dee shvee-guhR-toCH-tuhR*	daughter-in-law
der Schwiegervater	*deyR shvee-guhR-fah-tuhR*	father-in-law	die Schwiegermutter	*dee shvee-guhR-moo-tuhR*	mother-in-law
der Sohn	*deyR zohn*	son	die Tochter	*dee toCH-tuhR*	daughter
der Stiefbruder	*deyR shteef-bRew-duhR*	step-brother	die Stiefschwester	*dee shteef-shves-tuhR*	step-sister
der Stiefsohn	*deyR shteef-zohn*	stepson	die Stieftochter	*die shteef-toCH-tuhR*	step-daughter
der Vater	*deyR fah-tuhR*	father	die Mutter	*dee moo-tuhR*	mother

Here are some useful plurals and their spellings:

Plural	Pronunciation	English
die Eltern	*dee el-tuhRn*	the parents
die Großeltern	*dee gRohs-el-tuhRn*	the grandparents
die Kinder	*dee kin-duhR*	the children
die Schwiegereltern	*dee shvee-guhR-el-tuhRn*	the in-laws

Marking Relations?

We're all connected somehow. You're your mother's daughter or son, your uncle's nephew or niece, your wife's husband, or your husband's wife. There are two principal ways of showing possession in German: by using the genitive case and by using possessive adjectives.

The Genitive Case: Showing Possession

The genitive case shows possession or dependence. However, to show possession, you must also decline the noun and the noun marker correctly. Have you forgotten what a noun marker is? Noun markers refer to the definite article *the*, including the nominative *der*, *die*, *das*, or *die*; the indefinite article *ein*, the equivalent of *a* for nominative masculine or neuter nouns; or *eine*, the equivalent of *a* for nominative feminine nouns. Remember from Chapter 7 that masculine and neuter nouns take an ending, *-(e)s*, in the genitive case. Here is an abbreviated version of the genitive declension of the definite articles. When you use proper names or are speaking of family members expressing ownership or possession, you can use the *genitive -s* (add the *-s* without an apostrophe to the end of the word).

Masculine	Feminine	Neuter	Plural (All Genders)
des	der	des	der

DEFINITION

The **genitive –s** method of showing possession can be used with family members and proper names. For example, *Stephanies Vater* (*ste-fah-nees fah-tuhR*) means "Stephanie's father," and *Vaters Tochter* (*fah-tuhRs toH-tuhR*) means "father's daughter."

English frequently relies on the preposition *of* to express ownership, especially with inanimate objects. Note that the order of objects in German closely corresponds to the English possessive construction: *the X of the Y*, as in *die Farbe des Hauses*, or "the color of the house." In German, you identify the object first and then specify its owner, since logically, the most relevant item is that which is being modified—owned, possessed, had.

German	Pronunciation	Meaning
Das ist der Sohn des Mannes.	*dAs ist deyR zohn des mA-nuhs*	That is the man's son. (That is the son of the man.)
Das ist der Ehemann der Frau.	*dAs ist deyR ey-yuh-mAn deyR fRou*	That is the woman's husband. (That is the husband of the woman.)
Die Mutter des Kindes ist schön.	*dee moo-tuhR des kin-duhs ist shöhn*	The child's mother is beautiful. (The mother of the child is beautiful.)

Mine, All Mine

The *possessive adjectives my, your, his, her,* and so on show that something belongs to somebody. Singular possessive adjectives use the same endings as the declension of the indefinite article *ein* (declined in Chapter 7 and written out on a card by *you!*). You can think of this chart as the "*ein Wort*" chart—all of its members take the same endings and sort of rhyme: *ein, mein, dein, sein,* … well, you get my drift. The following examples show someone loving someone. The *someone* is the direct object and, therefore, takes the accusative case.

DEFINITION

Possessive adjectives (*mein, dein, sein, ihr, unser, euer,* and *ihr*) show that something belongs to someone, indicating possession or a special relationship. These are almost always followed by a noun and, therefore, like the *ein* words, need an ending.

English	German +	Pronunciation
He loves his father.	Er liebt **seinen** Vater.	*eyR leept zay-nuhn fah-tuhR*
He loves his mother.	Er liebt **seine** Mutter.	*eyR leept zay-nuh moo-tuhR*
She loves her father.	Sie liebt **ihren** Vater.	*zee leept ee-Ruhn fah-tuhR*
She loves her mother.	Sie liebt **ihre** Mutter.	*zee leept ee-Ruh moo-tuhR*

The following table lists the possessive adjectives.

Possessive Adjectives

Person	Singular	Meaning	Plural	Meaning
First	mein *mayn*	my	unser *oon-zuhR*	our
Second	dein *dayn*	your	euer *oy-uhR*	your
Third	sein, ihr, sein *zayn, eeR, zayn*	his, her, its	ihr *eeR*	their
(Formal)	Ihr *eer*	your	Ihr *eer*	your

ACHTUNG

The German word *ihr (eeR)* has many meanings. As a possessive adjective, it can mean "her," "their," or "your." One way of avoiding confusion in written German is by remembering to capitalize *Ihr* when it means "your."

The following two tables review the declension of possessive adjectives that exactly mirror the declension of the indefinite article, *ein.*

The Declension of Singular Possessive Adjectives

Nom.	dein Mann	deine Frau	dein Kind
	dayn mAn	*day-nuh fRou*	*dayn kint*
Acc.	deinen Mann	deine Frau	dein Kind
	day-nuhn mAn	*day-nuh fRou*	*dayn kint*
Dat.	deinem Mann	deiner Frau	deinem Kind
	day-nuhm mAn	*day-nuhR fRou*	*day-nuhm kint*
Gen.	deines Mann(e)s	deiner Frau	deines Kind(e)s
	day-nuhs mAn(uh)s	*day-nuhR fRou*	*day-nuhs kind(uh)s*

The Declension of Plural Possessive Adjectives

Case	Plural ("your children")
Nom.	deine Kinder
	day-nuh kin-duhR
Acc.	deine Kinder
	day-nuh kin-duhR
Dat.	deinen Kindern
	day-nuhn kin-duhRn
Gen.	deiner Kinder
	day-nuhR kin-duhR

Now that you know how to express possession with the genitive case and with possessive adjectives, see whether you can express these relationships in German when introducing them. Use either "Das ist ..." or "Das sind ...," depending on the subject and check your answers in Appendix A.

Example: her father

Answer: Das ist ihr Vater.

1. his sister

2. my uncle

3. our family

4. your (informal, pl.) children

5. the girl's brother

6. the man's mother

7. the child's parents

8. the husband of my sister

9. the parents of his wife

10. the aunt of your (informal, sg.) cousin (m.)

Using Possessive Adjectives to Show Your Preference

Everyone has favorites. What's your favorite color, song, or city? German uses the adjective *lieblings-* (*leep-links*) to express "favorite" after the appropriate possessive adjective: *mein* for a masculine (*der*) noun, *meine* for a feminine (*die*) noun, and *mein* for a neuter (*das*) noun in the nominative case. The word *lieblings-* is linked to the noun to form a compound noun: *die Lieblingsfarbe* (*leep-links-fAR-buh*) for "favorite color," *das Lieblingslied* (*leep-links-leet*) for "favorite song," and *die Lieblingsstadt* (*leep-links-shtAt*) for "favorite city." Recall that the gender of this new word will be determined by the gender of its component on the right.

Here's an example:

Mein Lieblingsschauspieler ist George Clooney.
mayn leep-links-shou-shpee-luhR ist joRj klew-ni
My favorite actor is George Clooney.

Try forming five sentences to express your favorite things! Sentence beginnings are in Appendix A.

Example: das Gemüse (*guh-mü-zuh*), vegetable

Answer: Mein Lieblingsgemüse ist Spinat (spinach).

1. der Film (movie)

2. der Schriftsteller/die Schriftstellerin

3. das Buch (book)

4. die Stadt (city)

5. der Sänger (singer)

Introductions

Practice a few of the following phrases to get the hang of introducing yourself.

German	Pronunciation	English
Darf ich mich vorstellen?	*dARf iH miH foR-shte-luhn*	May I introduce myself?
Mein Name ist ….	*Mayn nah-muh ist*	My name is ….
Ich möchte _____ vorstellen.	*iH möH-tuh _____ foR-shte-luhn*	I would like to introduce …
Kennen Sie (kennst du) meine Schwester Kathrin?	*ke-nuhn zee (kenst dew) may-nuh shves-tuhR kah-tReen*	Do you know my sister Katrin?
Kommen Sie (komm), ich stelle Ihnen (dir) meine Schwester Kathrin vor.	*ko-muhn zee (kom), iH shte-luh ee-nuhn (deeR) may-nuh shves-tuhR kah-tReen foR*	Come on, let me introduce my sister Katrin.
Das ist meine Schwester Kathrin.	*dAs ist may-nuh shves-tuhR kah-treen*	This is my sister Katrin.

You wouldn't greet the prime minister of England with a quick, "Hey, man, what's happenin'?" German has similar rules about the proper and improper way to deal with formal introductions. If you are being introduced to the head of a company at a business meeting, you will be given a formal introduction. Your response, in turn, should be expressed formally. Here are some formal ways of responding to an introduction:

Es freut mich, Sie kennenzulernen.
es froyt miH, zee ke-nuhn-tsew-leR-nuhn
It is a pleasure to meet you.

You're at a party and a friend wants to introduce you to someone; you'll probably find yourself caught up in an informal introduction. Here are some ways of responding to an introduction:

Freut mich.
froyt miH
What a pleasure.
(formal/informal)

Schön, dich kennenzulernen.
shön, diH ke-nuhn-tswe-leR-nuhn
Nice to meet you.
(informal)

(Sehr) Angenehm.
(zeyR) An-guh-neym
Delighted to meet you.
(formal)

Breaking the Ice

Okay, you've learned all about family names, possession, and introductions. Now you're ready to get out there and converse! Imagine that you and a few members of your family are taking a bus to a local museum. Soon after you board, a woman whom you seem to remember having seen somewhere before sits next to you and begins flipping through a magazine. See whether you can do the following. Check your accuracy in Appendix A.

1. Introduce yourself.

2. Tell where you are from.

3. Say what you do.

4. Ask your new acquaintance where she comes from.

5. Ask whether she knows a member of your family.

6. Introduce a member of your family to her.

7. Imagine that she introduces herself to you, and express pleasure at having met her.

Getting Involved in Conversation

One very useful verb is *haben* (*hah-buhn*), "to have." You can use this verb to express many things concerning yourself. Like the verb *sein*, *haben* is irregular (the second of the four irregular verbs in German). You'll have to memorize its conjugation, which shouldn't be too difficult—the irregularities of losing the *b* occur in the second and third person singular forms, exactly where the vowel changes occur in very strong verbs.

The Verb: *haben*

Person	Singular	Meaning	Plural	Meaning
First	ich habe *iH hah-buh*	I have	wir haben *veeR hah-buhn*	we have
Second	du hast *dew hAst*	you have	ihr habt *eeR hAbt*	You have
Third	er, sie, es, hat *eR, zee, es, hAt*	he, she, it has	sie haben *zee hah-buhn*	they have
Formal	Sie haben *zee hah-buhn*	you have	Sie haben *zee hah-buhn*	You have

Express Yourself with *haben*

Maybe you want to express how happy you are to have the opportunity (*die Gelegenheit haben*) to engage in conversation with someone, or how lucky you are (*wie viel Glück du hast*) to be able to visit Germany. The following table lists some idiomatic phrases that use *haben* to express luck, intention, and opportunity. You need merely combine these with the rest of your thoughts, involving another verb and possibly an idea housed in an infinitive phrase, to complete these expressions.

Expressions with *haben*

Idiom	Pronunciation	Meaning
die Gelegenheit haben	*dee guh-ley-guhn-hayt hah-buhn*	to have the opportunity
Es hat keinen Zweck.	*es hat kay-nuhn tsvek*	There's no point.
keine Lust haben	*kay-nuh loost hah-buhn*	to have no desire
die Zeit haben	*dee tsayt hah-buhn*	to have time

continues

Expressions with *haben* (continued)

Idiom	Pronunciation	Meaning
die Gewohnheit haben	*dee guh-vohn-hayt hah-buhn*	to have the habit
die Absicht haben	*dee Ap-siHt hah-buhn*	to have the intention
das Recht haben	*dAs ReHt hah-buhn*	to have the right
den Mut haben	*deyn moot hah-buhn*	to have the courage

Be sure to conjugate the verb *haben* correctly when you use it in a sentence.

AS A RULE

Adjectives that follow verbs, as in *Der Wein ist gut*, do not take endings. Because such adjectives are in the verb half of the sentence, they are referred to as predicate adjectives. However, if an adjective precedes the noun it modifies, its role becomes attributive and it takes an ending. All consecutive adjectives, no matter how many, that precede a noun have the same ending: *das schöne, lustige, kleine, intelligente Kind* (the pretty, funny, small, intelligent child).

Using Idioms with *Haben*

These idiomatic expressions are of little use to you in their base infinitive forms. See how successfully you've memorized them by completing the following sentences with the correctly conjugated form of the verb *haben*. Check your idioms in Appendix A.

das Glück haben	die Gewohnheit haben
die Absicht haben	die Zeit haben
Lust haben	den Mut haben

1. Dirk ist fröhlich und hat Zeit. Er _____ mitzukommen.

2. Eva ist sehr abenteuerlich (adventurous). Sie _____, Bungy-Jumping zu machen.

3. Hans ist verliebt. Er _____ zu heiraten.

4. Anne und Mark haben zwei Wochen Ferien. Sie _____, eine Reise nach Deutschland zu machen.

5. Ihr habt in der Lotterie gewonnen. Ihr _____ im Spiel.

What's It Like?

Using adjectives, you can paint pictures with words. If you want to describe someone or something, you will need to use descriptive adjectives. German adjectives take an ending when they come immediately before a noun so that noun and adjective agree in gender (masculine, feminine, or neuter), number (singular or plural), and case (nominative, accusative, dative, or genitive)—seems to be a recurring theme, eh? If an adjective doesn't precede a noun but rather comes after the verb, the adjective doesn't take an ending.

An attributive adjective—one taking an ending expressing agreement:

> Die freundliche Katze schnurrt viel.
> *dee froint-li-Huh kah-tsuh shnoort feel*
> The friendly cat purrs a lot.

A predicate (nonattributive) adjective—no noun follows it:

> Die Katze ist freundlich.
> *dee kah-tsuh ist froint-liH*
> The cat is friendly.

Figuring Out Adjective Endings

Adjectives can take different endings, depending on the type of word that precedes them; these words are commonly referred to as "limiting" words. When a *der Wort* (definite article) precedes an adjective, it performs the arduous task of expressing gender and grammatical function (case). Hence, the following adjective ending doesn't need to reflect this information and takes a so-called weak (*schwach*) ending (*-e/-en*): *der gute Film; Die nette Schwester besucht den alten Bruder.* If no limiting word comes before the adjective (which would mark gender and case), the adjective has to take on this responsibility and needs to be "strong" (*stark*) enough to indicate gender and case: *deutsches Bier; französischer Wein.* In the middle of this spectrum are adjectives that come after certain "*ein*" words. *Ein* words share characteristics of both weak and strong declensions. The grammatically ambiguous masculine nominative, neuter nominative, and neuter accusative *ein* words (*ein/ein/ein*) depend on the adjective for grammatical expression: *ein rotes Auto, mein neuer Ball.* The good news is that these declensions are all quite regular, and once you learn the corresponding paradigms, you won't have any trouble.

Some words, referred to as *der* words, are inflected just like the definite article *der*. These words behave just like definite articles, expressing all of the grammar in front of a noun, so the adjective that follows takes a weak ending. *Der* words include *der* ("the"), *dies-* ("this"), *jed-* ("each"), *jen-* ("that"), *manch-* ("many a"), *solch-* ("such"), and *welch-* ("which, what"). The following table gives *der* word declension with the corresponding adjective ending. You can make a useful chart to illustrate the adjective endings for adjectives preceded by a *der* word by setting up your paradigm with cases and genders and then filling in the bold-faced endings shown here.

The Weak (-e/-en) Declension of an Adjective Preceded by a *der Wort*

Case	Masculine "the little boy"	Feminine "the little cat"	Neuter "the little pig"	Plural "the little pigs"
Nom.	der klein**e** Junge *deyR klay-nuh yoon-guh*	die klein**e** Katze *dee klay-nuh kA-tsuh*	das klein**e** Schwein *dAs klay-nuh shvayn*	die klein**en** Schweine *dee klay-nuhn shvay-nuh*
Acc.	den klein**en** Jungen *deyn klay-nuhn yoon-guhn*	die klein**e** Katze *dee klay-nuh kA-tsuh*	das klein**e** Schwein *dAs klay-nuh shvayn*	die klein**en** Schweine *dee klay-nuhn shvay-nuh*
Dat.	dem klein**en** Jungen *deym klay-nuhn yoon-guhn*	der klein**en** Katze *deyR klay-nuhn kA-tsuh*	dem klein**en** Schwein *deym klay-nuhn shvayn*	den klein**en** Schweinen *dehn klay-nuhn shvay-nuh*
Gen.	des klein**en** Jungen *des klay-nuhn yoon-guhn*	der klein**en** Katze *deyR klay-nuhn kA-tsuh*	des klein**en** Schweins *des klay-nuhn shvayns*	der klein**en** Schweine *deyR klay-nuhn shvay-nuh*

Adjectives not preceded by a definite article, a *der* word, an indefinite article, or an *ein* word must indicate the gender and case of the noun they modify. Thus, when no article precedes a noun, adjectives take the strong declension and resemble a *der* word in their endings: *Schönes Wetter, was?* (*shö-nuhs ve-tuhR, vAs*), "Nice weather, isn't it?" The following table illustrates this similarity between unpreceded adjective endings and the *der* words, with the only exception found in the masculine and neuter genitive adjective endings.

The Strong Declension of an Adjective Not Preceded by a Limiting Word (Unpreceded Adjective Endings)

Case	Masculine *"green salad"*	Feminine *"cold milk"*	Neuter *"warm bread"*	Plural *"fresh fish"*
Nom.	grüner Salat *grü-nuhR zah-lAt*	kalte Milch *kAl-tuh milH*	warmes Brot *vAR-muhs bRot*	frische Fische *fri-shuh fi-shuh*
Acc.	grünen Salat *grü-nuhn zah-lAt*	kalte Milch *kAl-tuh milH*	warmes Brot *vAr-muhs bRot*	frische Fische *fri-shuh fi-shuh*
Dat.	grünem Salat *grü-nuhm zah-lAt*	kalter Milch *kAl-tuhR milH*	warmem Brot *vAr-muhm bRot*	frischen Fischen *fri-shuhn fi-shuhn*
Gen.	grünen* Salats *grü-nuhn zah-lAts*	kalter Milch *kAl-tuhR milH*	warmen* Brotes *vAr-muhn bRo-tuhs*	frischer Fische *fri-shuhR fi-shuh*

Note that the only adjective endings that do not resemble the der Wort paradigm are the genitive masculine and neuter, which take an -en rather than the predicted -es ending. But you still get to inflect the genitive masculine and neuter noun with an -(e)s, so take heart!

When adjectives come after an *ein Wort*, they have the responsibility to indicate the grammar *only* if the preceding limiting word doesn't—this is indicated by an asterisk in the following table. For the most part, the adjectives become wishy-washy and weak. Remember, *ein* words include *ein, mein, dein, sein* (m.), *ihr* (f.), *sein* (n.), *unser, euer, ihr* (pl.), and *Ihr* (formal).

Adjective Endings Following an *ein Wort*

Case	Masculine *"green salad"*	Feminine *"cold milk"*	Neuter *"warm bread"*	Plural *"fresh fish"*
Nom.	mein großer* Bruder *mayn gRoh-suhR bRew-duhR*	meine große Schwester *may-nuh gRoh-suh shve-stuhR*	mein großes* Haus *mayn gRoh-suhs hous*	meine großen Häuser *may-nuh gRoh- suhn hoy-zuhR*
Acc.	meinen großen Bruder *may-nuhn gRoh- suhn bRew-duhR*	meine große Schwester *may-nuh gRoh-suh shve-stuhR*	mein großes* Haus *mayn gRoh-suhs hous*	meine großen Häuser *may-nuh gRoh- suhn hoy-zuhRn*
Dat.	meinem großen Bruder *mayn-uhm gRoh- suhn bRew-duhR*	meiner großen Schwester *may-nuhR gRoh- suhn shve-stuhR*	meinem großen Haus *may-nuhm gRoh- suhn hous*	meinen großen Häusern *may-nuhn gRoh- suhn hoy-zuhRn*

continues

Adjective Endings Following an *ein Wort* (continued)

	Masculine	Feminine	Neuter	Plural
Gen.	meines groß**en** Bruders *may-nuhs gRoh-suhn bRew-duhRs*	meiner groß**en** Schwester *may-nuhR gRoh-suhn shve-stuhR*	meines groß**en** Hauses *may-nuhs gRoh-suhn hou-zuhs*	meiner groß**en** Häuser *may-nuhR gRoh-suhn hoy-zuhR*

Denotes instances in which the ein word itself has no ending; thus, it becomes the responsibility of the adjective to reflect case and gender.

Adjectives and Their Antonyms

Are you fickle? Knowing adjectives and their opposites comes in handy if you're constantly changing your mind. If you find something interesting one moment and boring the next, you may want to memorize the adjectives in the following table along with their opposites. Besides, if you learn adjectives with their opposites, you are economically acquiring two words for the memory price of one!

A List of Useful Adjectives

German	Pronunciation	Meaning	German	Pronunciation	Meaning
alt	*Alt*	old, aged	jung	*yoong*	young
blöd	*blöd*	stupid	intelligent	*in-te-li-gent*	intelligent
dick	*dik*	fat or thick	dünn	*dün*	thin
dreckig	*dRe-kiH*	dirty	sauber	*zou-buhR*	clean
falsch	*fAlsh*	wrong	richtig	*RiH-tiH*	right
fleißig	*flay-siH*	industrious	faul	*foul*	lazy
gesund	*guh-zoont*	healthy	krank	*kRAnk*	sick
groß	*gRohs*	big	klein	*klayn*	small
hart	*hArt*	hard	weich	*vayH*	soft
hell	*hel*	bright	dunkel	*doon-kuhl*	dark
hoch	*hoCH*	high	tief	*teef*	low
interessant	*in-tey-re-sAnt*	interesting	langweilig	*lAng-vay-liH*	boring
kalt	*kAlt*	cold	warm	*vahRm*	warm
klug	*klewk*	smart	dumm	*doom*	dumb
lang	*lAng*	long	kurz	*kooRts*	short

German	Pronunciation	Meaning	German	Pronunciation	Meaning
leer	*leyR*	empty	voll	*fol*	full
lustig	*loos-tiH*	funny	ernst	*eRnst*	serious
müde	*müh-duh*	tired	munter	*moon-tuhR*	awake
mutig	*mew-tiH*	brave	feige	*fay-guh*	cowardly
nass	*nAs*	wet	trocken	*tRo-kuhn*	dry
reich	*RayH*	rich	arm	*Arm*	poor
scharf	*shArf*	sharp	stumpf	*shtoompf*	blunt
schön	*shöhn*	beautiful	hässlich	*häs-liH*	ugly
schwer	*shveR*	hard or heavy	leicht	*layHt*	easy or light
stark	*shtARk*	strong	schwach	*shvACH*	weak
stolz	*shtolts*	proud	bescheiden	*buh-shay-duhn*	humble
süß	*zühs*	sweet	sauer	*zou-uhR*	sour
teuer	*toy-uhR*	expensive	billig	*bi-liH*	cheap
tolerant	*to-luh-Rant*	tolerant	intolerant	*in-to-luh-Rant*	intolerant
traurig	*tRou-RiH*	sad	glücklich	*glük-liH*	happy
wahr	*vahR*	true	falsch	*fAlsh*	untrue
weiß	*vays*	white	schwarz	*shvARts*	black

Applying Adjectives

Use the rules you've learned in this chapter to complete the following descriptions with German adjectives. Remember to first determine which type (if any) of limiting word precedes the adjective, and the case and the gender of the noun to be modified. To help you start, we've divided the following exercise into three parts. We'll let you figure out which limiting word is involved in each grouping! Check your accuracy in Appendix A.

    A. 1. Wo spielt dieser interessant _____ Film?

        2. Ich nehme das kalt _____ Bier.

        3. Jedes rot _____ T-Shirt ist billig.

        4. Wir besuchen die klein _____ Stadt.

        5. Sie lesen den best _____ Autor!

B. 1. Das ist warm _____ Brot.

2. Sie hat klug _____ Ideen. (pl.)

3. Frisch _____ Salat ist gesund.

4. Haben Sie schön _____ Blumen?

5. Lieb _____ Kerstin, ….

C. 1. Mainz ist eine schön _____, alt _____ Stadt.

2. Er ist mein best _____ Freund.

3. Ich sehe seine jung _____ Schwester.

4. Wo ist ein gut _____ Restaurant?

5. Wir kaufen ein neu _____ Auto.

The Least You Need to Know

- To show possession in German, use the genitive case or possessive adjectives such as *mein, dein,* and so on.
- *Haben* isn't just an important irregular verb that expresses physical conditions; it also can be used in certain idiomatic expressions of luck, intention, and opportunity.
- German adjectives agree with the noun they modify in gender, number, and case and take endings according to which kind of limiting word precedes them. But if you can't be bothered with memorizing paradigms, just use the adjective at the end of a sentence when it needs no ending!

At the Airport

In This Chapter

- Plane travel
- The verbs *gehen* and *fahren*
- Giving and receiving directions
- Useful prepositions for getting around

Ready to land in Germany, Austria, or Switzerland, you quickly make a mental list of all the things you have to do before you find your hotel. You have to pick up your bags, pass customs, and figure out whether you're going to take a taxi or locate a bus or commuter train that goes to the city. Don't worry: by the end of this chapter, you'll be able to accomplish all of these things in German.

Mainly on the Plane

Soon after the plane takes off, a voice on the overhead speaker begins referring to items on the plane that are above and around you. This familiarizes the passengers with safety features and with the actions taken in the event of an emergency. The vocabulary in the following table will help you understand this information as well as solve various flight-related problems.

Inside the Plane

German	Pronunciation	English
am Fenster	*Am fen-stuhR*	by the window
am Gang	*im gAng*	at the aisle
das Flugzeug	*dAs flook-tsoyk*	airplane
das Handgepäck	*dAs hAnt-guh-päk*	hand luggage
das Terminal	*dAs teR-mee-nahl*	terminal
der Abflug	*deyR ap-flook*	takeoff
der Flughafen	*deyR flook-hah-fuhn*	airport
der Flugsteig	*deyR flook-shtayk*	gate
der Notausgang	*deyR noht-ous-gAng*	emergency exit
der Passagier *or* der Fluggast	*deyR pA-sA-jeeR or deyR flook-gAst*	passenger
der Sitz	*deyR zits*	seat
die Fluggesellschaft *or* die Fluglinie	*dee flook-guh-zel-shAft or dee flook-li-nyah*	airline
die Rettungsweste *or* Schwimmweste	*dee Re-toongz-ves-tuh or shvim-ves-tuh*	life vest
die Sicherheitsvorkehrungen	*dee zi-HuhR-hayts-for-key-Run-guhn*	safety precautions
die Landung	*dee lAn-dung*	landing
im Notfall	*im noht-fAl*	in an emergency
notwendig	*noht-ven-diH*	necessary
(nicht) Raucher	*(niHt) Rou-CHuhR*	(no) smoking
rauchen	*Rou-CHuhn*	to smoke

Negotiating the Airport

Finally, the plane lands. You make it through customs without any difficulties and drag your bags off the luggage belt. Where should you go now? You may want to ask someone where the baggage carts are. After that, you'll probably want to hit an ATM or change some money the old-fashioned way at an exchange booth. Perhaps you need to freshen up a little. You can wander around looking for those signs with the generic men and women on them, or you can ask someone where the nearest *Toilette* (*toy-le-tuh*) is. The following table gives you much of the vocabulary you'll need to get around the airport.

Inside the Airport

German	Pronunciation	English
der Geldautomat	*das gelt-ou-toh-mAt*	ATM
das Gepäckstück	*dAs guh-päk-shtük*	piece of luggage
das Taxi	*dAs tah-xee*	taxi
das Ticket	*dAs ti-ket*	ticket
der Abflug	*deyR Ap-flook*	departure
der Aufzug	*deyR ouf-tsook*	elevator
der Ausgang	*deyR ous-gAng*	exit
der Autoverleih	*deyR ou-toh-feR-lay*	car rental
der Flug	*deyR flook*	flight
der Gepäckwagen	*deyR guh-pak-vah-guhn*	luggage cart
der Koffer	*deyR ko-fuhR*	suitcase
der Zoll	*deyR tsol*	customs
der Zwischenstop	*deyR tsvi-shuhn-shtop*	stopover
die Abflugszeit	*dee Ap-flook-tsayt*	departure time
die Ankunft	*dee An-koonft*	arrival
die Ankunftszeit	*dee An-koonf-tsayt*	arrival time
die Bushaltestelle	*dee boos-hAl-tuh-shte-luh*	bus stop
die Flugnummer	*dee flook-noo-muhR*	flight number
die Geldwechselstube	*dee gelt-vek-suhl-shtew-buh*	money exchange office
die Gepäckausgabe	*dee guh-pak-ous-gah-buh*	baggage claim
die Information	*dee in-foR-mah-tseeohn*	information
die Passkontrolle	*dee pAs-kon-tRo-luh*	passport control
die Sicherheitskontrolle	*dee zi-HuhR-hayts-kon-tRo-luh*	security check
die Toilette	*dee toy-le-tuh*	bathroom
einen Flug verpassen	*ay-nuhn flook veR-pA-suhn*	to miss a flight
kontrollieren	*kon-tRo-lee-Ruhn*	to inspect

Signage

While airline security has always been pretty tight on international flights, maybe it would be comforting to be able to decipher signs giving travelers tips and warnings and indicating rules and regulations in German. The following signs provide examples of information you might see in an airport that serves German-speaking populations. Read the signs, focus on words or parts of words you understand, and then try to match the sign with its corresponding summary from the list that follows. Check your answers in Appendix A.

A. ACHTUNG: Gefährden Sie nicht Ihre eigene Sicherheit: Nehmen Sie keine Gepäckstücke von anderen Personen an.

B. Ihr gesamtes Gepäck, einschließlich Ihres Handgepäcks, wird kontrolliert.

C. Das Benutzen von Gepäckwagen ist ausschließlich im Flughafen gestattet.

D. ACHTUNG: Aus Sicherheitsgründen werden alle zurückgelassenen Gepäckstücke von der Sicherheitspolizei zerstört.

Es ist dehalb notwendig, dass Sie Ihr Gepäck ständig mit sich führen.

E. AN DIE FLUGÄSTE: Das Mitführen von versteckten Waffen an Bord eines Flugzeugs ist gesetzlich verboten.

Es ist gesetzlich vorgeschrieben, dass alle Gepäckstücke, einschließlich des Handgepäcks, von der Sicherheitskontrolle überprüft werden.

Diese Durchsuchung kann verweigert werden. Passagiere, welche die Durchsuchung verweigern, sind nicht befugt, die Sicherheitskontrolle zu passieren.

Identify the sign that tells you:

1. _____ If you leave something behind, it will be destroyed.

2. _____ All of your luggage will be inspected, even carry-on.

3. _____ Carrying a concealed weapon onboard is forbidden.

4. _____ You can use the baggage carts only within the airport.

5. _____ Don't accept packages from strangers.

Getting Around

You will undoubtedly find the strong verb *gehen* ("to go") handy as you make your way out of the airport to the taxi stand. As you learned in Chapter 8, you must conjugate present tense verbs so that they agree with the subject. Now you need to apply these inflections (sg. *-e*, *-st*, *-t* and pl. *-en*, *-t*, *-en*) to the stem *geh-*. The verb for "to travel" is *fahren*. *Fahren*, a very strong verb, incurs a sound change ($a \rightarrow \ddot{a}$) in the present tense, like *fallen* does. The following table reviews this type of change, which occurs only in the second and third person singular forms.

The Very Strong Verb: *fahren*

Person	Singular	English	Plural	English
First	ich fahr**e** *iH fah-Ruh*	I travel	wir fahr**en** *veeR fah-Ruhn*	we travel
Second	du fähr**st** *dew fähRst*	you travel	ihr fahr**t** *eeR fahrt*	you travel
Third	er, sie, es fähr**t** *eR, zee, es fähRt*	he, she, it travels	sie fahr**en** *zee fah-Ruhn*	they travel
Formal	Sie fahr**en** *zee fah-Ruhn*	you travel	Sie fahr**en** *zee fah-Ruhn*	you travel

Contractions with *Gehen*

The verb *gehen* is often followed by the preposition *zu* (to). *Zu* is a preposition that always takes the dative case; therefore, when this preposition is used to indicate location, the entire prepositional phrase is in the dative. Recall the declination of the dative *der* words—*dem* (m.), *die* (f.), *dem* (n.). If the noun after the preposition is masculine or neuter (*dem*), *zu* can contract with the article *dem* to become *zum* ("to the"). A *contraction* is a single word made out of two words, as in the word *it's*. In German, contractions don't take an apostrophe. Some prepositions in German may take the accusative or dative. *Auf* and *in* are two prepositions that can be used to indicate motion, and when *gehen* is followed by one of these prepositions, the prepositional phrase is in the accusative (*den*, *die*, *das*). Because contractions make it faster and easier to express things, we can again combine the prepositions *in* and *auf* with the accusative neuter *das* to come up with *ins* and *aufs*. Here are some examples of these contractions, with the illustration of gender and case in parentheses—case is determined by the preceding preposition.

DEFINITION

A **contraction** is a shortened linguistic form attached to an adjacent form. In German, it's (a contraction in English!) a fusion of forms. Unlike their English counterparts, German contractions do not use apostrophes.

Ich gehe zum Bahnhof. (*der* Bahnhof + dative → dem)
iH gey-uh tsewm bahn-hohf
I'm going to the train station.

Ich gehe zum Geschäft. (*das* Geschäft + dative → dem)
iH gey-uh tsewm guh-shäft
I'm going to the store.

If the location toward which the subject is heading is feminine, *zu* ("to") can contract with the feminine dative article *der* ("the") to become *zur* ("to the").

Ich gehe zur Kirche. (*die* Kirche + dative → der)
iH gey-uh tsewR keeR-Huh
I'm going to the church.

Ich gehe ins Kino. (*das* Kino + accusative → das)
ich gey-uh inz kee-noh
I go to the movies.

How Do You Get To ...?

You may get disoriented in a new place; the best thing to do is to ask someone how to get to wherever you want to go. Here are some ways of asking questions:

Wo ist der Ausgang?
voh ist deyR ous-gAng
Where is the exit?

Wo sind die Taxis?
voh zint dee tah-xees
Where are the taxis?

If you're not sure whether what you're looking for is nearby, or if you just want to know whether whatever you're looking for is in the vicinity, use the phrase *gibt es* ("is there," "are there") and the prepositional phrase *in der Nähe* ("nearby"). It's a useful way of finding things out.

Gibt es Toiletten in der Nähe?
gipt es toy-le-tuhn in deyR näh-uh
Are there toilets nearby?

You Can't Get There from Here ...

What if the place you're looking for isn't within pointing distance? In this case, you'd better know the verbs people use when they give directions.

Verbs Used When Giving Directions

German	Pronunciation	English
abbiegen*	*Ap-bee-guhn*	to turn
gehen	*gey-uhn*	to go
laufen[S]	*lou-fuhn*	to walk
mitfahren*[S]	*mit-fah-Ruhn*	to ride with/along
nehmen[S]	*ney-muhn*	to take
weitergehen*	*vay-tuhR-gey-uhn*	to go on, to continue

* indicates a separable prefix verb.

[S] *indicates a very strong verb, incurring a sound change in the second and third person singular.*

Verbs with Separable Prefixes

Some verbs in the preceding table (the ones with asterisks next to them) have *separable prefixes*, verbal complements that are placed at the end of the sentence when the verb is conjugated (separable prefixes are addressed at greater length in Chapter 13). Some of the most common separable prefixes include *auf, hinüber, aus, an, hinunter, hinauf, weiter, bei, mit, nach*, and *zu*. Incidentally, the verbs marked with a superscript *S* are the *very strong*, or *sehr stark* verbs—those that incur a vowel change in the second and third person singular.

> **DEFINITION**
>
> **Separable prefixes** are verbal complements comprised of prepositions, adverbs, or particles that are placed at the end of the sentence when the verb is conjugated. This produces a two-part verb that alters or in some way affects the meaning of the main verb. These prefixes are always stressed.

Du biegst rechts ab.
dew beekst reHts Ap
You turn right.

Sie fährt mit?
zee fähRt mit?
Is she riding along/with?

Giving Commands

When someone tells you how to get somewhere, generally you are receiving a command, an imperative. Imperatives express commands, requests, or directives. The subject of the imperative is *you*. Because you can address someone formally or informally in German and speak to one or more than one person, German has several easily deducible imperative forms corresponding to the three grammatical forms expressing the second person pronoun "you": *Sie*, *du*, and *ihr*. Try to figure out which of the following *imperative* forms correspond to *du*, *ihr*, and *Sie*.

> **WE ARE FAMILY**
>
> English has numerous verbs that extend their meanings by adding certain prepositions, called *complements*: to go out, to come along/with, to drive back. German very neatly attaches this *complement* to the infinitive—hence, you get very similar constructions of *ausgehen, mitkommen, zurückfahren*. These separable prefixes occur sentence-final in statements and in questions. Some varieties of American English retain German word order, as in "Are you coming with?"

A. Gehen Sie nach rechts.
gey-uhn zee nACH reHts
Go right.

B. Geht nach rechts.
geyt nACH ReHts
Go right.

C. Geh(e) nach rechts.
Gey(-uh) nACH reHts
Go right.

If you deduced that answer A was the formal (*Sie*-address) imperative form, identical to the present-tense form, give yourself a point. Because it is a command, it begins with the verb because action is tantamount in getting one's way. And answer B? You guessed it—the familiar plural (*ihr*-address) imperative is identical to the *ihr* form in the present tense, except that the pronoun, *ihr*, is omitted. This pattern is easy enough to account for: commands in the familiar realm do not need to be formal, so we omit the pronoun. Likewise, we can account for answer C being the familiar singular (*du*-address) imperative, omitting the pronoun and even the ending (*-st*) on the verb! To pronounce that type of sliced-off stem more easily, often an *-e* is added, as in *Warte!* ("Wait!") or *Finde den Flugsteig!* ("Find the gate!")

Giving Orders

You need to practice giving and receiving commands before you can effectively do either. Complete the following exercise by filling in the appropriate command forms and their meanings. The entire chart appears in Appendix A.

Verb	Du	ihr	Sie	English
abbiegen*	_____	_____	_____	Turn!
gehen	Geh(e)!	Geht!	Gehen Sie!	Go!
weitergehen*	_____	_____	_____	Continue!
laufen[S]	_____	_____	_____	Walk!
mitfahren*[S]	_____	_____	_____	Ride along!

* *indicates a separable prefix verb.*

[S] *indicates a very strong verb, incurring a sound change in the second and third person singular.*

Prepositions: Little Words Can Make a Big Difference

Prepositions are useful for giving and receiving directions. They show the relationship of a noun to another word, adding supplemental information to a basic subject/verb sentence. Prepositions locate something—an entity, event, or situation—in relation to another referent in terms of space or time, or to designate the source and/or direction of motion. The following table contains some useful prepositions for getting where you want to go.

DEFINITION

A **preposition** is a word or phrase that shows the relation of a noun to another word in a sentence.

Prepositions

German	Pronunciation	English
an	*an*	to, on (vertical)
auf	*ouf*	to, in, at, on (horizontal)
aus	*ous*	out of
bei	*bay*	at, near
bis	*bis*	until, as far as
durch	*dooRCH*	through
gegen	*gey-guhn*	against
hinter	*hin-tuhR*	behind
in	*in*	in
nach	*nACH*	after
neben	*ney-buhn*	next to
ohne	*oh-nuh*	without
um	*ewm*	around
unter	*oon-tuhR*	under
von	*fon*	from
vor	*foR*	in front of
zu, nach	*tsew, nACH*	to, at
zwischen	*tsvi-shuhn*	between

Prepositions Are Particular!

Although the preceding table lists German prepositions, not all prepositions are created equal. Sure, you had it made in English, knowing that it's *for him* rather than *for he*. You intuitively and automatically change the case from nominative to objective after a preposition in English. German changes the form of the noun phrase (which might be a pronoun or a noun) after the preposition as well, relying on its various cases after specific prepositions. The following table contains the prepositions from the preceding table that are always dative. Note how some dative prepositions contract with the following definite article, as in *beim* and *zur*.

Dative Prepositions

German	Example	English
aus	aus dem Haus	out of the house
bei	beim Postamt	at the post office
	beim Arzt	at the doctor's
nach	nach einer Stunde	after an hour
	nach Wien	to Vienna
von	von Hamburg	from Hamburg
	von meinen Eltern	from my parents
zu	zur Bushaltestelle	to the bus stop

See whether you can fill in the correct form of the dative in the following dative prepositional phrases. Check your responses in Appendix A.

1. aus _____ Flugzeug (n.) (out of the airplane)

2. bei _____ Flughafen (m.) (near the airport)

3. von _____ Arbeit (f.) (from the workplace)

4. zu _____ Hotel (n.) (to the hotel)

Likewise, some prepositions always take the accusative case. Those relating to direction and duration are listed in the following table.

Accusative Prepositions

German	Example	English
bis	bis nächste Woche	by/until next week
	bis Mainz	as far as Mainz
durch	durch die Stadt	through the city
ohne	ohne den Bus	without the bus
um	um die Ecke	around the corner

Use the accusative case to finish these prepositional phrases. Check your responses in Appendix A.

1. durch _____ Land (n.) (through the country)

2. ohne _____ Koffer (m.) (without the suitcase)

3. um _____ Sitz (m.) (around the seat)

The prepositions *in* and *auf* belong to a nifty group of prepositions that can govern either the dative or the accusative, depending on the context. With verbs like *gehen* and *fahren* (introduced earlier in this chapter) that indicate motion *toward* a place, the preposition governs the accusative. To indicate moving around *within* a place, the preposition governs the dative. The following table provides examples of both instances for the two-way prepositions listed earlier in the table titled "Prepositions":

Two-Way Prepositions

German	Example	English
an	Ich gehe ans Fenster.	I'm going to the window.
	Ich bin am Fenster.	I'm at the window.
auf	Geh auf den Marktplatz!	Go to the town square!
	Parke auf dem Marktplatz!	Park on the town square!
hinter	Fahr hinter die Garage!	Drive behind the garage!
	Das Auto ist hinter der Garage.	The car is behind the garage.
in	Ich gehe in das Terminal.	I'm going (in)to the terminal.
	Ich bin im Terminal.	I'm in the terminal.
neben	Mein Koffer liegt neben der Gepäckablage.	My suitcase is lying next to the luggage rack.
unter	Die Rettungsweste ist unter dem Sitz.	The life vest is under the seat.
vor	Die Taxis warten vor dem Flughafen.	The taxis are waiting in front of the airport.
zwischen	Die Passkontrolle liegt zwischen der Sicherheitskontrolle und dem Flugsteig.	The passport control is between the security check and the gate.

Care to finish off your prepositional preoccupation with a few more exercises, this time concerning the two-way prepositions? Check your answers in Appendix A.

1. Ich werfe deinen Koffer auf dein _____ Sitz. (I'm throwing your suitcase onto your seat.)

2. Es gibt eine Passkontrolle an _____ Grenze. (There is passport control on/at the border.)

3. Klaus ist in _____ Toilette. (Klaus is in the bathroom.)

4. Stell dein Handgepäck neben _____ Bett. (Put your hand luggage next to the bed.)

5. Mein Ticket ist unter dein _____ Handgepäck! (My ticket is under your carry-on luggage!)

Pardon Me?

Track 7 We've all asked for directions and then immediately regretted it. Such remorse generally happens when the direction-giver enumerates more rights and lefts than we can handle. Thus, knowing how to show lack of understanding in a foreign country is extremely useful. In addition to scratching your head and cocking it to one side, use some of the phrases in the following table to let people know that you just don't understand. If you'd like to hear how these examples are pronounced, check out Track 7 on the CD included with this book.

Expressing Incomprehension and Confusion

German	Pronunciation	English
Entschuldigen Sie!	*ent-shool-dee-guhn zee*	Excuse me! (formal)
Entschuldigung, ich habe Sie nicht verstanden.	*ent-shool-dee-goong, iH hah-buh zee niHt feR-shtAn-duhn*	Excuse me, I didn't understand you.
Ich verstehe nicht.	*iH feR-shtey-uh niHt*	I don't understand.
Sprechen Sie langsamer, bitte.	*shpRe-Hun zee lAng-zah-muhR, bi-tuh*	Please speak more slowly.
Was haben Sie gesagt?/Wie bitte?	*vAs hah-buhn zee guh-zAkt/ vee bi-tuh*	What did you say?
Wiederholen Sie, bitte.	*vee-deR-hoh-luhn zee, bi-tuh*	Please repeat (what you just said).

The Least You Need to Know

- Learning a few useful vocabulary words will help you figure out airport traveling in German.
- The strong verb *gehen* is used to give directions. Useful also is the very strong verb *fahren*.
- German has three ways of forming commands, depending on the degree of formality and the number of addressees (one or more than one person).
- Prepositions are useful tools in expressing direction. Some of them govern the dative case, others govern the accusative, and still others can't quite make up their minds.
- If you don't understand the directions being given to you, don't be afraid to say, "Ich verstehe nicht. Wiederholen Sie, bitte (*iH feR-shtey-uh niHt, vee-deR-hoh-luhn zee, bi-tuh*)."

Getting Around Town on Time

In This Chapter

- Different modes of transportation
- Renting a car
- Determining *which, this, every,* or *such*
- Counting with cardinal numbers
- Telling time

The only way to get to know a city is to travel around in it. You have a number of options, of course. The mode of travel you choose will depend on many factors, including how near or distant your destination is. Whichever mode of travel is right for you, you should familiarize yourself with some terms.

Modes of Transportation

Whether you see yourself zipping along on the Autobahn or hobnobbing with the locals on a bus, knowing the words listed here will help you get around. You've already seen this vocabulary used with the dative preposition *mit* to indicate "by means of" in Chapter 5.

German	Pronunciation	English
das Auto	*dAs ou-toh*	car
das Taxi	*dAs tah-xee*	taxi
der Bus	*deyR boos*	bus
der Sportwagen	*deyR shpoRt-vah-guhn*	sports car
der Wagen	*deyR vah-guhn*	car
der Zug	*deyR tsewk*	train
die S-Bahn	*dee es-bahn*	commuter train
die Straßenbahn	*dee shtRah-suhn-bahn*	streetcar
die U-Bahn	*dee ew-bahn*	subway

You'll use the verb *nehmen (ney-muhn)*, "to take," to express how you are going to get from where you are to where you are going. *Nehmen* is a very strong verb whose stem vowel changes from e to i in the second and third person singular.

The Verb *nehmen*

Person	Singular	English	Plural	English
First	ich nehme *iH ney-muh*	I take	wir nehmen *veeR ney-muhn*	we take
Second	du nimmst *dew nimst*	you take	ihr nehmt *eeR neymt*	you take
Third	er, sie, es nimmt *eR, zee, es nimt*	he, she, it takes	sie nehmen *zee ney-muhn*	they take
Formal	Sie nehmen *zee ney-muhn*	you take	Sie nehmen *zee ney-muhn*	you take

Other verbs that incur the change from $e \rightarrow i$, and thus very much resemble *nehmen*, include *geben*, "to give"; *essen*, "to eat"; *sprechen*, "to talk"; *werfen*, "to throw"; and *sterben*, "to die."

See whether you can fill in the blanks in these sentences with the correct form of the verb *nehmen*. Check your answers in Appendix A.

1. Ich _____ ein Taxi zum Geschäft.

   I take the bus to the store.

2. Wir _____ die Straßenbahn in die Innenstadt.

   We take the streetcar to downtown.

3. Er _____ das Auto zur Kirche.

   He takes the car to the church.

4. Du _____ den Bus durch die Stadt.

   You take the bus through the city.

Which One?

Someone tells you that to get to the local museum, you must go straight past a building and then take a left on a street. *Which* building is the person talking about? *Which* street does he or she mean? When you're traveling—and particularly when you're asking directions—one word in German will be indispensable to you: *welcher* (*vel-HuhR*), the interrogative word for "which."

Welcher with Singular and Plural Nouns

When *welcher* comes immediately before a noun and introduces a question, it is considered an interrogative pronoun and must agree in number, gender, and case with the noun it precedes. Some common pronouns that follow the same declension patterns as *welcher* are *dieser* ("this"), *jeder* ("each," "every"), *mancher* ("many," "many a"), and *solcher* ("such," "such a"). The following table reviews the declension of *der* words, this time substituting *welch-* into the paradigm.

The *der* Wort *welch-*

Case	Masculine	Feminine	Neuter	Plural
	which bus	*which direction*	*which car*	*which cars*
Nom.	welcher Bus *vel-HuhR boos*	welche Richtung *vel-Huh RiH-toong*	welches Auto *vel-Huhs ou-toh*	welche Autos *vel-Huh ou-tohz*
Acc.	welchen Bus *vel-Huhn boos*	welche Richtung *vel-Huh RiH-toong*	welches Auto *vel-Huhs ou-toh*	welche Autos *vel-Huh ou-tohz*
Dat.	welchem Bus *vel-Huhm boos*	welcher Richtung *vel-HuhR RiH-toong*	welchem Auto *vel-Huhm ou-toh*	welchen Autos *vel-Huhn ou-tohz*
Gen.	welchen Buses *vel-Huhs boo-suhs*	welcher Richtung *vel-HuhR RiH-toong*	welchen Autos *vel-Huhs ou-to*	welcher Autos *vel-HuhR ou-tohz*

The Third Degree

You should be prepared for questions that begin with *welch-* (in its declined form). Here are some common questions you may be asked while traveling around the city. You should recognize a few of the prepositions from Chapter 11, including that tricky two-way preposition *in!*

Welchen Bus nehmen Sie? (m., acc.)
vel-Huhn boos ney-muhn zee
Which bus are you taking?

In welche Richtung fährt der Bus? (f., acc.)
in vel-Huh RiH-toong fähRt deyR boos
In which direction is the bus going?

Welches Auto mieten Sie? (n., acc.)
vel-Huhs ou-toh mee-tuhn zee
Which car are you renting?

Using Which

Have you ever spoken with someone who immediately assumes that you know what he or she is speaking about, no matter what the topic is? See whether you can properly decline the interrogative pronoun *welch-* to find out the specifics of the statements given here. Check your questions in Appendix A.

Example: Ich nehme die U-Bahn. (Welche U-Bahn?)

German	Pronunciation	English
1. Sie nehmen den Zug.	*zee ney-muhn deyn tsook*	They take the train.
2. Ich fahre in die Stadt.	*iH fah-Ruh in dee shtAt*	I'm driving into town.
3. Er mietet ein Auto.	*eR mee-tuht ayn ou-toh*	He rents a car.
4. Ich besuche einen Freund.	*iH buh-zew-CHuh ay-nuhn fRoynt*	I'm visiting a friend.
5. Wir gehen in ein Museum.	*veeR gey-uhn in ayn mew-zey-oom*	We're going to a museum.
6. Sie sucht ein Hotel.	*zee zewCHt ayn hoh-tel*	She's looking for a hotel.
7. Er nimmt ein Buch mit.	*eR nimt ayn buCH mit*	He's taking along a book.

On the Road

You may want to take a trip with your travel partners around the countryside or go on a castle quest. And the ideal way to do so is to rent a car. The following phrases are useful when renting a car.

> Ich möchte ein Auto mieten.
> *iH möH-tuh ayn ou-toh mee-tuhn*
> I would like to rent a car.

> Wie viel kostet es am Tag (in der Woche)?
> *vee feel kos-tuht es Am tahk (in deyR vo-CHuh)*
> How much does it cost per day (per week)?

Outside the Car

If you decide to rent a car, don't forget to check in the trunk for the regulation jack—in German, *der Wagenheber (deyR vah-guhn-hey-buhR)*—and the spare tire, or *der Ersatzreifen (deyR eR-zAts-Ray-fuhn)*.

Here are a few terms you might find useful when talking about the various features of a car.

German	Pronunciation	English
das Fenster	*dAs fen-stuhR*	window
das Nummernschild	*dAs noo-meRn-shilt*	license plate
das Rad	*dAs Raht*	wheel
das Rücklicht	*dAs Rük-liHt*	tail light
der Auspuff	*deyR ous-poof*	exhaust
der Benzintank	*deyR ben-zeen-tAnk*	gas tank
der Blinker	*deyR blin-kuhR*	turn signal
der Keilriemen	*deyR kayl-Ree-muhn*	fan belt
der Kofferraum	*deyR ko-fe-Roum*	trunk
der Kotflügel	*deyR koht-flü-guhl*	fender
der Kühler	*deyR küh-luhR*	radiator
der Motor	*deyR mo-tohR*	motor
der Scheibenwischer	*deyR shay-buhn-vi-shuhR*	windshield wiper
der Türgriff	*deyR tühR-gRif*	door handle

continues

continued

German	Pronunciation	English
der Vergaser	*deyR feR-gah-suhR*	carburetor
die Antenne	*dee An-te-nuh*	antenna
die Batterie	*dee bA-te-Ree*	battery
die Motorhaube	*dee mo-tohR-hou-buh*	hood
die Reifen	*dee Ray-fuhn*	tires
die Scheinwerfer	*dee shayn-veR-fuhR*	headlights
die Stoßstange	*dee shtob-shtAn-guh*	bumper
die Tür	*dee tühR*	door
die Windschutzscheibe	*dee vint-shutz-shay-buh*	windshield
die Zündkerzen	*dee tsünt-keR-tsuhn*	sparkplugs

Inside the Car

Here are a few useful terms for things inside a car.

German	Pronunciation	English
das Amaturenbrett	*dAs ah-mA-tew-Ruhn-bRet*	dashboard
das Antiblokiersystem	*dAs An-tee-bloh-keeR-süs-tem*	anti-lock brake system
das Gaspedal	*dAs gahs-pey-dahl*	accelerator
das Handschuhfach	*dAs hAnt-shew-fACH*	glove compartment
das Lenkrad	*dAs lenk-Raht*	steering wheel
das Radio	*dAs Rah-dee-oh*	radio
der Blinker	*deyR blin-kuhR*	turn signal
der Rückspiegel	*deyR Rük-shpee-guhl*	rearview mirror
die Alarmanlage	*dee ah-lArm-An-lah-guh*	alarm system
die Automatikgetriebe	*dee ou-toh-mah-tuhn-ge-tRee-buh*	automatic transmission
die Bremsen	*dee bRem-suhn*	brakes
die Hupe	*dee hew-puh*	horn
die Klimaanlage	*dee klee-mah-An-lah-guh*	air conditioning system
die Kupplung	*dee kup-lung*	clutch
die Schaltgetriebe	*dee shAlt-guh-tRee-buh*	manual transmission
die Schaltung	*dee shAl-tung*	gear shift
die Zündung	*dee tsün-dung*	ignition

You might want to ask someone whether you're heading in the right direction. You never know when you're going to get lost in the woods without your compass.

nach Norden	*nACH noR-duhn*	to the north
nach Süden	*nACH süh-duhn*	to the south
nach Westen	*nACH ves-tuhn*	to the west
nach Osten	*nACH os-tuhn*	to the east

Numbers

Sooner or later you're going to have to learn numbers in German. Numbers are used for telling time, for making dates, for counting, for finding out prices—they're even used to refer to the pages and chapters in this book!

Counting

Track 8 Numbers that express amounts are known as *cardinal numbers.* The sooner you learn cardinal numbers in German, the better. You're going to need to use numbers for everything—from renting a car to locating your gate in an airport. The following table lists the cardinal numbers. If you would like to hear pronunciation examples of cardinal numbers, check out Track 8 of the CD included with this book.

> **DEFINITION**
>
> A **cardinal number** is the basic form of a number; numbers used in counting.

Cardinal Numbers

German	Pronunciation	English
null	*nool*	0
eins	*aynts*	1
zwei	*tsvay*	2
drei	*dRay*	3
vier	*feeR*	4
fünf	*fünf*	5
sechs	*zeks*	6

continues

Cardinal Numbers (continued)

German	Pronunciation	English
sieben	*zee-buhn*	7
acht	*ACHt*	8
neun	*noyn*	9
zehn	*tseyn*	10
elf	*elf*	11
zwölf	*tsvölf*	12
dreizehn	*dRay-tseyn*	13
vierzehn	*feeR-tseyn*	14
fünfzehn	*fünf-tseyn*	15
sechzehn	*zeHs-tseyn*	16
siebzehn	*zeep-tseyn*	17
achtzehn	*ACH-tseyn*	18
neunzehn	*noyn-tseyn*	19
zwanzig	*tsvAn-tsiH*	20
einundzwanzig	*ayn-oont-tsvAn-tsiH*	21
zweiundzwanzig	*tsvay-oont-tsvAn-tsiH*	22
dreiundzwanzig	*dRay-oont-tsvAn-tsiH*	23
vierundzwanzig	*feeR-oont-tsvAn-tsiH*	24
fünfundzwanzig	*fünf-oont-tsvAn-tsiH*	25
sechsundzwanzig	*zeks-oont-tsvAn-tsiH*	26
siebenundzwanzig	*zee-buhn-oont-tsvAn-tsiH*	27
achtundzwanzig	*ACHt-oont-tsvAn-tsiH*	28
neunundzwanzig	*noyn-oont-tsvAn-tsiH*	29
dreißig	*dRay-siH*	30
vierzig	*feeR-tsiH*	40
fünfzig	*fünf-tsiH*	50
sechzig	*zeH-tsiH*	60
siebzig	*zeep-tsiH*	70
achtzig	*ACH-tsiH*	80
neunzig	*noyn-tsiH*	90
hundert	*hoon-deRt*	100
hunderteins	*hoon-deRt-aynts*	101

German	Pronunciation	English
hundertzwei	*hoon-deRt-tsvay*	102
zweihundert	*tsvay-hoon-deRt*	200
zweihundereins	*tsvay-hoon-deRt-aynts*	201
zweihunderzwei	*tsvay-hoon-deRt-tsvay*	202
tausend	*tou-zent*	1,000
zweitausend	*tsvay-tou-zent*	2,000
hunderttausend	*hoon-deRt-tou-zent*	100,000
eine million	*aynuh mee-leeohn*	1,000,000
zwei millionen	*tsvay mee-leeoh-nuhn*	2,000,000
eine milliarde	*ayn mee-leeAR-duh*	1,000,000,000
zwei milliarden	*tsvay mee-leeAR-duhn*	2,000,000,000

After you've learned the basics of counting in German, the main things to remember are …

- After the number 20, numbers are expressed in compound words with the 1, 2, 3 … coming first: 1-and-20, 2-and-20, 3-and-20 …. Don't forget to drop the -s from *eins* before *einundzwanzig, einunddreißig,* and so on.

- *Und* (and) is used to connect the numbers 1 through 9 to the numbers 20, 30, 40, 50, and so on.

- The -s is dropped from *sechs* to form *sechzehn* (16) and *sechzig* (60). Similarly, the -en is dropped from *sieben* to form *siebzehn* (17) and *siebzig* (70).

- Because the sounds of *zwei* (*tsvay*) and *drei* (*dRay*) are so similar, *zwo* (*tsvoh*) is often used for "two" in official language and when giving numbers on the telephone.

What Time Is It?

Now that you have familiarized yourself with German numbers, it should be relatively easy for you to tell time. The simplest way to question someone about the time is by saying:

Wie viel Uhr ist es?   Wie spät ist es?
vee feel ewR ist es   *vee shpäht ist es*
What time is it?   What time is it?

GERMAN CULTURE

In Germany, as in most European countries, colloquial time is given without any reference to A.M. or P.M. Often the 24-hour system—what we call official, or military, time—is used. Accordingly, 1:00 P.M. is 13:00, or *dreizehn Uhr* (*dray-tseyn ewR*); 2:00 P.M. is *vierzehn Uhr* (*feeR-tseyn ewR*); and so on. These may be expressed with a period separating the hour from the minutes 13.00 and 14.00.

Track 9

To say what time it is, start out with *Es ist* .... Look at the following table for some common phrases to help you tell time. If you would like to hear pronunciation examples for telling time, check out Track 9 of the CD included with this book.

Telling Time

German	Pronunciation	English
Es ist ein Uhr.	*es ist ayn ewR*	It is 1:00.
Es ist fünf nach zwei.	*es ist fünf nACH tsvay*	It is 2:05.
Es ist zehn nach drei.	*es ist tseyn nACH dRay*	It is 3:10.
Es ist zwanzig nach fünf.	*es ist tsvAn-tsiH nACH fünf*	It is 5:20.
Es ist halb acht.	*es ist hAlp ACHt*	It is 7:30.
Es ist fünf nach halb acht.	*es ist fünf nACH hAlp ACHt*	It is 7:35.
Es ist zwanzig vor neun.	*es ist tsvAn-tsiH foR noyn*	It is 8:40.
Es ist Viertel vor zehn.	*es ist feer-tuhl foR tseyn*	It is 9:45.
Es ist fünf vor zwölf.	*es ist fünf foR tsvölf*	It is 11:55.
Es ist Mitternacht.	*es ist mi-tuhR-nACHt*	It is midnight.
Es ist Mittag.	*es ist mi-tahk*	It is noon.

- To express the time after the hour, give the number of minutes past the hour first, then use *nach*, and then give the hour: *Es ist Viertel nach fünf.* ("It's a quarter past five.")

- To express the time before the hour, give the number of minutes before the hour first, then use *vor*, and then give the hour: *Es ist Viertel vor fünf.* ("It's a quarter to five.")

- With all other hours, *halb* is used to express half the way *to* the hour. *Halb sechs* does not mean half past six, but halfway to six (5:30).

- To express "at what time" something is occurring, use the preposition *um*: *Um halb sechs gehen wir.* ("We'll go at 5:30.")

> **DEFINITION**
>
> Usually, the preposition **um** means "around," but in time expressions, it means "at." *Um 9 Uhr beginnt das Theaterstück (oom noyn ewR buh-gint dAs tey-ah-teR-shtük)* means "The play begins at 9:00."

You'll also need to know more general time expressions. The following table provides some common time expressions.

Time Expressions

German	Pronunciation	English
eine Sekunde	*ay-nuh zey-koon-duh*	a second
eine Minute	*ay-nuh mee-new-tuh*	a minute
eine Stunde	*ay-nuh shtoon-duh*	an hour
morgens	*moR-guhnz*	mornings
am Morgen	*Am moR-guhn*	in the morning
abends	*ah-buhnts*	evenings
am Abend	*Am ah-buhnt*	in the evening (P.M.)
nachmittags	*nACH-mi-tahks*	afternoons (P.M.)
am Nachmittag	*Am nACH-mi-tahk*	in the afternoon
um wie viel Uhr	*oom vee feel ewR*	at what time
genau um Mitternacht	*guh-nou oom mi-tuhR-nACHt*	at exactly midnight
genau um ein Uhr	*guh-nou oom ayn ewR*	at exactly 1:00
um ungefähr/um etwa zwei Uhr	*oom oon-guh-fähR/oom et-vah tsvay ewR*	at about 2:00
ein Viertel	*ayn feeR-tuhl*	a quarter
eine halbe Stunde	*ay-nuh hAl-buh shtoon-duh*	half an hour
in einer Stunde	*in ay-nuhR shtoon-duh*	in an hour
bis zwei Uhr	*bis tsvay ewR*	until 2:00
vor drei Uhr	*foR dRay ewR*	before 3:00
nach drei Uhr	*nACH dRay ewR*	after 3:00
Seit wann?	*zayt vAn*	Since when?
seit sechs Uhr	*zayt zeks ewR*	since 6:00
vor einer Stunde	*foR ay-nuhR shtoon-duh*	an hour ago
jede Stunde	*yey-duh shtoon-duh*	every hour
stündlich	*shtünt-liH*	hourly

Time Expressions   (continued)

German	Pronunciation	English
früh	*fRüh*	early
spät	*shpäht*	late
gestern	*ges-tuhRn*	yesterday
heute	*hoy-tuh*	today
morgen	*moR-guhn*	tomorrow
vorgestern	*foR-ges-tuhRn*	the day before yesterday
übermorgen	*üh-buhR-moR-guhn*	the day after tomorrow

Wie spät ist es?

Take time now to read the following times aloud. Check your responses in Appendix A.

1. 7.38
2. 3.06
3. 14.00
4. 12.25
5. 19.30
6. 21.50

The Least You Need to Know

- You can use the very strong verb *nehmen* to indicate what transportation you are taking to get from one place to another.
- *Welcher* is the interrogative pronoun "which" or "what" and takes the same declination as the definite article.
- To rent and drive a car, you might need to know some basic vocabulary for the parts of a car.
- Whether you're telling someone the time or listening to a sales clerk count your change in a store, sooner or later you're going to need to know German cardinal numbers.

At the Hotel

Chapter 13

In This Chapter

- Checking out hotel facilities
- Counting with ordinal numbers (an excuse to review adjective endings!)
- Knowing and *knowing* something
- Verbs with prefixes, both separable and inseparable
- Exchanging money and figuring out currency
- The German equivalent of the English *let's*

You selected the method of transportation that suits your luggage situation and the purchasing power of your wallet. You pay the taxi driver, get off the bus, or exit the subway to find yourself in front of your hotel.

For some of us, a bed is all we look for in a hotel. For others, cable TV, a telephone, internet access, a sauna, and a garden-view balcony are the bare necessities. Whatever your personal needs may be, this chapter will help you get comfortable in a German hotel.

What a Hotel! Does It Have ...?

Before you hand over your credit card once you've arrived at your hotel, be sure to verify with the people at *die Hotel-Rezeption (dee hoh-tel Rey-tsep-tseeohn)* that they can provide you with whatever it is you need: a quiet room, a wake-up call, or coffee at 4 A.M. The following table will help you get the scoop on just about everything a hotel has to offer.

GERMAN CULTURE

Travelers interested in cheap, no-frills sleeping can stay at *eine Pension (ay-nuh pen-zeeohn)*, essentially a boarding house. Depending on whether you want all meals or just breakfast, you can choose *Vollpension* or *Halbpension*. If you want something cozier, try das *Gasthaus (dAs gAst-hous)*. And finally, there is *das Hotel (dAs hoh-tel)*.

At the Hotel

German	Pronunciation	English
das Einkaufszentrum	*dAs ayn-koufs-tsen-tRoom*	shopping center
das Fitnesscenter	*dAs fit-nes-sen-tuhR*	fitness center
das Geschäftszentrum	*dAs guh-shäfts-tsen-tRoom*	business center
das Hotel	*dAs hoh-tel*	hotel
das Restaurant	*dAs Re-stou-rohn*	restaurant
das Schwimmbad	*dAs shvim-baht*	swimming pool
das Zimmermädchen	*dAs tsi-muhR-mät-Huhn*	maid
der Aufzug	*deyR ouf-tsewk*	elevator
der (Gepäck)Träger	*deyR (guh-päk)tRäh-guhR*	porter
der Geschenkladen	*deyR guh-shenk-lah-duhn*	gift shop
der Internetzugriff	*deyR in-tuhR-net-tsew-grif*	internet access
der Kassierer	*deyR kA-see-RuhR*	cashier
der Parkplatz	*deyR pARk-plAts*	parking lot
der Pförtner	*deyR pföRt-nuhR*	concierge
der Portier	*deyR poR-ti-ey*	doorman
der Stock	*deyR shtok*	floor, story
der Zimmerservice	*deyR tsi-muhR-suhR-vis*	room service
die Etage	*dee e-tah-juh*	floor, story
die Reinigung	*dee Ray-ni-goong*	laundry and dry-cleaning service
die Sauna	*dee zou-nah*	sauna

Whenever you're about to book a room at a hotel, don't let the giddiness you feel at being in a new country prevent you from asking a few important questions about your room. Is it quiet? Does it look out onto the courtyard or onto the street? Is it a smoking room? Are there extra blankets in the cupboard? No matter how luxurious your hotel room, if you forget to ask any of these questions, you may find yourself spending a sleepless night shivering under your thin blanket, listening to the music from the discothek next door, and inhaling the secondhand smoke seeping in under your door. The following table has some words you may find useful when cross-examining hotel receptionists.

Hotel Basics

German	Pronunciation	English
das Badezimmer	*dAs bah-duh-tsi-muhR*	bathroom
das Dopplezimmer	*dAs do-pel-tsi-muhR*	double room
das Einzelzimmer	*dAs ayn-tsel-tsi-muhR*	single room
das Telefon	*dAs tey-ley-fon*	telephone
das Zimmer	*dAs tsi-muhR*	room
der Balkon	*deyR bAl-kohn*	balcony
der Fernseher	*deyR feRn-zey-uhR*	color television
das Kabelfernsehen	*dAs kA-bel-feRn-zey-uhn*	cable television
der Safe	*deyR zeyf*	safe
der Schlüssel	*deyR shlü-suhl*	key
der Wecker	*deyR ve-kuhR*	alarm clock
die Badewanne	*dee bah-duh-vA-nuh*	bathtub
die Dusche	*dee dew-shuh*	shower
die Halbpension	*dee hAlp-pen-zee-ohn*	just with breakfast
die Vollpension	*dee fol-pen-zee-ohn*	with meals
die Klimaanlage	*dee klee-mah-An-lah-guh*	air conditioning
die Toilette	*dee toee-le-tuh*	restroom
die Übernachtung	*dee üh-beR-nACH-toong*	overnight stay
ein Zimmer mit Aussicht	*ayn tsi-muhR mit ous-ziHt*	a room with a view
nach hinten	*nACH hin-tuhn*	at the back
nach vorne	*nACH foR-nuh*	at the front
zum Garten	*tsewm gAR-tuhn*	on the garden
zum Hof	*tsewm hof*	on the courtyard
zur Meerseite	*tsewR meeR-zay-tuh*	on the sea

Now, using the vocabulary you've learned, fill in the blanks of this dialogue between a hotel receptionist (*der Empfangschef*) and a client (*der Gast*). Check your accuracy in Appendix A.

1. **Gast:** Guten Tag. Haben Sie ein _____ (room) frei?

2. **Empfangschef:** Möchten Sie ein Zimmer mit einem _____ (balcony)? Wir haben ein wunderschönes _____ (room with a view) zur Meerseite.

3. **Gast:** Ja, warum nicht? Hat das Zimmer ein _____ (telephone)? Ich erwarte einen wichtigen Anruf.

4. **Empfangschef:** Selbstverständlich. Möchten Sie Vollpension oder _____ (just breakfast)?

   Gast: Vollpension, bitte.

5. **Empfangschef:** Gut. Die Zimmernummer ist 33. Hier ist Ihr _____ (key). Gute Nacht.

Calling Housekeeping

So what happens if you *do* forget to ask whether there are blankets in the closet and then the temperature drops 20 degrees shortly after you get into bed? Do you shiver all night, or do you call the concierge and ask for more blankets? Here are some expressions that will help you get whatever you need. Because you will usually be asking for *an* object or *a* thing, these nouns are listed with their indefinite articles followed by "m." for masculine nouns, "f." for feminine nouns, "n." for neuter nouns, and "pl." for plural nouns. See the following table.

Necessities

German	Pronunciation	English
das Briefpapier (n.)	*dAs bReef-pah-peeR*	stationery
die Ansichtskarte (f.)	*dee An-ziHts-kAR-tuh*	the postcard
die Eiswürfel (pl.)	*dee ays-vüR-fuhl*	ice cubes
die Streichhölzer (pl.)	*dee shtRayH-höl-tsuhR*	matches
ein Adapter (m.)	*ayn ah-dAp-tuhR*	an adapter
ein Aschenbecher (m.)	*ayn A-shuhn-be-HuhR*	an ashtray
ein Badetuch (n.)	*ayn bah-duh-tewCH*	a beach towel

German	Pronunciation	English
ein Handtuch (n.)	*ayn hAn-tewCH*	a towel
ein Kleiderbügel (m.)	*ayn klay-duhR-büh-guhl*	a hanger
ein Kopfkissen (n.)	*ayn kopf-ki-suhn*	a pillow
ein Mineralwasser (n.)	*ayn mi-nuh-Rahl-vA-suhR*	mineral water
ein Nähkasten (m.)	*ayn näh-kAs-tuhn*	a sewing kit
ein Stück Seife (n.)	*ayn shtük zay-fuh*	a bar of soap
ein Taschentuch (n.)	*ayn tA-shuhn-tewCH*	a handkerchief
eine Bettdecke (f.)	*ay-nuh bet-de-kuh*	a blanket

ACHTUNG

German bathrooms, like many European bathrooms, have what looks like a tiny bathtub, usually next to the toilet, known as a *bidet*. Non-Europeans sometimes make the mistake of thinking this bathroom fixture is for washing their clothes, but it is actually for cleansing one's nether regions.

Complete the following sentences. Keep in mind that the nouns you will be using are direct objects and take the accusative case: the masculine indefinite article *ein* becomes *einen*; the feminine and neuter indefinite articles *eine* and *ein* remain the same in the nominative and accusative cases (see Chapter 7).

Ich hätte gern …   Ich brauche …
iH hä-tuh geRn   *iH brou-CHuh*
I would like …   I need …

Using these expressions along with the vocabulary you've just learned, try to translate the following sentences into German. Check your translations in Appendix A.

1. I need an adapter.

2. I'd like a mineral water.

3. I need stationery.

4. I'd like an ashtray and matches.

5. I need a pillow.

6. I would like a beach towel.

Going Straight to the Top

Track 10 Now that you've had a good night's sleep, it's time to explore the hotel a little. To get around, you'll need to know how to get from one floor to another. The numbers used to refer to the floors of a building are known as *ordinal numbers*. An ordinal number refers to a specific number in a series. If your hotel is really fancy, someone in the elevator may ask you, "*Welcher Stock, bitte (vel-HuhR shtok, bi-tuh)*?" Study the ordinal numbers in the following table, and you'll be able to answer this question. You can also hear some pronunciation examples of ordinal numbers on Track 10 of the CD included with this book.

> **DEFINITION**
>
> **Ordinal numbers** are numbers that refer to a specific number in a series and answer the question: Which one? They may be preceded by a limiting word and, functioning as an adjective, be declined.

Ordinal Numbers

German	Pronunciation	English
1. erste	*eRs-tuh*	first
2. zweite	*tsvay-tuh*	second
3. dritte	*dRi-tuh*	third
4. vierte	*feeR-tuh*	fourth
5. fünfte	*fünf-tuh*	fifth
6. sechste	*zeks-tuh*	sixth
7. siebte	*zeep-tuh*	seventh
8. achte	*ACH-tuh*	eighth
9. neunte	*noyn-tuh*	ninth
10. zehnte	*tseyn-tuh*	tenth
11. elfte	*elf-tuh*	eleventh
12. zwölfte	*tsvölf-tuh*	twelfth
20. zwanzigste	*tsvAn-tsiHs-tuh*	twentieth
21. einundzwanzigste	*ayn-oont-tsvan-tsiHs-tuh*	twenty-first
100. hundertste	*hoon-deRt-stuh*	hundredth
1000. tausendste	*tou-zuhnt-stuh*	thousandth

- Ordinal numbers are formed by adding *-te* to the numbers 2 through 19 and by adding *-ste* from 20 on. *Erste* ("first"), *dritte* ("third"), *siebte* ("seventh"), and *achte* ("eighth") are exceptions.

- In English, we use letters (1st, 2nd, 3rd) to express ordinal numbers. In German, use a period after the numeral: 1., 2., 3., and so on.

- Ordinal numbers are, in fact, adjectives! Hence, they have the desire to agree with the noun they are modifying in gender (masculine, feminine, or neuter), number (singular or plural), and case (nominative, accusative, dative, genitive).

GERMAN CULTURE

In Germany, as in many European countries, the street-level floor is not numbered. It is referred to as *das Erdgeschoss* (*dAs eRt-guh-shos*). The German first floor is the equivalent of the American second floor.

The Declension of Ordinal Numbers

Ordinal numbers are treated as adjectives and can therefore be declined like any other adjective. They take normal adjective endings, as introduced in Chapter 10. In the sentence *Wir nehmen den ersten freien Aufzug zum Restaurant* (*veeR ney-muhn deyn eR-sten fRay-uhn ouf-tsewk tsewm Res-tou-RAn*), "We will take the first available elevator to the restaurant," the ordinal number *ersten* is modifying the singular noun *der Aufzug*.

Recall that adjectives needn't be burdened with the task of indicating gender, number, or case when they come after *der* words (words such as *dieser, welcher, jeder,* and so on) because the *der* word assumes that responsibility. The weak declension of adjectives illustrated with an ordinal number is shown in the table that follows.

Case	Singular Masculine	Singular Feminine	Singular Neuter	Plural All Genders
Nom.	der erste	die erste	das erste	die ersten
Acc.	den ersten	die erste	das erste	die ersten
Dat.	dem ersten	der ersten	dem ersten	den ersten
Gen.	des ersten	der ersten	des ersten	der ersten

Conversely, adjectives that are not preceded by any type of limiting word have to bear all of the grammar and thus resemble the definite article, also referred to as taking the strong declension: *Zimmer 33, erstes Zimmer auf der rechten Seite* ("room 33, first room on the right"). Why, you might wonder, is it *erstes* and not *erste* or *erster*? *Zimmer* is a neuter noun (*das*) and is functioning in this phrase as a subject, reflected by the nominative case. Remembering to stretch your mind to allow an *-es* for the *-as* in *das*, only two deviations from your *der* word chart occur when marking adjectives that are not preceded by any type of limiting word (genitive masculine and neuter).

Case	Singular Masculine	Singular Feminine	Singular Neuter	Plural All Genders
Nom.	erst**er**	erst**e**	erst**es**	erst**e**
Acc.	erst**en**	erst**e**	erst**es**	erst**e**
Dat.	erst**em**	erst**er**	erst**em**	erst**en**
Gen.	erst**en**	erst**er**	erst**en**	erst**er**

Adjectives preceded by an *ein* word (words such as *ein, mein, sein, ihr,* and so on) take a weak ending in all but three instances. You might recall that the *ein* in *ein Wagen* (masc., nom.), *ein Auto* (neut., nom.), and *Ich habe ein Auto* (neut., acc.) all look the same yet represent different gender and case. Therefore, given a second chance to reflect a bit of grammatical identity, the adjective following such a word will, indeed, strive to do so. See the table that follows for the mixed declension of adjectives.

Case	Singular Masculine	Singular Feminine	Singular Neuter	Plural All Genders
Nom.	ein erst**er**	eine erst**e**	ein erst**es**	die erst**en**
Acc.	einen erst**en**	eine erst**e**	ein erst**es**	die erst**en**
Dat.	einem erst**en**	einer erst**en**	einem erst**en**	den erst**en**
Gen.	eines erst**en**	einer erst**en**	eines erst**en**	der erst**en**

Ordinal Numbering

Complete the following sentences by supplying an ordinal number and adding the appropriate adjective ending. Check your answers in Appendix A.

Example: Sie hat Angst, ins Flugzeug zu steigen. Es ist ihr <u>erster</u> Flug. ("first"; masc., nom., after an *ein* word)

1. Wir haben nicht viel Geld. Wir fahren _____ ("second"; fem., dative, unpreceded) Klasse.

2. "Erster Stop ist in Marl; zweiter Stop ist in Haltern; _____ ("third"; masc., nom., unpreceded) Stop ist in Recklinghausen," sagt der Busfahrer.

3. Mein _____ ("first"; masc., nom., after an *ein* word) Beruf war Tellerwäscher. Heute bin ich Millionär.

4. Zuerst kommt die Post. Das _____ ("second"; neut., nom., after a *der* word) Gebäude auf der linken Seite ist ein Hotel.

5. Auf der zweiten Etage befindet sich das Restaurant. Auf der _____ ("third"; fem., dat., after a *der* word) Etage ist das Einkaufzentrum.

6. Er hat schon drei Söhne. Sein _____ ("fourth"; neut., nom., after an *ein* word) Kind wird ein Mädchen.

7. Wenn eine Katze schon acht Leben hatte, ist sie jetzt im _____ ("ninth"; neut., dat., after a *der* word) Lebensjahr!

Clams or Coal? It's All the Same in Money

Just as English has numerous *colloquial* expressions for money—clams, silverbacks, bucks, and so on—similar expressions are used in German, such as *Mäuse* (*moy-zuh*), "mice"; and *Knete* (*kney-tuh*), "dough." Perhaps one of the most culturally specific colloquialisms referring to money in German is *Kohle* (*koh-luh*), "coal." Now that you're wondering how to get your hands on some of that German spending money, you can hit the nearest ATM that is certain to be just around a corner or two, incurring a modest 4-5€ service charge from your home bank. You are guaranteed to get the fairest, most up-to-date exchange rate. Alternatively, you can get your *Euro-Banknoten*, "bank notes," and *Euro-Cent-Münzen*, "coins," at *Wechselstuben* (*vek-suhl-shtew-buhn*), "money exchange booths," at airports and at train stations. The *Deutsche-Verkehrs-Kredit Bank* has branches in train stations that stay open until 6 P.M. If all of the ATMs you encounter are out of service (*außer Betrieb*), look to exchange money at one of the larger branches of a bank in cities. The exchange rates at the larger bank branches are higher than at smaller, lesser-known banks, and the commission is lower. Most hotels also exchange money, but their rates are a complete rip-off, really—*ein totaler Nepp*. It's hardly even worth mentioning them.

On the odd chance that you still possess traveler's checks, you may exchange them in the same places you might go to exchange money: banks, money-exchange booths, and post offices. Post offices? Yes, *die Post.* The German post office will change your money for you, which is something you may want to keep in mind if you're cashless in the late afternoon and *still* can't locate a functioning ATM: Post offices stay open until 6 P.M.

Euro?

From 1948 through 2001, Germany's currency was the *Deutsche Mark, DM.* As of January 1, 2002, the *Euro, EUR* or €, replaced the German Mark. Similar to the former *Mark* and *Pfennig* (the breakdown of the Mark into 100 units), the *Euro* is divided into *Euro* and *Cent.* Thus, a book that costs 6,50€ will be read as *sechs Euro fünfzig* (*zeks oy-roh fünf-tsiH*). (Note that the German equivalent of a decimal point is a comma.) As of 2012, the *Euro* is used in 23 European countries; the *Euro-Banknoten* that come in differently colored and sized 5, 10, 20, 50, 100, 200, and 500 denominations are referred to in German as *ein 5-Euro* (*ayn fünf oy-roh*), *ein 10-Euro* (*ayn tseyn oy-roh*), and so on. *Euro-Münzen* are produced in every country that accepts them in 1-, 2-, 5-, 10-, 20-, and 50-cent denominations, as well as 1€ and 2€. The German 1- and 2-*Euro-Münzen* depict the *Bundesadler,* "federal eagle"; the 10-, 20-, and 50-*Cent-Stücke,* "cent pieces," show the *Brandenburger Tor,* "Brandenburg Gate"; and the three smallest coins portray an oak branch.

Read the following sentences aloud, checking your price enunciation in Appendix A.

1. Das Buch kostet 13,45€.

2. Die Blumen kosten 7,10€.

3. Die Ansichtskarte kostet 50€.

4. Ein Einzelzimmer kostet 81€.

5. Das Ticket kostet 36,99€.

Approximations and Oddities

In case you don't want to talk exact amounts of money or anything else that involves counting, you can always use the trusty approximate figures listed in the following table:

Approximate Figures

German	Pronunciation	English
circa	*tseeR-kuh*	about
etwa	*et-vah*	roughly
rund	*Roont*	around, about
über	*üh-buhR*	over, more than
ungefähr	*oon-guh-fähR*	approximately

AS A RULE

There are two German equivalents for the English "to know": *wissen,* which means to know something as a fact, and *kennen,* to be acquainted with a person, place, or thing. *Wissen* is frequently used to form an introductory clause about a fact: *Wissen Sie, ...? Ich weiß .... Kennen* takes only nouns as objects: *Ich kenne Berlin gut. Kennst du diesen Film? Kennen* is still used as a verb in Scottish, indicating perception or understanding.

You might recall from Chapter 12 that a million is a *Million,* but an American billion is a German *Milliarde,* whereas a German *Billion* is an American trillion. Aside from putting commas where we'd place decimals, and vice versa, Germans write the numeral 7 a wee bit differently: They put a line through it so that it looks like a backward capital *F.* Perhaps this feature is to distinguish it from the written 1, which has the initial stroke below the line.

More Action with Verbs

Do you remember what you learned about verbs in Chapter 8? Verbs are used to express action, motion, or states of being. This section looks at the irregular verb *wissen* and its weak partner, *kennen;* at the meanings of the simple present tense; and at verbs with prefixes.

Expressing Knowledge

The irregular verb *wissen (vi-suhn)* states knowledge of something as a fact: *Ich weiß die Adresse von Christoph nicht.* It never refers to persons. You'll recall the other two irregular verbs you've learned, *sein* and *haben.* Why, you might ask, must these verbs be irregular? Interestingly (or not) enough, the verbs *to be, to have, to know,* and *to become* (the fourth irregular verb to be learned later) are high-frequency verbs in most languages and thus mark themselves as meaningful and significant by retaining distinctive forms. In German, distinctiveness translates into changing the consonants, not just the vowels! Observe this behavior in the conjugation of *wissen* in the following table.

The Verb *wissen*

Personal	Singular	Plural
First	ich weiß	wir wissen
	iH vays	*veer vis-uhn*
Second	du weißt	ihr wisst
	dew vayst	*eer vist*
Third	er, sie, es weiß	sie wissen
	er, zee, es, vays	*zee vis-uhn*
Formal	sie wissen	sie wissen
	zee vi-suhn	*zee vi-suhn*

There you have it! Not only does a vowel-stem change occur in *all* of the singular conjugations, but you'll observe an ending omission in the *ich* and *er, sie,* and *es* forms (an *–e* and *–t*). We told you it was irregular! But take heart: to express knowing, as in indicating familiarity with something or somebody, you can also use a weak verb, *kennen.*

Care to exercise your choice? Try your hand at inserting the correct form of *wissen* or *kennen*! Answers and explanations appear in Appendix A.

1. _____ du, wo Kerstin wohnt?

2. Kerstin? Ich _____ niemanden mit dem Namen "Kerstin." Wer ist sie? (*niemand*, "no one"; *wer*, "who")

3. Ich _____, dass sie sehr hübsch und intelligent ist!

4. Na, ja. Vielleicht _____ Ronja sie.

5. _____ wir nicht Kerstins Mann, Frank?

6. Ach ja! Ich _____ ihren Mann vom Bus.

Verbs with Prefixes

The prefixes you're going to learn about here have nothing to do with prices you find on the menu in the restaurant of your fancy hotel. *Pre* means "to come before," and *fix* means "to join onto or with"; thus, a prefix is a series of letters (sometimes a word on its own) that you join to the beginning of another word. Verbs with prefixes, referred to as *two-part* or *compound verbs*, are not a singular German phenomenon. English also has many compound verbs: *to lead* evolves into *to mislead*; *to rate* develops into *to overrate* and *to underrate*; *to take* morphs into *to mistake, to retake, to undertake*, and *to overtake*. In German, as in English, the verb and the compound verb follow the same conjugation; *take* becomes *took* in the past tense, for example, and *mistake* becomes *mistook*.

DEFINITION

Compound verbs are verbs that are formed by adding a prefix to the stem verb. German has two types of compound verbs: those with separable prefixes and those with inseparable prefixes.

Coming Apart: Verbs with Separable Prefixes

When you were busy ordering people around and taking directions in Chapter 11, you used verbs with separable prefixes. You sent those prefixes to the end of the command. The rule still holds: separable prefixes like to get away from their stem verb and go to the end of a clause even in an ordinary statement or question: *Kommst du heute Abend mit? Ja, ich komme um 8 Uhr mit.* Just as the particle helpers in English stand on their own, so can the separable prefixes in German be words on their own, usually adverbs or prepositions. Although in the infinitive form they appear to be one word (as in the verb *weggehen*, which means "to go away"), the stem verb is conjugated and appears next the to subject while the prefix appears separately at the end of the sentence *Er geht jetzt weg* ("He's going away now").

AS A RULE

When a prefix is separated from a compound verb, the prefix occurs at the end of the clause, which also is often the end of the sentence: *Er geht jeden Morgen um sieben Uhr **aus**.*

Some common separable prefixes are *auf-, aus-, an-, bei-, mit-, nach-, vor-, weg-, weiter-, wieder-, zu-, zurück-,* and *zusammen-*.

The following sentences involve separable prefix verbs whose meanings you should be able to deduce from your general knowledge of German prepositions and verbs (see Chapter 8). Try to complete the sentences. Recall that a superscript "S" means that the verb is very strong and undergoes a stem-vowel change. The period indicates the separation between the separable prefix and the verb stem. Check your sentences in Appendix A.

1. Wann _____ Otto den Film _____? (an.sehen[S]) When is Otto viewing the film?

2. Tina _____ das Buch _____. (vor.lesen[S]) Tina is reading the book out loud.

3. Alicia _____ nie _____! (auf.geben[S]) Alicia never gives up!

4. Gretchen _____ ihr Bier immer _____! (aus.trinken) Gretchen always drinks up all of her beer.

Don't forget that the verbs with a superscript "s" incur a stem change in the present tense!

From now on in this book, separable prefix verbs will be marked in their infinitival form with a period between the prefix and the stem. Although these verbs are not normally represented this way, the period should help you identify them.

AS A RULE

The use of *doch, mal,* or *doch mal* in imperative constructions adds a subtle but noticeable layer of meaning. *Doch* adds a sense of urgency: *Lass uns doch japanisch essen,* or "Let's do eat Japanese." *Mal* adds a sense of impatience: *Tanz mal!* becomes *"Come on and dance!"* Combining *doch* with *mal* produces a tone that is a little more casual: *Kauf doch mal was,* or "Go ahead and buy something."

Sticking It Out Together: Verbs with Inseparable Prefixes

The German language has one more basic type of verb prefix: the inseparable variety. Inseparable prefixes cannot stand alone and must be attached to a verb. Also noteworthy is the fact that they are not stressed. Compare the separable prefix verb *aus.gehen* with the inseparable *ergeben*[S]. The following prefixes always remain attached to the verb, but if you are creative enough, you can build a "semantic bridge" and link the meaning of the stem with that of the newly formed verb!

Inseparable Prefix	German Verb	English
be- (*buh*)	bekommen	to get, receive
emp- (*emp*)	empfehlen[S]	to recommend
ent- (*ent*)	entdecken	to discover
er- (*eR*)	ergeben[S]	to yield, produce
ge- (*guh*)	gewinnen	to win
miss- (*mis*)	missverstehen	to misunderstand
ver- (*feR*)	vergessen[S]	to forget
zer- (*tseR*)	zerfallen[S]	to decay

From the preceding list, see whether you can fill in the following blanks with the correct verb—correctly conjugated, of course! Read these sentences aloud, remembering *not* to stress the prefix in these verbs. Check your verb choices in Appendix A.

1. Wo _____ Sie das? (Where do you get that?)

2. Ich _____ die Adresse. (I forget the address.)

3. Roger Federer _____ fast immer. (Roger Federer almost always wins.)

4. Welches Restaurant _____ du? (Which restaurant do you recommend?)

Let's ...

The German equivalent of the English *let's* utilizes that nifty imperative, or command form, you were exposed to in Chapter 11 but softens it up with the collective pronoun *wir.* You'll notice that the word order is verb-initial, just as it was in the regular imperative used to order people around. But now we've included ourselves, or "us" in the equation. Have a look:

Essen wir Eis.	Let's eat ice cream.
Kaufen wir ein.	Let's shop.
Finden wir das Museum.	Let's find the museum.

Another way to suggest to a friend that you do something together involves the expression *Lass uns ...* (*lAs oonz*), with the main verb arriving at the end of the suggestion in its infinitival form:

Lass uns ins Restaurant gehen.	Let's go to a restaurant.
Lass uns griechisch essen.	Let's eat Greek.

Suggest to your friends, using either the *Lass uns ...* or the *Verb + wir* constructions, the following activities. Check your suggestions in Appendix A.

1. Let's travel to Germany. _____

2. Let's go to the garden. _____

3. Let's take the bus. _____

4. Let's visit the city. _____

5. Let's learn German! _____

The Least You Need to Know

- If you familiarize yourself with a few basic vocabulary words, you should have no trouble getting what you need in your hotel room.

- Form ordinal numbers by adding *-te* to the numbers 2 through 19 and *-ste* to the numbers from 20 on. Memorize the exceptions to this rule: *erste, dritte, siebte,* and *achte.* Amaze yourself with all the new adjectives you've just acquired!

- The verbs *wissen* and *kennen* express knowledge and familiarity.
- Many German verbs are compound verbs—verbs with prefixes. These verbs can be either separable or inseparable.
- Use an ATM to get euros at the best rate.
- By beginning a sentence with the verb in its infinitive form followed by a *wir,* you'll be able to make suggestions in the vein of *let's* ....

Out and About in Germany

This part comprises chapters for sightseers, shopping addicts, sports fanatics, and gourmets. Once you've learned how to talk about the weather (an important ability in any language, particularly when making small talk), learning how to make suggestions about what you'd like to see, shop for, and eat will keep your outlook sunny!

A Date with the Weather

In This Chapter

* European countries with German-sounding names
* Describing weather conditions
* Learning the days of the week
* Naming the months of the year
* Breaking up the day

You've been in Germany for a while now, at least within the international borders of this book. You can get around, find a room, spout a few nouns, ask a question or two, tell a little time, and find a room. Now you've arrived in Frankfurt, and you're ready to plan your afternoon. You haven't written a single postcard. If you don't understand the local weather report, a walk to the post office could end up being a soggy sojourn. Weather can make or break your day and provide fodder for endless small talk with strangers.

In this chapter, you'll pick up the vocabulary you need to understand international communication and the weather forecast and how to make plans in a German city, inside or outside your hotel.

What's the Address?!

Preparing for your trip to Germany, you come across some funny-looking addresses on German websites. Easily enough explained. In Germany, after the line of the addressee come the street and then the house number/street address. Conversely, the ZIP code precedes the city in German correspondence. Guess there has to be some leveling out or reciprocation of numeral ordering somewhere! When in *Deutschland*, you'll want to use *Deutsch*-style addresses. Here's an example:

 ACHTUNG

It is not uncommon to find *Straße* abbreviated as *Str.* and to find more than one number for a house address. Never you mind—that is how the *Hausnummer,* the numerical sign on the street, will read.

German Style	U.S. Style
Bernadette Höfer	Bernadette Höfer
Feldbergstraße 3–7	300 Washington Avenue
55118 Mainz	Mainstreet, MD 21000

Identifying International Abbreviations

International abbreviations are used for the country names. You might have seen stickers on automobiles indicating countries of origin, bearing the same abbreviations. Some abbreviations you might not guess are listed here:

- CH for Switzerland (Confederatio Helvetica)
- SK for Slovakia (die Slowakei)
- PL for Poland (Polen)
- E for Spain (Spanien)

What is Germany's abbreviation? Why, *D* for *Deutschland*, of course!

Call Me (Maybe!)

Reading a German letter, business card, advertisement, or brochure, you're likely to encounter more than an address—most likely, a telephone number. Unlike American telephone numbers, which consist of a three-digit area code followed by a seven-digit number, the exact length of telephone numbers in Germany is variable. Most phone numbers have a city prefix consisting of three or four digits, and the actual phone number may be four to seven digits long. Go ahead and tack on another digit, a zero in front of the city code, if phoning from within Germany. Now do you feel the need to really learn your numbers? As an aid, the following table lists some useful communication terms. (For more in-depth information on telephone etiquette, cell phone usage, and a trip to the post office to get a phone card, see Chapter 23.)

GERMAN CULTURE

The postal service in Germany also provides phone service. Tell the postal worker behind the counter that you want to make a long-distance call, and he or she will indicate which phone booth is available. You pay (cash only) after your call. Long-distance calls made from the post office are considerably cheaper than those placed from a hotel.

Communication Terms

German	Pronunciation	English
die Adresse	*dee A-dRe-suh*	the address
die Ansichtskarte	*dee An-ziHts-kAR-tuh*	the postcard
der Brief	*deyR bReef*	the letter
die Hausnummer	*dee hous-noo-muhR*	the house number
das Land	*dAs lAnt*	the country
die Post	*dee post*	the post office
die Postkarte	*dee post-kAR-tuh*	the postcard
die Postleitzahl	*dee post-layt-tsahl*	the ZIP code
die Stadt	*dee shtAt*	the city
die Straße	*dee shtrA-suh*	the street
die Telefonnummer	*dee tey-ley-fo-noo-muhR*	the telephone number
der Wohnort	*deyR von-oRt*	the town of residence
Was bedeutet …?	*vAs buh-doy-tuht*	What does _____ mean?
Wie bitte?	*vee bi-tuh*	Excuse me?
Wie ist deine/ihre Telefonnummer?	*vee ist day-nuh ee-Ruh tey-ley-fo-noo-muhR*	What is your telephone number?
Wie schreibt man …?	*vee shraypt mAn*	How does one write …?

Using the information-gathering vocabulary you've just acquired, try to fill in the following blanks. Check your accuracy in Appendix A.

1. Ich kenne die Straße, aber nicht die _____. (house number)

2. Die _____ kommt vor der Stadt in der Adresse. (ZIP code)

3. Ich habe ein Telefon. Meine _____ ist 03-45-60. (telephone number)

4. Du schickst (send) eine _____ an deine Mutter. (postcard)

5. Sein Name ist sehr lang! _____ das? (Ask: How do you write that?)

Now try to fill in the information requested in German.

Name _____

Wohnort _____

Straße und Hausnummer _____

Postleitzahl und Stadt _____

Telefonnummer _____

European Countries, According to Germans

As an American (if you are), you come from America and speak *American*. Okay, maybe you speak *English* or some other variety. The point is that every language personalizes other countries' names to suit their language's sound systems. German names for countries should be fairly recognizable to you, but the pronunciation may be challenging. The following table lists some European countries:

Country Names

German	Pronunciation	English
Albanien	*Al-bah-neeuhn*	Albania
Belgien	*bel-geeuhn*	Belgium
Bulgarien	*bool-gah-Reeuhn*	Bulgaria
Dänemark	*däh-nuh-mARk*	Denmark
Deutschland	*Doytch-lAnt*	Germany
Finnland	*fin-lAnt*	Finland
Frankreich	*frAnk-rayH*	France
Griechenland	*gree-Huhn-lAnt*	Greece
Großbritannien	*gros-bRi-tah-neeuhn*	Great Britain

German	Pronunciation	English
Irland	*eer-lAnt*	Ireland
Italien	*ee-tah-leeuhn*	Italy
Lettland	*let-lAnt*	Latvia
Liechtenstein	*leeH-tuhn-shtayn*	Liechtenstein
Litauen	*lee-tou-uhn*	Lithuania
Luxemburg	*look-suhm-buHRk*	Luxembourg
die Niederlande	*dee nee-duhR-lAn-duh*	the Netherlands
Norwegen	*noR-vey-guhn*	Norway
Österreich	*ös-tuh-RayH*	Austria
Polen	*poh-luhn*	Poland
Portugal	*poR-too-gAl*	Portugal
Russland	*roos-lAnt*	Russia
die Schweiz	*dee shvayts*	Switzerland
Schweden	*Schvey-duhn*	Sweden
die Slowakei	*dee sloh-vah-kay*	Slovakia
Spanien	*shpah-neeuhn*	Spain
Tschechien	*tshe-Hee uhn*	Czech Republic
Ungarn	*ewn-gARn*	Hungary

Try your hand now at international abbreviations, indicating which country the following abbreviations represent. Check your answers in Appendix A.

1. CH _____

2. D _____

3. I _____

4. A _____

5. GB _____

6. F _____

And don't forget the good old United States: *die Vereinigten Staaten* (*dee feR-ayn-ik-tuh shtah-tuhn*)!

It's 20°, But They're Wearing Sandals!

Remember, Germans use Celsius (or centigrade), not Fahrenheit, the way we do in the United States. Twenty degrees in German weather terminology is actually 68° Fahrenheit!

GERMAN CULTURE

To convert Fahrenheit to Celsius, subtract 32 from the Fahrenheit temperature and multiply the remaining number by .5. To convert Celsius to Fahrenheit, multiply the Celsius temperature by 1.8 and then add 32.

Track 11 · The phrases in the following table will come in handy when the topic is weather. If you'd like to hear the pronunciation of some of these terms, check out Track 11 of the CD included with this book.

Weather Expressions

German	Pronunciation	English
Wie ist das Wetter?	*vee ist dAs ve-tuhR*	How is the weather?
Das Wetter ist herrlich.	*dAs ve-tuhR ist heR-liH*	The weather is wonderful.
Das Wetter ist furchtbar.	*dAs ve-tuhR ist fooRHt-bahR*	The weather is awful.
Das Wetter ist schlecht.	*dAs ve-tuhR ist shleHt*	The weather is bad.
Das Wetter ist schön.	*dAs ve-tuhR ist shöhn*	The weather is beautiful.
Das Wetter ist schrecklich.	*dAs ve-tuhR ist shRek-liH*	The weather is horrible.
Die Sonne scheint.	*dee zo-nuh shaynt*	The sun is shining.
Es blitzt und donnert.	*es blitst oont do-nuhRt*	There is lightning and thunder.
Es gibt Regenschauer.	*es gipt Rey-guhn-shou-uhR*	There are rain showers.
Es ist bewölkt.	*es ist buh-völkt*	It is cloudy.
Es ist feucht.	*es ist foyHt*	It is humid.
Es ist heiß.	*es ist hays*	It is hot.
Es ist heiter.	*es ist hay-tuhR*	It is clear.
Es ist kalt.	*es ist kAlt*	It is cold.
Es ist kühl.	*es ist kühl*	It is cool.
Es ist neblig.	*es ist ney-buh-liH*	It is foggy.
Es ist regnerisch.	*es ist Rek-nuh-Rish*	It is rainy.
Es ist sonnig.	*es ist zo-niH*	It is sunny.

German	Pronunciation	English
Es ist stürmisch.	*es ist shtüR-mish*	It is stormy.
Es ist windig.	*es ist vin-diH*	It is windy.
Es regnet.	*es Rek-nuht*	It is raining.
Es schneit.	*es shnayt*	It is snowing.
Es ist warm.	*es ist vARm*	It is warm.
Es regnet in Strömen.	*es Rek-nuht in shtRöh-muhn*	It is pouring.

How's the Weather?

Look at the weather map of Germany. Use complete sentences to describe the weather in the following cities. Check your weather predictions in Appendix A.

1. Erfurt

2. München

3. Schwerin

4. Kiel

5. Düsseldorf

What's the Temperature?

The following phrases will enable you to talk about and understand simple conversations about the weather. Note that German uses the plural form of "are," *sind*, to talk about the temperature because degrees are plural.

> Welche Temperatur ist es?
> *vel-Huh tem-puh-Rah-tewR ist es*
> What's the temperature?

> Es sind minus zehn Grad.
> *es zint mee-noos tseyn gRaht*
> It's -10°.

> Es sind zehn Grad unter Null.
> *es zint tseyn gRaht oon-tuhR nool*
> It's 10° below zero.

> Es sind zwanzig Grad.
> *es zint tsvAn-tsiH gRaht*
> It's 20°.

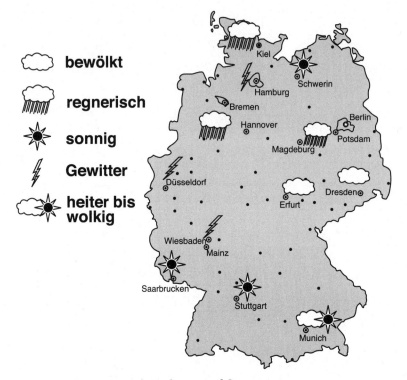

A weather map of Germany.

But the Weather's Supposed to Be …

German newspapers and internet sites contain information on the weather, just as American ones do. The maps often include Germany and Western Europe. Look at the table for the German terms commonly used to describe weather.

bewölkt	*buh-völkt*	cloudy
das Gewitter	*dAs ge-vi-tuhR*	thunderstorm
der Hagel	*deyR hah-guhl*	hail
der klare Himmel	*deyR klah-Ruh hi-muhl*	clear sky
der Regen	*deyR Rey-guhn*	rain
der Nebel	*deyR ney-buhl*	fog
der Regenschauer	*dee Rey-guhn-shou-uhR*	shower
der Schnee	*deyR shney*	snow

der Schneeregen	*deyR shney-Rey-guhn*	sleet
der Sprühregen	*deyR shpRüh-Rey-guhn*	drizzle
der Sturm	*deyR shtuRm*	storm
der Wind	*deyR vint*	wind
die Sonne	*dee zo-nuh*	sun
frisch	*fRish*	chilly
leicht	*layHt*	weak
leicht bewölkt	*layHt buh-völkt*	slightly cloudy
mäßig	*mäh-siH*	moderate
neblig	*ney-bliH*	foggy
stark bewölkt	*shtARk buh-völkt*	very cloudy
wechselhaft	*vek-suhl-hAft*	changeable

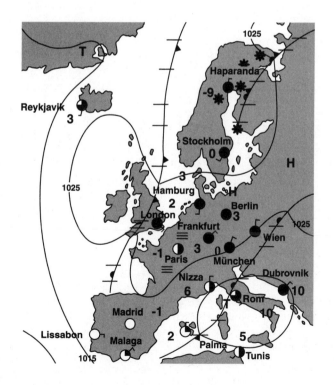

A weather map of Europe.

Days, Months, Seasons!

Remember sitting in kindergarten (a German word, by the way, which means "child garden") and learning the days of the week, the months of the year, and the seasons? This section focuses on precisely those elementary things: days, months, dates, and seasons.

ACHTUNG

According to traditional German law, all stores (with the exception of bakeries that opted to open for two hours) had to close on Sunday. Train stations could always have an open grocery store, florist, or card shop because train stations were *Touristenzonen,* tourist zones. This all changed in 2006, when German law-makers made the matter of shopping hours a state concern rather than a federal responsibility. Under the law in many German states, a total of 3 to 10 Sundays per year may be designated *Verkaufsoffene Sonntage,* "shopping Sundays." But most stores remain closed. Only larger stores and some shopping centers open their doors from 1:00 to 8:00 P.M. on that special Sunday.

What Day Is It?

Track 12 You've really been enjoying the great weather on your vacation, and now you've completely lost track of time. The days melt together like a dream. One day you wake up and leave your hotel to go shopping, only to find that all the stores are closed. It's early in the afternoon, the sun is shining, and cars are driving up and down the avenue. Is it a holiday? You stop a passerby and ask what day it is. "*Sonntag,*" he says. If you don't know the days of the week, you may think this *Sonntag* is some important date in German history or that he's talking about his favorite author. Of course, *Sonntag* is "Sunday," the day when, in Germany, most stores are closed. Study the German names for the days of the week in the following table. If you'd like to hear pronunciation examples of the days of the week, check out Track 12 of the CD included with this book.

AS A RULE

Remember, the days of the week, the months of the year, and the four seasons are masculine. Also, when you place them after an either accusative or a dative preposition, such as *an, in,* and *vor,* they take the dative case. When these prepositions appear in conjunction with time, they always take the dative case.

Days of the Week

German	Pronunciation	English
der Tag	*deyR tahk*	day
die Woche	*dee vo-CHuh*	week
die Wochentage	*dee vo-CHuhn-tah-guh*	days of the week
Montag	*mon-tahk*	Monday
Dienstag	*deenz-tahk*	Tuesday
Mittwoch	*mit-voCH*	Wednesday
Donnerstag	*deenz-tahk*	Thursday
Freitag	*fRay-tahk*	Friday
Samstag	*zAmz-tahk*	Saturday
Sonnabend	*zon-ah-bent*	Saturday
Sonntag	*zon-tahk*	Sunday
am Wochenende	*Am vo-CHuhn-en-duh*	on the weekend
Welcher Tag ist heute?	*vel-CHuhr tahk ist hoy-tuh*	What day is today?

To express *on* when talking about a specific day, Germans use the contraction *am*, a combination of the preposition *an* and *dem* (*dem* being the dative form of the masculine definite article, *der*).

> Am Montag gehe ich in die Stadt.
> *Am mohn-tahk gey-uh iH in dee shtAt*
> On Monday I go downtown.

To express that you do something on a specific day every week, simply add an *-s*, just as you do in English, to the end of the day, but don't capitalize it unless it begins the sentence:

> Ich gehe dienstags in die Stadt.
> *iH gey-uh deenz-tahks in dee shtAt*
> I go downtown on Tuesdays.

Try responding to the following questions in simple sentences:

1. Welcher Tag ist heute?
   vel-CHuhr tahk ist hoy-tuh
   What day is today?

2. Was machen Sie montags?
   vas mA-CHuhn zee mon-taks
   What do you do on Mondays?

3. Was machen Sie am Wochenende?
   vas mA-CHuhn zee Am vo-CHuhn-en-duh
   What do you do on the weekend?

4. Welcher Tag ist morgen?
   vel-CHuhR tahk ist moR-gen
   What day is tomorrow?

A Mouthful of Months

Track 13 Now that you know how to chat about the weather, you can ask friendly natives what the weather will be like in April, September, or even next month. The following table lists the months of the year. If you'd like to hear pronunciation examples of the months of the year, check out Track 13 of the CD included with this book.

> **GERMAN CULTURE**
>
> Every February before Lent, cities in Germany "go crazy." These days are referred to as the *Tolle Tage* (*to-luh tah-guh*), "crazy days." *Karneval* (*kAR-ne-vAl*), otherwise known down south as *Fasching* (*fah-sheeng*), is a major event in Catholic parts of the country. If you're in Köln, Mainz, or München during the final days before Lent, expect parades, partying, and costumes everywhere!

Months of the Year

German	Pronunciation	English
der Monat	*deyR moh-nAt*	month
das Jahr	*dAs yahR*	year
Januar	*yah-new-ahR*	January
Februar	*feb-Rew-ahR*	February
März	*marts*	March
April	*ah-pRil*	April
Mai	*mmay*	May
Juni	*yew-nee*	June

German	Pronunciation	English
Juli	*yew-lee*	July
August	*ou-goost*	August
September	*zep-tem-buhR*	September
Oktober	*ok-toh-buhR*	October
November	*noh-vem-buhR*	November
Dezember	*dey-tsem-buhR*	December
der Geburtstag	*guh-booRts-tahk*	birthday
der Urlaub	*deyr ewR-loup*	vacation

To make clear that something is expected to happen in a particular month, use the contraction *im*, a combination of the preposition *in* + *dem* expressing masculine dative case.

GERMAN CULTURE

Overall, the weather in many German-speaking countries is moderate: your sweat won't evaporate off your brow in summer, and in winter, your breath won't condense into ice cubes that fall clinking to the ground. If you're visiting Munich, pack a raincoat; it has more rainfall than other cities in Germany. In the mountainous regions of Switzerland and Austria, where glaciers keep the snow from melting all year round, you can get the best of both worlds—summer skiing in a T-shirt!

Mein Freund hat im Oktober Geburtstag.
mayn froynt hAt im ok-toh-buhR guh-booRts-tahk
My boyfriend's birthday is in October.

Now answer the following questions using *im* + *Monat*. Check your sentence structure in Appendix A.

1. Wann ist Ihr Geburtstag?
   vAn ist eeR guh-booRts-tahk
   When is your birthday?

2. Wann machen Sie in diesem Jahr Urlaub?
   vAn mA-CHuhn zee in dee-zuhm yahR ewR-loup
   When are you taking your vacation this year?

3. Welcher ist Ihr Lieblingsmonat?
   vel-CHuhR ist eeR leep-leenks-mon-nAt
   What's your favorite month?

4. Wann beginnt die Schule?
   van buh-gint dee shew-luh
   When does school begin?

The Four Seasons

As you engage in German conversations, you'll probably want to talk about the seasons. The information you need is in the following table. Notice how logical and concise the German for "season of the year" is: *Jahres (of the year)* + *Zeit (time)*.

The Seasons of the Year

German	Pronunciation	English
die Jahreszeit	*dee yah-Ruhs-tsayt*	season
der Winter	*deyR vin-tuhR*	winter
der Frühling	*deyR fRüh-ling*	spring
das Frühjahr	*das fRüh-yahR*	spring
der Sommer	*deyR zo-muhR*	summer
der Herbst	*deyR heRpst*	autumn, fall

Because seasons are comprised of months, it makes sense to use the same dative prepositional contraction, *im*, to express seasons:

> Ich fahre im Winter in die Alpen.
> *iH fah-Ruh im vin-tuhR in dee Al-puhn*
> I'm going in the winter to the Alps.

Try to answer the following questions concerning *die Jahreszeiten*. Responses are in Appendix A.

1. Wann schneit es viel?
   van shnayt es feel
   When does it snow lots?

2. Wann fallen die Blätter von den Bäumen?
   van fA-luhn dee blä-tuhR fon deyn boy-muhn
   When do the leaves fall from the trees?

3. Wann blühen die Blumen?
   van blüh-uhn dee blew-muhn
   When do the flowers bloom?

4. Wann scheint die Sonne oft?
   van shaynt dee zo-nuh oft
   When does the sun shine often?

Measures of Time

The Fourth of July, your own birthday, and the year you were first kissed: what do these things have in common? Well, if you want to chat about them, you have to learn a few words that deal with dates. You can start with some general terms that deal with chunks of time.

German	Pronunciation	English
eine Stunde	*ay-nuh shtoon-duh*	an hour
ein Tag	*ayn tahk*	a day
eine Woche	*ay-nuh vo-CHuh*	a week
ein Monat	*ayn moh-nAt*	a month
ein Jahr	*ayn yahR*	a year
zwei Jahre	*tsvay yah-Ruh*	two years
einige Jahre	*ay-ni-guh yah-Ruh*	some years
nächstes Jahr	*näH-stuhs yahR*	next year
letztes Jahr	*lets-tuhs yahR*	last year

Making a Date

Whether you have a dentist appointment or a romantic rendezvous, you will have to express the date of the appointment differently than you do in English. Here is a formula for expressing the date correctly in German:

day of the week + *der* (ordinal) number + month + year

Freitag, der fünfundzwanzigste April 2013
fray-tahk, deyR tsvay-oont-tsvAn-stiH-stuh ah-pRil tsvay-tau-zuhnt dray-tsayn
Friday, the 25th of April 2013

You write and punctuate dates in German differently than you do in English. Compare the following date (July 6, 2013) in English and in German.

July 6, 2013 (7/6/13)
der 6. Juli 2013 (6.7.13)

When writing letters in German, the place from which you are writing is given first, followed by the date. Note that the accusative *den* is used when expressing a definite time when no preposition is present.

Berlin, den 15.12.2013

Days of the month are expressed with ordinal numbers: *der erste Januar, der zweite Februar, der dritte März*, and so on.

At first glance, the way you express the year in German looks like it could take a year to say. If you were to express the year 2013, for example, you would say this:

Zweitausenddreizehn
tsvay-tau-zuhnt-dray-tsayn

To get information about the date, you should be able to ask the following questions:

Welcher Tag ist heute?
vel-CHuhR tahk ist hoy-tuh
What day is today?

Der Wievielte ist heute?
deyR vee-feel-tuh ist hoy-tuh
What's today's date?

Someone who answers your question will probably begin his or her response with one of the following phrases:

Heute ist der ....
hoy-tuh ist deyR
Today is the ....

Do you constantly forget important dates? Practice what you've just learned by listing the following dates in German. Check your sentences in Appendix A.

Example: Weihnachten

Answer: Weihnachten ist am 25. Dezember.

1. Valentinstag

2. Mein Geburtstag

3. Halloween

4. Neujahr

Time Expressions

You don't always speak in terms of exact dates—sometimes "in a week" or "a few days ago" will do. The expressions in the following table will help you schedule events, make plans, and arrange trysts. (Some of these expressions should already be familiar to you from Chapter 12.)

Time Expressions

German	Pronunciation	English
in	*in*	in
vor	*foR*	ago
nächste Woche	*näH-stuh vo-CHuh*	next week
letzte Woche	*lets-tuh vo-CHuh*	last week
der Abend	*deyR ah-buhnd*	evening
vorgestern	*foR-ges-tuhRn*	day before yesterday
gestern	*ges-tuhRn*	yesterday
heute	*hoy-tuh*	today
morgen	*moR-guhn*	tomorrow
übermorgen	*üh-buhR-moR-guhn*	day after tomorrow
am nächsten Tag	*Am näH-stuhn tahk*	the next day
heute in einer Woche	*hoy-tuh in ay-nuhR vo-CHuh*	a week from today
heute in zwei Wochen	*hoy-tuh in tsvay vo-CHuhn*	two weeks from today
der Morgen	*deyR moR-guhn*	morning
der Nachmittag	*deyR nACH-mi-tahk*	afternoon

Now translate the following sentences into English. Check your translations in Appendix A.

1. Heute in einer Woche habe ich Geburtstag.

2. Gestern war schönes Wetter.

3. Samstags spiele ich Tennis.

4. Übermorgen reisen wir nach Deutschland.

5. Am nächsten Tag essen wir im Restaurant.

The Least You Need to Know

- German addresses list the street first, followed by the house number. The ZIP code precedes the city. Phone numbers vary in length.
- The German word for Germany is *Deutschland,* Austria is *Österreich,* and Switzerland is *die Schweiz.*
- Learning a few weather expressions will help you figure out whether you should leave your umbrella in the closet.
- The days of the week in German are *Montag, Dienstag, Mittwoch, Donnerstag, Freitag, Samstag* (but *Sonnabend* in northern Germany), and *Sonntag.*
- The months of the year in German are *Januar, Februar, März, April, Mai, Juni, Juli, August, September, Oktober, November,* and *Dezember.*
- The four seasons are *Frühling, Sommer, Herbst,* and *Winter.*

Chapter 15

Let's Sightsee

In This Chapter

- Enjoying the pleasures of sightseeing
- Expressing your attitude with modals
- Expressing your reactions to suggestions
- Making suggestions in an inclusive way

You turn on the radio in your hotel room, and a voice says that today will be a warm, sunny day. If you're in Berlin, it's the perfect weather to see *das Brandenburger Tor* (the Brandenburg Gate), which stood as a symbol for the division of Germany after the Berlin Wall was built. If you're in Köln, you can visit the famous *Dom* and then sit down for a few hours at an outdoor café.

You look through your guidebook to see which museums are open and where they are located. Then you take the elevator downstairs and get a map of the city from the receptionist at the front desk. Now you are ready to venture out into a German, Swiss, or Austrian city to explore the parks, the streets, or the shopping districts. After reading this chapter, not only will you be able to find your way around, but you'll be well on your way to giving and responding to suggestions in German.

What Do You Want to See?

What's it going to be? The ancient rooms of a castle, the remains of the Berlin Wall, or the paintings in a museum? To express what you can see in a given place, you will need to use *man sieht* (*mAn zeet*), "one sees," which is colloquially expressed in English as "you see." Remember that *sehen* is a very strong verb. The complete conjugation for the present tense is given in Chapter 8.

AS A RULE

The basic word order rule for German can be expressed by the pseudomath-ematical expression XV_2, which translates to the verb always coming in the second position in the sentence (unless you're commanding or posing a yes/no question). X is the subject, an adverb, or a prepositional phrase, as in *Morgen gehe ich ins Kino*. In other words, if the subject does not begin the sentence, the subject will follow the verb. Either way, you end up with the verb in the second position!

The expression *man sieht* is quite versatile—you can use it to talk about practically anything. Practice the following expressions.

> In Berlin sieht man das Brandenburger Tor.
> *in beR-leen zeet mAn dAs bRAn-duhn-booR-guhR toR*
> In Berlin you see the Brandenburg Gate.

> Im Zirkus sieht man Elefanten.
> *im tsiR-koos zeet mAn ey-ley-fAn-tuhn*
> In the circus you see elephants.

> Im Kino sieht man einen Film.
> *im kee-non zeet mAn ay-nuhn film*
> In the cinema you see a movie.

Use the phrase *man sieht* to complete the following items. Because you'll be discussing "where" something is seen, and *in* is either an accusative or dative preposition (depending on whether there is motion), you'll be using the dative case and contractions for ease. Remember that the masculine *der* and neuter *das* become *dem* in the dative case, contracting with the preposition *in* to become *im*. The feminine *die* becomes *der* in the dative case. Check your sentences in Appendix A.

Example: das Aquarium/die Fische (the aquarium/the fish)

Answer: Im Aquarium sieht man die Fische.

1. der Nachtclub/eine Vorstellung (the nightclub/a show)

2. die Kathedrale/die Glasmalerei (the cathedral/the stained glass)

3. das Schloß/die Wandteppiche (the castle/the tapestries)

4. der Zoo/die Tiere (the zoo/the animals)

5. das Museum/die Bilder und Skulpturen (the museum/the paintings and sculptures)

6. das Kino/der Film (the cinema/the movies)

7. die Disco/die Tänzer (the disco/the dancers)

8. die Bibliothek/alte Bücher (the library/old books)

May, Must, Can—What Kind of Mode Are You In?

To make suggestions or express attitudes in German, you will need to use *modal verbs*—helping verbs used with other verbs. In the sentence *Wir müssen nach Hause gehen*, for example, the modal verb *müssen* modifies the act of the main verb, *gehen*, expressing the attitude of the speaker toward an action—the equivalent of *must*. Adding a modal to another verb is like having a puppy: life is never the same again. Modals modify the action of the main verb (just like Zane the Superpudel turns everything upside down) and significantly alter the meanings of sentences. For example, "We must go home" is much different from "We go home."

DEFINITION

A **modal verb** is a verb used with another verb (in its infinitival form) to signal contrasts in speaker attitude. The six principal modal verbs in German are *sollen, müssen, dürfen, können, wollen,* and *mögen.*

When a modal is used with another verb, the modal expresses the attitude of the agent (the subject of the sentence) to the main verb's meaning. The six principal modal auxiliary verbs in German and what they express are as follows:

- *sollen (zo-luhn)*, ought to: obligation, expectation

- *müssen (mü-suhn)*, to have to: necessity, probability

- *dürfen (düR-fuhn)*, to be allowed to: permission, politeness

- *können (kö-nuhn)*, to be able to: ability, possibility

- *wollen (vo-luhn)*, to want to: wish, desire, intention

- *mögen (möh-guhn)*, to like (something): liking, wish

Because the present tense of modal auxiliary verbs is irregular, the best thing for you to do is to memorize the conjugations (see the following six tables). A long time ago, the original present-tense forms of modals fell into disuse, and the original strong (vowel-changing) past tense assumed present tense meaning. This accounts linguistically for why all modals except *sollen* take a stem change in the singular. As you'll see, the first person and third person singular have the same form. Again, this phenomenon is related to the usage of the past-tense form. Simply put, learn the infinitive and the singular stem, and you'll have it made!

Conjugation of a Modal Auxiliary Verb: *sollen*

Person	Singular	English	Plural	English
First	ich soll *iH zol*	I ought to	wir sollen *veeR zo-luhn*	we ought to
Second	du sollst *dew zolst*	you ought to	ihr sollt *eeR zolt*	you ought to
Third	er, sie, es soll *eR, zee, es zol*	he, she, it ought to	sie sollen *zee zo-luhn*	they ought to
Formal	Sie sollen *zee zo-luhn*	you ought to	Sie sollen *zee zo-luhn*	you ought to

Did you notice that the first and third person singular are identical? These are also the only forms with modals that don't take the regular ending you've come to associate with present-tense verb conjugations. And did you pick up on how the first person and third person plural exactly resemble the infinitive?

Conjugation of a Modal Auxiliary Verb: *mögen*

Person	Singular	English	Plural	English
First	ich mag *iH mahk*	I like to	wir mögen *veeR möh-guhn*	we like to
Second	du magst *dew mahkst*	you like to	ihr mögt *eeR möhkt*	you like to
Third	er, sie, es mag *eR, zee, es mahk*	he, she, it likes to	sie mögen *zee möh-guhn*	they like to
Formal	Sie mögen *zee möh-guhn*	you like to	Sie mögen *zee möh-guhn*	you like to

Conjugation of a Modal Auxiliary Verb: *dürfen*

Person	Singular	English	Plural	English
First	ich darf *iH dARf*	I am allowed to	wir dürfen *veeR düR-fuhn*	we are allowed to
Second	du darfst *dew dARfst*	you are allowed to	ihr dürft *eeR düRft*	you are allowed to
Third	er, sie, es darf *er, zee, es dARf*	he, she, it is allowed to	sie dürfen *zee düR-fuhn*	they are allowed to
Formal	Sie dürfen *zee düR-fuhn*	you are allowed to	Sie dürfen *zee düR-fuhn*	you are allowed to

Conjugation of a Modal Auxiliary Verb: *können*

Person	Singular	English	Plural	English
First	ich kann *iH kAn*	I am able to	wir können *veeR kö-nuhn*	we are able to
Second	du kannst *dew kAnst*	you are able to	ihr könnt *eeR könt*	you are able to
Third	er, sie, es kann *er, zee, es, kAn*	he, she, it is able to	sie können *zee kö-nuhn*	they are able to
Formal	Sie können *zee kö-nuhn*	you are able to	Sie können *zee kö-nuhn*	you are able to

Conjugation of a Modal Auxiliary Verb: *müssen*

Person	Singular	English	Plural	English
First	ich muss *iH moos*	I have to	wir müssen *veeR mü-suhn*	we have to
Second	du must *dew moost*	you have to	ihr must *eeR müst*	you have to
Third	er, sie, es muss *er, zee, es moos*	he, she, it has to	sie müssen *zee mü-suhn*	they have to
Formal	Sie müssen *zee mü-suhn*	you have to	Sie müssen *zee mü-suhn*	you have to

Conjugation of a Modal Auxiliary Verb: *wollen*

Person	Singular	English	Plural	English
First	ich will *iH vil*	I want to	wir wollen *veeR vo-luhn*	we want to
Second	du willst *dew vilst*	you want to	ihr wollt *eeR volt*	you want to
Third	er, sie, es will *er, zee, es vil*	he, she, it wants to	sie wollen *zee vo-luhn*	they want to
(Formal)	Sie wollen *zee vo-luhn*	you want to	Sie wollen *zee vo-luhn*	you want to

The Power of Suggestion

Imagine that you are in a group traveling through Germany. A friend of yours who visited Hamburg a year ago has told you to be sure to visit the St. Pauli's Fischmarkt after going out dancing and reveling on a Saturday night. She says that people who don't feel like sleeping gather there in the early hours of Sunday morning with the market workers and eat breakfast. You don't know how others in your group would feel about going to St. Pauli's seafood fest, but you do know that there's only one way to find out: by suggesting it! To make suggestions in German, use the modals *sollen*, *dürfen*, *können*, or *wollen* plus the infinitive.

WE ARE FAMILY

While both the *can* of English and the *können* of German may be used in the contemporary sense of "receive permission," did you know that the Old English *cunnan* meant "know"? This meaning was retained until the sixteenth or seventeenth century (Early Modern English) and is still retained in German: *Ich kann Deutsch*, "I know German."

If you need more force behind your suggestions, use the modal *müssen* to express "must." Use *mögen* to express the things you like to do (on a regular basis). Note that the modal is the conjugated verb and, hence, is in the second position in the sentence. The verb carrying the main meaning and action is placed in infinitival form at the end of the sentence. You're inflecting the modal to show agreement with the subject (person, number); the accompanying verb is referred to as a *dependent infinitive*—unvarying in form and always sent to the end of the sentence. After all, why stack verbs if you can separate them?

Remember that five out of the six modal auxiliary verbs (*dürfen, können, mögen, müssen,* and *wollen*) change their stem vowel in the first, second, and third person singular forms.

sollen + gehen

German	Pronunciation	English
Sollen wir zum Fischmarkt gehen?	*zo-luhn veeR tsewm fish-mARkt gey-uhn*	Should we go to the fish market?
Wir sollen zum Fischmarkt gehen.	*veeR zo-luhn tsewm fish-mARkt gey-uhn*	We are supposed to go to the fish market.

wollen + gehen

German	Pronunciation	English
Wollt ihr zum Fischmarkt gehen?	*volt eeR tsewm fish-mARkt gey-uhn*	Do you want to go to the fish market?
Wir wollen zum Fischmarkt gehen.	*veeR vo-luhn tsewm fish-mARkt gey-uhn*	We want to go to the fish market.

mögen + gehen

German	Pronunciation	English
Magst du zum Fischmarkt gehen?	*mahkst dew tsewm fish-mARkt gey-uhn*	Do you like to go to the fish market?
Ich mag zum Fischmarkt gehen.	*iH mahk tsewm fish-mARkt gey-uhn*	I like to go to the fish market.

müssen + gehen

German	Pronunciation	English
Müssen sie zum Fischmarkt gehen?	*mü-suhn zee tsewm fish-mARkt gey-uhn*	Must they go to the fish market?
Sie müssen zum Fischmarkt gehen.	*zee mü-suhn tsewm fish-mARkt gey-uhn*	They must go to the fish market.

dürfen + gehen

German	Pronunciation	English
Darf ich zum Fischmarkt gehen?	*dARf iH tsewm fish-mARkt gey-uhn*	Am I allowed to go to the fish market?
Ich darf zum Fischmarkt gehen.	*iH dARf tsewm fish-mARkt gey-uhn*	I'm allowed to go to the fish market.

können + gehen

German	Pronunciation	English
Können wir nach Hause gehen?	*kö-nuhn veeR nACH hou-zuh gey-uhn*	Can we go home?
Wir können nach Hause gehen.	*veeR kö-nuhn nACH hou-zuh gey-uhn*	We can go home.

Making Suggestions

It's summertime … and the living is easy. Suggest five things you and your group of travelers can do together, and express each suggestion in three different ways. Use various modals in questions such as: *Sollen wir schwimmen gehen?* Don't forget to drag the accompanying verb—the dependent infinitive—to the end of your question!

Now try your hand at inserting the correct form of the modal (and sending the dependent infinitive to the end) in the following sentences. Check your sentences in Appendix A.

1. Ich komme später. (können)

2. Was machst du? (wollen)

3. Christina lernt viel. (müssen)

4. Dieser Film ist sehr gut. (sollen)

5. Wolfram kommt nicht mit. (dürfen)

Responding to Suggestions

You don't want to be someone who is always telling everyone else what you should do, what you must do, and what you can do all the time, do you? You'll probably want to give other people a chance to make suggestions, and when they do, you'll want to respond. In the following sections, you'll learn some common ways of responding to suggestions.

ACHTUNG

Don't confuse the first- and third-person singular forms of the modal *wollen* ("want to") with the English look-alike "will." *Beka will eine Radtour machen* means "Beka wants to go on a bike ride"—not that she will go on one!

Just Say Yes, No, Absolutely Not

You may want to decline a suggestion with more than a mere "yes" or "no," such as with a "Yes, but …."

Ja, ich bin daran interessiert.
yah, iH bin dah-RAn in-tuh-Re-seeRt
Yes, I'm interested in that.

Ja, es interessiert mich(sehr), aber ….
yah, es in-tuh-Re-seeRt miH (zeeR), ah-buhR
Yes, I'm (very) interested, but ….

Nein, leider interessiert es mich (überhaupt) nicht.
nayn, lay-duhR in-tuh-Re-seeRt es miH (üh-buhR-houpt) niHt
No, unfortunately, I'm not (at all) interested.

Nein, ich bin nicht daran interessiert.
nayn, iH bin niHt dah-RAn in-tuh-Re-seeRt
No, I'm not interested in that.

Das macht mir Spaß.
das maCHt meeR shpahs
That's fun.

Ich möchte lieber ….
iH möH-tuh lee-buhR
I would rather ….

To express boredom, dislike, or disgust, say:

German	Pronunciation	English
Ich mag ... nicht.	*iH mahk ... niHt*	I don't like ....
Ich habe keine Lust.	*iH hah-buh kay-nuh loost*	I don't feel like it.
Es ist langweilig.	*es ist lAng-vay-liH*	It's boring.
Das ist grauenhaft.	*das ist gRou-uhn-hAft*	That is horrible.

What Do You Think?

When someone suggests that the two of you go to the opera, and the suggestion appeals to you, answer with *Ich finde die Oper toll*. If you begin your answers with *Ich finde*, you can be pretty much assured that you're going to be saying something that makes sense. Here are some alternative ways to show your enthusiasm:

Ich liebe die Oper!   Ich mag die Oper.
iH lee-buh dee oh-puhR   *iH mahk dee oh-puhR*
I love opera!   I like opera.

To express joy, excitement, or anticipation at doing something, give your positive opinion by saying this:

Es ist ....   Das ist ....   Ich finde es ....
es ist   *dAs ist*   *iH fin-duh es*
It is ....   That is ....   I find it ....

Here are some common German superlatives:

German	Pronunciation	English
fantastisch!	*fAn-tAs-tish*	fantastic!
schön!	*shöhn*	beautiful!
sensationell!	*zen-zah-tseeon-el*	sensational!
super!	*zew-puhR*	super!
unglaublich!	*oon-gloup-liH*	unbelievable!
wunderschön!	*voon-deR-shöhn*	wonderful!

More Suggestions

Once again, it's time to put what you know to work. Imagine that you are planning a trip with a close friend. Your friend is a bit of a dreamer and keeps suggesting a million different things for the two of you to do. Practice letting your friend down gently by giving an affirmative answer and then a negative answer to his or her suggestions. Check possible responses in Appendix A.

Example: Lass uns nach Berlin reisen!

Answer: Super! Ich mag Berlin.

Nein, ich will nicht nach Berlin reisen.

1. Lass uns eine Kirche besichtigen!

2. Lass uns eine Ausstellung sehen!

3. Lass uns nach Europa reisen!

4. Lass uns Bilder anschauen!

5. Lass uns in die Oper gehen!

6. Lass uns Norwegisch lernen!

7. Lass uns ein Auto mieten!

The Least You Need to Know

- You can get around a city by knowing a few basic German words for sightseeing attractions and the phrases that describe what you plan to do there.
- After you've memorized the irregular conjugation of the six modal auxiliary verbs (*sollen, müssen, dürfen, können, wollen,* and *mögen*), making suggestions is easy: use the modal auxiliary verb + the dependent infinitive at the end of the sentence.
- You can begin your response to virtually any suggestion with the expression *Ich finde es* ….
- To make a suggestion, use the expression *Lass uns* and finish it with an infinitive, as in *Lass uns nach München fahren.*

You've Got to Go Shopping

Chapter 16

In This Chapter

- Stores and what they sell
- Clothing, colors, sizes, materials, and designs
- Accusative and dative personal pronouns
- Demonstrative adjectives: this, that, these, and those

Once you've seen the sights and been to the restaurants, you may want to spend a day or two shopping. Do you like to buy souvenirs for your friends? Do you enjoy shopping for yourself, or do you really dislike trying to locate the right size, color, material, and design in a jungle of hangers, racks, salespeople, and merchandise? Whether you love it or hate it, this chapter will help you prepare to shop.

Store-Bought Pleasures

One of the least expensive (and, for some, most enjoyable) ways to shop is with your eyes. The following table will start you on your way to guilt-free browsing by helping you identify stores and their offerings. Words that may form compounds with the meaning of "store" include *das Geschäft, der Laden, and die Handlung.* Hence, you might find a book (*Buch*) in a *Buchgeschäft*, in a *Buchladen*, or in a *Buchhandlung.* In the table, items that one might find in each store are listed in their plural form followed by their gender (m., f., or n.).

GERMAN CULTURE

Large department stores, *Kaufhäuser (kouf-hoy-zuhR)*, may be found in German cities. Aside from tendering the same goods and services as American department stores, they typically include a supermarket, indicated on the store directory as *Lebensmittel (ley-benz-mi-tuhl)*, in the basement, or *Untergeschoß (oon-tuhR-guh-shos)*.

Stores

Store	What You Can Buy There
das Bekleidungsgeschäft (*dAs buh-klay-doorgz-guh-shäft*) clothing store	die Bekleidung, f., (*dee buh-klay-doong*): clothes
das Blumengeschäft (*dAs blew-muhn-guh-shäft*) florist	die Blumen, f., (*dee blew-muhn*): flowers
das Lederwarengeschäft (*dAs ley-deR-vah-Ren-guh-shäft*) leather goods store	die Gürtel, m., (*dee güR-tuhl*); die Lederjacken, f., (*dee ley-duhR-yA-kuhn*); die Portemonnaies, n., (*dee poRt-mo-neyz*): belts, leather jackets, wallets
das Musikgeschäft (*dAs mew-zik-guh-shäft*) music store	die CDs, f., (*dee tse-dez*); die Kassetten, f., (*dee kA-se-tuhn*): CDs, tapes
das Schmuckgeschäft (*dAs shmook-guh-shäft*) or der Juwelier (*deyR yoo-vey-lee-uhR*) jewelry store	der Schmuck (*deyR shmook*): jewelry die Ohrringe (*dee oh-Ring-uh*): earrings das Armband (*dAs Arm-bAnt*): bracelet die Halskette (*dee hAls-ke-tuh*): necklace
das Sportgeschäft (*dAs shpoRt-guh-shäft*) sport shop	die Sportbekleidung, f., (*dee shpoRt-buh-klay-doong*); die Turnschuhe, m., (*dee tooRn-shew-uh*); die Sportgeräte, n., (*dee shpoRt-guh-Räh-tuh*): sports clothing, sneakers, sports equipment
der Geschenkartikelladen (*deyR guh-shenk-AR-ti-kuhl-lah-duhn*) gift shop	die Miniaturdenkmäler, n., (*dee mee-nee-ah-tooR-denk- mäh-luhR*); die Souvenirs, n., (*dee sew-vuh-neeRz*); die T-Shirts, n., (*dee tee-shiRts*); die Stadtpläne, m., (*dee shtAt-pläh-nuh*): miniature monuments, souvenirs, T-shirts, maps

Store	What You Can Buy There
der Kiosk (*deyR kee-osk*) newsstand	die Zeitungen, f., (*dee tsay-toon-guhn*); die Zeitschriften, f., (*dee tsayt-shRif-tuhn*): newspapers, magazines
der Tabakladen (*deyR tA-bAk-lah-duhn*) tobacconist	die Zigaretten, f., (*dee tsee-gah-Re-tuhn*); die Zigarren, f., (*dee tsee-gA-Ruhn*); die Feuerzeuge, n., (*dee foy-uhR-tsoy-guh*): cigarettes, cigars, lighters
die Apotheke (*dee ah-po-tey-kuh*) pharmacy	die Medikamente, n., (*dee me-dee-kah-men-tuh*): medicine
die Boutique (*dee boo-teek*) boutique	die Kleidung, f., (*dee klay-doong*): clothing der Schmuck, m., (*deyR shmook*): jewelry
die Buchhandlung (*dee bewCH-hAnt-loong*) bookstore	die Bücher, n., (*dee bü-CHuhR*): books
die Drogerie (*dee dRoh-guh-Ree*) drug store	die Schönheitsartikel, m., (*dee shön-hayts-AR-tee-kuhl*): beauty articles
die Schreibwarenladen (*shRayp-wah-Ruhn-lah-duhn*) stationery store	die Stifte, m., (*dee shtif-tuh*); die Schreibwaren, f., (*dee shRayp-vah-Ruhn*): pens, stationery
die Parfümerie (*dee pAR-fü-muh-Ree*) perfume store	das Parfüm (*dAs paR-füm*): perfume

Clothes Make the Mann

If you packed too little or want to check out European fashions, the vocabulary in the following table will help you identify something in the latest fashion, or *in der neusten Mode* (*in deyR noy-stuhn moh-duh*). Articles of clothing that occur in the plural are noted by a following (pl.). Note that *die Hose* (pair of pants or trousers) is singular, unlike its English equivalent.

Clothing

German	Pronunciation	English
das Hemd	*dAs hemt*	shirt
das Kleid	*dAs klayt*	dress
das Sakko	*dAs za-ko*	sports jacket
das T-Shirt	*dAs tee-shiRt*	T-shirt
der Anzug	*deyR An-tsewk*	suit
der Badeanzug	*deyR bah-duh-An-tsewk*	bathing suit
der Büstenhalter *or* der BH	*deyR bü-stuhn-hAl-tuhR* or *deyR bey-hah*	bra abbreviation for "bra"
der Gürtel	*deyR güR-tuhl*	belt
der Hut	*deyR hewt*	hat
der Mantel	*deyR mAn-tuhl*	coat
der Pullover	*deyR pool-oh-vuhR*	pullover
der Regenmantel	*deyR Rey-guhn-mAn-tuhl*	raincoat
der Rock	*deyR Rok*	skirt
der Schal	*deyR shahl*	scarf
der Schlafanzug	*deyR shlahf-An-tsook*	pajamas
der Schlips	*deyR schleps*	necktie
die Bluse	*dee blew-zuh*	blouse
die Größe	*dee gröh-suh*	size
die Handschuhe (pl.)	*dee hAnt-schew-uh*	gloves
die Hose	*dee hoh-zuh*	pair of pants
die Jacke	*dee yA-kuh*	jacket
die Jeans	*dee jeens*	jeans
die Krawatte	*dee kRah-vA-tuh*	necktie
die Mütze	*dee mü-tsuh*	cap
die Schuhe (pl.)	*dee shew-uh*	shoes
die Shorts (pl.)	*dee shorts*	shorts
die Socken (pl.)	*dee zo-kuhn*	socks
die Strumpfhose	*dee shtRoompf-hoh-zuh*	tights, stockings
die Tennisschuhe (pl.)	*dee te-nis-shew-uh*	tennis shoes
die Turnschuhe (pl.)	*dee toRn-shew-uh*	sneakers
die Unterwäsche	*dee oon-tuhR-vä-shuh*	underwear

Wear It Well

Now that you've bought it, you can finally wear it. The following table helps you express the concept of wearing clothing with the very strong verb *tragen* (*tRah-guhn*), "to wear" or "to carry."

The Verb *tragen*

Person	Singular	English	Plural	English
First	ich trage *iH tRah-guh*	I wear	wir tragen *veeR tRah-guhn*	we wear
Second	du trägst *dew tRähkst*	you wear	ihr tragt *eeR tRahkt*	you wear
Third	er, sie, es trägt *eR, zee, es tRäkt*	he, she, it wears	sie tragen *zee tRah-guhn*	they wear
Formal	Sie tragen *zee tRah-guhn*	you wear	Sie tragen *zee tRah-guhn*	you wear

What do you normally wear on your feet before you put on your shoes? What do you normally wear on your head when it's cold out? See whether you can fill in the blanks with the correct form of the verb *tragen* and appropriate vocabulary. Check your conjugations in Appendix A.

Example: Zum Sport _____ ich _____.

Answer: Zum Sport <u>trage</u> ich <u>Turnschuhe</u>.

1. In (in) unseren Schuhen _____ wir _____.

2. Wenn (when) ich schlafe, _____ ich einen _____.

3. Unter deiner Hose _____ du _____.

4. Wenn es regnet, _____ ich einen _____.

5. Im Winter _____ ihr warme _____.

6. Wenn man in die Oper (to the opera) geht, _____ man einen _____ mit einem _____.

7. Im Sommer _____ viele Leute (people) _____ und ein _____.

Colors

Certain colors are associated with certain moods or states of being. Don't be too quick to use the colors in the following table figuratively—at least, not in the same way you would use them in English. *Er ist blau* (*eR ist blou*), which translates into "he is blue," does not mean "he is sad." Germans use this phrase to indicate that someone has had too much to drink. However you use them, the colors (*die Farben*) in the following table will help you describe people, places, and things.

Colors

German	Pronunciation	English
beige	*Beyj*	beige
blau	*Blou*	blue
braun	*bRoun*	brown
gelb	*Gelp*	yellow
grau	*gRou*	gray
grün	*gRün*	green
lila	*lee-lah*	purple
orange	*oR-An-juh*	orange
rosa	*Roh-zah*	pink
rot	*Rot*	red
schwarz	*shvaRts*	black
weiß	*Vays*	white

To describe any color as light, simply add the word *hell* (*hel*) as a prefix to the color to form a compound adjective:

hellrot	hellgrün	hellblau
hel-Rot	*hel-gRün*	*hel-blou*
light red	light green	light blue

To describe a color as dark, add the word *dunkel* (*doon-kuhl*) as a prefix to the color to form a compound adjective:

dunkelrot	dunkelgrün	dunkelblau
doon-kuhl-Rot	*doon-kuhl-gRün*	*doon-kuhl-blou*
dark red	dark green	dark blue

The following table offers some additional adjectives that are useful when describing clothing.

Fashionable Adjectives

German	Pronunciation	English
breit	*brayt*	wide
eng	*eng*	narrow
gemustert	*guh-moos-tuhRt*	patterned
gepunktet	*guh-poonk-tuht*	polka-dotted
gestreift	*guh-shtRayft*	striped
kariert	*kah-ReeRt*	plaid
modisch	*moh-dish*	fashionable

To express need or desire, you can use *möchten. Ich möchte* is the equivalent of "I would like." Don't confuse it with *mögen*, which means "to like (something)." You can make a big mistake by confusing the two. If you're in a clothing store and you say, *"Ich möchte Kleider"* ("I would like some dresses") instead of *"Ich mag Kleider"* ("I like dresses"), you might end up with an armful of dresses and be expected to try them on, whether you're in the mood for trying on dresses or not. Now try to translate the following sentences into German. Remember that colors and patterns are adjectives, so they are declined according to what type of word precedes the adjective and the following noun (see Chapter 10). Also, the item that you "like" functions as the direct object in the sentence and thus takes the accusative case. Check your translations in Appendix A.

Example: I'd like a green dress.

Answer: Ich möchte ein grünes Kleid.

1. I'd like a light red skirt.
2. I'd like a dark blue suit.
3. I'd like a light yellow hat.
4. I'd like a gray jacket.
5. I'd like a polka-dotted tie.
6. I'd like a plaid pair of pants.
7. I'd like a fashionable bathing suit.
8. I'd like a striped shirt.

Fabric Preferences

Some people can't tolerate polyester, others find silk pretentious, and others won't wear anything that isn't at least 95 percent cotton. The following table will help you pick the material (*die Materialien*) you prefer when you shop.

Materials

German	Pronunciation	English
das Leder	*dAs ley-deR*	leather
das Leinen	*dAs lay-nuhn*	linen
das *Nylon*	*dAs nay-lon*	nylon
das *Polyester*	*dAs poh-lee-es-tuhR*	polyester
das *Wild*leder *or Velo*ursleder	*dAs vilt-ley-duhR or dAs vuh-looRz-ley-duhR*	suede
der *Flanell*	*deyR flah-nel*	flannel
der Kaschmir	*deyR kAsh-meeR*	cashmere
der Kord	*deyR koRt*	corduroy
die Baumwolle	*dee boum-wo-luh*	cotton
die *Seide*	*dee zay-duh*	silk
die *Wolle*	*dee vo-luh*	wool

To explain that you want something made out of a certain material, use the dative preposition *aus* followed by only the noun.

> Ich möchte ein Kleid aus Seide.
> *iH möH-tuh ayn klayt ous zay-duh*
> I'd like a silk dress.

What's the Object?

In Chapter 7, you learned about the accusative (*direct object*) case and the dative (*indirect object*) case relative to nouns. Now you're going to see how these cases affect pronouns.

If a friend tells you that she loves her favorite pair of shoes and that she wears her favorite pair of shoes all the time and that she takes off her favorite pair of shoes only when she gets blisters from dancing too much, you would probably want to take off one of *your* shoes and hit her over the head with it. She could be less long winded if she stopped repeating *favorite pair of shoes* (a direct object noun in English) and replaced it with *them* (a direct object pronoun in English). In German, the direct object is in the accusative case and is often called the accusative object. The animate object that is receiving the action of the verb is the indirect object and is marked in the dative case in German, also called the dative object. If you've forgotten what you learned about cases in Chapter 7, this summary should refresh your memory.

DEFINITION

A **direct object** is the noun or pronoun that receives the action of the verb. The verb assigns this object the accusative case.

The **indirect object** is the person, animal, or other animate object to whom/ which something is given or something is done. The dative case marks the indirect object in German.

Nouns or pronouns in the accusative case answer the question of whom or what the subject is acting on and can refer to people, places, things, or ideas.

	Nominative (Subj.)	Verb	Accusative (Direct Obj.)
With noun	Ich (I)	trage (wear)	meine Lieblingsschuhe. (my favorite shoes)
With pronoun	Ich (I)	trage (wear)	sie. (them)
With noun	Sie (they)	lieben (love)	das Leben. (life)
With pronoun	Sie (they)	lieben (love)	es. (it)

Indirect object nouns or pronouns (in German, nouns or pronouns in the dative case) answer the question of to whom or to what the action of the verb is being directed.

	Nominative (Subj.)	Dative Verb	Accusative (Indirect Obj.)	(Direct Obj.)
With noun	Ich (I)	kaufe (buy)	meinem Freund (my friend)	eine Mütze. (a cap)
With pronoun	Ich (I)	kaufe (buy)	ihm (him)	eine Mütze. (a cap)
With noun	Sie (she)	gibt (gives)	ihrer Schwester (her sister)	ein Geschenk. (a gift)
With pronoun	Sie (she)	gibt (gives)	ihr (her sister)	ein Geschenk. (a gift)

The English language uses direct and indirect pronouns to avoid repeating the same nouns over and over again. In German, direct object pronouns are in the accusative case, and indirect object pronouns are in the dative case. The following table provides a comprehensive chart of accusative personal pronouns in German. We've already used this paradigm to show subject (personal) pronouns and to conjugate verbs.

Accusative Personal Pronouns (Object Pronouns)

	Singular	**English**	**Plural**	**English**
First	mich (*miH*)	me	uns (*oonz*)	us
Second	dich (*diH*)	you	euch (*oyH*)	you
Third	ihn (*een*)	him	sie (*zee*)	them
	sie (*zee*)	her		
	es (*es*)	it		
Formal	Sie (*zee*)	you	Sie (*zee*)	you

The accusative case of the direct object should be easy enough to learn if you remember that the German *mich* has the same initial sounds as the English *me* (the object of a sentence or the object of a prepositional phrase). Then *dich* rhymes with *mich* but borrows the *d* sound from *du*. As far as third person singular masculine is concerned, it ends in an *n*, just like the accusative masculine *den* or *einen*. The German *uns* closely resembles the English *us*.

WE ARE FAMILY

The similarities between *uns* versus *us* and *fünf* versus *five* are more than coincidental. Old English (as well as Old Saxon and Old Frisian) underwent a sound change that resulted in the loss of nasals, like *n* before fricative sounds such as *f* and *s*. Can you guess what *Gans* means? "Goose!"

Try your hand at replacing the accusative noun phrases, indicated in boldface, with the appropriate accusative personal pronouns. Check your pronouns in Appendix A.

AS A RULE

When dealing with neuter nouns ending in *-chen* or *-lein*, you can use either the pronoun *es* (following the grammatical gender) or the pronoun *er* or *sie*, if the noun refers to a male or female.

1. Ich trage **eine enge Hose.**

2. Du trägst **einen schönen Hut.**

3. Kerstin trägt **ein breites Hemd.**

4. Frank trägt **weiße Tennisschuhe.**

Es is used as a direct object pronoun for neuter nouns, most of which are things. There are, however, a few exceptions. *Es* means "her," for example, in the sentence *Ich liebe es*, when *es* refers to *das Mädchen.*

Because English relies on prepositions to express the function of someone receiving something (indirect object) and German relies on the dative case to indicate this function, we've included that little English helper preposition for dative personal pronouns in the following table.

ACHTUNG

Remember, *ihn* and *ihm* are used for masculine, *sie* and *ihr* are used for feminine nouns, and *es* and *ihm* are used for neuter nouns. For all plural nouns, use *sie* for direct object pronouns and *ihnen* for indirect object pronouns.

Dative Personal Pronouns (Indirect Object Pronouns)

	Singular	English	Plural	English
First	mir (*meeR*)	(to) me	uns (*oonz*)	(to) us
Second	dir (*diH*)	(to) you	euch (*oyH*)	(to) you
Third	ihm (*eem*)	(to) him	ihnen (*ee-nuhn*)	(to) them
	ihr (*eeR*)	(to) her		
	ihm (*eem*)	(to) it		
Formal	Ihnen (*ee-nuhn*)	(to) you	Ihnen (*ee-nuhn*)	(to) you

Egads! How to assimilate this information? Again, recall the dative definite articles: masculine = *dem*, feminine = *der*, neuter = *dem*, plural = *den*. You'll notice that the ends of *ihm, ihr, ihm,* and *ihnen* share similarities in their final sounds. Latch on to your English *him* and *her* for another reminder.

And now for a little practice substituting the economical dative personal pronouns for the long-winded indirect object noun phrases, indicated in boldface. Check your pronouns in Appendix A.

1. Ich gebe **meinen lieben Studenten** Schokolade.

2. Bernadette schenkt **ihrer toleranten Schwester** Blumen.

3. Thomas dankt **seinem nervösen Freund** für den Kaffee.

4. Wir geben **dem freundlichen Kind** eine Olive.

Position of Object Pronouns

In swank social circles, position is everything. It's the same with direct and indirect objects in German. If we're dealing with noun phrases, the indirect (dative) object precedes the direct object (accusative):

> Ich schreibe dem Vater eine Postkarte.
> *iH shRay-buh deym fah-tuhR ay-nuh post-kAR-tuh*
> I write a postcard to the father.

However, if the direct object of a sentence is a pronoun, it precedes the indirect object:

> Ich schreibe sie ihm. Ich schreibe sie dem Vater.
> *iH shRay-buh zee eem iH shRay-buh zee deym fah-tuhR*
> I write it to him. I write it to the father.

Note that *eine Postkarte* is replaced with the feminine pronoun *sie*, not with the ubiquitous inanimate neuter English "it" equivalent (*es*).

GERMAN CULTURE

European sizes (*Größen*) vary greatly from American sizes. While with clothing you might find S, M, L, and XL, you'll more than likely encounter numbered sizes such as 34 to 44 for women (*Damen*) and 36 to 54 for men (*Herren*). Shoe sizes for both men and women range from 36 upward.

Using Direct Object Pronouns

A German friend invites you to accompany her shopping in Düsseldorf. Use direct object pronouns to answer the questions she asks you in the dressing room. Try answering both positively and negatively. Check your answers in Appendix A.

Example:

Magst du die graue Bluse?

Ja, ich mag <u>sie</u>.

Nein, ich mag <u>sie</u> nicht.

1. Magst du den schwarzen Schal?

2. Magst du die dunkelgrünen Schuhe?

3. Magst du die hellrote Hose?

4. Magst du das blaue Hemd?

Using Indirect Object Pronouns

When she finishes shopping for herself, your friend wants to buy a few presents for certain members of her family. Unfortunately, she can't think of anything interesting to buy them. Offer her suggestions (in the form of commands using *schenken*, "to give as a gift"), replacing the indirect object (dative noun phrase) with a pronoun and expressing the direct object in the accusative case according to the following example. Remember that *ein* in the accusative masculine becomes *einen*. Check your sentences in Appendix A.

Example:

Hans/ ein Hut (m., der Hut) Schenke ihm einen Hut.

1. die Eltern/ ein Schal (m., der Schal)

2. die Schwester/ ein Kleid (n., das Kleid)

3. der Bruder/ eine kurze Hose (f., die kurze Hose)

4. die Oma/ eine Strumpfhose (f., die Strumpfhose)

Now rewrite these four commands using *only* pronouns. Because the direct object will be a pronoun, the direct object pronoun will precede the indirect object. Verify your pronouns in the appendix—they'll be numbered 5 through 8.

Example:

Schenke ihm einen Hut. = Schenke ihn ihm.

Asking for Something

Here are some phrases to help you through the most common in-store shopping situations:

Kann ich Ihnen helfen?
kAn iH ee-nuhn hel-fuhn
May I help you?

Nein danke, ich schaue mich nur um.
nayn dAn-kuh, iH shou-uh miH nooR oom
No, thank you, I am (just) looking.

Ja, ich würde gern (+ accusative object) sehen.
yah, iH vüR-duh geRn ... zey-uhn
Yes, I would like to see ...

Was wünschen Sie?
vAs vün-shuhn zee
What would you like?

Ich suche (+ accusative object).
iH zew-CHuh
I'm looking for ....

Welche Größe brauchen Sie?
vel-Huh gröh-suh brou-CHuhn zee
What size do you need?

Größe ...
gröh-suh
Size ...

Was ist im Sonderangebot?
vAs ist im zon-duhR-An-guh-bot
What's on sale?

I'll Take This

To ask your salesperson (or the cashier, or anyone else within asking distance) for his or her opinion about a suit, tie, hat, or skirt, you'll need to use a *demonstrative adjective*. The demonstrative adjective *dieser* ("this") allows you to be specific about an item. You encountered these types of *der* words in Chapter 12. The important thing to remember is that, in German, demonstrative adjectives must agree in number, gender, and case with the noun they modify. Because demonstrative adjectives inflect like definite articles, the following table reviews the declension of *dieser*, a *der Wort*, in all four cases.

DEFINITION

Demonstrative adjectives are adjectives such as *dieser* ("this") that point out someone or something specific—a particular noun.

Demonstrative Adjectives: *This, That, These, Those*

Case	Masculine	Feminine	Neuter	Plural
Nom.	dies**er** Hut *dee-zuhR hewt*	dies**e** Hose *dee-zuh hoh-zuh*	dies**es** Kleid *dee-zuhs klayt*	dies**e** *dee-zuh*
Acc.	dies**en** Hut *dee-zuhn hewt*	dies**e** Hose *dee-zuh hoh-zuh*	dies**es** Kleid *dee-zuhs klayt*	dies**e** *dee-zuh*
Dat.	dies**em** Hut *dee-zuhm hewt*	dies**er** Hose *dee-zuhR hoh-zuh*	dies**em** Kleid *de-zuhm klayt*	dies**en** *dee-zuhn*
Gen.	dies**es** Hutes *dee-zuhs hewts*	dies**er** Hose *dee-zuhR hoh-zuh*	dies**es** Kleides *dee-zuhs klayts*	dies**er** *dee-zuhR*

Expressing Opinions

You've tried on a million hats, and not one of them is right. Just when you're about to give up, you find the perfect hat. If you're happy with an item, you may want to express your pleasure. On the other hand, perhaps you are dissatisfied with the fit or style of something. You may express your opinion with the phrases in the following table. Note that *gefallen* and *stehen* use the dative case to express the person whom (indirect object) something (the direct, accusative object) pleases or fits.

German	Pronunciation	English
Das gefällt mir.	*dAs guh-fält miR*	I like it. (Literally: it is pleasing to me.)
Das steht mir gut.	*dAs shteyt miR gewt*	That suits me well.
Es ist angenehm.	*es ist An-guh-neym*	It is nice.
Es ist elegant.	*es ist ey-ley-gAnt*	It's elegant.
Es ist praktisch.	*es ist pRAk-tish*	It's practical.
Es gefällt mir nicht.	*es guh-fält miR niHt*	I don't like it.
Das steht mir nicht.	*dAs shteyt miR niHt*	That doesn't suit me.
Es ist schrecklich.	*es ist shRek-liH*	It is horrible.
Es ist zu klein.	*es ist tsew klayn*	It's too small.
Es ist zu groß.	*es ist tsew gRohs*	It's too big.
Es ist zu eng.	*es ist tsew eng*	It's too tight.
Es ist zu lang.	*es ist tsew lAng*	It's too long.
Es ist zu kurz.	*es ist tsew kooRts*	It's too short.

What's Your Preference?

Many questions concerning style and size begin with the interrogative pronoun *welcher*, another *der* word introduced in Chapter 12. *Welcher* follows the same declension as the demonstrative pronoun *dieser*, shown in the demonstrative adjectives table.

Sample question:

Welches Hemd gefällt Ihnen am besten?
vel-Huhs hemt guh-fält ee-nuhn Am bes-tuhn
Which shirt do you like best?

Answer:

Dieses Hemd dort gefällt mir am besten.
dee-suhs hemt doRt guh-fält meeR Am bes-tuhn
I like that shirt there best.

Now it's time to practice what you've learned about the interrogative pronoun *welcher* to determine "which." Respond to the questions in the following exercise with the correctly declined form of *welcher*. Check your questions in Appendix A.

Example: Ich suche ein Geschäft.

Answer: Welches Geschäft?

1. Diese Krawatte gefällt uns.

2. Der Anzug steht dir gut.

3. Das T-Shirt schenke ich meinem Bruder.

4. Ich suche meine Schuhe.

5. Ich mag dieses Kleid.

6. Sie möchte diesen Schlafanzug dort.

Did you figure out that the article of clothing in the first three sentences was the subject and, hence, in the nominative case? And what about the final three sentences? Yup, direct objects, thus expressed in the accusative case.

The Least You Need to Know

- You should be able to recognize the German names of stores and what they sell.

- You can use the verb *tragen* to talk about what you are wearing.

- In German, direct object pronouns are in the accusative case, and indirect object pronouns are in the dative case.

- The demonstrative adjective *dieser* helps you to indicate someone or something by expressing this or that (and, in the plural form, these or those). Its interrogative partner, *welcher,* can help you clarify which one.

Eating on the Go: *Auf dem Markt*

In This Chapter

- Where to buy various kinds of food
- How to read a wine label and a beer menu
- How to express quantity
- Identifying what you want and asking for it

In Chapter 16, you learned how to shop for fashion items. You told the salespeople what you wanted and answered their questions. You learned about colors, patterns, and preferences. Now your wallet is a little lighter, your suitcase is a little heavier, and your stomach feels a little emptier than it did when you set out earlier in the day. It's too early for dinner, so you decide to stop for a snack.

What do you feel like eating? You could get a sandwich (ein belegtes Brot, *ayn buh-lek-tuhs bRoht*) at a Café (*dAs kah-fey*) or a Bäckerei (*ay-nuh bä-kuh-Ray*), or stop in a Supermarkt (*deyR zew-peR-mARkt*) for bread (das Brot, *dAs bRoht*) and cheese (der Käse, *deyR käh-zuh*) and make your own. This chapter will help you get the food you want in just the right amount.

Shopping Around

One way to save money when you're traveling is to buy the fixings to make your own lunches and snacks or learn where to eat cheaply and easily. The list of foods and food shops in the following table should help you keep your appetite sated while you shop and sightsee. Bear in mind that the supermarket and an open-air market are the only two establishments where you are likely to find exclusively foodstuff.

Foods and Food Shops

German	Pronunciation	English
das Brot	*dAs bRoht*	bread
das Fischgeschäft	*dAs fish-guh-shäft*	fish store
das Fleisch	*dAs flaysh*	meat
das Gebäck	*dAs guh-bäk*	pastry (sweet)
das Gemüse	*dAs guh-müh-zuh*	vegetables
das Lebensmittelgeschäft	*dAs ley-buhnz-mi-tuhl-guh-shäft*	grocery store
das Obst	*dAs opst*	fruit
der Bäcker	*deyR bä-kuhR*	baker
der Fisch	*deyR fish*	fish
der Metzger	*deyR mets-guhR*	butcher
der Nachtisch	*deyR nACH-tish*	dessert
der Proviant	*deyR pRoh-vee-Ant*	provisions
der Supermarkt	*deyR zew-peR-mARkt*	supermarket
der Wein	*deyR vayn*	wine
die Bäckerei	*dee bä-kuh-Ray*	bakery
die Früchte	*dee fRüH-tuh*	fruits
die Konditorei	*dee kon-dee-toR-ay*	café, pastry shop
die Meeresfrüchte	*dee mee-Ruhs-fRüH-tuh*	seafood
die Metzgerei	*dee mets-guh-Ray*	butcher shop
die Obst- und Gemüsehandlung	*dee opst oont guh-müh-zuh-hAnt-loong*	produce shop
die Spirituosen	*dee Spee-Ree-too-oh-zuhn*	liquors
die Süßigkeiten	*dee züh-siH-kay-tuhn*	candies
die Weinhandlung	*dee vayn-hAnt-loong*	wine store

Getting There

You've familiarized yourself with all the food and pastry shops near your hotel. You're armed with nothing but your appetite and some euros! When it's time to go out into the world for supplies to stock your miniature hotel refrigerator or your backpack, use the verb *gehen* and the preposition *zu* + the correctly declined definite article to identify the store you're about to visit. Keep in mind that the preposition *zu* is always followed by the dative case. Of course, once you're there, you are *in* + dative case!

Dative Preposition and Article	Contraction	Example	English
zu + dem = (masc. and neut.)	zum	Ich gehe zum Supermarkt. *iH gey-uh tsoom zew-peR-mARkt*	I go/am going to the supermarket.
zu + der = (fem.)	zur	Ich gehe zur Weinhandlung. *iH gey-uh tsooR vayn-hant-loong*	I go/am going to the liquor store.

You know what you want—now figure out where to go to get those items! Check your responses in Appendix A.

Example: Gemüse: Ich gehe zur Obst- und Gemüsehandlung.

1. Gebäck

2. Fleisch

3. Brot

4. Fisch

Okay! So you've figured out where to go for certain items. Of course, there is more than one alternative and source for food. Some cities have a daily open-air market; in other cities, these markets might be open just one or two days a week. You can always go to a supermarket, but don't overlook the smaller stores and produce handlers proudly displaying their offerings along the sidewalk underneath awnings. Because most produce is labeled in the plural (think "tomatoes"), the following charts list most items in their plural forms, providing the singular gender afterward.

GERMAN CULTURE

To grab a quick bite to eat, stop at the German fast-food option—*der Imbiss* or *Schnellimbiss*. Located on virtually every busy corner, this is a small booth or stand where you can get a variety of sausages (*eine Curry-, Weiß-, or Knackwurst*) served on a small hard roll with mustard, French fries, and *Pommes frites* (*pomes*) to eat with a small plastic fork. Or, you can get *einen Hamburger* or *eine Frikadelle*, a hamburger without a roll.

Vegetables

German	Pronunciation	English
das Gemüse	*dAs guh-müh-zuh*	vegetables
das Sauerkraut	*dAs zou-uhR-kRout*	pickled cabbage
der Blumenkohl	*deyR blew-muhn-kohl*	cauliflower
der Brokkoli	*deyR bRo-koh-lee*	broccoli
der Champignon	*deyR sham-peen-yon*	mushrooms
der Kohl	*deyR kohl*	cabbage
der Kopfsalat	*deyR Kopf-zah-laht*	lettuce
der Mais	*deyR mays*	corn
der Sellerie	*deyR ze-luh-Ree*	celery
der Spargel	*deyR shpAR-guhl*	asparagus
der Spinat	*deyR spee-naht*	spinach
die Aubergine	*dee oh-beR-jee-nuh*	eggplant
die Bohnen, f.	*dee boh-nuhn*	beans
die Erbsen, f.	*dee eRp-suhn*	peas
die Gurken, f.	*dee gooR-kuhn*	cucumbers
die Karotten, f.	*dee kah-Ro-tuhn*	carrots
die Kartoffeln, f.	*dee kAR-to-fuhln*	potatoes
die Pilze, m.	*dee pil-tsuh*	mushrooms
die Tomaten, f.	*dee toh-mah-tuhn*	tomatoes
die Zwiebeln, f.	*dee zvee-buhln*	onions
eingelegte Gurken, f.	*ayn-gu-leyk-tuh gooR-kuhn*	pickles

Auf dem Markt is the way to express being at the open-air market. While there, you can find almost anything: fresh flowers, produce, eggs, cheese, meat, sausage, fish, bread, and so on. Because most items are labeled by name along with a price, the market is also an opportune place to learn vocabulary.

Fruits and Nuts

German	Pronunciation	English
das Obst	*dAs opst*	fruit
die Ananas	*dee A-nah-nAs*	pineapple
die Äpfel, m.	*dee Âp-fel*	apples
die Aprikosen, f.	*dee Ap-Ree-koh-zuhn*	apricots

German	Pronunciation	English
die Pfirsiche, m.	*dee pfeeR-ziH-uh*	peaches
die Bananen, f.	*dee bah-nah-nuhn*	bananas
die Birnen, f.	*dee beeR-nuhn*	pears
die Blaubeeren, f.	*dee blou-bey-Ruhn*	blueberries
die Erdbeeren, f.	*dee eRt-bey-Ruhn*	strawberries
die Haselnüsse, f.	*dee hah-zuhl-nüh-suh*	hazelnuts
die Himbeeren, f.	*dee him-bey-Ruhn*	raspberries
die Johannisbeeren, f.	*dee yoh-hA-nis-bey-Ruhn*	currants
die Kastanien, f. *or* die Maronen, f.	*dee kAs-tah-nee-uhn or dee mah-Roh-nuhn*	chestnuts
die Kirschen, f.	*dee keeR-shuhn*	cherries
die Mandeln, f.	*dee mAn-duhln*	almonds
die Melone	*dee mey-loh-nuh*	melon
die Nüsse, f.	*dee nü-suh*	nuts
die Orangen, f. *or* die Apfelsinen, f.	*dee oh-RAn-juhn or dee Ap-fel-zee-nuhn*	oranges
die Pflaumen, f.	*dee pflou-muhn*	plums
die Preiselbeeren, f.	*dee pRay-zuhl-bey-Ruhn*	cranberries
die Trauben, f.	*dee trou-buhn*	grapes
die Walnüsse, f.	*dee vAl-nüh-suh*	walnuts
die Wassermelone	*dee vA-suhR-mey-loh-nuh*	watermelon
die Rosinen, f.	*dee Roh-zee-nuhn*	raisins
die Zitronen, f.	*dee tsee-tRoh-nuhn*	lemons

At the Butcher or Delicatessen (*beim Metzger*)

German	Pronunciation	English
das Fleisch	*dAs flaysh*	meat
das Huhn *or* das Hähnchen	*dAs hewn or dAs hähn-Hen*	chicken
das Kalbfleisch	*dAs kAlp-flaysh*	veal
das Lammfleisch	*dAs lAm*	lamb
das Rindfleisch	*dAs Rint-flaysh*	beef
das Rippensteak	*dAs Ri-puhn-steyk*	rib steak

continues

At the Butcher or Delicatessen (*beim Metzger*) (continued)

German	Pronunciation	English
das Rumpfsteak	*dAs Roompf-steyk*	rump steak
das Schnitzel	*dAs shnit-suhl*	cutlet
das Schweinefleisch	*dAs shvay-nuh-flaysh*	pork
das Wiener Schnitzel	*dAs vee-nuhR-shnit-suhl*	breaded veal cutlet
der Aufschnitt	*deyR ouf-shnit*	sliced cold meat
der Hammelbraten	*deyR hA-mel-bRah-tuhn*	roast mutton
der Rinderbraten	*deyR Rin-deR-bRah-tuhn*	roast beef
der Schinken	*deyR shin-kuhn*	ham
der Speck	*deyR shpek*	bacon
die Bratwurst	*dee bRaht-vooRst*	fried sausage
die Leber	*dee ley-buhR*	liver
die Leberwurst	*dee ley-buhR-vooRst*	liver sausage
die Wurst	*dee vooRst*	sausage

Most fishmongers at the market offer sandwiches of pickled herring, smoked salmon, shrimp salad, or fried fish on crusty rolls at quite a reasonable price.

At the Fish Store (*auf dem Markt*)

German	Pronunciation	English
der Fisch	*deyR fish*	fish
der Hering	*deyR hey-ring*	herring
der Hummer	*deyR hoo-muhR*	lobster
der Kabeljau	*deyR kah-bel-you*	cod
der Krebs	*deyR kReyps*	crab
der Lachs	*deyR lAks*	salmon
der Matjes	*deyR mAt-yeyz*	young herring
der Thunfisch	*deyR tewn-fish*	tuna
der Tintenfisch	*deyR tin-tuhn-fish*	squid
die Auster	*dee ous-tuhR*	oyster
die Flunder/der Rochen	*dee floon-duhR/deyR Ro-CHuhn*	flounder
die Forelle	*dee foh-Re-luh*	trout

German	Pronunciation	English
die Garnele	*dee gahR-ney-luh*	shrimp
die Krabben (f.)	*dee kRA-buhn*	shrimp, prawns
die Meeresfrüchte (pl.)	*dee mey-Ruhs-früH-tuh*	seafood
die Seezunge	*dee zey-tsoon-guh*	sole

At the Dairy (*auf dem Markt*)

German	Pronunciation	English
das Ei/die Eier (pl.)	*dAs ay/dee ay-eR*	eggs
der Joghurt/Jogurt	*deyR yoh-gooRt*	yogurt
der Käse	*deyR käh-zuh*	cheese
der Quark	*deyR kvaRk*	soft curd cheese
die Butter	*dee boo-tuhR*	butter
die Magermilch	*dee mah-guhR-milH*	skim milk
die Sahne	*dee zah-nuh*	cream
die saure Sahne	*dee zou-Ruh zah-nuh*	sour cream
die Schlagsahne	*dee shlAk-zah-nuh*	whipped cream
die Vollmilch	*dee fol-milH*	whole milk

Although many supermarkets offer a combined bakery and pastry shop, selling both bread items and pastries, outside of that setting you will most likely encounter *eine Bäckerei* that sells only bread items and flat coffee cakes, probably some to-go type sandwiches, and coffee for drinking at a stand-up table in the bakery. If you desire a torte, piece of cake, or other delectable pastry, frequent *eine Konditorei*, where you may point to the type of pastry you'd like to savor in the establishment or get the sweet *zum Mitnehmen* to take with you. Sandwiches from a *Bäckerei* are typically open faced, so you can see what you get.

At the Bakery and Pastry Shop (*in der Bäckerei und in der Konditorei*)

German	Pronunciation	English
das Brot	*dAs broth*	bread
das Brötchen *or* die Semmel	*dAs bRöht-Huhn or deyR ze-muhl*	roll

continues

At the Bakery and Pastry Shop (*in der Bäckerei und in der Konditorei*) (continued)

German	Pronunciation	English
das Plätzchen *or* die Kekse (pl.)	*dAs pläts-Huhn or dee kek-suh*	cookie
das Roggenbrot	*dAs Ro-guhn-bRoht*	rye bread
das Toastbrot *or* der Toast	*dAs tohst-bRoht or deyR tohst*	white bread (toast)
das Vollkornbrot	*dAs fol-koRn-bRoht*	whole-grain bread
das Weißbrot	*dAs vays-bRoht*	white bread
der Apfelstrudel	*deyR Ap-fuhl-shtRew-duhl*	apple strudel
der Berliner	*deyR beR-lee-nuhR*	jelly doughnut
der Kuchen	*deyR kew-CHuhn*	cake
die Torte	*dee toR-tuh*	tart
die Kirschtorte	*dee kiRsh-toR-tuh*	cherry pie
die Schwarzwälder kirschtorte	*dee shvARts-väl-duhR-keeRsh-toR-tuh*	Black Forest (cake)

At the Supermarket (*im Supermarkt*)

German	Pronunciation	English
die Getränke	*dee guh-tRän-kuh*	drinks
das Bier	*dAs beeR*	beer
das Mineralwasser	*dAs mi-nuh-Rahl-vA-suhR*	mineral water
der Kaffee	*deyR kA-fey*	coffee
der Saft	*deyR zAft*	juice
der Tee	*deyR tey*	tea
der Wein	*deyR vayn*	wine
die Cola	*dee koh-luh*	cola
die Cola Light	*dee koh-luh layt*	diet cola
die Limonade	*dee lee-moh-nah-duh*	lemonade, or a type of soft drink
die Milch	*dee milH*	milk
kohlensäurehaltig	*koh-len-zoy-Ruh-hAl-tiH*	carbonated
nicht kohlensäurehaltig	*niHt koh-len-zoy-Ruh-hAl-tiH*	noncarbonated

When you go into a grocery store, be prepared to either bring your own reusable cloth bags or pay a small fee for the shop's sturdy plastic bags. At discount grocery stores like *Aldi*, you'll also need to put a deposit on the cart. Expect the checker to push the items into your cart, after which you'll bag them at another counter. Also bear in mind that Germany is environment friendly (*umweltfreundlich*), and you'll be charged for a deposit on most glass containers.

Prost! ("Cheers!")

On wine labels in Germany, you will come across four different categories of grapes used for wines: *Spätlese* (*shpät-ley-zuh*), indicating a dry wine; *Auslese* (*ous-ley-zuh*), indicating a fairly dry wine made from ripe grapes; *Beerenauslese* (*beyR-uhn-ous-ley-zuh*), indicating a sweet wine made from a special kind of very ripe grape; and *Trockenbeer enauslese* (*tRo-kuhn-bey-Ruhn-ous-ley-zuh*), indicating a very sweet (usually quite expensive) wine. Here are some terms you should know if you're a wine lover:

GERMAN CULTURE

Terms for beer and wine differ in different parts of Germany. In southern Germany, where most of the wine is produced, *ein Schoppen* refers to a glass of wine. Thus, to order a glass of Riesling, you would say, *Einen Schoppen Riesling, bitte!* Depending where the *Kneipe* or *Biergarten* is in Germany, you might be able to sample *eine Berliner Weiße,* beer with raspberry syrup; *ein Alsterwasser,* half beer and half Sprite; *einen Radler,* the southern Germany equivalent of beer and Sprite; or *ein Diesel,* a mixture of beer and cola.

German	Pronunciation	English
leicht	*layHt*	light
lieblich	*leep-liH*	sweet
mild	*milt*	mild
(sehr) trocken	(*zeyR*) *tRo-kuhn*	(very) dry

If you're a beer drinker, put down this book, go to your local brew pub, and take a sip of a good German beer. Your taste buds will tell you more about German beer than we possibly can. Here are a few terms and phrases that might help you in a German *Kneipe* (*knay-puh*, f.), or pub:

German	Pronunciation	English
ein Altbier	*ayn Alt-beeR*	a bitter ale
ein Bier, bitte	*ayn beeR, bi-tuh*	a beer, please
ein Bier vom Fass	*ayn beeR fom fAs*	a draft beer
ein dunkles Bier	*ayn doon-kluhs beeR*	a dark beer
ein helles Bier	*ayn he-luhs beeR*	a light beer
ein Pils	*ayn pilts*	a pilsner (light beer)

You can use the verb *trinken* to order a beer or that special glass of wine. The following table is not quite complete. Because *trinken* is a normal strong verb (incurring no stem-vowel change in the present tense), you can go ahead and prove your mastery of present tense verb endings by applying them to the stem here so conveniently provided!

Conjugation of the Verb *trinken*

Person	Singular	English	Plural	English
First	ich trink**e**	I drink	wir trink**en**	we drink
Second	du trink**st**	you drink	ihr trink**t**	you drink
Third	er, sie, es trink**t**	he, she, it drinks	sie trink**en**	they drink
Formal	Sie trink**en**	you drink	Sie trink**en**	you drink

Worked up a thirst, have you? Picture yourself in a *Biergarten* in München. How would you ask someone what he or she wants to drink? How would you answer someone if you were asked? How would you explain to someone what the people around you are imbibing? Fill in the blanks with the correct form of *trinken*. Check your conjugations in Appendix A.

Example: Der Mann _____ ein Bier vom Fass.

Answer: Der Mann <u>trinkt</u> ein Bier vom Fass.

    1. Was möchten Sie _____?

    2. Ich _____ ein Bier.

    3. Die beiden Frauen am Nachbartisch _____ Kaffee.

    4. Mattias und ich _____ gern lieblichen Wein.

5. Am liebsten _____ ich Limonade.

6. Was _____ du am liebsten?

It's the Quantity That Counts

Track 14 You've been invited to an outdoor buffet in the countryside. The hostess has asked you to bring cheese and meat. The hostess has invited just a few other people, so you figure a pound each of cheese and meat ought to be enough. When you go to *der Supermarkt*, however, the man behind the counter does not understand how much cheese or meat you want. In Germany, the metric system is used for measuring quantities of food. Liquids are measured in liters. Let the following table help you order the right amounts of meat and cheese so you don't have any leftovers. Also, check out Track 14 of the CD included with this book to hear the pronunciation of some of these examples.

AS A RULE

You'll notice that the German measurements and weights are in the singular. That's rather economical, if you consider it. The *zwei* in front of *Pfund* already conveys the idea of more than 1 pound! Speaking of pounds, *ein Pfund* is approximately *ein halbes Kilo* (half a kilogram). Naturally, any rule of the fist (*Faustregel*) has exceptions—the feminine measurement quantities take the plural: *zwei Flaschen Mineralwasser*.

Getting the Right Amount

German	Pronunciation	Amount
ein Becher	*ayn be-HuhR*	a container of
ein Dutzend	*ayn doo-tsent*	a dozen
ein Gefäß	*ayn guh-fähs*	a jar of
ein Glas	*ayn glAs*	a glass
ein halbes Pfund (250 Gramm)	*ayn hAl-buhs pfoont (250 gRAm)*	a half pound of (250 grams)
ein Liter	*ayn lee-tuhR*	a liter of
ein Packet	*ayn pA-keyt*	a package of

continues

Getting the Right Amount (continued)

German	Pronunciation	Amount
ein Pfund (ein halbes Kilo) (500 Gramm)	*ayn pfoont* *(ayn hAl-buhs kee-loh)* *(500 gRAm)*	a pound of (a half kilo) (500 grams)
ein Sack	*ayn zAk*	a bag of
ein Stück	*ayn shtük*	a piece of
ein Viertel	*ayn feeR-tuhl*	a quarter of
eine Dose	*ay-nuh doh-zuh*	a can of
eine Flasche	*ay-nuh flA-shuh*	a bottle of
eine Kiste	*ay-nuh kis-tuh*	a case of
eine Schachtel	*ay-nuh shACH-tuhl*	a box of
eine Scheibe	*ay-nuh shay-buh*	a slice of
eine Tüte	*ay-nuh tüh-tuh*	a sack
zwei Pfund (ein Kilo)	*tsvay pfoont* *(ayn kee-loh)*	2 pounds of (1 kilo)

ACHTUNG

To ask for a slice of cheese in German, you say, *Ich möchte eine Scheibe Käse* (iH möH-tuh ay-nuh shay-buh käh-zuh). To ask for a specific kind of cheese, however, you say (pointing at the cheese), *Ich möchte eine Scheibe von diesem Käse dort* (iH möH-tuh ay-nuh shay-buh fon dee-zuhm käh-zuh doRt), or, "I would like a slice of that cheese there."

What if you want to try a bit of something before buying it, or if you simply want to have a taste or a bite of someone else's dessert after dinner? Here are a few expressions you may find useful.

German	Pronunciation	English
ein bisschen	*ayn bis-Huhn*	a little bit of
etwas	*et-vAs*	some
genug	*guh-newk*	enough
mehr	*meyR*	more
viel	*feel*	a lot of

German	Pronunciation	English
wenig	*vey-niH*	little/not much
weniger	*vey-nee-guhR*	less/fewer
zu viel	*tsew feel*	too much
zu wenig	*tsew vey-niH*	too little/not enough

A Trip to the Market

You have written a list of foods you will need for a picnic (*ein Picknick*) with a group of friends. As you approach the outdoor farmer's market where you want to do your shopping, however, you realize that your English list of ingredients will be of little use to you. As you pass by the stands, someone calls out: "Frische Äpfel!" Someone else calls out: "Zwölf Eier für nur ein Euro!" To make yourself understood, you must translate everything on your list into German and politely request the items. Check your translations in Appendix A.

Example: (a jar of pickles)

Answer: Ich möchte ein Glas eingelegte Gurken, bitte.

1. Three bottles of wine

2. A half pound of shrimp

3. One fourth of a pound of cheese

4. A bag of cherries

5. A dozen eggs

6. One kilogram of salmon

7. Three pounds of potatoes

8. A half kilogram of sausage

9. A liter of cream

10. A case of beer

Getting What You Want

Are you tired of the crowds in supermarkets? Go to one of the smaller neighborhood stores on a less-frequented side street near your hotel. These are sometimes referred to as a *Tante-Emma-Laden* (literally, an "Aunt Emma Store"). Although the selection is less extensive than at a supermarket, you'll find most everything you desire. Someone there will probably be happy to help you with your shopping. Be prepared for the following questions:

> Was möchten Sie?
> *vAs möH-tuhn zee*
> What would you like?

> Was wünschen Sie?
> *vAs vün-shuhn zee*
> What can I do for you?

> Kann ich Ihnen helfen?
> *kAn iH ee-nuhn hel-fuhn?*
> May I help you?

 Track 14 You might begin your answer with one of the following phrases (if you'd like to hear how to pronounce these responses, check out Track 14 of the CD included with this book):

> Ich möchte ….
> *iH möH-tuh*
> I would like ….

> Können Sie mir … geben?
> *kö-nuhn zee meeR … gey-buhn*
> Could you give me …?

> Bitte
> *bi-tuh*
> please

You might then be asked:

Sonst noch etwas?	Ist das alles?
zonst noH et-vAs	*ist dAs A-luhs*
Something else?	Is that all?

An appropriate response would be to give additional items you need or to answer:

> Ja (Danke), das ist alles.
> *ya (dAn-kuh), dAs ist ah-luhs*
> Yes (thank you), that's all.

You are *auf dem Markt*. Can you construct a dialogue between you and a clerk? Are you prepared to state specific amounts and to respond to the clerk's questions? Review this chapter and try to construct a useful dialogue.

The Least You Need to Know

- You should know the names of German foods and types of stores.
- *Ich möchte* followed by the desired item (and amount) will get you almost anything you want.
- Don't forget your "please" and "thank you" with *bitte* and *danke schön*.

Chapter 18

Restaurant Hopping

In This Chapter

- Figuring out the gastronomic possibilities
- How to order in a restaurant, bar, or café
- How to figure out exactly what you want
- Dietary preferences

Germany is a country well-known for hearty, satisfying repasts. Of course, before you can even begin to satisfy your hunger by venturing into an eating venue, you must know how to order whatever you want in German (it wouldn't hurt to be able to understand the specials when the waiter recites them, either). By the end of this chapter, you will be able to order meals in German and make specific requests.

Where Can I Get Something to Eat Around Here?
(*Wo kann ich denn hier etwas zu essen bekommen?*)

You'll be happy to know that when hunger strikes, many types of eating establishments are waiting to feed you. The one you choose depends on the following factors: the kind of meal you want, the kind of service you want, and the size of your budget. Are you looking for breakfast, *das Frühstück* (*dAs fRüh-shtük*); for lunch, *das Mittagessen* (*dAs mi-tahk-e-suhn*); or for dinner, *das Abendessen* (*dAs ah-buhnt-e-suhn*)?

Germany has many different words for places where one can eat or drink something. Try one of these:

- *der Imbiss (deyR im-bis)*, fast-food stand or snack counter
- *das Café (dAs kA-fey)*, coffee house serving mainly desserts and light dishes such as open-faced sandwiches
- *das Restaurant (dAs Res-tou-Rohn)*, general word for "restaurant"
- *das Lokal (dAs loh-kAl)*, general word for an establishment that serves food and drinks
- *die Gaststätte (dee gAst-shtä-tuh)*, full-service restaurant
- *der Gasthof/das Gasthaus (deyR gAst-hof, dAs gAst-hous)*, small inn with pub or restaurant
- *die Kneipe (dee knay-puh)*, small, simple pub or bar
- *die Studentenkneipe (dee shtew-den-tuhn-knay-puh)*, typical place where students gather, serving drinks and simple food
- *das Wirtshaus (dAs veeRts-hous)*, pub serving mainly alcoholic beverages and some food

GERMAN CULTURE

Water, water everywhere and not a drop to drink! In Germany, you won't find the obligatory glass of water on your table. A word of caution: if you ask for water in a restaurant (*ein Glas Wasser, bitte*), you will most likely get and be charged for a glass of mineral water—and a bubbly one, at that. If you really want just plain (free) tap water, ask for *Leitungswasser (lay-tungz-vA-suhr)*.

When you do finally pick a restaurant, you'll probably have to know how to do a few things before you get there. You may have to call to find out the exact location of the restaurant. If the restaurant is a good one and it's the weekend, you'll need to make a reservation. But never forgo the opportunity to stumble across a wonderful *Lokal* by strolling around, perusing the menu posted outside, and sneaking in for a peek. You'll also get an idea of what time a restaurant serves until by finding the phrase *warme Küche bis …*—literally, "warm cuisine until …." The following list contains some phrases you may find useful when dining out:

German	Pronunciation	English
Ich möchte einen Tisch reservieren …	*iH möH-tuh ay-nuhn tish Re-zuhR-vee-Ruhn*	I would like to reserve a table …
für heute Abend.	*führ hoy-tuh ah-bent*	for this evening.
für morgen Abend.	*führ moR-guhn ah-bent*	for tomorrow evening.
für Samstag Abend.	*führ zAmz-tahk ah-bent*	for Saturday night.
für zwei Personen.	*führ tsvay peR-zoh-nuhn*	for two people.
auf der Terrasse, bitte.	*ouf deyR te-RA-suh, bi-tuh*	on the terrace, please.
im Biergarten.	*im beeR-gAR-tuhn*	in the beer garden.
am Fenster.	*Am fen-stuhR*	at the window.
im Raucherbereich.	*im Rou-CHuhR-buh-RayH*	in the smoking section.
im Nichtraucherbereich.	*im niHt-Rou-HuhR-buh-RayH*	in the nonsmoking section.
an der Theke.	*An deyR tey-kuh*	at the bar.

Remember that when you use the modal verb *möchte*, the dependent infinitive, *reservieren*, should come at the end of the sentence, as in the following examples:

> Ich möchte einen Tisch für heute Abend reservieren.
> *iH möH-tuh ay-nuhn tish führ hoy-tuh ah-bent Re-zuhR-vee-Ruhn*
> I'd like to reserve a table for this evening.

> Ich möchte einen Tisch für Samstag Abend für zwei Personen auf der Terasse reservieren.
> *iH möH-tuh ay-nuhn tish führ zAmz-tahk ah-bent führ tsvay peR-zoh-nuhn ouf deyR te-RA-suh Re-zuhR-vee-Ruhn*
> I'd like to reserve a table for two on the terrace for Saturday evening.

Dining Out

It's Saturday night, and you want to try the fare at one of the fanciest restaurants in Berlin. Call and make a reservation. Be aware that smoking is more accepted and much more widely tolerated in Germany than in the United States. The person on the other end of the line may ask you this question:

> Einen Tisch für wie viele Personen?
> *ay-nuhn tish fühR vee fee-luh peR-zoh-nuhn*
> A table for how many people?

Answer this way:

> Einen Tisch für vier Personen, bitte.
> *ay-nuhn tish fühR feeR peR-zoh-nuhn, bi-tuh*
> A table for four, please.

You've arrived at the restaurant, and the hostess has seated you. Now what? Bear in mind that German restaurant service is different from American service. Your server in Germany will not rush you. In fact, you may have to assert yourself to get certain things done. Not to say that you have to be pushy, but you are in control of your dining experience—you own that table until you are ready to depart. But before you depart, did you hold your utensils in the European fashion? Germans hold the knife in the right hand and the fork in the left and don't switch them around. They also tend to keep their hands on the table at all times rather than resting a hand in their laps.

AS A RULE

In all but the most exclusive restaurants in German-speaking countries, if the restaurant is very crowded, it is acceptable and quite normal for people to ask to share a table. In fact, there is typically no host for seating, so simply ask an occupied table: *Ist hier noch frei?* "Is this seat taken?" If it is still available, you'll hear, *Ja, hier ist noch frei.* If it's already taken, listen for the word *besetzt* (*buh-zetst*), as in *Nein, hier ist besetzt,* telling you that the seat is taken.

Track 15 Regardless of *how* you eat, the next chart provides some useful phrases *im Restaurant.* Check out Track 15 of the CD included with this book to hear some of the examples.

Eating Out

German	Pronunciation	English
Wir/ich möchten/möchte gern bestellen.	*veer/iH möH-tuhn/ möH-tuh geRn buh-shte-luhn*	We/I would like to order.
Bitte schön. Was darf's sein?	*bi-tuh shön, vAs dARfs zayn*	What would you like?
Was bekommen Sie?	*vas buh-ko-muhn zee*	What would you like?

German	Pronunciation	English
Ich möchte gern ...	*iH möH-tuh geRn*	I would like ...
Ich nehme ...	*iH ney-muh*	I'll take ...
Was empfehlen Sie?	*vAs em-pfey-luhn zee*	What do you recommend?
Und zu trinken?	*oont tsew trin-kuhn*	And to drink?
Bringen Sie mir bitte ...	*brin-guhn zee meer bi-tuh*	Please bring me ...
Hat's geschmeckt?	*hAts guh-shmekt*	Did it taste good?
Ja, es hat sehr gut geschmeckt.	*ya, es hAt zeyR gewt guh-shmekt*	Yes, it was very tasty.
Ja, sehr.	*ya, zehR*	Yes, very good.
Zahlen, bitte!	*tsah-luhn, bi-tuh*	Check, please.
die Speisekarte	*dee shpay-zuh-kAR-tuh*	menu
kalte Teller	*kAl-tuh te-luhR*	cold dishes
warme Teller	*wAR-muh te-luhR*	warm dishes
die Vorspeise	*dee foR-shpay-zuh*	appetizer
das Gericht	*dAs guh-riHt*	dish (of food)
das Hauptgericht	*dAs houpt-guh-RiHt*	main dish
die Beilage	*dee bay-lah-guh*	side dish
die Nachspeise *or* der Nachtisch	*dee nACH-shpay-zuh* or *deyR nACH-tish*	dessert

What if, when your appetizer comes, you have no cutlery with which to eat? Also, if you're thirsty, you'll need a glass of something. The terms in the following table should be of use to you when you are in a restaurant and want to identify and label everything on your table.

ACHTUNG

Do not confuse *das Menü (dAs mey-nüh)* with the printed menu, *die Speisekarte (dee shpay-zuh-kAR-tuh)*. *Das Menü* is a set combination of items from the menu at a specific price. There may be several offered each day.

A Table Setting

German	Pronunciation	English
das Besteck	*dAs buh-stek*	cutlery
das Geschirr	*dAs guh-sheeR*	tableware
die Gabel	*dee gah-buhl*	fork
das Glas	*dAs glAs*	glass
der Löffel	*deyR lö-fuhl*	spoon
die Kellnerin	*dee kel-nuh-Rin*	waitress
der Kellner	*deyR kel-nuhR*	waiter
das Messer	*dAs me-suhR*	knife
die Pfeffermühle	*dee pfe-fuhR-müh-luh*	pepper mill
der Salzstreuer	*deyR zAlts-shtRoy-uhR*	salt shaker
die Serviette	*dee zeR-vee-e-tuh*	napkin
der Suppenlöffel	*deyR zoo-puhn-lö-fuhl*	soup spoon
der Suppenteller	*deyR zoo-puhn-te-luhR*	soup dish
die Tasse	*dee tA-suh*	cup
der Teelöffel	*deyR tey-lö-fuhl*	teaspoon
der Teller	*deyR te-luhR*	dinner plate
die Tischdecke	*dee tish-de-kuh*	tablecloth
die Untertasse	*dee oon-teR-tA-suh*	saucer

Something's Missing

If something is missing from your table setting and you need to ask the waiter for it, the verb *fehlen* (*fey-luhn*) will empower you to state what is missing; *fehlen* takes the dative case. The great thing about dative verbs in general is that they allow the subject (focus) of the utterance to be on the item being discussed. For instance, your fork is missing: *Mir fehlt die Gabel* translates literally into "To me is missing the fork." But isn't this what you really mean? And doesn't this give you a chance to practice all the dative personal pronouns you learned in Chapter 16?

Try your hand at describing what's missing from the table by using the dative verb *fehlen*. Begin with the dative pronoun for the person who's missing the item.

Example: your napkin is missing, thus, *Dir fehlt die Serviette*. Note that the form of the verb is in the third person singular because the subject of the sentence is *die Serviette*, the napkin. You will begin each statement with the dative personal pronoun that reflects who is missing something, followed by the verb that is conjugated to agree with the subject—the thing that is missing! Check your command of dative pronouns with the verb *fehlen* in Appendix A.

1. My cup is missing.

2. His spoon is missing.

3. Her knife is missing.

4. Our salt shaker is missing.

You Need What?

Suppose that the table isn't already set, and you *need* something. Remember how to express a need? In Chapter 12, you learned how to ask for extra amenities for your hotel room. Now tell your waiter what you need by using those items from the preceding table and the verb *brauchen*. Remember, the items following the verb will bein the accusative case and must be declined correctly. Check your sentences in Appendix A.

Example: How would you say you need a plate?

Ich brauche einen Teller.

1. How would you ask for a menu?

2. How would you ask for a glass?

3. How would you ask for a napkin?

4. How would you ask for a saucer?

Waiter, I'd Like ...

To get the attention of your server, simply signal with your hand, or say *Bedienung*, which covers both male and female servers. Your waiter tonight asks whether you want to start with something to drink. Use the phrase *ich hätte gern (iH hä-tuh geRn)* followed by whatever you would like (in the accusative case). To tell the waiter that you want mineral water, for example, you would say: *Ich hätte gern ein Mineralwasser, bitte* (*hätte* = would like to have). The following table lists popular German dishes for a hearty appetite, *für den großen Hunger.*

GERMAN CULTURE

You'll find loads of international cuisine in Germany. You can eat *griechisch* (Greek), *chinesisch* (Chinese), *indisch* (Indian), *japanisch* (Japanese), and so on. If you opt for *italienisch* (Italian), expect *eine Pizza* to be individual sized. And do not order a *Pizza mit Peperoni* unless you want a pizza with hot chili peppers. If you want something closer to the American "pepperoni pizza," order a *Pizza mit Salami.*

Meat or Fish as a Main Course (*Fleisch oder Fisch als Hauptgericht*)

German	Pronunciation	English
das Bündnerfleisch	*dAs bünt-nuhR-flaysh*	thinly sliced, air-dried beef
das deutsche Beefsteak	*dAs doy-tshuh beef-steyk*	Salisbury steak
das Gulasch	*dAs goo-lAsh*	beef stew with spicy paprika
das Lammkotelett	*dAs lAm-kot-let*	lamb chop
das Spanferkel	*dAs shpAn-feR-kuhl*	suckling pig/pig roast
die Leber	*dee ley-buhR*	liver
das Naturschnitzel	*dAs nah-tooR-shnit-suhl*	unbreaded veal cutlet
das Schweinskotlett	*dAs shvaynz-kot-let*	pork chop
das Wienerschnitzel	*dAs vee-nuhR-shnit-suhl*	breaded veal cutlet
das Jägerschnitzel	*dAs yäh-guhR-shnit-suhl*	veal/pork cutlet with mushrooms and peppers
das Zigeunerschnitzel	*dAs tsi-goy-nuhR-shnit-suhl*	cutlet with a spicy sauce of red and green peppers
der Bauernschmaus	*deyR bou-uhRn-shmous*	smoked pork, sausages, dumpling, tomato, and sauerkraut
der Hackbraten	*deyR hAk-bRah-tuhn*	meatloaf
der Kalbsbraten	*deyR kAlps-bRah-tuhn*	roast veal
der Rinderbraten	*deyR Rin-duhR-bRah-tuhn*	roast beef
der Sauerbraten	*deyR zou-uhR-bRah-tuhn*	marinated pot roast
die Hühnerbrust	*dee hüh-nuhR-broost*	chicken breast
der Huhn vom Rost	*deyR hewn fom Rost*	grilled chicken

German	Pronunciation	English
die Ente mit Rotkohl	*dee en-tuh mit Rot-kohl*	duckling with red cabbage
der Leberkäs	*deyR ley-buhR-kähs*	a type of meatloaf in southern Germany
Matjes nach Hausfrauenart	*mA-tyeyz nACH hous-frou-uhn-ARt*	young herring in cream with apples and onions
der Stockfisch in Rahmsauce	*deyR shtok-fish in Rahm-Zos*	salt cod in cream
die geräucherte Forelle	*dee guh-Roy-HuhR-tuh fo-Re-luh*	smoked trout

That's the Way I Like It

With certain dishes, you have a choice about how they're served or cooked. For example, if you order eggs, you'll want to let the waiter know how you like them cooked. Your waiter may ask you something like this:

> Wie wollen (möchten) Sie sie (ihn, es)?
> *vee vo-luhn (möH-tuhn) zee zee (een, es)*
> How do you want them (it)?

The adjectives and egg items in the following table provide you with possibilities.

How Would You Like It Prepared?

German	Pronunciation	English
angebräunt	*An-guh-bRoynt*	browned
blutig/halb durch	*blew-tiH/hAlp dooRCH*	rare
gut durchgebraten	*gewt dooRCH-guh-bRA-tuhn*	well-done
gebacken	*guh-bA-kuhn*	baked
gebraten	*guh-bRA-tuhn*	roasted
gedünstet	*guh-düns-tuht*	steamed
paniert	*pah-neeRt*	breaded
püriert	*püh-ReeRt*	puréed/mashed
das Omelett	*dAs om-let*	omelet
das Spiegelei	*dAs shpee-guhl-ay*	fried eggs

continues

How Would You Like It Prepared?   (continued)

German	Pronunciation	English
die Rühreier	*dee RühR-ay-uhR*	scrambled eggs
hartgekocht	*hARt-guh-koCHt*	hard-boiled
pochiert	*po-sheeRt*	poached
weichgekocht	*vayH-guh-koCHt*	soft-boiled

Is anything more frustrating in a restaurant than having your favorite food arrive at your table overcooked, undercooked, too greasy, or over easy instead of scrambled? Practice expressing what you want the way you want it. These words may come in handy when someone else is doing the cooking. Check your orders in Appendix A.

Example: Ich möchte meine Eier _____ (soft-boiled).

Answer: Ich möchte meine Eier <u>weich gekocht</u>.

1. Sie möchte ihr Steak _____ (well-done).

2. Hans möchte seinen Fisch _____ (breaded).

3. Wir möchten unsere Kartoffeln _____ (mashed).

4. Ich möchte mein Gemüse _____ (steamed).

5. Ich hätte gern _____ (fried eggs).

Spice It Up

If your tongue's idea of heaven is hot chilies and spicy salsa, German food might seem a little bland. Spice things up with seasonings. The following table provides a list of some common herbs, spices, and condiments.

Herbs, Spices, and Condiments

German	Pronunciation	English
das Basilikum	*dAs bah-zee-lee-koom*	basil
die Butter	*dee boo-tuhR*	butter
der Dill	*deyR dil*	dill
der Essig	*deyR e-siH*	vinegar
der Honig	*deyR hoh-niH*	honey

German	Pronunciation	English
der Knoblauch	*deyR knobb-louCH*	garlic
die Konfitüre	*dee kon-fi-tüh-Ruh*	jam
die Kräuter (pl.)	*dee kroy-tuhR*	herbs
die Marmelade	*dee mAR-muh-lah-duh*	jam
die Mayonnaise	*dee mah-yoh-nay-zuh*	mayonnaise
der Meerrettich	*deyR mey-Re-tiH*	horseradish
das Öl	*dAs öhl*	oil
der Oregano	*deyR oh-Rey-gah-no*	oregano
der Pfeffer	*deyR pfe-fuhR*	pepper
das Salz	*dAs zAlts*	salt
der Senf	*deyR zenf*	mustard
der Zucker	*deyR tsoo-kuhR*	sugar

Special Diets

Do you get little red spots all over your face when you eat strawberries? Are you on a restricted diet? Be prepared to use the following phrases to express your special needs.

AS A RULE

An important way to express negation is to use the negative article, *kein*. The declination of *kein* mirrors that of *ein*. It may be used to negate a noun that would be preceded by the indefinite article *ein* or no article. *Wir haben keine Speisekarte* means "We don't have a menu." The negative of *Ich habe Hunger,* "I am hungry," is *Ich habe keinen Hunger,* "I am not hungry."

German	Pronunciation	English
Ich bin auf (einer) Diät.	*iH bin ouf (ay-nuhR) dee-eyt*	I am on a diet.
Ich bin Vegetarier/Vegetarierin.	*iH bin vey-gey-tah-Ree-uhR*	I'm a vegetarian.
Ich kann nichts essen, was … enthält.	*iH kAn niHst e-suhn, vAs … ent-hält*	I can't eat anything with … in it.
Ich kann kein (e, -en) … essen (trinken).	*iH kAn kayn (uh, -uhn) e-suhn (tRin-Kuhn)*	I can't have …

continues

continued

German	Pronunciation	English
die Meeresfrüchte	*dee mey-Ruhs-fRüH-tuh*	seafood
die gesättigten Fette	*dee guh-zä-tiH-tuhn fe-tuh*	saturated fats
Ich suche nach einem Gericht mit niedrigem Cholesteringehalt.	*iH zew-CHuh nACH ay-nuhm guh-RiHt mit nee-dRee-guhm ko-les-tey-Reen-guh-hAlt*	I'm looking for a dish (that is) low in cholesterol.
niedrigem Fettgehalt	*nee-dRee-guhm fet-guh-hAlt*	low in fat
niedrigem Natriumgehalt	*nee-dRee-guhm nA-tRee-oom-guh-hAlt*	low in sodium
keine Milchprodukte	*kay-nuh milH-pRo-duk-tuh*	non-dairy
salzfrei	*zAlts-fRay*	salt-free
zuckerfrei	*tsoo-kuhR-fRay*	sugar-free

Something Light

If you're not a big eater or you aren't very hungry, tell the server *Ich habe keinen großen Hunger*—literally, "I don't have a big hunger" or "I'm not very hungry." Or, state that you want something small: *Ich möchte eine Kleinigkeit essen.* Numerous soups, potato dishes, and salads will fit the bill. You might find the following items on a menu listed under the heading *für den kleinen Hunger* (for a small appetite).

Soups, Potatoes, and Salads (*Suppen, Kartoffeln, und Salate*)

German	Pronunciation	English
die Bauernsuppe	*dee bou-uhRn-zoo-puh*	cabbage and sausage soup
die Bohnensuppe	*dee boh-nuhn-zoo-puh*	bean soup
die Frühlingssuppe	*dee fRüh-links-zoo-puh*	spring vegetable soup
die Kraftbrühe mit Ei	*dee kRAft-bRüh-huh mit ay*	beef broth with egg
die Linsensuppe	*dee lin-zuhn-zoo-puh*	lentil soup
die Ochsenschwanzsuppe	*dee ok-suhn-shvAnts-zoo-puh*	oxtail soup
die Tomatensuppe	*dee toh-mah-tuhn-zoo-puh*	tomato soup
das Bauernfrühstück	*dAs bou-uhRn-früh-shtük*	bacon and potato omelet

German	Pronunciation	English
die Bratkartoffeln	*dee bRAt-kAR-to-fuhln*	hash browns, roasted potatoes
die Ofenkartoffel	*dee oh-fuhn-kAR-to-fuhl*	baked potato
die Salzkartoffeln	*dee zAlts-kAr-to-fuhln*	salted, boiled potatoes
Kartoffelpuffer/brei/püree	*kAR-to-fuhl poo-fuhR/bray/ püh-rey*	whipped potatoes
eine große Portion	*ay-nuh gro-suh poR-tseeon*	a large portion
eine kleine Portion	*ay-nuh klay-nuh poR-tseeon*	a small portion
ein kleiner Salat	*ayn klay-nuhR zah-lAt*	a small salad
der Bauernsalat	*deyR bou-uhRn-zah-lAt*	green salad with cheese, tomatoes, onions, and olives in a vinaigrette
der Bohnensalat	*deyR boh-nuhn-zah-lAt*	pickled bean salad
ein gemischter Salat	*ayn guh-mish-tuhR zah-lAt*	a green salad with pickled vegetables
der Gurkensalat	*deyR gooR-kuhn-zah-lAt*	pickled cucumber salad
der Geflügelsalat	*deyR guh-flüh-guhl-zah-lAt*	chicken salad

And now you're done. Where's the check (*die Rechnung*)? In the server's mind and pocket, of course. Unlike in the United States, where the server places the bill on the table fairly soon after you put down your fork, the Germans let you take your time. You pay the bill when you're ready by telling your server *Zahlen, bitte*. The server will calculate the bill at the table and expect you to pay on the spot. Separate checks are the norm.

How About Some Strudel, Sweetie?

Do you have a sweet tooth? Then your favorite part of the meal is probably the end of it. In Germany, your sweet tooth will be satisfied. Cake is normally eaten around 4:00 in the afternoon for *Kaffee* (*kA-fey*), an early afternoon coffee break. The following table lists some of the most delicious desserts.

Delectable Desserts (*leckere Nachspeisen*)

German	Pronunciation	English
der Apfelstrudel	*deyR ap-fuhl-shtrew-duhl*	apple strudel
der Kuchen	*deyR kew-CHuhn*	coffee-cake type of cake, often including fruit or poppyseeds
der Obstsalat	*deyR opst-zah-laht*	fruit salad
der Pfirsich Melba	*deyR pfeeR-ziH mel-bah*	peach Melba
der Schokoladenpudding	*deyR shoh-koh-lah-duhn-poo-ding*	chocolate pudding
die Pfannkuchen (pl.)	*dee pfAn-kew-CHuhn*	crepes (pl.)
die Rote Grütze	*dee Roh-tuh gRü-tsuh*	red berry compote
die Sachertorte	*dee zA-CHuhR-toR-tuh*	chocolate cake
die Schwarzwalder kirschtorte	*dee shvARts-väl-duhR keeRsh-toR-tuh*	Black Forest cake
die Torte	*dee toR-tuh*	layered cake or fruit tart

If you're an ice cream lover, of course, you'll want to go to an ice cream vendor—just look for anything containing the word *Eis.* You'll find ice cream parlors where you can sit and relax for a long while at cute little tables. Or, if you prefer eating on the run, find an ice cream vendor who sells ice cream by the very small scoop—*eine Kugel.* You'll want to try at least three varieties! The following terms will help you get the amount and flavor you want.

German	Pronunciation	English
das Eis	*dAs ays*	ice cream
as Erdbeereis	*dAs eRt-beyR-ays*	strawberry ice cream
das Haselnusseis	*dAs hah-zuhl-noos-ays*	hazelnut ice cream
das Pistazieneis	*dAs pi-stah-tsee-uhn-ays*	pistachio ice cream
das Schokoladeneis	*dAs shoh-koh-lah-den-ays*	chocolate ice cream
das Vanilleeis	*dAs vah-ni-lee-uh-ays*	vanilla ice cream
der Eisbecher	*deyR ays-be-HuhR*	dish of ice cream
mit Schlagsahne	*mit shlAk-zah-nuh*	with whipped cream
mit Schokoladensoße	*mit shoh-koh-lah-den-zoh-suh*	with chocolate sauce
in einer Waffel	*in ay-nuhR vA-fuh*	in a waffle cone

Are You Thirsty? (*Hast du Durst?*)

If you're not a wine or beer drinker, you may want to know how to order certain nonalcoholic beverages with your dinner. The following table provides a list of drinks you might enjoy at any time before, during, or after dinner or at the *Eiscafé* in the late afternoon.

ACHTUNG

Although many establishments in Germany accept credit cards, plastic is a less widespread phenomenon in Germany than it is in the United States. Be sure that you see the imprimatur of your credit card company on the window or menu of the establishment where you're about to eat!

Beverages (*Getränke*)

German	Pronunciation	English
der Kaffee	*deyR kA-fey*	coffee
ein Kaffee mit Milch	*ayn kA-fey mit milH*	a coffee with milk
ein Kaffee mit Zucker	*ayn kA-fey mit tsoo-kuhR*	a coffee with sugar
ein schwarzer Kaffee	*ayn shvAr-tsuhR kA-fey*	a black coffee
ein entkoffinierter Kaffee	*ayn ent-ko-fi-neeR-tuhR kA-fey*	a decaffeinated coffee
ein Eiskaffee	*aynn ays-kA-fey*	an iced coffee
der Cappuccino	*deyR ka-poo-chee-no*	cappuccino, often served with whipped cream
mit Schlagsahne	*mit shlAk-zah-nuh*	with whipped cream
eine Cola	*ay-nuh ko-lA*	a coke
eine Cola Light	*ay-nuh ko-lA layt*	a diet coke
der Tee	*deyR tey*	tea
ein Tee mit Zitrone	*ayn tey mit tsee-tRoh-nuh*	a tea with lemon
das Mineralwasser	*dAs mi-nuh-Rahl-vA-suhR*	mineral water

Good Morning, Say Cheese

In Germany, cheese often accompanies *Wurst* as a part of a fortifying breakfast. Yogurt, coffee, tea, juice, fresh rolls, cereal, butter, jam, honey, fresh fruit, and other yummy things help round out the typical German breakfast. Here are some expressions that will help you determine the cheese that is most to your liking.

GERMAN CULTURE

In most German restaurants, *das Trinkgeld* (tRink-gelt)—the tip—is included in the price of the meal (generally 15 percent). Still, it is common practice to round up the bill. If your bill is 10,50€, for example, you might give the waiter 11€ or 12€ and say, (*Es*) *stimmt so*, the equivalent of "Keep the change."

German	Pronunciation	English
der Käse	*deyR käh-zuh*	cheese
hart	*hARt*	hard
mild	*milt*	mild
scharf	*shARf*	sharp
weich	*vayH*	soft
würzig	*vüR-tsiH*	spicy

As for the rest of breakfast, most places where you might stay overnight offer a buffet-style breakfast. You merely choose between *Kaffee oder Tee* and select whatever else you desire. You danced till dawn, and now you are hungry. You think, *Ich habe Hunger!* Go over to that *Frühstücksbuffet* and talk about what you would like to eat, remembering to place whatever it is that you are desiring in the accusative case.

Ich möchte ….

Ich nehme ….

Ich hätte gern ….

It Was Delicious

Don't keep your satisfaction to yourself when you like what you've eaten. To express joy, pleasure, amazement, and wonder when a meal has been exceptional, use the following superlative phrases.

Das Essen war ausgezeichnet!
dAs e-suhn vahR ous-guh-tsayH-nuht
The meal was great!

Das Steak war vorzüglich!
dAs steyk vahR foR-tsühk-liH
The steak was excellent!

Die Bedienung ist großartig!
dee buh-dee-nung ist gRohs-AR-tiH
The service is great!

This chapter ends with the very last thing you need to know in a restaurant: how to ask for your bill. Remember, *Zahlen, bitte!* Well, there's another way of expressing yourself. Take your pick!

Die Rechnung bitte.
dee ReH-noong bi-tuh
The check, please.

The Least You Need to Know

- You can find someplace to eat by asking, *Wo kann ich denn hier etwas zu essen bekommen?*
- In Germany, the customer controls the pace of service in a restaurant.
- You can read a German menu with very little difficulty and satiate a large or a small appetite.
- You can express dietary preferences and pleasures.

You're Invited: "Would You Like to ...?"

Chapter 19

In This Chapter

- Having fun in Germany
- Extending, accepting, and refusing invitations
- Using adverbs to describe abilities

You've visited tourist attractions, you've strolled through quiet parks, and you've bought souvenirs for your friends back home. The meals you've eaten have been delicious. Now that both your appetite and your curiosity have been satisfied, you want to have a little fun. After reading this chapter, you'll be ready to try almost anything, to brag about your talents and skills, and to invite someone to join you for a drink, a stroll, or a night on the town.

Are You a Sports Fan?

Whatever your sport, you will probably be able to participate in it while in Germany (if your favorite sports are spectator sports, you're in luck—soccer is the national favorite). In the following sections, you will learn the terms for many sports, where these sports are played, and how to tell someone which games you enjoy.

What's Your Game?

Even those who claim to detest spectator sports have a game they play or used to play that is close to their hearts. No doubt you can find at least one game you enjoy playing out of those listed in the following table.

Sports (*Sportarten*)

German	Pronunciation	English
Aerobic machen	*eh-Roh-bik mA-CHuhn*	to do aerobics
amerikanischen Fußball spielen	*A-meR-i-kAn-i-shun fews-bAl shpee-luhn*	to play football
angeln	*An-geln*	to fish
Badminton spielen	*bAt-min-tohn shpee-luhn*	to play badminton
Baseball spielen	*beys-bAl shpee-luhn*	to play baseball
Basketball spielen	*bAs-ket-bAl shpee-luhn*	to play basketball
Billiard spielen	*bee-lee-ahRt shpee-luhn*	to play billiards
Bergsteigen	*beRk-shtay-guhn*	to climb mountains
Bodybuilding machen	*bo-dee bil-ding mA-CHuhn*	to do weight training
Fahrrad/Rad fahren	*Rat fah-Ruhn*	to bicycle
Fußball spielen	*fews-bAl shpee-luhn*	to play soccer
Handball spielen	*hant-bAl shpee-luhn*	to play team handball
Kanu/Kayak fahren	*kah-new/kay-Ak fah-Ruhn*	to canoe/kayak
reiten	*Ray-tuhn*	to ride horseback
Schach spielen	*shACH shpee-luhn*	to play chess
Schlittschuh laufen	*shlit-shew lou-fuhn*	to go ice skating
schwimmen	*shvi-muhn*	to swim
segeln	*zey-guhln*	to sail
Ski fahren	*skee fah-Ruhn*	to ski
spazieren gehen	*spA-tsee-Ruhngey-uhn*	to go for a walk
Sport treiben	*shpoRt tRay-buhn*	to play sports
Tennis spielen	*te-nis shpee-luhn*	to play tennis
Tischtennis spielen	*tish-te-nis shpee-luhn*	to play table tennis
wandern	*vAn-duhRn*	to hike
Wasserski fahren	*vA-suhR-skee lou-fuhn*	to water ski

Welchen Sport treibst du gern? What sport do *you* like to play? To say that you enjoy a sport, use this construction:

> *Ich* + conjugated verb + *gern*
>
> Ich schwimme gern.
> *iH shvi-muh geRn*
> I like to swim.

For sports that are made up of a noun and a verb (*Rad fahren*, *Wasserski laufen*), use the following construction:

> *Ich* + conjugated verb + *gern* + noun

> Ich fahre gern Wasserski.
> *iH lou-fuh geRn vA-suhR-skee*
> I like to water ski.

Where to Play

Whether you're a participant or a spectator, the expressions in the following table will help you identify where to go to indulge your athletic passions.

Where to Go for Sports

German	Pronunciation	English
das Eisstadion	*dAs ays-shtah-deeon*	ice-skating rink
das Freibad	*dAs fray-baht*	outdoor swimming pool
das Gebirge	*dAs guh-beeR-guh*	mountain
das Hallenbad	*dAs hA-luhn-baht*	indoor swimming pool
das Schwimmbad	*dAs shvim-baht*	swimming pool
das Sportstadion	*dAs shpoRt-shtah-dee-on*	sports stadium
der Basketballplatz	*deyR bAs-ket-bAl-plAts*	basketball court
der Boxring	*deyR box-Ring*	boxing arena
der Fußballplatz	*deyR fews-bAl-plAts*	soccer field
der Sportplatz	*deyR shpoRt-plAts*	playing field
der Tennisplatz	*deyR te-nis-plAts*	tennis court
die Autorennbahn	*dee ou-toh-Ren-bahn*	car-racing track
die Skipiste	*dee skee-pis-tuh*	ski slope
die Sporthalle	*dee shpoRt-hA-luh*	gymnasium
der Fluss	*deyR floos*	river
der See	*deyR zey*	lake
der Wald	*deyR vAlt*	forest
die Wiese	*dee vee-zuh*	meadow

Now put what you've learned to use by filling in the blanks with the appropriate vocabulary. Notice that if you're talking about *where* you can engage in these sports, the construction involves a two-way preposition—those that take either the accusative case indicating motion or the dative case indicating position. When discussing *where* something occurs, you use the dative case. But if you're going there, the construction is accusative. Here we've provided the appropriate prepositions and articles for you. Check your responses in Appendix A.

Example: Tennis spiele ich auf dem _____.

Answer: Tennis spiele ich auf dem <u>Tennisplatz</u>.

1. Ich wandere am liebsten im _____.

2. Fußball spielen wir auf dem _____.

3. Zum Skifahren gehe ich auf die _____.

4. Anna schwimmt gern im _____.

5. Wir segeln gern auf dem _____.

6. Schlittschuh lauft ihr im _____.

Express Your Desire with *Mögen*

In Chapter 15, you learned to use modals in the present tense to express your attitude. To tell someone that you would like to do something, use the verb *mögen* (*möh-guhn*) "to like" in the *subjunctive* mood—that is, make it sound a little politer and more inviting: *ich möchte* (*iH möH-tuh*), or "I would like." Of course, you end the sentence with a dependent infinitive; otherwise, no one will know what you would like to do. You'll notice that the first and third person singular have the same ending, which is consistent with what you already know about modals. Naturally, the plural forms are as you would expect. *Mögen* is conjugated in the following table.

DEFINITION

The **subjunctive** is a type of mood, grammatically speaking, that marks speakers' attitudes toward the truth of their assertions or obligation, permission, or suggestion. The verb form in the subjunctive mood indicates that something is relatively unlikely or contrary to fact.

The Verb *Mögen* in the Subjunctive ("Would Like To")

Person	Singular	English	Plural	English
First	ich möchte *iH möH-tuh*	I would like	wir möchten *veeR möH-tuhn*	we would like
Second	du möchtest *dew möH-test*	you would like	ihr möchtet *eeR möH-thut*	you would like
Third	er, sie, es möchte *eR, zee, es möH-tuh*	he, she, it would like	sie möchten *zee möH-tuhn*	they would like
Formal	Sie möchten *zee möH-tuhn*	you would like	Sie möchten *zee möH-tuhn*	you would like

Now fill in the blanks with the appropriate form of *möchten*. Check your verb conjugations in Appendix A.

> **GERMAN CULTURE**
>
> Although Germans are tennis fans, they are soccer fanatics. No single U.S. game can compete with it in popularity. Few Germans are immune to the excitement of the matches played among the country's 18 best first-division teams, the *Fußball-Bundesliga*. But when they're not watching *Fußball*, Germans can be found engaging in leisure activities at sport clubs, *Sportvereine*, where healthful exercise is balanced with social interaction.

Example: Ich _____ Fußball spielen.

Answer: Ich <u>möchte</u> Fußball spielen.

1. Anne _____ bergsteigen.

2. Wir _____ wandern.

3. Franz und Klara _____ reiten.

4. Ihr _____ in der Sporthalle Badminton spielen.

5. Hans und Franz _____ am Fluss angeln.

Extending an Invitation

If you are traveling alone, or if your traveling companion starts to snore in his or her chair after lunch, you may need to find someone with whom to play your favorite sport.

Use the verb *mögen* in the subjunctive (*möchten*), followed by the subject and whatever verb you choose, as illustrated in the following construction:

> *Möchten Sie* or *möchtest du* + (sport) verb

> Möchten Sie Bergsteigen gehen?
> *möH-tuhn zee beRk-shtay-guhn*
> Would you like to go mountain climbing?

> Möchtest du Tennis spielen?
> *möH-test dew te-nis shpee-luhn*
> Would you like to play tennis?

Accepting an Invitation

 Not only is accepting an invitation a way of showing the natives that you're friendly, but you'll probably end up having a great time if you do! Whether it's a romantic dinner, a doubles tennis match, or simply a walk in the park, the following phrases will help you gracefully accept any invitation. Check out Track 16 of the CD included with this book to hear some of these examples.

German	Pronunciation	English
Selbstverständlich.	*zelpst-feR-shtänt-liH*	Of course.
Natürlich.	*nah-tüR-liH*	Naturally.
Warum nicht?	*vah-Room niHt*	Why not?
Ja, das ist eine gute Idee.	*yah, dAs ist ay-nuh gew-tuh ee-dey*	Yes, that's a good idea.
Wenn du (Sie) willst (wollen).	*ven dew (zee) vilst (vo-luhn)*	If you like.
Fantastisch.	*fAn-tAs-tish*	Fantastic.

Refusing an Invitation

 Of course, if you always say yes to invitations, you probably won't have any time left for yourself. In fact, if you love traveling, chances are good that you also enjoy spending time alone in museums, cathedrals, cafés, airports, and sleeping compartments on trains. It may be just as important for you to learn how to gracefully refuse an invitation as it is for you to learn how to gracefully accept one. Sooner or later, you'll probably find the following phrases useful. Check out Track 16 of the CD included with this book to hear some of these examples.

German	Pronunciation	English
Das ist unmöglich. *or* Das geht leider nicht.	*dAs ist oon-mök-liH or das geyt lay-duhR niHt.*	That's impossible.
Nein, ich habe keine Lust.	*nayn, iH hah-buh kay-nuh loost*	No, I don't feel like it.
Nein, ich habe keine Zeit.	*nayn, iH hah-buh kay-nuh tsayt*	No, I have no time.
Es tut mir Leid.	*es toot meeR layt*	I'm sorry.

Showing Indecision and Indifference

Your best buddy asks you to go ice skating. You haven't been ice skating since you were nine, and you figure you may look a little foolish trying, but you're a good sport. So you shrug and let him know it's all the same to you. Try a few of these useful phrases to show your indifference.

German	Pronunciation	English
Das ist mir egal.	*dAs ist meeR ey-gahl*	It makes no difference to me.
Was du willst.	*vAs dew vilst*	Whatever you'd like.
Ich weiß nicht.	*iH vays niHt*	I don't know.
Vielleicht.	*fee-layHt*	Maybe.
Mal sehen.	*mahl zeh-uhn*	We'll see.

Do You Accept or Refuse?

If you know how to tell someone which sports you like, chances are good that you'll be asked to play sooner or later. Practice what you've learned in this chapter to accept and refuse invitations. Give the German for the following sentences. Questions and possible responses appear in Appendix A.

Example: Would you like to play tennis? No, I don't feel like it.

Answer: Möchten Sie Tennis spielen? Nein, ich habe keine Lust.

1. Would you like to play basketball? Yes, that's a good idea.

2. Would you like to hike? No, I'm tired.

3. Would you like to play soccer? Why not?

4. Would you like to fish? No, I don't have the time.

5. Would you like to play badminton? No, I'm tired.

6. Would you like to ride bikes? Naturally.

Let's Do Something Else

There are many reliable ways of having a good time, and new ways are being invented every day. If sports aren't your thing, you may want to suggest some other kind of activity. To tell someone that you would like to go to the opera, you might say this:

> Ich möchte in die Oper gehen.
> *iH möH-tuh in dee oh-puhR gey-uhn*
> I would like to go to the opera.

If you'd like to go to the movies, you could say this:

> Ich möchte ins Kino gehen.
> *iH möH-tuh ins kee-noh gey-uhn*
> I'd like to go to the movies.

Use the phrases in the following table to make creative suggestions.

Places to Go and Things to Do

Place	English	Activity	English
in die Disko gehen *in dee dis-ko gey-uhn*	to go to the discotheque	tanzen *tAn-tsuhn*	to dance
in die Oper gehen *in dee oh-puhR gey-uhn*	to go to the opera	Musik hören *mew-zeek höh-Ruhn*	to listen to music
ins Ballett gehen *ins bA-let gey-uhn*	to go to the ballet	die Tänzer anschauen *dee tän-tsuhR An-shou-uhn*	to watch the dancers

Place	English	Activity	English
ins kasino gehen *ins kah-zee-noh gey-uhn*	to go to the casino	spielen *shpee-luhn*	to play
ins kino gehen *ins kee-noh gey-uhn*	to go to the movies	einen film sehen *ay-nuhn film zey-uhn*	to see a movie
ins konzert gehen *ins kon-tseRt gey-uhn*	to go to a concert	ein orchester/einen chor hören *ayn oR-kes-tuhR höh-Ruhn*	to hear an orchestra/a choral concert
ins theater gehen *ins tey-ah-tuhR gey-uhn*	to go to the theater	ein theaterstück sehen *ayn tey-ah-tuhR-shtük zey-uhn*	to see a play
zu hause bleiben *tsew hou-zuh blay-buhn*	to stay at home	meditieren *me-dee-tee-Ruhn*	to meditate
		faulenzen *fou-len-tsuhn*	to lie around
zum strand gehen *tsewm stRAnt gey-uhn*	to go to the beach	schwimmen, sich sonnen *shvi-muhn, siH zo-nuhn*	to swim, to lie in the sun

Entertaining Options

Sometimes, after the shops and the restaurants, the sightseeing and the sweating, there's nothing better than sitting in front of the television and chilling out. You could cozy up with the *Fernsehzeitung* (*feRn-zey-tsay-toong*, the German *TV Guide*) and settle in for a pleasant evening. Alternatively, you might go to the local movie theater. In the following sections, you will learn some important entertainment vocabulary.

At the Movies and on TV

Go ahead and switch on the set. Television advertisements are a great way to test your knowledge of German because they use relatively simple language, speak in the present tense, and rely on visuals. If you flip through the *Fernsehzeitung*, you'll discover that movie listings contain not only a synopsis of the plot, but also a category or genre. The different kinds of movies and shows are listed for you in the following table. First, some useful phrases regarding television viewing follow:

Was gibt es im Fernsehen?
vAs gipt es im feRn-zey-uhn
What's on TV?

Welche Art von Film gibt es?
vel-Huh Art fon film geept es
What kind of film is it?

Television Programs and Movies (*Fernsehprogramme und Filme*)

German	Pronunciation	English
der Abenteuerfilm	*deyR ah-ben-toy-uhR-film*	adventure film
der Dokumentarfilm	*deyR doh-kew-men-tAR-film*	documentary
das Drama	*dAs dRah-mah*	drama
der Horrorfilm	*deyR ho-Ror-film*	horror movie
die Komödie	*dee koh-möh-dee-uh*	comedy
der Krimi	*deyR kRee-mee*	thriller
die Liebesgeschichte	*dee lee-buhs-guh-shiH-tuh*	love story
die Nachrichten	*dee nACH-RiH-tuhn*	news
die Seifenoper	*dee zay-fuhn-oh-puhR*	soap opera
die Serie	*dee zeyR-eeyuh*	series
der Spielfilm	*deyR shpeel-film*	feature film
der Trickfilm	*deyR tRik-film*	cartoon
der Wetterbericht	*deyR ve-tuhR-buh-RiHt*	weather

At a Concert

If you go to a concert in Germany, you'll certainly want to tell your friends about it. In Germany, as in America, when referring to the cellist or to the pianist, you can simply refer to the instrument: "The cello was exceptional," or *Das Cello war außergewöhnlich* (*dAs che-loh vAR ou-suhR-guh-vöhn-liH*). The following table lists the most common musical instruments.

Musical Instruments (*Musikinstrumente*)

German	Pronunciation	English
das Akkordeon	*dAs A-koR-de-ohn*	accordion
das Cello	*dAs che-loh*	cello
die Flöte	*dee flöh-tuh*	flute
die Geige	*dee gay-guh*	violin
die Gitarre	*dee gee-tA-Ruh*	guitar
die Harfe	*dee hAR-fuh*	harp
das Horn	*dAs horn*	horn
die Klarinette	*dee klah-Ree-ne-tuh*	clarinet
das Klavier	*dAs klA-veeR*	piano
die Oboe	*dee oh-boh-uh*	oboe
die Pauke	*dee pou-kuh*	bass drum
die Posaune	*dee po-zou-nuh*	trombone
das Saxophon	*dAs zak-soh-fohn*	saxophone
das Schlagzeug	*dAs shlAk-tsoyk*	drums
die Trommel	*dee tRo-muhl*	drum
die Trompete	*dee tRom-pey-tuh*	trumpet

AS A RULE

The word "adverb" implies its principal function, which is to be added to, or to modify, a verb. But don't let the name fool you. Adverbs can also modify adjectives, as they do in the following sentences:

Das Frühstück war sehr gut.
dAs fRüH-shtük vAR zeyR gewt
The breakfast was very good.

Seine Geschichte war höchst langweilig.
zay-nuh guh-shiH-tuh vAR höHst lAng-vay-liH
His story was very boring.

Expressing Your Enjoyment or Disappointment

When you enjoy a film or a concert, you can express your enjoyment by using the following phrases. When referring to a movie (*der Film*), use the masculine pronoun *er.* Likewise, use the neuter *es* when referring to a *Konzert* (*das*):

German	Pronunciation	English
Ich liebe den Film/das Konzert!	*iH lee-buh deyn film/dAs kon-tseRt*	I love the film/the concert!
Es ist ein guter Film/ein gutes Konzert.	*es ist ayn gew-tuhR film/ayn gew-tuhs kon-tseRt*	It is a good film/a good concert.
Er/es ist orginell.	*eR/es ist o-Ri-gee-nel*	It is original.
Er/es ist interessant.	*eR/es ist in-tey-Re-sAnt*	It is interesting.
Es ist amüsant.	*es ist ah-müh-zAnt*	It is amusing.
Es ist spannend.	*es ist shpA-nuhnt*	It is suspenseful.
Es ist bewegend.	*es ist buh-vey-guhnt*	It is moving.

If you found the film or show disappointing, use any of these phrases to show your disapproval:

German	Pronunciation	English
Ich hasse den Film/das Konzert.	*iH hA-suh deyn film/dAs kon-tseRt*	I hate the film/the concert.
Er/es ist schlecht.	*eR/es ist shleHt*	It is bad.
Er/es ist absoluter Schrott.	*eR/es ist ap-soh-lew-tuhR shRot*	It is total garbage.
Es ist immer wieder das Gleiche.	*es ist i-muhR vee-duhr dAs glay-Huh*	It is always the same thing.

Adverbs: Modifying Verbs

Adverbs are used to modify verbs or adjectives. You can use adverbs to describe how well, how badly, or in what way something is done, as in "He plays the piano wonderfully" or "I swim amazingly well." English adverbs are formed by adding the ending *-ly* to adjectives, resulting in words like *happily, quickly, slowly, moderately,* and so on.

> **DEFINITION**
>
> **Adverbs** are words used to modify verbs or adjectives.

In German, almost all adjectives can be used as adverbs. In addition, many words are adverbs only. To form the comparative of adjectives or adverbs, add *-er* to the adverb: *der Abenteuerfilm ist spannender als* (more suspenseful than) *der Dokumentafilm.* To compare two things, simply insert *als* between the items to be compared. To form the superlative, add *am* before the superlative and *-sten* to the adverb: *Der Abenteuerfilm ist am spannendsten* (the most suspenseful). Naturally, something that is best/worst/ most does not need a comparison: *Kalte Suppe ist am schlechtesten* (the worst)!

The best way to understand the difference between adverbs and adjectives is to know that adjectives modify nouns (and, therefore, take an ending if they precede a noun), whereas adverbs modify verbs, in the sense of specifying the time, manner, or place. Compare the use of *gut* and *laut* as adjectives and adverbs in the following sentences.

> Roger Federer ist ein guter Tennisspieler. (adj.)
> *Roh-jeR fey-deR-eR ist ayn gew-tuhR te-nis-shpee-luhR*
> Roger Federer is a good tennis player.

> Ich kann auch gut spielen. (adv.)
> *iH kAn ouH gewt shpee-luhn*
> I can also play well.

> In der Disko hört man nur laute Musik. (adj.)
> *in deyR dis-koh höRt mAn newR lou-tuh mew-zeek*
> In the disco, you hear only loud music.

> Das Orchester spielt das Stück viel zu laut. (adv.)
> *dAs oR-kes-tuhR shpeelt dAs shtük feel tsew lout*
> The orchestra plays the piece far too loudly.

Exclusively Adverbs

Although most adjectives can be used as adverbs, many words can be used only as adverbs. The following table lists common adverbs that do not double as adjectives.

> **ACHTUNG**
>
> The adverb of time *morgen* means "tomorrow." *Der Morgen,* however, means "the morning." To say "tomorrow morning," use *morgen früh,* not *morgen Morgen.* For example, you would say, *Wir gehen morgen früh nach Hause* ("We're going home tomorrow morning").

Common Adverbs

German	Pronunciation	English
anschließend	*An-shlee-suhnt*	then, afterward
bald	*bAlt*	soon
da	*dA*	there
danach	*dA-nACH*	then/after that
dort	*doRt*	there
endlich	*ent-liH*	at last
früh	*fRüh*	early
ganz	*gAnts*	quite, entirely
gelegentlich	*guh-ley-guhnt-liH*	occasionally
gestern	*ges-tuhRn*	yesterday
heute	*hoy-tuh*	today
hier	*heeR*	here
immer	*i-muhR*	always
jetzt	*yetst*	now
manchmal	*mAnH-mahl*	sometimes
nie	*nee*	never
noch	*noCH*	still
nur	*nuR*	only
oft	*oft*	often
plötzlich	*plöts-liH*	suddenly
sehr	*zeyR*	very
sofort	*zoh-foRt*	immediately
spät	*shpäht*	late
zusammen	*tsew-zA-muhn*	together

Here are some sample sentences that use these adverbs:

> Heute spielen wir Fußball.
> *hoy-tuh shpee-luhn veeR fews-bAl*
> Today we play soccer.

> Ich möchte sofort ins Schwimbad gehen.
> *iH möH-tuh zo-foRt ins shvim-bAt gey-uhn*
> I'd like to go into the swimming pool immediately.

Position of Adverbs

Brace yourself: you're not finished with adverbs yet. Adverbs can be divided into categories. The most common categories of adverbs are time, manner, and place. *Heute* in *Sie geht heute ins Kino* (*zee geyt hoy-tuh ins kee-noh*), or "Today she goes to the movies," uses an adverb of time; *langsam* in the sentence *Er läuft langsam* (*eR loyft lang-zahm*), or "He runs slowly," is an adverb of manner; and *hier* in *Hier fühle ich mich wie zu Hause* (*heeR füh-luh iH miH vee tsew hou-zuh*), or "I feel at home here," is an adverb of place.

> **AS A RULE**
>
> *Nicht* is the German negative particle. It follows the inflected verb (*Mein Bruder raucht nicht*), pronouns, and most noun objects (*Du kennst meinen Bruder [ihn] nicht*). *Nicht* precedes most other elements, such as adjectives, adverbs, and prepositional phrases: *Ich bin <u>nicht</u> nervös. Ich fahre <u>nicht</u> gern. Dieses Bier ist <u>nicht</u> für mich.*

So what happens when you stack adverbs in one sentence? How do you know which adverb to put where? In English, it's a matter of topicalization—whatever you want to stress occurs first. But in German, there are rules. And these rules are easily learned. Simply remember this clue: TeMPo. Adverbs of *time* come first. Adverbs of *manner* come next. Then come adverbs of *place*. Or, if you prefer, use the German acronym *ZAP: Zeit, Art, Platz*. Note that the English word order does not correspond to this.

> Er fährt heute mit dem Fahrrad dorthin. (time, manner, place)
> *eR fähRt hoy-tuh mit deym fah-RAt doRt-hin*
> He rides (to) there today on his bicycle.

If two adverbs of the same type occur in a sentence, the more general adverb precedes the more specific adverb. After all, isn't it more logical to know the broad span of time before narrowing it down?

> Er fährt morgen um 8 Uhr dorthin. (general time, specific time)
> *eR fähRt moR-guhn oom ACHt ewR*
> He is driving there at 8:00 tomorrow morning.

How Well Do You Do Things?

Now you're ready to use adverbs to describe your stunning abilities. The following table contains some common adverbs (all of which, incidentally, can be used as adjectives) that you can use to tell someone how well (or poorly) you can do something.

Common Adverbs for Describing Abilities

German	Pronunciation	English
schnell	*shnel*	fast
langsam	*lAng-zahm*	slow
ausgezeichnet	*ous-guh-tsayH-nuht*	excellent
gut	*gewt*	good
schlecht	*shleHt*	bad
grauenhaft	*gRou-uhn-hAft*	horribly
schrecklich	*shRek-liH*	terribly
wunderbar	*voon-duhR-bAR*	wonderfully

Adverbs in Action

Are you a good golfer? How well do you sing? Can you run for miles, or are you a good sprinter? How well do you dance? Use adverbs to tell how well you perform the following activities. Remember to conjugate the verb to agree with *ich*. Check your accuracy in Appendix A.

Example: (Deutsch sprechen) Ich spreche Deutsch langsam.

1. tanzen

2. Klavier spielen

3. kochen

4. Golf spielen

5. laufen

6. singen

7. Tennis spielen

8. wandern

The Least You Need to Know

- *Sport treiben* is the expression for playing sports, but the verb *spielen* is used to express participation in a specific sport: *Ich treibe viel Sport. Jeden Tag spiele ich Tennis.*

- If you like to do something, use the adverb *gern* + a noun or a verb.

- The verb *möchten* can be used to politely extend, accept, and refuse invitations.

- Adverbs are words that modify both verbs and adjectives. Most German adverbs can also function as adjectives.

Angst: Solving Problems on the Go

All the fun and games you've been enjoying have left you frazzled and worn out. This part introduces many useful terms you'll need to confront and remedy some problems concerning repair of your beauty, health, clothing, and other possessions. Better yet, you'll also learn how to ask for the kind of haircut you want and to express various kinds of aches and pains (along with their locations on your body).

What to Say when You're Looking for Help

Chapter 20

In This Chapter

- Personal services
- Locating solutions to your problems
- Understanding banking terms
- Comparing and contrasting

You've been eating, buying things, watching TV—to put it mildly, having a good old time. And then, all of a sudden, the problems start. You've stained your favorite silk shirt, and your shoes have worn down so much that you can actually feel the city streets through the soles when you walk! And that's not all. Yesterday you sat on your glasses and broke one of the lenses, and you ripped the hem of your jacket on a door handle. Don't worry. Everything you need to repair yourself is just a few blocks—or perhaps even just a phone call—away. And if you need some extra money to pay for these services, you can get help at the bank. By the end of this chapter, all your problems will be under control.

A Bad Hair Day!

Is your hair getting shaggy? Are your roots showing? Maybe you just want to return to your native land with a new do. Whatever your reasons for wanting to venture into a hair salon, you will need to have the basic vocabulary to get your hair styled just so.

Beautify Yourself

In Germany, *der Friseursalon* (*deyR fRee-zühR-zah-lon*), the hairdresser, is generally for both men and women. You'll also find gender-specific hairdressers: *der Herrenfriseur* (*deyR he-Ruhn fRee-zühR*) and *der Damenfriseur* (*deyR dah-muhn-fRee-zühr*). To say you're going to get your hair cut or done: *Ich gehe zum Friseur* (*iH gey-uh tsewm fRee-zühR*). If you want special services such as pedicures, manicures, or facials, you go to a beauty salon: *Ich gehe zum Kosmetiksalon* (*iH gey-uh tsewm kos-mey-tik-zah-lon*).

To get what you would like to have, begin your requests to the beauty consultant with the following phrase:

> Ich hätte gern ....
> *iH hä-tuh geRn*
> I would like ....

Most salons provide the services listed in the following table.

> **AS A RULE**
>
> Unlike English, which uses the possessive adjective when referring to body parts (*my* hair, *my* finger), German makes use of the handy dative case to refer to the person whose appendage something is and the simple definite article: *Könnten Sie mir bitte die Haare fönen?* You used a similar concept when you were missing a fork back in Chapter 18: *Mir fehlt die Gabel.* Also, unlike in English, hair is used in German in the plural: *die Haare.*

Hair Care

German	Pronunciation	English
ein Bürstenschnitt (m.)	*ayn büR-sten-shnit*	a crewcut
ein Haarschnitt (m.)	*ayn hahR-shnit*	a haircut
eine Dauerwelle (f.)	*ay-nuh dou-uhR-ve-luh*	a perm
eine Färbung (f.)	*ay-nuh fäR-boong*	a coloring
eine Gesichtsmassage (f.)	*ay-nuh guh-ziHts-mA-sah-juh*	a facial
eine Haarwäsche (f.)	*ay-nuh hahR-vä-shuh*	a shampoo
eine Maniküre (f.)	*ay-nuh mA-nee-küh-Ruh*	a manicure
eine Pediküre (f.)	*ay-nuh pey-dee-küh-Ruh*	a pedicure
eine Tönung (f.)	*ay-nuh töh-noong*	a tint

The article following the phrase *ich hätte gern* should be in the accusative case. To let someone know you'd like a haircut, say this:

Ich hätte gern einen Haarschnitt.
iH hä-tuh geRn ay-nuhn hahR-shnit
I'd like a haircut.

Another way of getting services in a beauty salon is to use the subjunctive mood of the modal verb *können*. The following table contains some phrases that use *können* in the subjunctive to help you make polite requests.

Other Services

German	Pronunciation	English
Könnten Sie mir bitte den Pony zurechtschneiden?	*kön-tuhn zee meeR bi-tuh deyn po-nee tsew-ReHt-shnay-duhn*	Could you please cut my bangs?
Könnten Sie mir bitte die Haare nachschneiden?	*kön-tuhn zee meeR bi-tuh dee hah-Ruh nACH-shnay-duhn*	Could you please trim my hair?
Könnten Sie mir bitte die Haare glätten?	*kön-tuhn zee meeR bi-tuh dee hah-Ruh glä-tuhn*	Could you please straighten my hair?
Könnten Sie mir bitte die Haare fönen?	*kön-tuhn zee meeR bi-tuh dee hah-Ruh föh-nuhn*	Could you please blow-dry my hair?

Expressing Your Style

Getting a haircut in a foreign country is truly a brave thing to do because, let's face it, it's hard enough to get the kind of haircut you want when both you and your hairdresser speak the same language. The phrases in the following table might help.

Hairstyles and Colors

German	Pronunciation	English
kurz	*kooRts*	short
lang	*lAng*	long
mittellang	*mi-tuhl-lAng*	medium length
gewellt	*guh-velt*	wavy
glatt	*glAt*	straight
lockig	*lo-kiH*	curly
stufig	*shtew-fiH*	layered
geflochten	*guh-floCH-tuhn*	braided
blond	*blont*	blond
kastanienbraun	*kAs-tah-nee-uhn-bRoun*	auburn
rot	*Rot*	red
schwarz	*shvARts*	black
in einer dunkleren Farbe	*in ay-nuhR doonk-luh-Ruhn fAR-buh*	in a darker color
in einer helleren Farbe	*in ay-nuh he-luh-Ruhn fAR-buh*	in a lighter color
in der gleichen Farbe	*in deyR glay-Huhn fAR-buh*	in the same color

Suppose you are allergic to particular beauty products, chemicals, or lotions. Or perhaps you can't abide certain smells. Do you detest the way most hairspray leaves your hair feeling like straw? If you don't like certain hair care products, speak up. Begin your request to the hairdresser with either of the following phrases:

> Ich möchte kein(-e, -en) ….
> *iH möH-tuh kayn(-uh, -uhn)*
> I don't want any ….

> Bitte, benutzen Sie kein(-e, -en) ….
> *bi-tuh, buh-noot-tsuhn zee kayn(-uh, -uhn)*
> Please, don't use ….

German	Pronunciation	English
das Haargel	*dAs hahR-geyl*	gel
das Haarspray	*dAs hahR-shpRey*	hairspray
das Shampoo	*dAs shAm-pew*	shampoo

German	Pronunciation	English
der Haarschaum	*deyR hahR-shoum*	mousse
die Haarlotion	*dee hahR-loh-tseeohn*	lotion
die Pflegespülung	*dee pfley-guh-shpüh-loong*	conditioner

I Need a Helping Hand

There will undoubtedly be times, particularly if you take what you've learned of the German language and venture into a German-speaking country, when you will find yourself in need of a helping hand. The problem is, how do you get this helping hand to help you? The sections that follow will help you prepare for an encounter at the dry cleaner's, at the laundromat, at the shoemaker's, and so on.

When you have minor problems—a stain, a broken shoelace, a ripped contact lens—that occur in a universe where chaos seems to dispel what little order there is, you will find the following phrases useful.

Um wie viel Uhr öffnen Sie?
oom vee feel ewR öf-nuhn zee
What time do you open?

Um wie viel Uhr schließen Sie?
oom vee feel ewR shlee-suhn zee
What time do you close?

An welchen Tagen haben Sie geöffnet (geschlossen)?
An vel-Huhn tah-guhn hah-buhn zee guh-öf-net (guh-shlo-suhn)
What days are you open (closed)?

Können Sie mein(-e, -en) … reparieren?
kö-nuhn zee mayn(-uh, -uhn) … Re-pah-Ree-Ruhn
Can you fix my … for me?

Können Sie ihn (es, sie) heute reparieren?
kö-nuhn zee een (es, zee) hoy-tuh Re-pah-Ree-Ruhn
Can you fix it (them) today?

Kann ich bitte eine Quittung bekommen?
kAn iH bi-tuh ay-nuh kvi-toong buh-ko-muhn
Can I have a receipt, please?

At the Dry Cleaner—*in der Reinigung*

Stains, spills, and tears happen to clothing no matter how careful you are or where you are. Why not take your shirt to the cleaner and remedy the unsightliness? The person helping you will probably ask you something like, *"Wo liegt das Problem?"* (*vo leekt dAs pRo-blem*). Knowing how to explain your problem and ask for the necessary type of service is crucial.

> Das Hemd ist schmutzig.
> *dAs hemt ist shmoot-siH*
> The shirt is dirty.

> Mir fehlt ein Knopf.
> *meeR feylt ayn knopf*
> I'm missing a button.

> Ich habe ein Loch in meiner Hose.
> *iH hah-buh ayn loCH in may-nuhR hoh-zuh*
> I have a hole in my pants.

> Da ist ein Flecken.
> *dA ist ayn fle-kuhn*
> There's a stain.

You've explained the problem. Now you must be clear about what you want done to correct it. Try these phrases, inserting the appropriate form of *dies-* in the accusative with the following clothing items (refer back to Chapter 16 to brush up on articles of clothing vocabulary). Check your accuracy in Appendix A.

> Können Sie diese(-s, -n) ... für mich reinigen, bitte?
> *kö-nuhn zee dee-zuh(-s, -n) ... fühR miH ray-ni-guhn, bi-tuh*
> 1. Can you clean this (these) for me, please (blouse, sports jacket, tie)?

> Können Sie diese(-s, -n) ... für mich bügeln, bitte?
> *kö-nuhn zee dee-zuh(-s, -n) ... fühR miH büh-guhln, bi-tuh*
> 2. Can you iron this (these) for me, please (jacket, shorts, scarf)?

> Können Sie diese(-s, -n) ... für mich stärken, bitte?
> *kö-nuhn zee dee-zuh(-s, -n) ... fühR miH shtäR-kuhn, bi-tuh*
> 3. Can you starch this (these) for me, please (pair of pants, shirt, skirt)?

> Können Sie diese(-s, -n) ... für mich nähen bitte?
> *kö-nuhn zee dee-zuh(-s, -n) ... fühR miH näh-uhn, bi-tuh*
> 4. Can you sew this (these) for me, please (dress, suit, socks)?

At the Laundromat—*im Waschsalon*

If the laundry that has piled up in the corner of your hotel room is made up of basic, run-of-the-mill dirty clothes, you may want to stuff everything into a bag and wander the city streets in search of the nearest laundromat if you are in a large city. These phrases will be of use to you in your search:

> Ich suche einen Waschsalon/eine Münzwäscherei.
> *iH zew-CHuh ay-nuhn vAsh-zah-lohn/ay-nuh münts-vä-sheR-ay*
> I'm looking for a laundromat.

> Ich habe viel dreckige Wäsche.
> *iH hah-buh feel dRe-ki-guh vä-shuh*
> I have a lot of dirty clothes.

> Ich möchte meine Wäsche waschen lassen.
> *iH möH-tuh may-nuh vä-shuh vA-shuhn lA-suhn*
> I want to have my clothes washed.

> Welche Waschmaschine kann ich benutzen?
> *vel-Huh vAsh-mA-shee-nuh kAn iH buh-noo-tsuhn*
> Which washing machine can I use?

> Welcher Trockner ist frei?
> *vel-HuhR tRok-nuhR ist fRay*
> Which dryer is free to use?

> Wo kann ich Waschpulver kaufen?
> *vo kAn iH vAsh-pool-vuhR kou-fuhn*
> Where can I buy laundry soap?

Now create your own vocabulary list from the previous phrases and check your vocabulary in Appendix A.

Example: laundry = die Wäsche

1. dryer =

2. laundromat =

3. washing machine =

4. laundry soap =

5. to wash =

6. to look for =

7. to buy =

8. to use =

9. dirty =

At the Shoemaker—*beim Schuster*

Did both heels snap off your favorite leather boots? Have you been walking so much that you have worn away the soles of your shoes? Perhaps you simply want to be able to see your smiling face reflected in your polished patent leather dress shoes. Whatever your reasons for visiting a shoe repair shop, the following phrases will help you make your desires clear.

AS A RULE

To form a yes/no question in German, place the inflected verb first, as you do in English: are you looking for a laundromat? *Suchen Sie einen Waschsalon?* If the question begins with a question word, such as *wann* (when), *warum* (why), *wo* (where), or *wie viel* (how much), the inflected verb comes in second position, followed by the subject: *Wo finde ich einen Waschsalon?*

Können Sie ... für mich reparieren?
kö-nuhn zee ... führ miH re-pah-ree-Ruhn
Can you fix ... for me?

diese Schuhe
dee-zuh shew-uh
these shoes

diese Stiefel
dee-zuh shtee-fuhl
these boots

diesen Absatz
dee-zuhn ap-zAts
this heel

diese Sohle
dee-zuh zoh-luh
this sole

Haben Sie Schnürsenkel?
hah-buhn zee shnüR-zen-kuhl
Do you have shoelaces?

Können Sie meine Schuhe putzen, bitte?
kö-nuhn zee may-nuh shew-uh poot-zuhn, bi-tuh
Can you polish my shoes, please?

I Need This Fixed

Your clothes are filthy. Your best dress is ripped. Your shoes are a wreck. The heels are worn down, and the shoes themselves are encrusted with mud. You have a party to go to later in the evening! What should you do? You can start by using what you've learned to translate the following sentences into German. Check your translation in Appendix A.

Example: Can you fix these shoes for me?

Answer: Können Sie diese Schuhe für mich reparieren?

1. I'm looking for a laundromat.

2. Can you dry clean this dress for me?

3. What time do you close?

4. Can you polish my boots, please?

5. I have lots of dirty clothes.

6. Where can I polish these shoes?

At the Optometrist—*beim Optiker*

Almost everyone with less than perfect vision has had the unfortunate experience of looking and looking for misplaced glasses. Finally, you plop yourself down on a chair to the muffled sound of breaking glass. If you happen to sit on your glasses while in Deutschland, these phrases may come in handy:

Können Sie diese Brille reparieren, bitte?
Kö-nuhn zee dee-zuh bRi-luh Re-pah-Ree-Ruhn, bi-tuh
Can you repair these glasses for me, please?

Das Glas (das Gestell) ist zerbrochen.
dAs glAs (dAs guh-shtel) ist tseR-bRo-CHuhn
The lens (the frame) is broken.

Können Sie diese Kontaktlinsen ersetzen?
kö-nuhn zee dee-zuh kon-tAkt-lin-zuhn eR-ze-tsuhn
Can you replace these contact lenses?

Verkaufen Sie Sonnenbrillen?
feR-kou-fuhn zee zo-nuhn-bRi-luhn
Do you sell sunglasses?

I Have Lost My ...

Track 17

Here are the phrases you will need to get through some common angst-inducing situations. Check out Track 17 of the CD included with this book to hear the pronunciation for these examples.

Wo ist ...?	die Polizei/das Polizeirevier
vo ist	*dee po-li-tsay/dAs po-li-tsay-reh-vee-RuhR*
Where is ...?	the police station

das amerikanische Konsulat/Botschaft
dAs ah-mey-Ree-kah-ni-shuh kon-zew-laht/bot-shAft
the American consulate/embassy

Ich habe ... verloren.	meinen Pass (m., acc.)
iH hah-buh ... feR-loh-Ruhn	*may-nuhn pAs*
I have lost	my passport

mein Portemonnaie (n., acc.)	meine Handtasche (f., acc.)
mayn poRt-moh-ney	*may-nuh hAn-tA-shuh*
my wallet	my purse

Helfen Sie mir, bitte.	Spricht hier jemand Englisch?
hel-fuhn zee meeR, bi-tuh	*shpRiHt heeR yeh-mAnt eng-lish*
Help me, please.	Does anyone here speak English?

Ich brauche einen Dolmetscher.
iH bRou-CHuh ay-nuhn dol-met-chuhR
I need an interpreter.

To the Bank!

After all of this beautifying and repairing, you probably need to locate an ATM or exchange money.

Wo findet man einen Geldautomat?
voh fin-det mAn ay-nuhn gelt-ou-toh-maht?
Where can one find an ATM?

If you need to do anything involving a bank, you'll have to acquaint yourself with the banking terms in the following table. Much of this vocabulary is useful outside of the financial institution realm.

GERMAN CULTURE

Most German banks are open Monday through Friday from approximately 8 or 9 A.M. to 4 or 5 P.M. Open hours of German banks *do* differ; some of them close for a lunch break, while others may remain open longer on Thursdays but close earlier on Fridays. Still others may take a certain weekday afternoon off. Your best bet is to consult the posted open hours. The largest banks are the Commerzbank, the Deutsche Bank, the Dresdner Bank, and the Volksbank.

Banking Terms

German	Pronunciation	English
abheben*	*Ap-hey-buhn*	withdraw
ausfüllen*	*ous-fü-luhn*	fill out
das Bankkonto	*dAs bAnk-kon-toh*	bank account
das Bargeld	*dAs bahR-gelt*	cash
das Geldwechselbüro	*dAs gelt-vek-suhl-büh-Roh*	money-exchange bureau
das Sparkonto	*dAs shpAR-kon-toh*	savings account
das Wechselgeld	*dAs vek-suhl-gelt*	change (coins)
der (Kassen) Schalter	*deyR (kA-suhn) shAl-tuhR*	(teller's) window
der Geldautomat	*deyR gelt-ou-toh-maht*	ATM
der Geldschein	*deyR gelt-shayn*	bill
der Kontostand	*deyR kon-toh-shtAnt*	balance
der Wechselkurs	*deyR vek-suhl-kooRs*	exchange rate
die Abhebung	*dee Ap-hey-boong*	withdrawal
die Einzahlung	*dee ayn-tsah-loong*	deposit
die Filiale	*dee fi-lee-ah-luh*	branch
die Münze	*dee mün-tsuh*	coin
die Quittung	*dee kvi-toong*	receipt
die Überweisung	*dee üh-buhR-vay-zoong*	transfer
die Unterschrift	*dee oon-tuhR-shRift*	signature
einzahlen*	*ayn-tsah-luhn*	to deposit
das Konto überziehen	*dAs kon-toh üh-buhR-tsee-uhn*	to overdraft
sparen	*shpah-Ruhn*	save
überweisen	*üh-buhR-vay-zuhn*	transfer
unterschreiben	*oon-tuhR-shRay-buhn*	sign (to)

Indicates that these are separable-prefix verbs.

If you plan to settle down in Germany, you'll probably need to use some of the following phrases that relate to exchanging money, making a deposit or a withdrawal, or opening an account.

Ich möchte …
iH möH-tuh
I would like …

etwas Geld wechseln
et-vAs gelt vek-suhln
to change some money

eine Einzahlung machen
ay-nuh ayn-tsah-loong mA-CHuhn
to make a deposit

eine Abhebung machen
ay-nuh ap-hey-boong …
to make a withdrawal

ein Konto eröffnen
ayn kon-toh eR-öf-nuhn
to open an account

ein Konto schließen
ayn kon-toh shlee-suhn
to close an account

Comparison Shopping

Just because you're in a foreign country doesn't mean you shouldn't shop around. Whether it's a hotel or a clothing store, ask about prices. Then go elsewhere and ask about their prices. Find the best deal and take it!

When you are explaining to someone why you bought this here and that there, you will have to know how to use adjectives and adverbs to compare things.

Adverbs and Adjectives Compared

Adverbs and adjectives have three forms: the *positive form, billig (bi-liH,* "cheap"); the *comparative form, billiger (bi-li-guhR,* "cheaper"); and the *superlative form, der/die/das billigste (deyR/dee/dAs bi-lik-stuh)* or *am billigsten (Am bi-lik-stuhn).* All of these mean "the cheapest." The form of the definite article and the ending on the adjective vary according to case and gender.

DEFINITION

Simple adverbs or adjectives are in **positive form**—for example, big.

Comparative form is the *more* form that adjectives and adverbs take when compared—for example, bigger.

Superlative form is the *most* form that adjectives and adverbs take when they are compared—for example, biggest.

Adjectives and adverbs show levels of degree in English either by adding *-er* (or modifying the adjective with *more*) to form the comparative or by adding *-est* (or using *most*) to form the superlative. The process is quite similar and even simpler in German: the ending *-er* is used to form the comparative for both adjectives and adverbs of any length (*intelligenter*), and *-(e)st* is used to form the superlative (*der intelligenteste*). An *-e* is added to the *-st* superlative inflection when the adjective or adverb ends in *t, ß, ss,* or *z,* so that there aren't numerous *s* sounds piling up on each other.

WE ARE FAMILY

In present-day German, most monosyllabic adjectives and adverbs incur a sound change in the comparative and superlative forms. This sound change can be traced back to the days of Old High German (500–1050), when adjectives and adverbs took an ending that promoted the shifting in sounds. The endings have been lost, but the sound change remains: *alt* becomes *älter.* Hmm … is there a similarity between that German comparison for *old* and the English old and *elder?*

Notice that, when used attributively, adjectives in the superlative take adjective endings. For example, in "the tastiest cheese," *der leckerste Käse, lecker* precedes a nominative masculine noun. Thus, the superlative ending for that adjective is *-ste* because it takes an inflection to agree with the noun it's modifying. For adverbs, the superlative ending becomes *-(e)sten* because the preposition/article contraction *am* precedes it (*an + dem*).

The following list gives you the adjective *stark* (*shtARk,* "strong") in the base, comparative, and superlative forms. Notice the addition of an umlaut in the comparative and superlative forms. This sound mutation occurs quite frequently with adjectives and adverbs of one syllable with the vowels *a, o,* or *u.*

AS A RULE

The superlative of an adjective is formed by adding *-st* to the positive form. The *-st* is expanded to *-est* if the adjective stem ends in *-d, -t,* or a silibant such as *-s, -st, -ß,* or *-z,* as in *Im Winter sind die Tage am kürzesten.* Remember that if the adjective precedes a noun, it is attributive in function and takes an adjective ending to agree in number, gender, and case: *Trier ist die älteste Stadt in Deutschland.* The one exception to this rule of adding an *-e* before the *-st* is the superlative of *groß: größt-,* as in *Bayern ist das größte Land Deutschlands.*

Adjective Degree	German	Pronunciation	English
Positive	der starke Regen	*deyR shtahR-kuh rey-guhn*	the heavy rain
Comparative	der stärkere Regen	*deyR shtäR-kuh-Ruh rey-guhn*	the heavier rain
Superlative	der stärkste Regen	*deyR shtäRk-stuh rey-guhn*	the heaviest rain

The following list gives you the adverb *stark* in the positive, comparative, and superlative forms.

Adjective Degree	German	Pronunciation	English
Positive	Es regnet stark.	*es Reyg-nuht shtARk*	It rains hard.
Comparative	Es regnet stärker.	*es Reyg-nuht shtäR-kuhR*	It rains harder.
Superlative	Es regnet am stärksten.	*es Reyg-nuht Am shtäRk-stuhn*	It rains the hardest.

The following two tables list the adjectives you will need (in their comparative and superlative forms) to be a good comparison shopper.

> **ACHTUNG**
>
> To express that someone or something is "more and more so" in German, the adverb *immer* is used with a comparative form, a base adjective followed by the comparative suffix -er. *Die Autos fahren immer schneller* means "Cars are going faster and faster."

Adjectives Used to Compare

Positive	English	Comparative	Superlative
billig *bi-liH*	cheap	billiger *bi-li-guhR*	am billigsten *Am bi-liH-stuhn*
bunt *boont*	colorful	bunter *boon-tuhR*	am buntesten *Am boon-tuhs-tuhn*
groß *gRoß*	big	größer *gRöß-suhR*	am größten *Am gRös-tuhn*
klein *klayn*	small	kleiner *klay-nuhR*	am kleinsten *Am klayn-stuhn*

Positive	English	Comparative	Superlative
schön	beautiful	schöne	am schönsten
shöhn		*shöh-nuhR*	*Am shöhn-stuhn*
teuer	expensive	teurer	am teuersten
toy-uhR		*toy-RuhR*	*Am toy-uhR-stuhn*
warm	warm	wärmer	am wärmsten
vARm		*väR-muhR*	*Am väRm-stuhn*
weich	soft	weicher	am weichesten
vayH		*vay-HuhR*	*Am vay-Huhs-tuhn*

Remember, when forming the comparative with adverbs, add the ending *-er* to the positive form of the adverb. To form the superlative, use the formula *am* + positive form of adverb + the ending *-(e)sten*.

Irregular Comparisons

Some adjectives and adverbs have irregular comparative and superlative forms. You should be able to discern the similarities between some of the irregular German degree forms and their irregular English counterparts. And yes, you guessed it: you're simply going to have to commit these to memory.

Positive	English	Comparative	English	Superlative	English
gern	gladly	lieber	more gladly	am liebsten	most gladly
geRn		*lee-buhR*		*Am leep-stuhn*	
gut	good	besser	better	am besten	the best
gewt		*be-suhR*		*Am be-stuhn*	
hoch	high	höher	higher	am höchsten	the highest
hoCH		*höh-uhR*		*Am höH-stuhn*	
nah	close	näher	closer	am nächsten	the closest
nah		*näh-uhR*		*Am näH-stuhn*	
oft	often	öfter	more often	am öftesten	the most often
oft		*öft-uhR*		*Am of-tuh-stuhn*	
viel	much	mehr	more	am meisten	the most
feel		*meyR*		*Am may-stuhn*	

Make Degree Evaluations

Try your hand at applying comparative and superlative judgments to hair, laundry, and shoes—topics covered in this chapter—and translate the following English phrases into German. Don't forget to add adjective endings where appropriate! Check your mastery in Appendix A.

Example: the prettiest hair coloring = die schönste Färbung

1. the shortest haircut

2. the curliest perm

3. a darker color

4. the dirtiest shirt

5. the cheapest laundromat (m.)

6. This dryer is bigger.

7. the nearest dry cleaner (f.)

8. This heel (m.) is the highest.

The Least You Need to Know

- You can get the services you need and put your angst-ridden hours to an end with a few simple phrases.
- You will be able to recognize the locations offering these services because the German expressions *Wäscherei* and *Waschsalon* contain the English cognate *wash*; *Schuster* sounds like *shoe*; and *Optiker* resembles the English *optician*.
- Familiarity with banking terms will be your greatest asset when you are in a German bank.
- The comparative and superlative forms in German are formed in much the same way as they are in English: by adding *-er* and *-(e)st*.
- The irregular forms of *gut, besser,* and *am besten* and *viel, mehr,* and *am meisten* also mirror their English equivalents.

Doctor, Doctor: "Ich bin krank"

Chapter 21

In This Chapter

- Your body
- Symptoms, illnesses, and cures
- The irregular verb *tun* in the expression *weh tun*
- Expressing how long
- How to use reflexive verbs

Now you know from Chapter 20 how to take care of all those little things that go wrong when you're traveling. But what about personal health issues? What happens if you get sick? Unfortunately, many travelers have minor aches, pains, headaches, and upset stomachs. In this chapter, you'll learn the key words and phrases you need to complain in German about everything from a headache to a not-so-happy tummy.

Where Does It Hurt?

The first thing you need to know is how to tell the doctor where, specifically, you're experiencing pain or discomfort. Try some of the words in the following table. If you'd like to hear how some of these terms are pronounced, check out Track 18 of the CD included with this book.

Parts of the Body

German	Pronunciation	Plural	Pronunciation	English
der Fußknöchel *or* der Knöchel	*deyR fews-knö-Huhl* or *deyR knö-Huhl*	die Fußknöchel or die Knöchel	*dee fews-knö-Huhl* or *dee knö-Huhl*	ankle(s)
der Arm	*deyR ARm*	die Arme	*dee Ar-muh*	arm(s)
der Rücken	*deyR Rü-kuhn*	die Rücken	*dee Rü-kuhn*	back(s)
der Körper	*deyR köR-puhR*	die Körper	*dee köR-puhR*	body(ies)
das Gehirn	*dAs guh-hiRn*	die Gehirne	*dee guh-hiR-nuh*	brain(s)
der Busen	*deyR bew-zuhn*	die Busen	*dee bew-zuhn*	breast(s)
die Brust	*dee bRoost*	die Brüste	*dee bRüs-tuh*	chest(s)
das Kinn	*dAs kin*	die Kinne	*dee kin-nuh*	chin(s)
das Ohr	*dAs ohR*	die Ohren	*dee oh-Ruhn*	ear(s)
das Auge	*dAs ou-guh*	die Augen	*dee ou-guhn*	eye(s)
das Gesicht	*dAs guh-ziHt*	die Gesichter	*dee guh-ziH-tuhR*	face(s)
der Finger	*deyR fin-guhR*	die Finger	*dee fin-guhR*	finger(s)
der Fingernagel	*deyR fin-guR-ney-guhl*	die Fingernägel	*dee fin-guR-ney-guhl*	fingernails
der Fuß	*deyR fews*	die Füße	*dee fü-suh*	foot (feet)
die Hand	*dee hAnt*	die Hände	*dee hän-duh*	hand(s)
der Kopf	*deyR kopf*	die Köpfe	*dee köp-fuhf*	head(s)
das Herz	*dAs heRts*	die Herzen	*dee heR-tsuhn*	heart(s)
das Knie	*dAs knee*	die Knie	*dee knee-uh*	knee(s)
das Bein	*dAs bayn*	die Beine	*dee bay-nuh*	leg(s)
die Lippe	*dee li-puh*	die Lippen	*dee li-puhn*	lip(s)
der Mund	*deyR moont*	die Münder	*dee Mün-duhR*	mouth(s)
der Hals	*deyR hals*	die Hälse	*dee häl-zuh*	neck(s)
die Nase	*dee nah-zuh*	die Nasen	*dee nah-zuhn*	nose(s)
die Schulter	*dee shool-tuhR*	die Schultern	*dee shool-tuhRn*	shoulder(s)
die Haut	*dee hout*	die Häute	*dee hoy-tuh*	skin(s)
die Wirbelsäule	*dee viR-buhl-zoy-luh*			spine
der Magen	*deyR mah-guhn*	die Mägen	*dee mä-guhn*	stomach(s)
die Kehle	*dee key-luh*	die Kehlen	*dee key-luhn*	throat(s)

German	Pronunciation	Plural	Pronunciation	English
der Zeh	*deyR tsey*	die Zehen	*dee tsey-hun*	toe(s)
die Zunge	*dee tsoon-guh*	die Zungen	*dee tsoon-guhn*	tongue(s)
der Zahn	*deyR tsahn*	die Zähne	*dee tsäh-nuh*	tooth (teeth)
das Handgelenk	*dAs hAnt-guh-lenk*	die Handgelenke	*dee hAnt-guh-len-kuh*	wrist(s)

Expressing Your Pain

How would you tell a German that you have a headache? a sore throat? a stomachache? You could point to your head, your throat, or your stomach and contort your face in agony, perhaps grunting or yowling for emphasis. Or, you could learn how to express these things in German. In the following sections, you will learn how to express pains, aches, and illnesses in German.

What Seems to Be the Problem?

When you go to the doctor, the first question will probably be *Was haben Sie?* (*vAs hah-buhn zee*), or "What's troubling you?" Use the following formula to answer:

> *Ich habe* + body part that hurts + *-schmerzen*

Examples:

Ich habe Bauchschmerzen.	*iH hah-buh bouCH-shmeR-tsuhn*	I have a stomachache.
Ich habe Zahnschmerzen.	*iH hah-buh tsahn-shmeR-tsuhn*	I have a toothache.
Ich habe Kopfschmerzen.	*iH hah-buh kopf-shmeR-tsuhn*	I have a headache.

Maybe your traveling companion was crazy enough to stay out all night trying to carry on a conversation over the music at a *Disko*. To speak about someone else's pains, conjugate the verb *haben*:

Er hat Halsschmerzen.	*eR hAt hAlz-shmeR-tsuhn*	He has a sore throat.

Another way of talking about your symptoms is to use the expression *weh tun* (*vey tewn*), "to hurt," which is a dative expression that requires an indirect object pronoun (dative personal pronoun). Before you learn how to use this expression, familiarize yourself with the very strong verb *tun* (*toon*), "to do."

Person	Singular	English	Plural	English
First	ich tue *iH tew-uh*	I do	wir tun *veeR tewn*	we do
Second	du tust *dew tewst*	you do	ihr tut *eeR tewt*	you do
Third	er, sie, es tut *eR, zee, es tewt*	he, she, it does	sie tun *zee tewn*	they do
Formal	Sie tun *zee tewn*	you do	Sie tun *zee tewn*	you do

The basic formula you will need to create a sentence using the expression *weh tun* is as follows:

Body part + conjugated form of *tun* + indirect object pronoun + *weh*

Your indirect object pronoun must agree with the subject. Here's a review of the indirect object pronouns you learned in Chapter 16.

Dative Pronouns	English	Dative Pronouns	English
mir	to me	uns	to us
dir	to you	euch	to you
ihm, ihr, ihm	to him, to her, to it	ihnen	to them
Ihnen	to you		

Use the definite article with the body part!

Example:

> Mein Fuß tut weh.
> *mayn fews tewt vey*
> My foot hurts me.

More Symptoms

You may need to come up with something more specific than a vague ache or pain to give your doctor a shot at curing you. You'll then want to be able to understand, or at least anticipate, some of the questions the doctor might pose you. Consult the following table for specific symptoms.

AS A RULE

The order of the words in sentences that use *weh tun* can change without altering the meaning of the sentence. The subject remains "marked" as such in the nominative case:

> Mir tut der Fuß weh.
>
> Der Fuß tut mir weh.

Other Symptoms

German	Pronunciation	English
der Abzess	*deyR Ap-ses*	abscess
die Blase	*dee blah-zuh*	blister
der gebrochene Knochen	*deyR ge-bRo-CHuh-nuh kno-CHuhn*	broken bone
der blaue Fleck	*deyR blou-uh flek*	bruise
die Beule	*dee boy-luh*	bump
der Schüttelfrost	*deyR shü-tuhl-fRost*	chills
der Husten	*deyR hew-stuhn*	cough
der Krampf	*deyR kRAmpf*	cramps
der Durchfall	*deyR dooRCH-fAl*	diarrhea
das Fieber	*dAs fee-buhR*	fever
die Magenverstimmung	*dee mah-guhn-feR-shti-moong*	indigestion
der Knoten	*deyR knoh-tuhn*	lump
der Schmerz	*deyR shmeRts*	pain
der (Haut)Ausschlag	*deyR (hout)ous-shlahk*	rash

> Hatten Sie jemals ...?
> *hA-tuhn zee yey-mAlz*
> Have you ever had ...?
>
> Haben Sie eine Krankenversicherung?
> *hah-buhn zee ay-nuh kRAn-kuhn-feR-zi-Huh-Roong*
> Do you have health insurance?

Leiden Sie unter ...?
lay-duhn zee oon-tuhR
Do you suffer from ...?

What's Wrong?

After your visit to the doctor, you may want to call your friends and relatives and give them a detailed description of your illness. Most maladies can be expressed with the verb *haben*. Here's the basic formula:

Subject pronoun + conjugated form of *haben* + (indefinite article) noun

Common Nouns Used for Expressing Health Conditions

German	Pronunciation	English
die Angina	*dee An-gee-nah*	angina
die Blinddarmentzündung	*dee blint-dahRm-ent-tsün-doong*	appendicitis
das Asthma	*dAs Ast-mah*	asthma
die Bronchitis	*dee bRon-Hee-tis*	bronchitis
der Krebs	*deyR kReyps*	cancer
die Windpocken	*dee vint-po-kuhn*	chicken pox
die Erkältung	*dee eR-käl-toong*	cold
die Erschöpfung	*dee eR-shö-pfoong*	exhaustion
die Grippe	*dee gRi-puh*	flu
die Röteln	*dee Röh-tuhln*	German measles
die Gicht	*dee giHt*	gout
die Kopfschmerzen	*dee kopf-shmeR-tsuhn*	headache
der Herzinfarkt	*deyR heRts-in-fARkt*	heart attack
die Leberentzündung	*dee ley-buhR-ent-tsün-doong*	hepatitis
die Masern (pl.)	*dee mah-zuhRn*	measles
die Lungenentzündung	*dee loon-guhn-ent-tsün-doong*	pneumonia
die Kinderlähmung	*dee kin-deR-ley-moong*	poliomyelitis
die Bauchschmerzen (pl.)	*dee bouCH-shmeR-tsuhn*	stomachache
der Schlaganfall	*deyR shlahk-An-fAl*	stroke
der Sonnenstich	*deyR zo-nuhn-shtiH*	sunstroke

You may also hear the following expressions. They take the verb *sein*, followed by an adjective.

German	Pronunciation	English
Ich bin erkältet.	*iH bin eR-käl-tuht*	I have a cold.
Ich bin krank.	*iH bin kRAnk*	I'm sick.

Symptoms

You've been beleaguered by a series of illnesses. Use what you've learned to express your symptoms to a doctor. Check your complaints in Appendix A.

Example: toothache

Answer: Ich habe Zahnschmerzen.

1. a cold
2. cough
3. headache
4. stomachache
5. a blister
6. fever

GERMAN CULTURE

When you travel in Germany, try to get sick during business hours weekdays. You will find that pharmacies, *die Apotheken* (*dee ah-poh-tey-kuhn*), easily identified by a large red A, are open anywhere from 8:00 A.M. to 7:00 P.M. Monday through Friday and until 2:00 P.M. on Saturday, depending on the region and the size of the city. German pharmacists will give you helpful advice (free!) and often refer you to a doctor. Don't confuse pharmacies with *die Drogerien* (*dee dRoh-guhR-eeuhn*), which do not carry over-the-counter drugs; they sell toiletries and other consumer items.

How Long Have You Felt This Way?

One question a nurse or doctor will ask is, *Seit wann haben Sie diese Krankheit?* (*zayt vAn hah-buhn zee dee-zuh kRAnk-hayt*), or "How long have you had this illness?" The doctor may also ask, *Wie lange haben Sie diese Beschwerden schon?* (*vee lAn-guh hah-buhn zee dee-zuh buh-shveR-duhn shon*), or "How long have you had these problems?" Answer either of these questions with the following construction:

Seit + amount of time you've been sick

Don't forget that the prepositional phrase following the preposition *seit* is a dative preposition and always requires the dative case.

Example:

seit einer Woche	seit einem Tag	seit zwei Tagen
zayt ay-nuhR vo-CHuh	*zayt ay-nuhm tahk ...*	*tsvay tah-guhn*
for a week	for a day	for two days

If the aches and pains you're experiencing are too minor to merit the attention of a doctor—let's say you have a headache or a sore throat—you'll probably want to try a little self-care. Why not visit your local pharmacy, *Apotheke* (*ah-poh-tey-kuh*), where the pharmacist can offer advice on nonprescription medicines, ointments, and other products you can use to treat minor ailments?

Finding Medications and Toiletries

Track 19

Whether you're looking for medication or a can of hairspray, you want to be sure you're looking in the right place. You can find most of the items listed in the following table in a *Drogerie*, drugstore, or one of the smaller supermarkets in Germany. If you'd like to hear how some of the examples are pronounced, check out Track 19 of the CD included with this book.

GERMAN CULTURE

Das Rezept means both a prescription for medication and a recipe. Stemming from the Latin meaning "to receive," *das Rezept* was initially used by pharmacists referring to instructions for medication from doctors. Its meaning became more generalized to refer to instructions in the kitchen.

Drugstore Items

German	Pronunciation	English
die Aknemedizin	*dee Ak-nuh-mey-dee-tseen*	acne medicine
der Alkohol	*deyR Al-koh-hohl*	alcohol
ein Mittel gegen Sodbrennen	*ayn mi-tuhl gey-guhn zohd-bRe-nuhn*	an antacid
das Aspirin	*dAs As-pey-Reen*	aspirin
die Heftpflaster	*dee heft-pflA-stuhR*	Band-Aids
die Flasche	*dee flA-shuh*	bottle

German	Pronunciation	English
der Kamm	*deyR kAm*	brush
die Kondome (pl.)	*dee kon-doh-muh*	condoms
die Watte	*dee vA-tuh*	cotton
die Wattestäbchen	*dee vA-tuh-shtäp-Huhn*	cotton swabs
die Hustenbonbons (pl.)	*dee hew-stuhn-bon-bonz*	cough drops
der Hustensaft	*deyR hew-stuhn-sAft*	cough syrup
das Deodorant	*dAs dey-oh-doh-Rant*	deodorant
die Enthaarungscreme	*dee ent-hah-Roongz-kReym*	depilatory cream
das Enthaarungswachs	*dAs ent-hah-Roongz-vAks*	depilatory wax
die Windeln (pl.)	*dee vin-duhln*	diapers
die Augentropfen (pl.)	*dee ou-guhn-tRo-pfuhn*	eye drops
der Erste-Hilfe-Kasten/ Verbandkasten	*deyR eR-stuh-hil-fuh-kA-stuhn/ veyR-bAnt-kA-stuhn*	first-aid kit
die Mullbinde	*dee mool-bin-duh*	gauze bandage
das Heizkissen	*dAs hayts-ki-suhn*	heating pad
der Eisbeutel	*deyR ays-boy-tuhl*	ice pack
das (milde) Abführmittel	*dAs (mil-duh) Ap-fühR-mi-tuhl*	laxative (mild)
der Spiegel	*deyR shpee-guhl*	mirror
die Feuchtigkeitscreme	*dee foyH-tiH-kayts-kreym*	moisturizer
das Mundwasser	*dAs moont-vA-suhR*	mouthwash
die Nagelfeile	*dee nah-guhl-fay-luh*	nail file
die Nasentropfen	*dee nah-zuhn-tRo-pfuhn*	nose drops
der Schnuller	*deyR shnoo-luhR*	pacifier
der (elektrische) Rasierer	*deyR (ey-lek-tRi-shuh) Rah-zee-RuhR*	razor (electric)
die Rasierklinge	*dee Rah-zeeR-klin-guh*	razor blade
die Sicherheitsnadeln (pl.)	*dee zi-HuhR-hayts-nah-duhln*	safety pins
die Schere	*dee shey-Ruh*	scissors
das Shampoo	*dAS shAm-pew*	shampoo
die Rasiercreme	*dee Rah-zeeR-kReym*	shaving cream
die Schlaftabletten (pl.)	*dee shlahf-tA-ble-tuhn*	sleeping pills
das Körperpuder	*dAs köR-peR-pew-duhR*	talcum powder
das Thermometer	*dAs teR-moh-mey-tuhR*	thermometer

continues

Drugstore Items (continued)

German	Pronunciation	English
die Taschentücher (pl.)	*dee tA-shuhn-tüh-HuhR*	tissues
die Zahnbürste	*dee tsahn-büR-stuh*	toothbrush
die Zahnpasta	*dee tsahn-pAs-tuh*	toothpaste
die Pinzette	*dee pin-tse-tuh*	tweezers
die Vitamine	*dee vee-tah-mee-nuh*	vitamins

Special Needs Items

Did you break your leg skiing? Do you need a wheelchair? Many pharmacies (*Apotheken*) in Germany specialize in medical appliances. The following table details items you may need if you are temporarily or permanently physically challenged. Start by asking the pharmacist this:

> Wo kann ich ein(-e, -en) … bekommen?
> *vo kAn iH ayn(-uh, -uhn) … buh-ko-muhn*
> Where can I get …?

Special Needs

German	Pronunciation	English
der (Spazier) Stock	*deyR (shpah-tseeR) shtok*	cane
die Krücken (pl.)	*dee kRü-kuhn*	crutches
das Hörgerät	*dAs höR-guh-Räht*	hearing aid
die Gehhilfe	*dee gey-hil-fuh*	walker
der Rollstuhl	*deyR Rol-shtewl*	wheelchair

Have It on Hand

Imagine that you rent a small apartment in Düsseldorf. Which items do you need to ensure that you have a well-stocked medicine cabinet? Use a form of *brauchen* and check your translations in Appendix A.

Example: to freshen breath

Answer: Ich brauche Mundwasser.

1. for headaches
2. when you break your foot
3. for minor cuts and burns
4. to blow your nose
5. when you can't sleep

6. when you have a cough
7. when you need to shave
8. when you have a uni-brow
9. when you get a hangnail

Expressing How You Feel

To express how you feel, use the *reflexive verb sich fühlen*. The *sich* in front of this verb is known as a *reflexive pronoun* because it refers back to the subject. In other words, the action performed "reflects back" onto the subject performing the action. The following table shows you how to conjugate the reflexive verb *sich fühlen* using the correct reflexive pronouns (remember, in the infinitive form, reflexive verbs are marked as reflexive with the preceding reflexive pronoun *sich*).

DEFINITION

A **reflexive verb** always takes a reflexive pronoun because the action of the verb reflects back on the subject of the sentence. The subject and the object relate to the same entity.

A **reflexive pronoun** forms a part of a reflexive verb in which the action refers back to the subject. These are identical to personal pronouns except for the third person singular and plural and the formal *Sie*-form, all of which are *sich*. Reflexive pronouns must agree in terms of number and gender with the subject.

The Verb: *sich fühlen*

Person	Singular	English	Plural	English
First	ich fühle mich *iH füh-luh miH*	I feel	wir fühlen uns *veeR füh-luhn oonz*	we feel
Second	du fühlst dich *dew fühlst diH*	you feel	ihr fühlt euch *eeR fühlt oyH*	you feel

continues

The Verb: *sich fühlen* (continued)

Person	Singular	English	Plural	English
Third	er, sie, es fühlt sich *eR, zee, es fühlt ziH*	he, she, it feels	sie fühlen sich *zee füh-luhn ziH*	they feel
Formal	Sie fühlen sich *zee füh-luhn ziH*	you feel	Sie fühlen sich *zee füh-luhn ziH*	you feel

Reflexive Verbs

Reflexive pronouns show that a subject is performing the action of the verb on itself. In other words, the subject and the reflexive pronoun both refer to the same person(s) or thing(s); for example, "he hurt himself" and "we enjoyed ourselves." The following table shows reflexive pronouns as they should appear with their reflexive verbs in both the dative and the accusative. You'll notice that the only thing new under the sun is the appearance of *sich*, which actually simplifies matters because the third person singular and plural (and formal, of course) in both the accusative and the dative are the same: *sich!*

Accusative and Dative Reflexive Pronouns

Accusative Pronouns	Pronunciation	English	Dative Pronouns	Pronunciation	English
mich	*miH*	myself	mir	*meeR*	for myself
dich	*diH*	yourself	dir	*deeR*	for yourself
sich	*ziH*	himself herself itself	sich	*ziH*	for himself for herself for itself
uns	*oonz*	ourselves	uns	*oonz*	for ourselves
euch	*oyH*	yourselves	euch	*oyH*	for yourselves
sich	*ziH*	themselves	sich	*ziH*	for themselves
sich (formal)	*ziH*	yourself/ yourselves (formal)	sich (formal)	*ziH*	for yourself/ yourselves (formal)

Compare the pronouns in the following sentences:

1. Du fühlst dich schlecht.
   dew fühlst diH shleHt
   You feel bad.

2. Du kaufst dir ein Medikament.
   dew koufst deeR ayn me-dee-kah-ment
   You buy yourself medicine.

AS A RULE

The reflexive pronoun follows the conjugated verb except in a question, when the subject must first frame the verb, followed by the reflexive pronoun:

Ich wasche mich. I wash myself.

Warum fühlst du dich schlecht? Why are you feeling poorly?

Do you see the difference? The second-person singular reflexive pronoun (it's a mouthful, but there's no other way of putting it) in the first sentence appears in the accusative case. Why? Because in the first sentence, the reflexive pronoun serves as a direct object. The second-person singular reflexive pronoun in the second sentence appears in the dative case. In the second sentence, the pronoun serves as an indirect object because the reflexive pronoun, *dir*, is receiving a direct object, *ein Medikament*.

Now, using what you've learned about reflexive pronouns and about the verb *sich fühlen*, you should be able to express how you and others feel:

Ich fühle mich schlecht.   Ihr fühlt euch gut.
iH füh-luh miH shleHt   *eeR fühlt oyH gewt*
I feel bad.   You all feel good.

Reflexive or Not?

You can't always tell from the English verb whether the German verb will be reflexive. So your best bet is simply to learn the common reflexive verbs in German.

ACHTUNG

When reflexive verbs are used in German, the reflexive pronoun must be stated. (In many cases the reflexive pronoun can be omitted in English, as in the sentence "I shaved before going to the wedding.")

Common Reflexive Verbs

German	Pronunciation	English
sich die Zähne putzen	*ziH dee tsäh-nuh poo-tsuhn*	to brush one's teeth
sich erkälten	*ziH eR-käl-tuhn*	to catch a cold
sich umziehen*	*ziH oom-tsee-uhn*	to change (oneself)
sich kämmen	*ziH kä-muhn*	to comb (oneself)
sich ankleiden*	*ziH An-klay-duhn*	to dress (oneself)
sich anziehen*	*ziH An-tsee-uhn*	to dress (oneself)
sich fertig machen	*ziH fer-tiH mah-CHuhn*	to get (oneself) ready
sich verletzen	*ziH feR-le-tsuhn*	to injure (oneself)
sich fit halten[S]	*ziH fit hAl-tuhn*	to keep (oneself) fit
sich hinlegen*	*ziH hin-lay-guhn*	to lie down
sich treffen[S]	*ziH tRe-fuhn*	to meet (each other)
sich schminken	*ziH shmin-kuhn*	to put make-up on (oneself)
sich erholen	*ziH eR-hoh-luhn*	to recuperate (oneself)
sich entspannen	*ziH ent-shpA-nuhn*	to relax (oneself)
sich rasieren	*ziH Rah-zee-Ruhn*	to shave (oneself)
sich anmelden*	*ziH An-mel-duhn*	to sign (oneself) up
sich setzen	*ziH ze-tsuhn*	to sit (oneself) down
sich stricken	*ziH shtre-kuhn*	to stretch (oneself)
sich duschen	*ziH doo-shun*	to take a shower
sich ausziehen*	*ziH ous-tsee-uhn*	to undress (oneself)
sich waschen[S]	*ziH vA-shuhn*	to wash (oneself)

[S]*denotes a very strong verb, incurring a stem-vowel change in the present tense: waschen becomes wäscht; treffen becomes trifft.*

denotes a separable prefix verb.

Reflexive Verbs in Action

Use what you've learned about reflexive verbs to describe all the different things you must do to get ready before leaving your hotel room in the morning. Then talk about the things you do before going to bed at night. Check your sentences in Appendix A.

1. sich waschen
2. sich rasieren
3. sich anziehen
4. sich fertig machen
5. sich strecken
6. sich ausziehen
7. sich hinlegen

Commanding Reflexively

When you use reflexive verbs to tell your husband to shave or to tell your children to wash their hands before dinner, the reflexive pronoun usually comes at the end of the sentence unless the reflexive verb has a separable prefix or you have an object or adverb in the command. Remember, when you use the formal second person singular or plural, you must always include *Sie* as part of the command:

Verletz dich nicht!	*feR-letst diH niHt*	Don't hurt yourself!
Waschen Sie sich!	*vA-shun zee ziH*	Wash yourself!
Wascht euch!	*vAsht oyH*	Wash yourselves!
Zieh(e) dich an!	*tsee(-uh) diH An*	Get dressed!

Be Bossy

You're traveling with a group of friends, and you're all getting ready to go out. Practice using reflexive verbs by telling a friend (use the *du* imperative) to do and then not to do the following. Check your imperatives in Appendix A.

1. wash up
2. change clothing
3. shave
4. get ready
5. sit down
6. relax

The Least You Need to Know

- If you become ill in a German-speaking country, your recovery will be a lot easier if you know how to express your symptoms or medical condition correctly.
- You can express illness in various ways. For starters, use the conjugated form of the verb *haben* + the body part that hurts + the ending *-schmerzen*. Alternatively, use the expression *weh tun*.
- Reflexive pronouns show that the action of reflexive verbs reflects back on the subject of the sentence.

In the Past: *Die Vergangenheit*

Chapter 222

In This Chapter

- Using the present perfect
- All about the helping verbs *haben* and *sein*
- Asking questions and giving answers in the past tense

So far, you've been navigating through Deutschland in the present tense. Imagine now that, after purchasing the items you need for a well-stocked medicine cabinet in Chapter 21, you walk out of the pharmacy without taking the bag filled with items you've already paid for. You don't realize that the bag is missing until a taxi has driven you halfway home. What do you do now?

Talking About the Past

You must, of course, go back to the pharmacy and tell the person behind the counter (someone new—the person who was there earlier has stepped out for lunch) what happened. To do so, you will have to talk about the past, known in German as *die Vergangenheit (dee feR-gAn-guhn-hayt)*.

You can speak in the past tense in various ways. In English, for example, you can say, "I went to the store." In German, this tense is referred to as *das Präteritum (dAs pRä-tey-Ree-toom)*, or the simple past—so simple that it needs only one verb form to express it. You also can say, "I have gone to the store." This tense is referred to as *das Perfekt (dAs peR-fekt)*, or the present perfect tense. When you say "I had gone to the store," you are speaking in the past in yet another way, referred to as *das Plusquamperfekt (dAs ploos-kvahm-peR-fekt)*, or the past perfect tense. This chapter focuses on the formation of *das Perfekt*, the most common way of speaking in the past in German.

Strong Verbs

You already have a head start on the formation of the perfect tense in German. English and German form the perfect tense in much the same way. Both languages use an *auxiliary* or helping verb (have/*haben*) with the past participle to form the present perfect tense: "I have bought"/*ich habe gekauft.* The only hitch is that some verbs in German use the verb *to be* (*sein*) as an auxiliary: *Ich bin gegangen* ("I have gone"). Here's the basic formula for forming the *Perfekt:*

Subject + the conjugated form of *sein* or *haben* in the present + past participle

The important thing to remember is that after you learn how to form the past participle, you won't have any trouble speaking in the past. The past participle never changes. Only the auxiliary verbs *haben* and *sein* change to agree with the subject. So how is the past participle formed? Most past participles take *ge-* at the beginning of the verb (when you're dealing with verbs with separable prefixes, however, the *ge-* comes after the separable prefix in the formation of the past participle).

DEFINITION

An **auxiliary verb** serves as the specifier of the main verb—it *helps* the main verb. In the case of the German *Perfekt* tense, the auxiliary verb enables the main verb to pop up in its past participial form at the end of the phrase: *Dagmar hat mich geliebt.*

All strong verbs have a past participle ending in *-en,* as do some in English, such as *taken, eaten,* and *spoken.* Do you remember strong verbs from Chapter 8? The main difference between strong and weak verbs is that strong verbs have a vowel change in one of their principal parts. If they're very strong (*sehr stark*), they incur a change already in the third person singular, present; if they're merely *stark,* the change comes out in the simple past and the past participle forms. English verbs follow this pattern, too: *sing, sang, sung* (in German, *singen, sang, gesungen*). Think of strong verbs as verbs so stubborn that they insist on having their own way. Although these verbs follow certain patterns of vowel changes, it would probably take you longer to memorize the patterns than to memorize the past participle for the strong verbs you use. Our advice? Start memorizing. In the following list, *hat* means that the auxiliary verb is *haben,* and *ist* means that it is *sein.*

AS A RULE

Although it may seem as if most verbs are strong (and, therefore, must be memorized by rote), less than 20 percent of German verbs fall into this category. Bear in mind that you need memorize a strong verb only one time. Once you establish the paradigm for the very strong verb "to eat"—*essen/isst/hat gegessen*—you can automatically conjugate "to forget": *vergessen, vergisst, hat vergessen.*

Infinitive	Third Person Singular + Past Participle	Pronunciation	English Past Participle
backen[S]	hat gebacken	*hAt guh-bA-kuhn*	baked
bleiben	ist geblieben	*ist guh-blee-buhn*	stayed
essen	hat gegessen	*hAt guh-ge-suhn*	eaten
fahren[S]	ist gefahren	*ist guh-fah-Ruhn*	driven
geben[S]	hat gegeben	*hAt guh-gey-buhn*	given
gehen	ist gegangen	*ist guh-gAn-guhn*	gone
genießen	hat genossen	*hAt guh-no-suhn*	enjoyed
heben	hat gehoben	*hAt guh-hoh-buhn*	lifted, raised
laufen[S]	ist gelaufen	*ist guh-lou-fuhn*	run, walked
nehmen[S]	hat genommen	*hAt guh-no-muhn*	taken
schlafen[S]	hat geschlafen	*hAt guh-shlah-fuhn*	slept
singen	hat gesungen	*hAt guh-zoon-guhn*	sung
sprechen	hat gesprochen	*hAt guh-shpRo-CHuhn*	spoken
stehen	hat gestanden	*hAt guh-shtAn-duhn*	stood
trinken	hat getrunken	*hAt guh-tRoon-kuhn*	drank
tun	hat getan	*hAt guh-tahn*	did
waschen[S]	hat gewaschen	*hAt guh-vA-shuhn*	washed
ziehen	hat gezogen	*hAt guh-tsoh-guhn*	pulled

[S]*denotes a very strong verb that takes a vowel change in the second and third person singular.*

In the following sentences, two verbs from the list are used along with the conjugated auxiliary verbs *haben* or *sein* to form sentences in the *Perfekt*.

Sie hat ihre Schlaftabletten genommen.
zee hAt ee-Ruh shlahf-tAb-le-tuhn guh-no-muhn
She has taken her sleeping pills.

Du bist zur Drogerie gegangen.
dew bist tsewR dRoh-guh-Ree guh-gAn-guhn
You have gone to the drugstore.

> **ACHTUNG**
>
> Make sure you send that past participle (your *ge-* form) to the end of the sentence. Make them wait for the verb! After all, you've already given your listener a conjugated helping verb next to the subject. And patience is a virtue!

As you can see, to form the *Perfekt* with strong verbs, all you have to do is conjugate *haben/sein* correctly and add *ge-* to the beginning of the strong verb in its altered past participle form. Yes, that form is not highly predicable and needs to be learned by rote. At least you can anticipate that the past participle form of a strong verb will end in *-en!*

Forming the Past Participle with Weak Verbs

The difference between the formation of the *Perfekt* with strong and weak verbs is that the past participles of weak verbs end in *-t*, resembling the English dental suffix *-ed*. For this reason, when you are forming a past participle, you need to know whether the verb is weak or strong. *Gehen* is a strong verb. Giving it the weak verb ending *-t* in the past participle (resulting in the unfortunately ungrammatical *Ich habe gegangt*) would be as incorrect as saying "I have goed" in English.

Weak verbs were discussed in Chapter 8. When conjugated, weak verbs follow a set pattern of rules and retain the same stem vowel throughout the conjugation. That is, add a *ge-* prefix to the *stem* (infinitive minus final *-en*) and a *-t* suffix. After you come up with the past participle, just plug it into the same formula:

Subject (noun or pronoun) + the conjugated form of *sein* or *haben* in the present tense + past participle

Here are some common weak verbs and their past participles:

Infinitive	Third Person Singular + Past Participle	Pronunciation	English Past Participle
antworten	hat geantwortet	*hAt guh-Ant-voR-tuht*	answered
arbeiten	hat gearbeitet	*hAt guh-AR-bay-tuht*	worked
benutzen (NS)	hat benutzt	*hAt buh-nootst*	used
brauchen	hat gebraucht	*hAt guh-bRouCHt*	needed
kaufen	hat gekauft	*hAt guh-kouft*	bought
kochen	hat gekocht	*hAt guh-koCHt*	cooked
kosten	hat gekostet	*hAt guh-kos-tuht*	cost, tasted
kratzen	hat gekratzt	*hAt guh-krA-tsuhn*	scratched
lehren	hat gelehrt	*hAt guh-leyRt*	taught
lernen	hat gelernt	*hAt guh-leRnt*	learned
rauchen	hat geraucht	*hAt guh-rouCHt*	smoked
sagen	hat gesagt	*hAt guh-zAkt*	said
studieren (oo-la-la)	hat studiert	*hAt shtew-deeRt*	studied
trauen	hat getraut	*hAt guh-tRout*	trusted, dared
träumen	hat geträumt	*hAt guh-tRoymt*	dreamt
versuchen (NS)	hat versucht	*hAt feR-zooCHt*	tried

What in the world does "oo-la-la" after the verb *studieren* mean? Why, that German verbs that end in *-ieren* are of French origin, of course! Thus, they are a bit resistant to totally resembling a German past participle, and although they will accept the *-t* suffix, they will not accept the *ge-* prefix. Oh! And what does "NS" after *benutzen* and *versuchen* mean? Only that *be-* and *ver-* are inseparable prefixes and, thus, will not tolerate a *ge-* prefix, either.

Forming the Past Participle with Mixed Verbs

The final German verb type is known as "mixed" because, like a codependent couple, these verbs share both strong and weak tendencies. Mixed verbs add the *-t* ending to form their past participle, just as weak verbs do. However, like strong verbs, the stem vowel of the infinitive changes in the past tense. Here is a list of the infinitives and past participles of some common mixed verbs.

Infinitive	Third Person Singular + Past Participle	Pronunciation	English Past Participle
brennen	hat gebrannt	*hAt guh-bRAnt*	burnt
bringen	hat gebracht	*hAt guh-bRACHt*	brought
denken	hat gedacht	*hAt guh-dACHt*	thought
kennen	hat gekannt	*hAt guh-kAnt*	known
nennen	hat genannt	*hAt guh-nAnt*	named
rennen	ist gerannt	*ist guh-Rant*	run
senden	hat gesandt	*hAt guh-zAnt*	sent
wenden	hat gewandt	*hAt guh-vAnt*	turned
wissen	hat gewusst	*hAt guh-voost*	known

Using *sein* in the *Perfekt*

The present perfect tense in German is made up of the present tense of the auxiliary *haben* or *sein* and the past participle of the verb. Because most verbs are *transitive*—that is, they can take a direct object—*haben* is used very frequently in the formation of the *Perfekt*. Some verbs, however, use *sein* instead of *haben* as an auxiliary in the present perfect (you are already familiar with some of them). Verbs that take *sein* are *intransitive verbs* that almost always express motion or a change of condition. Familiarize yourself with the past participles of the most commonly used of these verbs.

> **DEFINITION**
>
> **Intransitive verbs** do not take a direct object. **Transitive verbs** can take a direct object.

Past Participle	Third Person Singular	Pronunciation	English Infinitive/Past Participle
bleiben	ist geblieben	*ist guh-blee-buhn*	to stay/stayed
fliegen	ist geflogen	*ist guh-flo-guhn*	to fly/flown
gehen	ist gegangen	*ist guh-gAn-guhn*	to go/gone
kommen	ist gekommen	*ist guh-ko-muhn*	to come/come
laufen[S]	ist gelaufen	*ist guh-lou-fuhn*	to run/run
reisen	ist gereist	*ist guh-Rayst*	to travel/travelled

Past Participle	Third Person Singular	Pronunciation	English Infinitive/Past Participle
sein	ist gewesen	*ist guh-vey-zuhn*	to be/been
steigen	ist gestiegen	*ist guh-shtee-guhn*	to climb/climbed
sterben[S]	ist gestorben	*ist guh-shtoR-buhn*	to die/died
wandern	ist gewandert	*ist guh-vAn-duhRt*	to hike/hiked, to wander/wandered
werden	ist geworden	*ist guh-voR-duhn*	to become/became

[S]*denotes a very strong verb that incurs a sound change in the second and third person singular present tense.*

Producing the *Perfekt*

Now try to explain to someone how you happened to leave your purchases behind. English translations are provided so that you know exactly what happened in the past. Check your production in Appendix A.

Example: Ich _____ zur Drogerie _____ (kommen).

Answer: Ich <u>bin</u> zur Drogerie <u>gekommen</u>. (I came to the drugstore.)

1. Ich _____ in die Drogerie _____ (gehen). (I went into the drugstore.)

2. Ich _____ Aspirin und Rasiercreme aus dem Regal _____ (nehmen). (I took aspirin and shaving cream from the shelf.)

3. Ich _____ meine Einkäufe zur Kasse _____ (bringen). (I brought my purchases to the cash register.)

4. Sie _____ nicht viel _____ (kosten). (They didn't cost much.)

5. Ich _____ der Kassiererin _____ (antworten). (I answered the sales clerk.)

6. Ich _____ nicht an meine Einkaufstasche _____ (denken). (I didn't think about my shopping bag.)

7. Ich _____ sie nicht _____ (mitnehmen*). (I didn't take it with me.)

*denotes separable prefix verb.

Position of *nicht*

As a general rule, when you say "not" in the past, *nicht* comes after the auxiliary verb *sein*. With verbs that take *haben*, *nicht* comes after the direct object. *Nicht* always precedes the past participle.

Ich bin nicht in die Drogerie gegangen.
iH bin niHt in dee dRoh-guh-Ree guh-gAn-guhn
I did not go to the drugstore.

Ich habe meine Vitamine nicht genommen.
iH hah-buh may-nuh vee-tah-mee-nuh niHt guh-no-muhn
I did not take my vitamins.

Sie hat das Rezept nicht gelesen.
zee hAt dAs Rey-tsept niHt guh-ley-zuhn
She did not read the prescription.

Er ist nicht nach Hause gefahren.
eR ist niHt nACH hou-zuh guh-fah-Ruhn
He did not drive home.

All You Did

Sometimes it seems like there just aren't enough hours in the day! But look at all that your friends accomplished. Explain in the past tense what you and your friends managed to get done today in the following exercise. Don't forget that verbs of motion are typically intransitive—don't take direct objects—and as such, use *sein* as the auxiliary. Check your sentences in Appendix A.

Example: (ich/die Blumen kaufen)

Answer: Ich <u>habe</u> die Blumen <u>gekauft</u>.

1. du/ins Museum gehen

2. er/die Einkäufe vergessen

3. sie (sg.)/zum Friseur fahren

4. Sie/den Anruf machen

5. wir/den Film sehen

6. ihr/an eure Eltern denken

7. ich/Toast machen

8. du/in den Bergen wandern

9. sie (pl.)/die Oper genießen

10. ich/ein Glas Wein trinken

Forming a Question in the Past

In case you're afraid that you are going to have to learn something entirely new to form questions in the past tense, don't be: you can use intonation. To ask a question, just speak with a rising inflection.

> Du hast an die Reise gedacht?
> *Dew hAst An dee Ray-zuh guh-dACHt*
> Have you thought about the trip?

Another way of asking questions is to add the word *oder* (*oh-duhR*) or the phrase *nicht wahr* (*niHt vahR*) to the end of your statements:

> Du hast an die Reise gedacht, oder?
> *Dew hAst An dee Ray-zuh gu-dACHt, oh-duhR*
> You have thought about the trip, right?

> Du hast an die Reise gedacht, nicht wahr?
> *Dew hAst An dee Ray-zuh gu-dACHt, niHt vahR*
> You have thought about the trip, haven't you?

The most common way of forming questions is to reverse the word order of the subject nouns or pronouns and the conjugated form of the verb (this change is called *inversion*):

> Du bist nach Hause gegangen.
> Bist du nach Hause gegangen?

Answering a Question Negatively in the Past

To answer negatively, use *nein* (*nayn*) at the beginning of the statement and then follow the auxiliary verb with *nicht* (*niHt*). Remember, both questions and answers in the past usually end with the past participle.

Haben Sie geraucht?
hah-buhn zee guh-RouCHt

Nein, ich habe nicht geraucht.
nayn, iH hah-buh niHt guh-RouCHt

When the action of the verb is referring to a thing not preceded by a definite article, you can use the expression *kein* to give a negative answer in the past: *Ich habe kein Fleisch gegessen* ("I ate no meat").

Ask Questions

Keep questioning. Form negative and affirmative questions in the past out of the following sentences. Check your questions in Appendix A.

Example: Du bist nach Berlin gefahren.

Answers: Bist du nach Berlin gefahren?

           Bist du nicht nach Berlin gefahren?

1. Ihr seid zum Friseur gegangen.

2. Sie haben den Hustensaft getrunken.

3. Du hast an die Einkaufstasche gedacht.

4. Thomas hat geraucht.

5. Susanne hat Käse gegessen.

The Least You Need to Know

- You can form the past tense by using the auxiliary verbs *haben* or *sein* and a past participle.
- To speak in the present perfect tense (in German, *das Perfekt*), use the following formula: subject + conjugated present tense (*das Präsens*) of *haben* or *sein* + past participle.
- To ask questions in the past tense in German, use intonation, add the tag *oder* or *nicht wahr* to the end of the statement, or use inversion.

When in Germany, Do as the Germans Do

You may decide that the German life is for you. Learn how to communicate in the twenty-first century or via old, reliable snail mail and telephone. You can even find a place to hang out—be it a room in a boardinghouse or a castle in the Alps—and learn how to pay for it!

Communicating: Phone, Mail, and Internet

In This Chapter

- Figuring out phones
- How to use reflexive verbs in the past tense
- Internet access in Germany
- Sending snail mail
- All about the verbs *schreiben* ("to write") and *lesen* ("to read")
- Expressing polite requests or wishes

Now that you've spent some time sight seeing, shopping, and living, you'll probably want to phone home or communicate in some way with those you left behind. Readers used to the American phone system will find calling home from Germany a challenge. If you don't want to bother with the hassle of figuring out roaming charges and international cell phone plans, you can always search for a pink-lavender Deutsche Telekom booth found in post offices, train stations, airports, and urban pedestrian areas.

Because most pay phones no longer accept coins, first you'll have to purchase a phone card from a post office or *T-Punkt* shop. And then there's Wi-Fi (*W-LAN*)—free or paid—for your electronic communication. This chapter teaches you how to place a local or international call from Germany, Switzerland, or Austria and offers cell phone solutions and internet options. Along the way, you'll also learn about using reflexive verbs in the past tense.

Using the Phone

Before you even get near a Deutsche Telekom phone booth, be prepared for something new. Expect the procedure you will use to make local and long-distance calls to be a challenge. Fortunately, phone booths have instructions in English. If you need to make an operator-assisted call, you'll have to learn to identify the type of call you're trying to make. The following table lists your options.

Types of Phone Calls

German	Pronunciation	English
das Auslandsgespräch	*dAs ous-lAnts-guh-shpRähH*	out-of-the-country call
das Ferngespräch	*dAs feRn-guh-shpRähH*	long-distance call
das Ortsgespräch	*dAs oRts-guh-shpRähH*	local call
das R-Gespräch	*dAs eR-guh-shpRähH*	collect call

Perhaps you're lucky enough to have a German friend explain the whole procedure of making a long-distance call to you before you even step into a phone booth. To be able to understand what's being said, you'll have to familiarize yourself with the parts of a German phone and these other helpful words.

The Telephone (*das Telefon*)

German	Pronunciation	English
das Freizeichen *or* der Wählton	*dAs fray-tsay-Huhn* or *deyR vahl-tohn*	dial tone
das öffentliche Telefon	*dAs ö-fent-li-Huh tey-ley-fohn*	public phone
das Telefon	*dAs tey-ley-fohn*	telephone
das Telefonbuch	*dAs tey-ley-fohn-bewCH*	telephone book
das tragbare (schnurlose)	*dAs tRahk-bah-Ruh (shnooR-loh-zuh)*	cordless phone
der Fernsprechautomat *or* die Telefonkabine	*deyR feRn-shpRähH-ou-toh-mAt* or *dee tey-ley-fohn-kah-bee-nuh*	phone booth
der Lautsprecher	*deyR lout-shpRe-HuhR*	speaker telephone
der Telefonhörer	*deyR tey-ley-fohn-höh-RuhR*	receiver
die Auskunft	*dee ous-koonft*	information

German	Pronunciation	English
die Tastatur	*dee tA-stah-tewR*	keypad
die Telefonkarte	*dee tey-ley-fohn-kAR-tuh*	phone card
die Telefonnummer	*dee tey-ley-fohn-noo-muhR*	telephone number
die Telefonzelle	*dee tey-ley-fohn-tse-luh*	booth
die Vermittlung	*dee feR-mit-loong*	operator
die Wählscheibe	*dee vähl-shay-buh*	dial
die Wähltaste	*dee vähl-tA-stuh*	button
Telefon	*tey-ley-fohn*	portable phone

Making a Call

Most public phone booths in Germany and Austria take only phone cards, *Telefonkarten* (*tey-ley-fohn-kAR-tuhn*), that you can get from the post office or a *T-Punkt* store in 5€, 10€, or 20€ denominations. In Germany, information in English for numbers within Germany is 11837 or 11834 for numbers elsewhere (*Deutsche Telekom*) or at www.teleauskunft.de. It's cheaper to make calls on weekends and after 8 P.M.

ACHTUNG

Each American long-distance or cell phone service has its own toll-free number in Germany, Austria, and Switzerland. You simply dial that number to reach a U.S. operator or to direct dial anywhere you want to call. You can charge the call to your American phone card or call collect. The downside to this is that you may arrive home to a phone bill much larger than you anticipated. These toll-free numbers are subject to change, so be sure to verify the latest access numbers before heading abroad.

Now that you know a little bit about placing a phone call in a German-speaking country, a few more vocabulary items might come in handy if an automated recording speaks to you or an answering machine picks up on the other end. At the very least, it would be to your advantage to understand that you are being asked to leave a message!

Phoning Vocabulary

German	Pronunciation	English
anrufen*S	*An-Rew-fuhn*	to call
der Anrufbeantworter	*deyR An-rewf-buh-Ant-voR-tuhR*	answering machine
auf ein Freizeichen warten	*ouf ayn fray-tsay-Huhn vAR-tuhn*	to wait for the dial tone
auflegen*	*ouf-ley-guhn*	to hang up (the receiver)
den Hörer abnehmen*S	*deyn höh-RuhR Ap-ney-muhn*	to pick up the receiver
die (Telefon) Leitung	*dee (tey-ley-fohn) lay-toong*	the (telephone) line
die Leitung ist besetzt	*dee lay-toong ist buh-zetst*	the line is busy
die Vorwahl kennen	*dee fohR-vahl ke-nuhn*	to know the area code
eine Nachricht hinterlassen*S	*ay-nuh nACH-RiHt hin-tuhR-lA-suhn*	to leave a message
eine Telefonkarte (f.) einführen*	*ay-nuh tey-ley-fohn-kAR-tuh ayn-füh-Ruhn*	to insert the card
mit der Vermittlung sprechenS	*mit deyR feR-mit-loong shpRe-Huhn*	to speak to the operator
telefonieren (m.)	*tey-ley-foh-nee-Ruhn*	to telephone
wählen	*väh-luhn*	to dial
sich verwählen	*feR-väh-luhn*	to misdial
zurückrufen*S	*tsew-Rük-Rew-fuhn*	to call back
das Telefon klingelt	*dAs tey-ley-fohn klin-guhlt*	the phone rings
Auf Wiederhören	*ouf-vee-duhR-höh-Ruhn*	good-bye (on the phone)
außer Betrieb	*ou-suhR buh-tReep*	out of order

*The verbs with an * have separable prefixes, while the verbs with an S are strong—the past participles end in -en and may incur a stem change.*

Phoning Home

You've been trying to make a long-distance call via Deutsche Telekom, and you can't get through. The operator asks you what you've been doing, and you explain the problem. Fill in the blanks of the following sentences using the correctly conjugated verb (use what you learned in Chapter 22 about the *Perfekt* to use verbs in the past tense—auxiliary verb + past participle). To form the past participle with verbs with separable prefixes, add *ge-* after the prefix before the stem: *Ich habe meinen Freund angerufen.* Check your answers in Appendix A.

Example: Das Telefon _____ oft _____ (klingeln).

Answer: Das Telefon <u>hat</u> oft <u>geklingelt</u>.

1. Ich _____ den Hörer _____ (abnehmen*S).

2. Ich _____ die Telefonkarte _____ (einführen*).

3. Dann _____ ich die Telefonnummer _____ (wählen).

4. Ich _____ eine Nachricht _____ (hinterlassen*S)

5. Danach _____ ich den Hörer _____ (auflegen*).

GERMAN CULTURE

Calling long distance from a hotel is much more expensive than calling from a phone booth. Long-distance phone calls can be made from most phone booths in Germany, Switzerland, and Austria (you should look for the sign *Ausland/ International* near the phone). The most economical way to make a call is to purchase a phone card (these can be purchased at a post office). The magnetic strip, similar to the strip on credit cards, enables you to use phone booths all over Europe. To make an international call, dial 00 + the country code + the area code + the phone number of the person you are trying to reach. You'll see the area codes for local numbers on the sign next to the phone.

An Actual Phone Conversation

You've read the lists, you've memorized the verbs, and you've studied the vocabulary. Now, can you put what you've learned into practice? See whether you understand this telephone dialogue between Johannes and Frau Gehring. Check your comprehension with a translation in Appendix A.

1. Frau Gehring: Gehring, Guten Tag.

2. Johannes: Hallo, hier ist Johannes. Kann ich bitte Tanja sprechen?

3. Frau Gehring: Einen Moment, bitte. Es tut mir Leid. Sie ist nicht zu Hause.

4. Johannes: Wann kann ich sie erreichen?

5. Frau Gehring: Ich weiß nicht, wann sie wiederkommt. Möchtest du eine Nachricht hinterlassen?

6. Johannes: Nein, danke. Ich rufe später nochmal an. Auf Wiederhören.

7. Gehring: Auf Wiederhören.

Did you notice how a German answers the phone? Not with the American "Hello," but rather with his or her last name (*der Familienname*). Also, the caller immediately identifies herself after the greeting. Instead of "Is so-and-so there?", you'll say, *"Kann ich so-und-so sprechen?"* How about the closing salutation? It's rather logical to say that you'll hear from someone again, *"Auf Wiederhören,"* rather than see someone because, after all, you *are speaking* to the person. On a mobile, however, most young people answer with a simple, "Hallo."

Talking to an Operator

You can run into many problems when you're making a phone call. You may dial the wrong number, get a never-ending busy signal, or get an answering machine instead of a person. Here are some phrases you may hear (or need to say) when you run into rough times on the phone.

Welche Nummer haben sie gewählt?
vel-Huh noo-muhR hah-buhn zee guh-vählt
What number did you dial?

Es tut mir Leid. Ich muss mich verwählt haben.
es toot miR layt. iH moos miH feR-vählt hah-buhn
I'm sorry. I must have dialed the wrong number.

Wir wurden unterbrochen.
veeR vooR-duhn oon-tuhR-bRo-CHuhn
We got disconnected.

Bitte wählen Sie die Nummer noch einmal.
bi-tuh väh-luhn zee dee noo-muhR noCH ayn-mahl
Please redial the number.

Diese Telefonleitung wurde abgestellt.
dee-zuh tey-ley-fohn-lay-toong vooR-duh ap-guh-shtelt
This telephone number has been disconnected.

Das Telefon ist defekt (außer Betrieb).
dAs tey-ley-fohn ist dey-fekt (ou-suhR be-tReep)
The telephone is out of order.

Rufen Sie mich später zurück.
Rew-fuhn zee miH shpäh-tuhR tsew-Rük
Call me back later.

Ich kann Sie akustisch nicht verstehen.
iH kAn zee A-koos-tish niHt feR-shtey-uhn
I can't hear you.

Es meldet sich niemand.
es mel-det ziH nee-mAnt
There's no answer.

Melden (melde) Sie sich (dich) wieder!
mel-duhn (mel-duh) zee ziH (diH) vee-duhR
Keep in touch!

Ich muss auflegen.
iH moos ouf-ley-guhn
I have to hang up.

I Have Misdialed: Reflexive Verbs in the Past

Were you unable to phone someone who was expecting your call? You'll probably have to give the person a reason. To explain your situation, you may need to use reflexive verbs in the *Perfekt*. All reflexive verbs use *haben* as an auxiliary verb in the present perfect. Here are the various conjugations for "I have misdialed—I dialed the wrong number":

Ich habe mich verwählt.	Wir haben uns verwählt.
Du hast dich verwählt.	Ihr habt euch verwählt.
Er/Sie/Es hat sich verwählt.	Sie haben sich verwählt.
Sie haben sich verwählt. (formal)	

To form the negative with reflexive verbs, *nicht* follows the reflexive pronoun.

Er hat sich nicht gemeldet. (He didn't answer.)

You can form negative questions in the past with reflexive verbs in several ways:

- Through inversion: *Hat er sich nicht gemeldet?*

- Through intonation: *Er hat sich nicht gemeldet?*

- By using the tag *oder* or *nicht wahr*: *Er hat sich nicht gemeldet, nicht wahr?*

They're Busy

Tell what these people were doing when the phone was ringing, replacing the proper noun with a personal pronoun. Remember that the form of *haben* must agree with the subject and that the past participle appears at the end. Strong verbs (those whose past participles end in an *–en* and may incur a stem-vowel mutation) are indicated with an ^S, while separable ones are followed by an asterisk. Check your sentences in Appendix A.

Example: (Anna/sich die Haare waschen^S)

Answer: Sie hat sich die Haare gewaschen.

1. Maria/sich anziehen^S*

2. Stefan/sich rasieren

3. Mark und ich/sich waschen^S

4. Ben und Uli/sich die Zähne putzen

5. Christoph/sich umziehen^S*

6. Karl/sich kämmen

7. Theresa/sich schminken

8. Heinz-Friedrich/sich fertig machen

Und ein Handy/Mobiltelefon/Funktelefon?

You can obtain cellular service for overseas use in various ways. You can purchase or rent a GSM (Global System for Mobile communication) phone from your current cell phone provider, sign up for the service, and then roam internationally or rent a cell phone from a cell phone rental company. The obvious advantage to using your current cell phone provider is that this allows you to retain your U.S. phone number: people can call your regular cell phone number and reach you in Germany. Although this is convenient for people calling from the United States, it is expensive for those calling within Germany. Also, roaming rates tend to be very expensive.

To rent a phone through a cellular rental company, find an online vendor who will send you a handset that is compatible for overseas use, along with a foreign cell phone number (*die Handynummer*). You are billed for the handset rental plus minute usage, generally with a minimum per-day usage quota. You mail back the rental once you return from your trip and are billed for airtime use and the handset rental. Again, your bill could be more than you expected. Another option is to rent a cell phone directly at an international airport. Having this last-minute option is convenient, although you won't have the luxury of comparison shopping online. Bear in mind that phone rental rates are expensive, and the per-minute airtime costs are based on the roaming rates of your provider.

If you're willing to make the effort, your best bet is to obtain two items: a cell phone that works overseas and a Subscriber Information Module (SIM) card, a small chip that easily slips into the phone and stores important information. Rates vary, but domestic calls are, on average, less than 25¢ per minute and about 50¢ per minute to call the United States. More important, perhaps, is that incoming calls from anywhere in the world are always free. You simply purchase a prepaid SIM card for Germany that allows for pay-as-you-go cellular communication. After you slip it into the phone and phone away, you can purchase reload vouchers to add more talk time if you run out of call credit. You may purchase one by simply walking into a cell phone store in Germany.

CellularAbroad.com offers country-specific SIM cards. If you are traveling to more than one country, you can purchase a prepaid international SIM card that works in nearly all countries. You retain one phone number internationally, but the rates are not as good as those with country-specific cards, and you won't get free incoming calls.

If you are going to use a cell phone in Germany, you'll want to know the following terms:

German	Pronunciation	English
das Handy *or* das Mobiltelefon	*dAs hAn-dee* or *dAs mob-eel-te-le-fon*	cell phone
(den Akku)laden	*deyn Ak-ew lah-duhn*	charge (battery)
neue Meldung	*nou-uh mel-doonk*	new message
die Signalstärke	*dee zig-nAl-shtäR-kuh*	signal strength
das Smartphone	*dAs smart-fon*	smartphone
die SMS	*dee es-em-es*	text message
simsen	*zim-suhn*	texting

Really Using the World Wide Web

Maybe your mode of communication involves a computer. If you're into Skype, Jamba, Apple's iChat, any other web video and/or audio chat service, or just plain email, you'll want to know the following terms:

German	Pronunciation	English
der Anhang	*deyR An-hAng*	attachment
der App	*deyR Ap*	app
die Maus	*dee mous*	mouse
herunterladen	*heR-un-tuhR-lah-duhn*	download
aufladen	*ouf-lah-duhn*	upload
der Podcast	*deyR pod-kAst*	podcast
das Internet	*dAs in-teR-net*	internet
der Internetanschluss	*deyR in-teR-net-An-shloos*	internet connection
auf einen Link klicken	*ouf ay-nuhn link kli-kuhn*	to click on a link
die Email	*dee ee-meyl*	email
neue Mails (pl.)	*noy-uh meylz*	new messages
ungelesene Mails (pl.)	*oon-guh-ley-zuhn-uh meylz*	unread mail
eine Nachricht senden	*dee nACH-RiHt zen-duhn*	to send a message
die Email Adresse	*dee ee-meyl A-dRe-suh*	email address
der Drucker	*deyR dRü-kuhr*	printer
der Computer	*deyR kom-pyew-tuhR*	computer
die Taste	*dee tAs-tuh*	key
die Tastatur	*dee tAs-tuh-tewR*	keyboard
der Bildschirm	*deyR bilt-sheeRm*	computer screen

If you depend on email to stay connected to your friends, family, work, you name it, you'll be relieved to learn that most computer jargon, even in Germany, is in English. Take, for example, the idiomatic expression *auf die Tasten hämmern (ouf dee tAs-tuhn hä-muhRn)*. Can you guess what noun the verb *hämmern* comes from, in both English and German? If you figured out that *auf die Tasten hämmern* is the equivalent of the English "to hammer on the keyboard," you might be good enough to *hämmern*.

Do you want to chat? *(Wollen Sie chatten?)* Join a German *Chat-Raum* and investigate the local *Chat-Events*. One of the many German search engines to start you off is www.google.de. Next to English, the most popular language of the internet is German. From a German website (often ending with the letters *de*), you'll be able to keep abreast of the current weather and news, order a pizza, read a magazine, plan your next destination, or connect with real Germans!

> **WE ARE FAMILY**
>
> German is becoming more like English, believe it or not! Take into consideration the recently coined *emailen*, "to email." Seems simple enough to coin a new verb, eh? Simply add the German infinitive ending of *–en*. But it gets better! The past tense of *emailen* is *geemailt!*

Should You Bring Your Laptop or Tablet Computer to Germany?

Germany has thousands of wireless internet "hotspots" available at hotels, gas stations, bars, and restaurants. Many of them are free of charge, but locations are subject to change, so do a web search to find the most current list of locations near you. Most German business hotels offer Ethernet or Wi-Fi, or in German, *W-LAN (vey-lahn)*, for either an hourly or a daily charge. If you will need internet access from your hotel, ask before booking.

If you didn't feel like schlepping your laptop or tablet computer with you on your travels, you could search out an internet café. While these cafés are becoming fewer and fewer, they can provide you with the opportunity to stay connected while traveling without a computer. Internet cafés are located throughout the larger cities or in the technology section in department stores. Get universal access offered by having a web-based email account offered at no charge by services like Yahoo! or Gmail. Web cafés charge from €1 to €2.50 per hour of online time.

Connecting with Social Media

Social media usage in Germany is not as ubiquitously popular as it is in the United States. Germans are fairly cautious about using social media and are particularly concerned with security issues. While Germany is very wired, only about 50 percent of the population in Germany is active on one or more social media sites. However, this doesn't mean that the people of Deutschland don't use social media or that it isn't growing in popularity.

Germans who are on social media can choose from a variety of platforms, including those familiar to people around the world—Facebook and Twitter—as well as from some local platforms like SchuelerVZ, Wer-Kennt-wen, and Xing. The Hamburg-based social network, Xing, allows you to easily locate potential business opportunities, collaborate with other industry professionals, and seek out employment both in Germany and worldwide.

Snail Mail

You've spent the whole day in a museum visually imbibing the brilliant hues of German Expressionism. Now you're dying to get to a café where you can sit down and whip off a few postcards telling friends and family what you've seen.

> **GERMAN CULTURE**
>
> You'd better check your calendar before heading off to the Postamt because Germany celebrates many holidays, many of them religious. The most important are Christmas (*Weihnachten*), New Year (*Neujahr*), and Easter (*Ostern*), which are celebrated for two days each. The various German states also observe regional holidays, especially around Easter. An important nonreligious holiday in Germany is the Day of German Unity (*Tag der deutschen Einheit*) on October 3.

You've spent a couple of hours writing your own postal masterpieces. Now you want to be sure that everything you've written reaches its destination. Whatever you send by the *Deutsche Post* (*doy-tchuh post*) will, of course, get to wherever it's going (the German postal system is famous worldwide for its efficiency). The question is, how soon will it get there? Before you do any letter or postcard writing, you're going to want to know how to ask for paper, envelopes, and other items. The following table will help you.

Alles über die Post: Mail and the Post Office

German	Pronunciation	English
das Paket	*dAs pah-keyt*	package, parcel
das Porto	*dAs poR-toh*	postage
das Postfach	*dAs post-fACH*	post office box
der Brief	*deyR bReef*	letter
der Briefkasten	*deyR bReef-kAs-tuhn*	mailbox
der Briefträger	*deyR bReef-tRäh-guhR*	mailman

German	Pronunciation	English
der Briefumschlag	*deyR bReef-oom-shlahk*	envelope
der Empfänger	*deyR emp-fän-guhR*	addressee
das Postamt	*dAs post-amt*	post office
der Postbeamte	*deyR post-be-Am-tuh*	postal worker
der Absender	*deyR Ap-zen-duhR*	sender
der Telefondienst	*deyR tey-ley-fohn-deenst*	telephone service
die Briefmarke	*dee bReef-maR-kuh*	stamp
der Briefmarkenautomat	*deyR bReef-maR-kuhn-ou-to-mat*	stamp machine
der Briefwechsel	*deyR bReef-vek-suhl*	correspondence
die Bundespost	*dee boon-duhs-post*	federal postal service
die Luftpost	*dee looft-post*	airmail
die Postanweisung	*dee post-An-vay-zoong*	postal order
die Postkarte	*dee post-kAR-tuh*	postcard
ein Bogen (m.) Briefmarken	*ayn boh-guhn bReef-mAR-kuhn*	a sheet of stamps

Track 20 You've written your postcard or letter. Now all you have to do is find a mailbox. If you don't know where one is, ask this (check out Track 20 of the CD included with this book to hear how the following questions and phrases are pronounced):

> Wo ist die nächste Post?
> *voh ist dee näH-stuh post*
> Where is the nearest post office?

> Wo finde ich den nächsten Briefkasten?
> *voh fin-duh iH deyn näH-stuhn bReef-kA-stuhn*
> Where do I find the nearest mailbox?

AS A RULE

When you're in the post office requesting stamps, use the counting term *mal* to tell the clerk how many of a certain stamp you need: *sechs ein Euro Briefmarken* (*zeks ayn oy-Roh bReef-maR-kuhn*) indicates that you want six 1€ stamps. A word useful for expressing quantity is *mal*. It can be used with cardinal numbers, as in *zweimal die Woche,* "two times per week"; or *hundertmal im Monat,* "a hundred times per month." And "ten times"? *Zehnmal.* Just remember to combine the particle for "times" and the number.

Whoops! You forgot about stamps. Regarding postage … you're in luck if you're into simplicity. The *Deutsche Post* instituted reform in 2011 that standardized international rates. Letters and postcards both get posted at a single rate: 0.75€, whether they go to the United States or Japan. Once you've found a post office (it has a yellow sign with black letters that say "Deutsche Post"), you should be able to ask for the type of service you need:

> Was kostet das Porto?
> *vAs kos-tuht dAs poR-toh*
> What's the postal rate?

German	Pronunciation	English
für die Vereinigten Staaten	*führ dee feR-ay-nik-tuhn shtah-tuhn*	for the United States
für eine Eilpost	*führ ay-nuh ayl-post*	for a special delivery
für einen Eilbrief	*führ ay-nuhn ayl-bReef*	for an express letter
für einen Einschreibebrief	*führ ay-nuhn ayn-shRay-buh-bReef*	for a registered letter
für einen Luftpostbrief	*führ ay-nuhn looft-post-bReef*	for an airmail letter

Here are a few more useful phrases:

> Ich möchte diesen Brief (per Luftpost, per Eilpost) verschicken.
> *iH möH-tuh dee-zuhn bReef (peR looft-post, peR ayl-post) feR-shi-kuhn*
> I would like to send this letter (by airmail, special delivery).

> Wie viel wiegt dieser Brief?
> *vee-feel veekt dee-zuhR bReef*
> How much does this letter weigh?

> Wie lange dauert es, bis der Brief ankommt?
> *vee lAn-guh dou-eRt es, bis deyR bReef An-komt*
> How long will it take for the letter to arrive?

Readin' and Writin'—Yesterday

If you're filling out forms to send a package at the post office, you may have some trouble figuring out what goes where. To ask a postal worker where you should write what information, use the strong verb *schreiben* (*shRay-buhn*), "to write." *Schreiben* is a normal strong verb, so its conjugation in the present tense is thoroughly predictable. What you need to learn is its past participle, the equivalent of the English "written": *hat geschrieben.* Now you are equipped to talk about what you wrote yesterday!

Speaking of writing, you'll also be doing a lot of reading—of signs, of forms, of your own letters, and of other people's letters. The very strong verb *lesen (ley-zuhn),* "to read," will help you express exactly what kind of reading you are doing. The stem vowel *e* changes to *ie* in the second and third person singular, as illustrated in the following table. Incidentally, the past tense form for *lesen* is *hat gelesen.*

The Verb *lesen*

Person	Singular	English	Plural	English
First	ich lese *iH ley-zuh*	I read	wir lesen *veeR ley-zuhn*	we read
Second	du **lie**st *dew leest*	you read	ihr lest *eeR leyst*	you read
Third	er, sie, es **lie**st *eR, zee, es leest*	he, she, it reads	sie lesen *zee ley-zuhn*	they read
Formal	Sie lesen *zee ley-zuhn*	you read	Sie lesen *zee ley-zuhn*	you read

Can You Read This?

Have you been glancing at German magazines and newspapers whenever you pass a newsstand? Why don't you buy something that looks interesting? One of the best ways to improve your reading skills is to read. The following table lists some of the things you can read when you are in Germany.

Things to Read

German	Pronunciation	English
die Anzeige	*dee an-tsay-guh*	ad
die Werbung	*dee ver-boong*	ad
das Buch	*dAs bewCH*	book
das Kinderbuch	*dAs kin-duhR-bewCH*	children's book
das Tagebuch	*dAs tah-guh-bewCH*	journal/diary
der Fahrplan	*deyR fahR-plAn*	train/bus schedule

continues

Things to Read (continued)

German	Pronunciation	English
die Zeitschrift	*dee tsayt-shRift*	news magazine
die Illustrierte	*dee i-lew-stReeR-tuh*	magazine
die Speisekarte	*dee shpay-zuh-kAR-tuh*	menu
die Zeitung	*dee tsay-toong*	newspaper
der Roman	*deyR Roh-mahn*	novel
die Quittung	*dee kvi-toong*	receipt
das Schild	*dAs shilt*	sign
die Warnung	*dee vAR-noong*	warning

Getting It Right

Now that you're familiar with reading and writing in German, see whether you can fill in the blanks with the correct forms of *lesen* and *schreiben*. Check your conjugations in Appendix A.

Example: Er _____ eine Zeitung.

Answer: Er <u>liest</u> eine Zeitung.

1. Ich _____ meinem Freund einen Brief.

2. Wir _____ ein Buch.

3. Sie _____ ihren Eltern eine Postkarte.

4. Du _____ die Wohnungsanzeigen.

5. Ich _____ eine Illustrierte.

6. Wolfram _____ gern Kinderbücher.

7. Ihr _____ uns jede Woche.

Would You Please ...

Remember that prodding, kind of sweet-sounding form of the modal *mögen* (*möchten*) and the polite form of *können* (*könnten*)? Well, those were the modals in the subjunctive mood. How about a surefire way to be able to express any verb, sentiment, or thought in a more tentative, modest, or polite way? In spoken German, like the English *would*, the subjunctive form of *würden* can be used with almost any infinitive to express polite requests or wishes or to give advice. As with any verb phrase, the unconjugated verb—in this case, the infinitive—goes at the end of the sentence. Observe:

> Würdest du mir helfen?
> *vüR-duhst dew meer hel-fuhn*
> Would you help me?

> Ich würde gern mitkommen.
> *iH vüR-duh geRn mit-ko-muhn*
> I would like to come along.

> Ich würde nicht so viel essen.
> *iH vür-duh niHt zo feel e-suhn*
> I wouldn't eat so much.

The Subjunctive Verb *würden*

Person	Singular	English	Plural	English
First	ich würde *iH vüR-duh*	I would	wir würden *veeR vüR-duhn*	we would
Second	du würdest *dew vüR-duhst*	you would	ihr würdet *eeR vüR-duht*	you would
Third	er, sie, es würde *eR, zee, es vüR-duh*	he, she, it would	sie würden *zee vüR-duhn*	they would
Formal	Sie würden *zee vüR-duhn*	you would	Sie würden *zee vüR-duhn*	you would

Now it's your turn to express yourself politely to your friends and family (informally). Rather than blurting out commands, seduce your audience into doing what you want them to do using a *würden*. Check your polite requests in Appendix A.

Example: Komm schnell! → Würdest du bitte schnell kommen?

1. Schreib oft!

2. Lies gute Zeitungen!

3. Nimm dein Medikament!

Instead of stating what you want to do (*ich will*), suggest it coyly.

Example: Ich will griechisch essen. → Ich würde gern griechish essen.

1. Ich will nach Spanien fahren.

2. Ich will lang schlafen.

3. Ich will nur tanzen.

Finally, rather than telling someone what to or not to do, go ahead and give gentle advice:

Example: Studier mehr! → Ich würde mehr studieren.

1. Geh in die Oper!

2. Trink mehr Milch!

3. Kauf nicht alles!

If you're not sure whether you're going to get everything done, you will probably want to use the subjunctive mood. This will allow you to speculate and wish something were done, perhaps contrasting the reality that may not be what you had envisioned. Thank goodness for the subjunctive mood.

I'm in a Subjunctive Mood

German has separate forms for verbs that are in the subjunctive mood, forms that are used to express wishes or contrary-to-fact statements. It's worth learning the subjunctive of certain high-frequency German verbs because it is very useful to be able to express yourself politely or hope and long for something that is not. Because we're nearing the end of the book, and you've already been exposed to the subjunctive form of *haben* (when you ordered food or requested other items), let's look at it. The entire subjunctive conjugation of *haben* appears in the following table.

The Subjunctive Forms for *haben*

Person	Singular	Plural
First	ich hätte	wir hätten
	iH hä-tuh	*veeR hä-tuhn*
Second	du hättest	ihr hättet
	dew hä-tuhst	*eeR hä-tuht*

Person	Singular	Plural
Third	er, sie, es hätte	sie hätten
	eR, zee, es hä-tuh	*zee hä-tuhn*
Formal	Sie hätten	Sie hätten
	see hä-tuhn	*see hä-tuhn*

That's all fine and dandy, but what does it mean? Well, the German subjunctive can be translated into English a couple of ways. One way to understand the subjunctive employs the adverb *gern* as a crutch:

> Ich hätte gern zwei Brötchen.
> *iH hä-tuh geRn tsvay bRöt-Huhn*
> I would like to have two rolls.

In this utterance, the *gern* helps to express the "like" part of the equation. The *hätte* expresses "would have." Nice and neat to have one sound-adulterated word express two English words, huh?

You Have Three Wishes

You are walking along a path in the woods when you come upon a pear-shaped blue bottle. You try to twist the cork free, and finally, it comes loose. You are surrounded by smoke, and a genie in *Lederhosen* and suspenders and a long beard is floating in the air before you. *"Sie haben drei Wünsche frei,"* the genie says. *"Was würden Sie am liebsten haben?"* ("You have three wishes. What would you most like to have?") Come up with a list of things you'd like to have using the following suggestions and *"Ich hätte gern …"* Check your wishes in Appendix A.

Example: einen BMW

Answer: Ich hätte am liebsten einen BMW.

1. ein Schloss

2. ein Stück Schwarzwälder Kirschtorte

3. viel Geld

4. ein Haus in den Alpen

5. ein großes Bier

6. viele schöne Blumen

The Least You Need to Know

- Even though spoken German might seem more difficult to understand over the phone, the protocol of telephoning will be familiar to you. If you feel utterly bewildered, you can always respond with, "Wie, bitte?" to request repetition or explanation.

- Reflexive verbs use *haben* as an auxiliary verb in the present perfect.

- Sending mail in Germany is easy once you figure out where the nearest post office is and master the polite phrase for "I would like": *Ich möchte.*

- Knowing the conjugations for *schreiben* ("to write") and *lesen* ("to read") will help you fill out forms at the post office and will aid in your exploration of a large selection of newspapers, magazines, and various books and maps at a train station.

- To express yourself politely with any verb, supply a form of the subjunctive würde plus an infinitive at the end. (Ich würde …)

- With the subjunctive mood of haben (hätten), you can express what you would like to have, be it food, cars, castles, or a good cup of coffee.

The Future Is Now: Staying a While in Germany

Chapter

24

In This Chapter

- Apartments and houses
- Rooms, furnishings, amenities, and appliances
- Speaking in the future tense
- Bureaucracy of residence and car registration

In this chapter, you'll learn how to get furnishings and appliances in case you decide to stay a while and explore the country in greater depth. You'll also learn how to express your plans for the future.

Lodgings

You never know when you may decide that you want to start a new life in the *Bundesrepublik* and rent an apartment or even buy a house of your own. In any case, you should be prepared to read and understand the apartments-for-rent and houses-for-sale sections of the *Zeitung* and be able to speak with real estate agents about properties to rent or to buy. The following table has the vocabulary you'll need to describe your ideal dwelling. To hear how the terms are pronounced, check out Track 21 of the CD included with this book.

The House, the Apartment, the Rooms

German	Pronunciation	English
das Arbeitszimmer	*dAs AR-bayts-tsi-muhR*	study
das Badezimmer	*dAs bah-duh-tsi-muhR*	bathroom
das Dach	*dAs dACH*	roof
das Dachgeschoss	*dAs dACH-guh-shos*	attic
das Erdgeschoss	*dAs eRt-guh-shos*	ground floor
das Esszimmer	*dAs es-tsi-muhR*	dining room
das Fenster	*dAs fen-stuhR*	window
das Schlafzimmer	*dAs shlahf-tsi-muhR*	bedroom
das Treppenhaus	*dAs tRe-puhn-hous*	staircase
das Wohnzimmer	*dAs vohn-tsi-muhR*	living room
der Abstellraum	*deyR Ap-shtel-Roum*	storage room
der Aufzug	*deyR ouf-tsewk*	elevator
der Balkon	*deyR bAl-kon*	balcony
der Besitzer	*deyR buh-zi-tsuhR*	owner
der Fußboden	*deyR fews-boh-duhn*	floor
der Hinterhof *or* der Garten	*deyR hin-tuhR-hohf or deyR gAR-tuhn*	backyard/garden
der Innenhof	*deyR i-nuhn-hohf*	courtyard
der Kamin	*deyR kah-meen*	fireplace
der Keller	*deyR ke-luhR*	basement
der Mieter	*deyR mee-tuhR*	tenant
der Mietvertrag	*deyR meet-feR-tRahk*	lease
der Portier	*deyR poR-tee-eR*	doorman
der Schrank	*deyR shRAnk*	closet
der Stock	*deyR shtok*	floor (story)
der Vermieter	*deyR feR-mee-tuhR*	landlord
die Decke	*dee de-kuh*	ceiling
die Dusche	*dee dew-shuh*	shower
die elektrische Heizung	*dee ey-lek-tRi-shuh hay-tsoong*	electric heating
die Gasheizung	*dee gahs-hay-tsoong*	gas heating
die Instandhaltung	*dee in-shtAnt-hAl-toong*	maintenance

German	Pronunciation	English
die Klimaanlage	*dee klee-mah-An-lah-guh*	air-conditioning
die Küche	*dee küh-Huh*	kitchen
die Miete	*dee mee-tuh*	rent
die Sauna	*dee zou-nah*	sauna
die Terrasse	*dee te-RA-suh*	terrace
die Wand	*dee vAnt*	wall
die Waschküche	*dee vAsh-küh-Huh*	laundry room
die Wohnung	*dee voh-noong*	apartment

Buying or Renting

Do you want to rent an apartment? Would you prefer to buy a house? Whether you're buying or renting, these phrases will serve you well.

Ich suche ….
iH zew-CHuh
I'm looking for ….

einen Immobilienmakler (m.)
ay-nuhn i-moh-bee-lee-uhn-mAk-luhR
a real estate agency

den Anzeigenteil für Immobilien
deyn An-tsay-guhn-tayl führ i-moh-bee-lee-uhn
the real estate advertising section

Ich möchte … mieten (kaufen)
iH möH-tuh … mee-tuhn (kou-fuhn)
I would like to rent (buy) …

eine Wohnung
ay-nuh voh-noong
an apartment

eine Eigentumswohnung
ay-nuh ay-guhn-tewmz-voh-noong
a condominium

Wie hoch ist die Miete?
vee hohCH ist dee mee-tuh
What is the rent?

Gibt es Einbrüche?
gipt es ayn-bRü-Huh
Are there break-ins?

Wie teuer ist die Instandhaltung der Wohnung (des Hauses)?
vee toy-uhR ist dee in-shtAnt-hAl-toong deyR voh-noong (des hou-zuhs)
How much is the maintenance of the apartment (house)?

Wie hoch sind die monatlichen Zahlungen?
vee hohCH zint dee moh-nAt-li-Huhn tsah-loon-guhn
How much are the monthly payments?

Wie hoch sind die Nebenkosten?
vee hohCH zint dee ney-bunn kos-tuhn
How much are the utilities?

Ich möchte eine Hypothek aufnehmen.
iH möH-tuh ay-nuh hüh-poh-teyk ouf-ney-muhn
I'd like to apply for a mortgage.

Muss ich eine Kaution hinterlassen?
moos iH ay-nuh kou-tsee-ohn hin-tuhR-lA-suhn
Do I have to leave a deposit?

All the Comforts of Home

Start living in your new home; soon enough your needs become clear. When you go to close the curtains, you'll realize that they're missing. When you walk across the living room floor, the echo of your footsteps against the wood reminds you that a carpet would come in mighty handy. As evening falls and the rooms grow dark, you'll wish you had a lamp. The following table gives you a head start on the furniture and accessories you may not know you need until you really start to miss them.

Furniture and Accessories

German	Pronunciation	English
bequem	*buh-kveym*	comfortable
das Bett	*dAs bet*	bed
das Bücherregal	*dAs bü-HuhR-Rey-gahl*	bookshelf
das Eisfach	*dAs ays-fACH*	freezer
das Sofa	*dAs zoh-fuh*	sofa
der Couchtisch	*deyR coutch-tish*	coffee table
der Fernseher	*deyR feRn-zey-uhR*	television
der Kühlschrank	*deyR kühl-shRAnk*	refrigerator
der Ofen	*deyR o-fuhn*	oven

German	Pronunciation	English
der Schreibtisch	*deyR shRayp-tish*	desk
der Sessel	*deyR ze-suhl*	armchair
der Stuhl	*deyR shtewl*	chair
der Teppich	*deyR te-piH*	carpet
der Tisch	*deyR tish*	table
der Trockner	*deyR tRok-nuhR*	dryer
die Gardinen	*dee gAR-dee-nuhn*	curtains
die Kommode	*dee ko-moh-duh*	dresser
die Möbel (pl.)	*dee möh-buhl*	furniture
die Spülmaschine	*dee shpühl-mA-shee-nuh*	dishwasher
die Uhr	*dee ewR*	clock
hell	*hel*	bright
Küchengeräte	*küh-Huhn-guh-Räh-tuh*	appliances
möbliert	*möh-bleeRt*	furnished
ruhig	*Ru-iH*	calm
unmöbliert	*oon-möh-bleeRt*	unfurnished

Auf Möbelsuche (In Search of Furniture)

Suppose you've found an unfurnished house or apartment. What kinds of furniture do you need? Formulate sentences (using *brauchen* and the accusative case for the direct object) saying that you need the following items. Refer to Chapter 10 if you need some adjectival adjustment. Check your sentences in Appendix A.

Example: a big bed   Ich brauche ein großes Bett.

1. A comfortable sofa

2. A small chair

3. A stylish clock

4. A bright lamp

5. An inexpensive table

German Culture

In Germany, the kitchen and bathroom are not counted as "rooms" when describing the number of rooms in an apartment. Thus, a *Zweizimmerwohunung* has one bedroom and a living room.

Read this advertisement and then try to describe in English what you can expect if you shop at this particular furniture store. Check your comprehension in Appendix A.

1. Möbelhaus Müller.

2. Absolute Qualitätsgarantie.

3. Wir garantieren kostenlose Reparatur der Möbel innerhalb der ersten zwei Jahre.

4. Wir liefern Ihnen Ihre Möbel kostenlos nach Hause.

5. Wir kaufen Ihre alten Möbel auf.

6. Wir versichern Ihnen absolute Preis- und Qualitätsgarantie.

There's Hope for the Future

If you're planning to stay in Germany longer than anticipated, or you even acquire some property, the first thing you're going to have to do is learn how to express your plans in the *future tense*.

DEFINITION

To form the **future tense,** use the present tense of the auxiliary verb *werden* with the infinitive of the verb.

Here is the formula to produce the future tense:

Subject + conjugated present tense of werden + the infinitive of the verb

Expressing the Future

To express the future in German colloquial speech, the present tense is often used in reference to the future, utilizing adverbs such as *soon* and *next week*. This also is done in English, though not as commonly. Another way of speaking in the future is to use the future tense. To form the future tense, use the present tense of the auxiliary verb *werden* (veR-duhn) along with the infinitive of the main verb. *Werden* literally means "to become," but it loses this meaning when utilized as a helping verb to form the future tense. Earlier you learned that German has four irregular verbs. Well, *werden* is the fourth! You'll observe that it is, indeed, irregular: it not only changes the stem vowel, but it also goofs around with consonants and endings. *Werden* is also used to indicate the speaker's intent of a future promise or to make a definite point.

The following table conjugates the auxiliary verb *werden* to produce the future tense of *kaufen*.

werden + *kaufen* = Future Tense of *kaufen*

Person	Singular	English	Plural	English
First	ich werde kaufen *iH veR-duh kou-fuhn*	I will buy	wir werden kaufen *veeR veR-duhn kou-fuhn*	we will buy
Second	du wirst kaufen *dew virst kou-fuhn*	you will buy	ihr werdet kaufen *eeR veR-duht kou-fuhn*	you will buy
Third	er, sie, es wird kaufen *eR, zee, es virt kou-fuhn*	he, she, it will buy	sie werden kaufen *zee ver-duhn kou-fuhn*	they will buy
Formal	Sie werden kaufen *zee veR-duhn kou-fuhn*	you will buy	Sie werden kaufen *zee veR-duhn kou-fuhn*	you will buy

Tomorrow's Plans

Make a list of all the things you and your friends are going to do tomorrow, using subject pronouns, the appropriate form of *werden* + infinitive. Check your sentences in Appendix A.

Example: ich/ein Auto kaufen

Answer: Ich werde ein Auto kaufen.

1. Christa und Inge/ins Kino gehen

2. Klaus/Brot backen

3. Ingo und ich/Tennis spielen

4. Meine Mutter/zum Zahnarzt gehen

5. ich/Norbert anrufen

6. Liesel und ich/ein Buch lesen

7. ihr/Rad fahren

8. Wolfram und Catharina/viel Deutsch sprechen

So You Want to Live in Germany?

If you want to live and work in Germany (and you're not a citizen of the European Union), be prepared for *sehr viel:* red tape. You'll need to acquire a residence permit at the residents' registration office (*Einwohnermeldeamt*) within two weeks of moving to a new community. This rule applies to everyone, even students living in a community temporarily. (In addition, you must notify the same *Einwohnermeldeamt* when you move out of a community.) You'll also need a work permit, which itself requires a written offer of employment sufficient to convince the bureaucracy that only you—and no European with the right to work in Germany—can do the job. Hey, the United States subjects all foreign workers to the same routine, after all.

GERMAN CULTURE

Be forewarned that the way many Germans drive might require you, as a passenger or a driver, to have nerves of steel. Most stretches of the *Autobahn* do not have a speed limit, and drivers generally tend to ignore the "recommended" speed of 130 kilometers per hour—around 80 miles per hour. Slower traffic is not only supposed to keep to the right, but it does, as those in the left lane overtake at breakneck speed. If you are in that left lane and see a faint flash of headlights behind you, figure that you have two seconds, tops, to get the heck over to the right, lest you become a hood ornament.

Sound like a lot? Well, you might make it easier by contacting your local German diplomatic representative before you leave home. That way, you'll find out in advance where you stand, which documents and photos to take along, whether you'll have to take a physical at the public health department, and various other bureaucratic sundries. Once you get to Germany, you'll have ample time to try out your German because you'll be skipping from one permit-issuing office to another and back again if you get something wrong. Oh! Did we mention that permits need to be renewed at set intervals? Ah! The fun never ends!

I Need My Wheels!

All right, so you figured out you're in it for the long haul, and you desire the freedom and independence that an automobile can provide. Well, by now you're accustomed to searching out various governmental agencies and standing in line. Thus, you won't be surprised to learn that registering a car is about the same (and perhaps as bothersome) as registering yourself. Naturally, if you change your address during your car's lifetime, you have to re-register the car, in person, after you have re-registered yourself. Of course, you'll need to clear your car through the motor vehicle inspection department (*TÜV*) before you can register it—and thereafter once every two years. If your car passes that inspection, you can feel pretty proud to be driving in Germany and can rest assured that your car is in pretty good shape.

The Least You Need to Know

- After you learn a few basic phrases, you should have no trouble buying or renting an apartment, house, or castle (you never know!) from a German real estate agent.
- To furnish specific rooms, you will have to know the vocabulary for furnishings, amenities, and appliances.
- To speak of something you plan to do in the future, use the perfect tense with an implication of future action, or use the future tense, which is formed with the helping verb *werden* conjugated in the present + the verb in the infinitive.
- If you intend to stay in Germany somewhat permanently, you'll need to register yourself and, if you'll be working, obtain a work permit.
- A car, if you have one, adheres to the same rules of registration as you do!

Answer Key

You will find the answers to the exercises in this book arranged here by chapter and heading.

Chapter 1

Time to Change

1. seine Anschrift ändern
2. (sich) verwandeln in
3. sich umziehen
4. wechseln
5. umsteigen

Chapter 4

How Much Do You Understand Already?

1. Der Bandit ist blond.
2. Die Bank ist modern.
3. Die Olive ist parallel.
4. Der Wind ist warm.
5. Das Chaos ist irrational.

Cognate Conversation

1. Das Wetter ist gut.
2. Ist das Buch interessant?
3. Der Autor ist populär.
4. Das Parfüm ist attraktiv.
5. Der Wind ist warm.
6. Der Charakter ist primitiv.
7. Das Herz ist wild.
8. Das Salz ist weiß.

Putting It All Together

1. The president and the bandit bake tomatoes.
2. The uncle drinks wine.
3. The tiger and the elephant swim in the ocean.
4. The film begins in the supermarket.

5. "Religion and chaos? A modern problem," says the young, intelligent author.

6. The doctor and the detective find the lamp interesting.

7. My brother and my father have a guitar.

8. The alligator costs $10,000.

Chapter 5

1. Ich fliege <u>mit dem Flugzeug</u> von Wisconsin nach Vancouver.

2. Ich fahre <u>mit dem Auto</u> vom Flughafen zum See.

3. Ich fahre <u>mit dem Schiff</u> über den See.

4. Ich reite <u>mit dem Pferd zum Haus.</u>

5. Dann gehe ich <u>zu Fuß.</u>

Expressing Time

1. bis bald/auf Wiedersehen/bis später

2. bis später/bis bald/bis heute Abend

3. pünktlich

4. (zu) spät

5. (zu) früh

6. von Zeit zu Zeit

7. regelmäßig/täglich/jeden Tag

8. wöchentlich

Stating Location

1. Gegenüber der Post ist <u>der Bahnhof.</u>

2. Vor dem Museum ist <u>der Parkplatz.</u>

3. Links neben dem Hotel ist <u>der Bahnhof.</u>

4. Hinter dem Café ist <u>der Spielplatz.</u>

5. Neben der Bäckerei ist <u>das Café.</u>

What's Your Opinion?

1. <u>Ich weiß nicht.</u>/Ich habe keine Ahnung. Ich habe den Wetterbericht nicht gelesen.

2. Das finde ich gut./<u>Das ist eine tolle Idee.</u>/Bestimmt. Ich schwimme sehr gern!

3. <u>Du hast Recht.</u> Das Wetter ist nie stabil.

4. Das macht nichts./<u>Das ist mir egal.</u> Alle Wetterwebseiten haben einen guten Wetterbericht.

5. Bestimmt./Natürlich./<u>Klar.</u> Ich will den neusten Arnold Schwarzenegger Film sehen.

How Are You?

1. Ich bin <u>müde.</u>

2. Mir ist <u>kalt.</u>

3. Sie weint. Sie ist <u>traurig.</u>

4. Ich bin <u>froh,</u> dass das Wetter gut ist.

5. Mein Magen knurrt. Ich bin <u>hungrig.</u>

6. Ich bin <u>verliebt</u>.

7. Ich kann nicht mehr! Ich bin <u>fertig</u>/schlapp.

8. Ich bin <u>fit</u>.

9. Ich bin <u>gut gelaunt</u>.

Chapter 6

Compound Nouns

1. die Hotelkette

2. das Musikgeschäft

3. das Geschenkpapier

4. die Telefonnummer

5. der Briefkasten

6. die Schwerkraft (gravity)

7. der Treffpunkt

Practice Those Plurals

1. die Zimmer

2. die Gärten

3. die Wände

4. die Bilder

5. die Bücher

6. die Schüsseln

7. die Briefe

8. die Zeitungen

Chapter 7

Identifying Function

1. (Den Studenten) findet <u>der Detektiv</u> intelligent.

2. [Dem Vater] schicken <u>die Kinder</u> (den Kaffee).

3. <u>Die Menschen</u> helfen [den Kindern].

4. (Das Paket) packt <u>der Lehrer</u>.

5. <u>Die Mütter</u> bringen [den Vätern] (die Blumen).

Du, Ihr, or Sie?

1. Wie finden <u>Sie</u> Amerika?

2. Was machen <u>Sie</u>?

3. Was bringt <u>ihr</u> zum Park?

4. Was trinkst <u>du</u>?

5. Warum stinkst <u>du</u>?

6. Was planen <u>Sie</u>?

Er, Sie, Es?

1. **Es** ist blau. (The perfect house is blue.)

2. **Er** telefoniert regelmäßig. (The friendly uncle telephones regularly.

3. **Sie** ist modern. (The red wall is modern.)

4. **Er** ist lang. (The elegant letter is long.)

5. **Es** singt oft. (The blonde child sings often.)

Chapter 8

Painless Conjugation

1. Ich suche das Museum. (I look/am looking for the museum.)

2. Klaus reserviert ein Hotelzimmer. (Klaus reserves a hotel room.)

3. Sie warten auf den Bus. (She waits/is waiting for the bus.)

4. Ihr mietet ein Auto. (You all rent/are renting a car.)

5. Wir fragen nach der Adresse. (We ask/are asking for the address.)

6. Ich lerne Deutsch. (I learn/am learning German.)

7. Ich reise nach Hamburg. (I travel/am traveling to Hamburg.)

8. Er braucht ein Taxi. (He needs a taxi.)

9. Du besuchst deine Mutter. (You visit your mother.)

10. Tina bestellt ein Glas Wein. (Tina orders/is ordering a glass of wine.)

11. Christoph, du tanzt gut! (Cristoph, you dance well!)

12. Der Professor arbeitet jeden Tag. (The professor works every day.)

13. Die Professorin öffnet das Fenster. (The professor opens the window.)

14. Die Pizza kostet nur 10 Euro. (The pizza costs only 10 euros.)

Change and Conjugate

1. Hans isst gern Bratwurst.

2. Er gibt mir einen guten Tip.

3. Christoph sieht einen Biergarten.

4. Petra trifft ihre deutsche Brieffreundin.

5. Du sprichst sehr gut Englisch.

6. Karl liest die Süddeutsche Zeitung.

7. Almut fährt nach Berlin.

8. Der Bus hält vor der Kirche.

9. Der Bayer bläst das Horn.

10. Meine Freundin empfiehlt das Restaurant.

11. Du schläfst sehr lange.

12. Du wäschst jede Woche die Wäsche.

13. Paul läuft sehr schnell und oft.

14. Er schlägt den Tennisball.

15. Die Professorin trägt einen Mini-Rock.

Ask Me If You Can

1. Kostet das Ticket 200 Euro?

2. Ist das das Terminal für internationale Flüge?

3. Steht die Flugnummer auf dem Ticket?

4. Gibt es Toiletten auf dieser Etage?

5. Dauert der Flug zwei Stunden?

6. Ist das Abendessen inklusiv?

Chapter 9

To Be or Not to Be?

1. Ich bin Kellner (Kellnerin).

2. Er ist Krankenpfleger.

3. Sie ist Ärztin.

4. Ich bin Rechtsanwalt (Rechtsanwältin).

5. Du bist Student (Studentin).

6. Er ist Polizist.

7. Sie ist Geschäftsführerin.

8. Sie sind Schriftsteller (Schriftstellerin).

Ask Away

A: Sample Questions

2. Woher kommst du?

3. Mit wem reist du?

4. Wohin reist du?

5. Was trinkst du?

6. Wo trinkst du?

7. Wie lang(e) trinkst du?

B: Sample Questions

1. Wie heißen Sie?

2. Woher kommen Sie?

3. Wie lang(e) reisen Sie?

4. Wo reisen Sie?

5. Wie finden Sie die Schweiz?/Finden Sie die Schweiz sehr schön?

6. Wann reisen Sie zurück?/Reisen Sie bald zurück?

Chapter 10

Mine, All Mine

1. Das ist seine Schwester.

2. Das ist mein Onkel.

3. Das ist unsere Familie.

4. Das sind eure Kinder.

5. Das ist der Bruder des Mädchens.

6. Das ist die Mutter des Mannes.

7. Das sind die Eltern des Kindes.

8. Das ist der Ehemann meiner Schwester.

9. Das sind die Eltern seiner Frau.

10. Das ist die Tante deines Cousins.

Using Possessive Adjectives to Show Your Preference

1. Mein Lieblingsfilm ist ....

2. Mein Lieblingsschriftsteller/Meine Lieblingsschriftstellerin ist ....

3. Mein Lieblingsbuch ist ....

4. Meine Lieblingsstadt ist ....

5. Mein Lieblingssänger ist ....

Breaking the Ice

1. Darf ich mich vorstellen? Mein Name ist ….

2. Ich komme aus ….

3. Ich bin ….

4. Woher kommen Sie?

5. Kennen Sie (meinen Bruder, meine Schwester, meine Mutter, meinen Vater …)?

6. Das ist ….

7. Es freut mich, Sie kennenzulernen.

Using Idioms with *haben*

1. Er hat Lust mitzukommen.

2. Sie hat den Mut/hat Lust, Bungy-Jumping zu machen.

3. Er hat die Absicht zu heiraten.

4. Sie haben die Zeit, eine Reise nach Deutschland zu machen.

5. Ihr habt Glück im Spiel.

Applying Adjectives

A. 1. Wo spielt dieser interessante Film?

2. Ich nehme das kalte Bier.

3. Jedes rote T-Shirt ist billig.

4. Wir besuchen die kleine Stadt.

5. Sie lesen den besten Autoren.

B. 1. Das ist warmes Brot.

2. Sie hat kluge Ideen.

3. Frischer Salat ist gesund.

4. Haben Sie schöne Blumen?

5. Liebe Kerstin, ….

C. 1. Mainz ist eine schöne, alte Stadt.

2. Er ist mein bester Freund.

3. Ich sehe seine junge Schwester.

4. Wo ist ein gutes Restaurant?

5. Wir kaufen ein neues Auto.

Chapter 11

Signage

1. D   4. C

2. B   5. A

3. E

Giving Orders

Verb	du	ihr	Sie	English
abbiegen	Biege ab!	Biegt ab!	Biegen Sie ab!	Turn!
gehen	Geh(e)!	Geht!	Gehen Sie!	Go!
weiterge-hen	Geh(e) weiter!	Geht weiter!	Gehen Sie weiter!	Con-tinue!
laufen	Lauf(e)!	Lauft!	Laufen Sie!	Walk!
mitfahren	Fahr(e) mit!	Fahrt mit!	Fahren Sie mit!	Ride along!

Prepositions Are Particular!

Dative Prepositions

1. aus <u>dem</u> Flugzeug

2. bei <u>dem</u> (beim) Flughafen

3. von <u>der</u> Arbeit

4. zu <u>dem</u> (zum) Hotel

Accusative Prepositions

1. durch <u>das</u> (durchs) Land

2. ohne <u>den</u> Koffer

3. um <u>den</u> Sitz

Two-Way Prepositions

1. auf dein<u>en</u> Sitz (accusative)

2. an <u>der</u> Grenze (dative)

3. in <u>der</u> Toilette (dative)

4. neben <u>das</u> Bett (accusative)

5. unter dein<u>em</u> Handgepäck (dative)

Chapter 12

Modes of Transportation

1. Ich <u>nehme</u> ein Taxi zum Geschäft.

2. Wir <u>nehmen</u> die Straßenbahn in die Innenstadt.

3. Er <u>nimmt</u> das Auto zur Kirche.

4. Du <u>nimmst</u> den Bus durch die Stadt.

Using Which

1. Welchen Zug nehmen Sie?

2. In welche Stadt fährst du?

3. Welches Auto mietet er?

4. Welchen Freund besuchst du?

5. In welches Museum geht ihr?

6. Welches Hotel sucht sie?

7. Welches Buch nimmt er mit?

Wie spät ist es?

1. sieben Uhr achtunddreißig

2. drei Uhr sechs/sechs (Minuten) nach drei

3. vierzehn Uhr

4. zwölf Uhr fünfundzwanzig/fünf vor halb eins

5. neunzehn Uhr dreißig/halb acht

6. einundzwanzig Uhr fünfzig/zehn vor zehn

Chapter 13

What a Hotel! Does It Have ...?

1. **Gast:** Guten Tag. Haben Sie ein <u>Zimmer</u> frei?

2. **Empfangschef:** Möchten Sie ein Zimmer mit einem <u>Balkon</u>? Wir haben ein wunderschönes <u>Zimmer mit Aussicht</u> zur Meerseite.

3. **Gast:** Ja, warum nicht? Hat das Zimmer ein <u>Telefon</u>? Ich erwarte einen wichtigen Anruf.

4. **Empfangschef:** Selbstverständlich. Möchten Sie Vollpension oder <u>Halbpension</u>?

   Gast: Vollpension, bitte.

5. **Empfangschef:** Gut. Die Zimmernummer ist 33. Hier ist Ihr <u>Schlüssel</u>. Gute Nacht.

Calling Housekeeping

1. Ich brauche einen Adapter.

2. Ich hätte gern ein Mineralwasser.

3. Ich brauche Briefpapier.

4. Ich hätte gern einen Aschenbecher und Streichhölzer.

5. Ich brauche ein Kopfkissen.

6. Ich möchte ein Badetuch.

Ordinal Numbering

1. Wir haben nicht viel Geld. Wir fahren <u>zweiter</u> Klasse.

2. "Erster Stop ist Marl; zweiter Stop ist Haltern; <u>dritter</u> Stop ist Recklinghausen," sagt der Busfahrer.

3. Mein <u>erster</u> Beruf war Tellerwäscher. Heute bin ich Millionär.

4. Zuerst kommt die Post. Das <u>zweite</u> Gebäude auf der linken Seite ist ein Hotel.

5. Auf der zweiten Etage befindet sich das Restaurant. Auf der <u>dritten</u> Etage ist das Einkaufszentrum.

6. Er hat schon drei Söhne. Sein <u>viertes</u> Kind wird ein Mädchen.

7. Wenn eine Katze schon acht Leben gehabt hat, ist sie jetzt im <u>neunten</u> Lebensjahr!

Euro?

1. Das Buch kostet dreizehn (Euro) fünfundvierzig.

2. Die Blumen kosten sieben Euro zehn.

3. Die Ansichtskarte kostet fünfzig Cent.

4. Ein Einzelzimmer kostet einundachtzig Euro.

5. Das Ticket kostet sechsunddreißig (Euro) neunundneunzig.

Expressing Knowledge

1. <u>Weißt</u> du, wo Kerstin wohnt? (You're inquiring about a known fact—where Kerstin lives.)

2. Kerstin? Ich <u>kenne</u> niemanden mit dem Namen "Kerstin." Wer ist sie? (You are not familiar with this person.)

3. Ich <u>weiß</u>, dass sie sehr hübsch und intelligent ist! (You know the fact that she is cute and smart.)

4. Na, ja. Vielleicht <u>kennt</u> Ronja sie. (Maybe Ronja knows—is familiar with—her.)

5. <u>Kennen</u> wir nicht Kerstins Mann, Frank? (Again, knowing or being acquainted with a person uses *kennen*.)

6. Ach ja! Ich <u>kenne</u> ihren Mann vom Bus. (Got it figured out? "I know (am acquainted with) her husband from the bus.")

Coming Apart: Verbs with Separable Prefixes

1. Wann <u>sieht</u> Otto den Film <u>an</u>?

2. Tina <u>liest</u> das Buch <u>vor</u>.

3. Alicia <u>gibt</u> nie <u>auf</u>!

4. Gretchen <u>trinkt</u> ihr Bier immer <u>aus</u>!

Sticking It Out Together: Verbs with Inseparable Prefixes

1. Wo <u>bekommen</u> Sie das?

2. Ich <u>vergesse</u> die Adresse.

3. Roger Federer <u>gewinnt</u> fast immer.

4. Welches Restaurant <u>empfiehlst</u> du?

Let's ...

1. Lass uns nach Deutschland reisen!/ Reisen wir nach Deutschland!

2. Lass uns in den Garten gehen!/Gehen wir in den Garten!

3. Lass uns den Bus nehmen!/Nehmen wir den Bus!

4. Lass uns die Stadt besuchen!/Besuchen wir die Stadt!

5. Lass uns Deutsch lernen!/Lernen wir Deutsch!

Chapter 14

Call Me (Maybe!)

1. Ich kenne die Straße, aber nicht die <u>Hausnummer</u>.

2. Die <u>Postleitzahl</u> kommt vor der Stadt in der Adresse.

3. Ich habe ein Telefon. Meine <u>Telefonnummer</u> ist 03-45-60.

4. Du schickst eine <u>Postkarte/ Ansichtskarte</u> an deine Mutter.

5. Sein Name ist sehr lang! <u>Wie schreibt man</u> das?

European Countries, According to Germans

1. die Schweiz

2. Deutschland

3. Italien

4. Österreich

5. Großbritannien

6. Frankreich

How's the Weather?

1. Erfurt ist bewölkt.

2. München ist heiter bis wolkig.

3. Schwerin ist sonnig.

4. Kiel ist regnerisch.

5. In Düsseldorf gibt es Gewitter/gewittert es.

A Mouthful of Months

1. Mein Geburtstag ist im …

2. Ich mache Urlaub im …

3. Mein Lieblingsmonat ist der …

4. Die Schule beginnt im …

The Four Seasons

1. Es schneit viel im Winter.

2. Die Blätter fallen im Herbst von den Bäumen.

3. Die Blumen blühen im Frühling.

4. Die Sonne scheint oft im Sommer.

Making a Date

1. Valentinstag ist am 14. Februar.

2. Mein Geburtstag ist am ….

3. Halloween ist am ….

4. Neujahr ist am 1. Januar.

Time Expressions

1. My birthday is a week from today.

2. Yesterday the weather was good.

3. Saturdays I play tennis.

4. We travel to Germany the day after tomorrow.

5. We are eating in a restaurant the next day.

Chapter 15

What Do You Want to See?

1. Im Nachtclub sieht man eine Vorstellung.

2. In der Kathedrale sieht man die Glasmalerei.

3. Im Schloss sieht man (die) Wandteppiche.

4. Im Zoo sieht man (die) Tiere.

5. Im Museum sieht man (die) Bilder und Skulpturen.

6. Im Kino sieht man den Film.

7. In der Disco sieht man (die) Tänzer.

8. In der Bibliothek sieht man (die) Bücher.

Making Suggestions

1. Ich <u>kann</u> später kommen.

2. Was <u>willst</u> du machen?

3. Christina <u>muss</u> viel lernen.

4. Dieser Film <u>soll</u> sehr gut sein.

5. Wolfram <u>darf</u> nicht mitkommen.

More Suggestions

1. Lass uns eine Kirche besichtigen!
Fantastisch! Ich liebe Kirchen.
Nein, das interessiert mich nicht.

2. Lass uns eine Ausstellung sehen!
Ja, das interessiert mich.
Nein, das ist langweilig.

3. Lass uns nach Europa reisen!
Ja, ich liebe Europa.
Nein, ich mag Europa nicht.

4. Lass uns Bilder anschauen!
Ja, das interessiert mich.
Nein, ich habe keine Lust.

5. Las uns in die Oper gehen!
Ja, das interessiert mich.
Nein, das interessiert mich nicht.

6. Lass uns Norwegisch lernen!
Ja, ich mag das.
Nein, ich mag das nicht.

7. Lass uns ein Auto mieten!
Wunderschön! Das macht mir Spaß!
Nein, ich kann nicht Auto fahren!

Chapter 16

Wear It Well

1. In unseren Schuhen <u>tragen</u> wir <u>Socken</u>.

2. Wenn ich schlafe, <u>trage</u> ich einen <u>Schlafanzug</u>.

3. Unter deiner Hose <u>trägst</u> du <u>Unterwäsche</u>.

4. Wenn es regnet, <u>trage</u> ich einen <u>Regenmantel</u>.

5. Im Winter <u>tragt</u> ihr warme <u>Handschuhe</u>.

6. Wenn man in die Oper geht, <u>trägt</u> man einen <u>Anzug</u> mit einem <u>Schlips/ mit einer Krawatte</u>.

7. Im Sommer <u>tragen</u> viele Leute <u>Shorts</u> und ein <u>T-Shirt</u>.

Colors

1. Ich möchte einen hellroten Rock.

2. Ich möchte einen dunkelblauen Anzug.

3. Ich möchte einen hellgelben Hut.

4. Ich möchte eine graue Jacke.

5. Ich möchte eine/einen gepunktete/ gepunkteten Krawatte/Schlips.

6. Ich möchte eine karierte Hose.

7. Ich möchte einen modischen Badeanzug.

8. Ich möchte ein gestreiftes Hemd.

What's the Object?

Accusative Pronouns

1. Ich trage <u>sie</u>.

2. Du trägst <u>ihn</u>.

3. Kerstin trägt <u>es</u>.

4. Frank trägt <u>sie</u>.

Dative Pronouns

1. Ich gebe <u>ihnen</u> Schokolade.

2. Bernadette schenkt <u>ihr</u> Blumen.

3. Thomas dankt <u>ihm</u> für den Kaffee.

4. Wir geben <u>ihm</u> eine Olive.

Using Direct Object Pronouns

1. Ja, ich mag <u>ihn</u>./Nein, ich mag <u>ihn</u> nicht.

2. Ja, ich mag <u>sie</u>./Nein, ich mag <u>sie</u> nicht.

3. Ja, ich mag <u>sie</u>./Nein, ich mag <u>sie</u> nicht.

4. Ja, ich mag <u>es</u>./Nein, ich mag <u>es</u> nicht.

Using Indirect Object Pronouns

1. Schenk ihnen einen Schal!

2. Schenk ihr ein Kleid!

3. Schenk ihm eine kurze Hose!

4. Schenk ihr eine Strumpfhose!

5. Schenke ihn ihnen!

6. Schenke es ihr!

7. Schenke sie ihm!

8. Schenke sie ihr!

What's Your Preference?

1. Welche Krawatte?

2. Welcher Anzug?

3. Welches T-Shirt?

4. Welche Schuhe?

5. Welches Kleid?

6. Welchen Schlafanzug?

Chapter 17

Getting There

1. Ich gehe zur Konditorei.

2. Ich gehe zum Metzger/zur Metzgerei.

3. Ich gehe zur Bäckerei/zum Bäcker.

4. Ich gehe zum Fischgeschäft.

Prost! ("Cheers!")

1. Was möchten Sie <u>trinken</u>?

2. Ich <u>trinke</u> ein Bier.

3. Die beiden Frauen am Nachbartisch <u>trinken</u> Kaffee.

4. Mattias und ich <u>trinken</u> gern milden Wein.

5. Am liebsten <u>trinke</u> ich Limonade.

6. Was <u>trinkst</u> du am liebsten?

A Trip to the Market

1. Ich möchte drei Flaschen Wein, bitte.

2. Ich möchte ein halbes Pfund Garnelen, bitte.

3. Ich möchte ein Viertel Pfund Käse, bitte.

4. Ich möchte eine Tüte Kirschen, bitte.

5. Ich möchte ein Dutzend Eier, bitte.

6. Ich möchte ein Kilo Lachs, bitte.

7. Ich möchte drei Pfund Kartoffeln, bitte.

8. Ich möchte ein halbes Kilo/ein Pfund Wurst, bitte.

9. Ich möchte einen Liter Sahne, bitte.

10. Ich möchte eine Kiste Bier, bitte.

Chapter 18

Something's Missing

1. Mir fehlt die Tasse.

2. Ihm fehlt der Löffel.

3. Ihr fehlt das Messer.

4. Uns fehlt der Salzstreuer.

You Need What?

1. Ich brauche eine Speisekarte.

2. Ich brauche ein Glas.

3. Ich brauche eine Serviette.

4. Ich brauche eine Untertasse.

That's the Way I Like It

1. Sie möchte ihr Steak gut durchgebraten.

2. Hans möchte seinen Fisch paniert.

3. Wir möchten unsere Kartoffeln püriert.

4. Ich möchte mein Gemüse gedünstet.

5. Ich hätte gern ein Spiegelei.

Chapter 19

Where to Play

1. Ich wandere am liebsten im Gebirge/Wald.

2. Fußball spielen wir auf dem Fußballplatz.

3. Zum Skifahren gehe ich auf die Skipiste.

4. Anna schwimmt gern im Schwimmbad.

5. Wir segeln gern auf dem Meer.

6. Schlittschuh lauft ihr im Eisstadion.

Express Your Desire with *Mögen*

1. Anne möchte bergsteigen.

2. Wir möchten wandern.

3. Franz und Klara möchten reiten.

4. Ihr möchtet in der Sporthalle Badminton spielen.

5. Hans und Franz möchten am Fluss angeln.

Do You Accept or Refuse?

1. Möchten Sie Basketball spielen? Ja, das ist eine gute Idee.

2. Möchten Sie wandern? Nein, ich bin müde.

3. Möchten Sie Fußball spielen? Warum nicht?

4. Möchten Sie angeln? Nein, ich habe keine Zeit.

5. Möchten Sie Badminton spielen? Nein, ich bin müde.

6. Möchten Sie Radfahren? Natürlich.

Adverbs in Action

1. Ich tanze ….

2. Ich spiele … Klavier.

3. Ich koche ….

4. Ich spiele … Golf.

5. Ich laufe ….

6. Ich singe ….

7. Ich spiele … Tennis.

8. Ich wandere ….

Chapter 20

At the Dry Cleaner—*in die Reinigung*

1. diese Bluse, dieses Sakko, diese Krawatte/diesen Schlips

2. diese Jacke, diese Shorts, diesen Schal

3. diese Hose, dieses Hemd, diesen Rock

4. dieses Kleid, diesen Anzug, diese Socken

At the Laundromat—*im Waschsalon*

1. dryer = der Trockner

2. laundromat = der Waschsalon/die Münzwäscherei

3. washing machine = die Waschmaschine

4. laundry soap = der Waschpulver

5. to wash = waschen (sehr stark)

6. to look for = suchen

7. to buy = kaufen

8. to use = benutzen

9. dirty = dreckig/schmutzig

I Need This Fixed

1. Ich suche einen Waschsalon/eine Münzwäscherei.

2. Können Sie dieses Kleid für mich reinigen?

3. Um wie viel Uhr schließen Sie?

4. Können Sie meine Stiefel putzen, bitte?

5. Ich habe viel dreckige Wäsche.

6. Wo kann ich diese Schuhe putzen?

Make Degree Evaluations

1. der kürzeste Haarschnitt
2. die lockigste Dauerwelle
3. eine dunklere Farbe
4. das schmutzigste/dreckigste Hemd
5. der/die billigste Waschsalon/ Münzwäscherei
6. Dieser Trockner ist größer.
7. die nächste Reinigung
8. Dieser Absatz ist am höchsten.

Chapter 21

Symptoms

1. Ich habe eine Erkältung.
2. Ich habe Husten.
3. Ich habe Kopfschmerzen.
4. Ich habe Bauchschmerzen.
5. Ich habe eine Blase.
6. Ich habe Fieber.

Have It on Hand

1. Ich brauche Aspirin.
2. Ich brauche Krücken.
3. Ich brauche Heftpflaster.
4. Ich brauche Taschentücher.

5. Ich brauche Schlaftabletten/ein Heizkissen.
6. Ich brauche Hustenbonbons/ Hustensaft.
7. Ich brauche Rasiercreme/eine Rasierklinge.
8. Ich brauche eine Pinzette.
9. Ich brauche eine Nagelfeile.

Reflexive Verbs in Action

1. Ich wasche mich.
2. Ich rasiere mich.
3. Ich ziehe mich an.
4. Ich mache mich fertig.
5. Ich strecke mich.
6. Ich ziehe mich aus.
7. Ich lege mich hin.

Be Bossy

1. Wasch(e) dich! Wasch(e) dich nicht!
2. Zieh dich um! Zieh dich nicht um!
3. Rasier dich! Rasier dich nicht!
4. Mach(e) dich fertig! Mach(e) dich nicht fertig!
5. Setz dich! Setz dich nicht!
6. Entspann dich! Entspann dich nicht!

Chapter 22

Producing the *Perfekt*

1. Ich bin in die Drogerie gegangen.

2. Ich habe Aspirin und Rasiercreme aus dem Regal genommen.

3. Ich habe meine Einkäufe zur Kasse gebracht.

4. Sie haben nicht viel gekostet.

5. Ich habe der Kassiererin geantwortet.

6. Ich habe nicht an meine Einkaufstasche gedacht.

7. Ich habe sie nicht mitgenommen.

All You Did

1. Du bist ins Museum gegangen.

2. Er hat die Einkäufe vergessen.

3. Sie ist zum Friseur gefahren.

4. Sie haben den Anruf gemacht.

5. Wir haben den Film gesehen.

6. Ihr habt an eure Eltern gedacht.

7. Ich habe Toast gemacht.

8. Du bist in den Bergen gewandert.

9. Sie haben die Oper genossen.

10. Ich habe ein Glas Wein getrunken.

Ask Questions

1. Seid ihr zum Friseur gegangen? Seid ihr nicht zum Friseur gegangen?

2. Haben sie den Hustensaft getrunken? Haben sie den Hustensaft nicht getrunken?

3. Hast du an die Einkaufstasche gedacht? Hast du nicht an die Einkaufstasche gedacht?

4. Hat Thomas geraucht? Hat Thomas nicht geraucht?

5. Hat Susanne den Käse gegessen? Hat Susanne den Käse nicht gegessen?

Chapter 23

Phoning Home

1. Ich habe den Hörer abgenommen.

2. Ich habe die Telefonkarte eingeführt.

3. Dann habe ich die Telefonnummer gewählt.

4. Ich habe eine Nachricht hinterlassen.

5. Danach habe ich den Hörer aufgelegt.

An Actual Phone Conversation

1. Frau Gehring: Gehring, Hello.

2. Johannes: Hi, this is Johannes. May I please speak with Tanja?

3. Frau Gehring: One moment, please. I'm sorry. She's not home.

4. Johannes: When can I reach her?

5. Frau Gehring: I don't know when she'll be back. Would you like to leave a message?

6. Johannes: No, thanks. I'll call back again later. Good-bye.

7. Gehring: Good-bye.

They're Busy

1. Sie hat sich angezogen.

2. Er hat sich rasiert.

3. Wir haben uns gewaschen.

4. Sie haben sich die Zähne geputzt.

5. Er hat sich umgezogen.

6. Er hat sich gekämmt.

7. Sie hat sich geschminkt.

8. Er hat sich fertig gemacht.

Getting It Right

1. Ich schreibe meinem Freund einen Brief.

2. Wir lesen ein Buch.

3. Sie schreibt ihren Eltern eine Postkarte.

4. Du liest die Wohnungsanzeigen.

5. Ich lese eine Illustrierte.

6. Wolfram liest gern Kinderbücher.

7. Ihr schreibt uns jede Woche.

Would You Please ...

1. Würdest du bitte oft schreiben?

2. Würdest du bitte gute Zeitungen lesen?

3. Würdest du bitte dein Medikament nehmen?

4. Ich würde gern nach Spanien fahren.

5. Ich würde gern lang schlafen.

6. Ich würde gern nur tanzen.

7. Ich würde in die Oper gehen.

8. Ich würde mehr Milch trinken.

9. Ich würde nicht alles kaufen.

You Have Three Wishes

1. Ich hätte am liebsten ein Schloss.

2. Ich hätte am liebsten ein Stück Schwarzwälder Kirschtorte.

3. Ich hätte am liebsten viel Geld.

4. Ich hätte am liebsten ein Haus in den Alpen.

5. Ich hätte am liebsten ein großes Bier.

6. Ich hätte am liebsten viele schöne Blumen.

Chapter 24

Auf Möbelsuche (in Search of Furniture)

1. Ich brauche ein bequemes Sofa.

2. Ich brauche einen kleinen Stuhl.

3. Ich brauche eine modische Uhr.

4. Ich brauche eine helle Lampe.

5. Ich brauche einen billigen Tisch.

German Culture

1. Müller's Furniture Store

2. Absolute guarantee of quality

3. We'll guarantee free furniture repair within the first two years.

4. We'll deliver your furniture for free.

5. We'll buy your old furniture back.

6. We ensure this price and quality.

Tomorrow's Plans

1. Sie werden ins Kino gehen.

2. Er wird Brot backen.

3. Wir werden Tennis spielen.

4. Sie wird zum Zahnarzt gehen.

5. Ich werde Norbert anrufen.

6. Wir werden ein Buch lesen.

7. Ihr werdet Rad fahren.

8. Sie werden viel Deutsch sprechen.

Lexicon: English to German, German to English

How to Use This Lexicon

As you learn in *The Complete Idiot's Guide to Learning German, Fourth Edition*, some German nouns have articles in front of them. These articles label the words as feminine (*f*), masculine (*m*), or neutral (*n*). If a word occurs primarily in its plural form and you find it listed as such in this appendix, it will bear the plural marker, *die*. Also, you know that German nouns are capitalized, whereas in English, only proper nouns and adjectives are capitalized. Strong verb conjugations are given in parentheses. A period separates the infinitive form of separable prefix verbs.

English to German

A

a lot of   viel (*feel*)

about   circa (*tseeR-kuh*)

actor   Schauspieler/
Schauspielerin (*shou-shpee-luhR/in*) m./f.

address   Adresse (*A-dre-suh*) f.

advice   Rat (*Raht*) m.

advise (to)   raten (rät, hat geraten) (*Rah-tuhn*)

after   nach (*nACH*)

afternoon   Nachmittag (*nACH-mi-tahk*) m.

ago   vor (*foR*)

air   Luft (*looft*) f.

air-conditioning
Klimaanlage (*klee-mah-An-lah-guh*) f.

airline   Fluglinie (*flewk-lee-nyah*) f.

airplane   Flugzeug (*flewk-tsoyk*) n.

airport   Flughafen (*flewk-hah-fuhn*) m.

airport gate   Flugsteig (*flewk-shtayk*) m.

alarm clock   Wecker (*ve-kuhR*) m.

all   alle (*ah-luh*)

allergic   allergisch (*A-leR-gish*)

almond   Mandel (*mAn-duhl*) f.

along   entlang (*ent-lAng*)

almost   fast (*fAst*)

always   immer (*i-muhR*)

angry   ärgerlich (*äR-guhR-liH*)

ankle   Fußknöchel (*fews-knö-CHuhl*) m.

answer (to)   antworten (*Ant-voR-tuhn*)

answering machine   Anrufbeantworter
(*An-Rewf-buh-Ant-vohR-tuhR*) m.

apartment   Wohnung (*voh-noong*) f.

appetizer   Vorspeise (*foR-shpay-zuh*) f.

apple   Apfel (*Ap-fuhl*) m.

approximately   ungefähr (*oon-guh-fähR*)

April   April (*Ah-pril*) m.

apricot   Aprikose (*Ap-Ree-koh-zuh*) f.

app   App (*Ap*) m.

armchair   Sessel (*ze-suhl*) m.

around   rund (*Roont*)

arrive (to)   an.kommen (ist angekommen)
(*An-ko-muhn*)

art   Kunst (*koonst*) f.

ashtray   Aschenbecher (*ah-shun-be-HuhR*) m.

ask (to)   fragen (*fRah-guhn*)

asparagus   Spargel (*shpAR-guhl*) m.

at   bei (*bay*)

at home   zu Hause (*tsew hou-zuh*)

at last   endlich (*ent-liH*)

at the side   seitlich (*zayt-liH*)

attachment   der Anhang (*An-hAng*) m.

ATM   Bankautomat (*bAnk-ou-toh-mAt*) m.

aunt   Tante (*tAn-tuh*) f.

August   August (*ou-goost*) m.

autumn   Herbst (*heRpst*) m.

awake   munter (*moon-tuhR*)

awful   furchtbar (*fooRCHt-bahR*)

B

back   Rücken (*Rü-kuhn*) m.

backyard   Hinterhof (*hin-tuhR-hohf*) m.

bacon   Speck (*shpek*) m.

bad   schlecht (*shleHt*)

bag   Tüte (*tüh-tuh*) f.

bake (to)   backen (backt, hat gebacken) (*bA-kuhn*)

baker   Bäcker/Bäckerin (*bä-kuhR/in*) m./f.

bakery   Bäckerei (*bä-kuh-Ray*) f.

balcony   Balkon (*bAl-kon*) m.

bar (pub)   Kneipe (*knay-puh*) f.

basement   Keller (*ke-luhR*) m.

basil   Basilikum (*bah-zee-lee-koom*) n.

bathe (to)   baden (*bah-duhn*)

bathing suit   Badeanzug (*bah-duh-An-tsewk*) m.

bathroom   Badezimmer (*bah-duh-tsi-muhR*) n., Toilette (*toy-le-tuh*) f.

be allowed (to)   dürfen (darf) (*dür-fuhn*)

bean soup   Bohnensuppe (*boh-nuhn-zoo-puh*) f.

beans   Bohnen (*boh-nuhn*) pl.

beautiful   schön (*shöhn*)

become (to)   werden (wird, ist geworden) (*veR-duhn*)

bed   Bett (*bet*) n.

bedroom   Schlafzimmer (*shlahf-tsi-muhr*) n.

beef   Rindfleisch (*Rint-flaysh*) n.

beef broth   Kraftbrühe (*krAft-bRüh-uh*) f.

beer   Bier (*beeR*) n.

begin (to)   beginnen (hat begonnen) (*buh-gi-nuhn*)

behind   hinter (*hin-tuhR*)

beige   beige (*beyj*)

believe (to)   glauben (*glou-buhn*)

belt   Gürtel (*güR-tuhl*) m.

beneath   unter (*oon-tuhR*)

beside   neben (*ney-buhn*)

best (the)   am besten (*Am bes-tuhn*)

better   besser (*be-suhR*)

between   zwischen (*tsvi-shuhn*)

bicycle   Fahrrad (*fah-Rat*) n.

big   groß (*gRohs*)

bind (to)   binden (hat gebunden) (*bin-duhn*)

birthday   Geburtstag (*guh-booRts-tahk*) m.

black   schwarz (*shvARts*)

blanket   Bettdecke (*bet-de-kuh*) f.

blouse   Bluse (*blew-zuh*) f.

blow (to)   blasen (bläst, hat geblasen) (*blah-zuhn*)

blue   blau (*blou*)

blueberries   Blaubeeren (*blou-bey-Ruhn*) pl.

blunt   stumpf (*shtoompf*)

boat   Boot (*boht*) n.

body   Körper (*köR-puhR*) m.

book   Buch (*bu-CH*) n.

bookshelf   Bücherregal (*büh-HuhR-Rey-gal*) n.

bookstore   Buchhandlung (*bewCH-hAnt-loong*) f.

boots   Stiefel (*shtee-fuhl*) pl.

boring   langweilig (*lAng-vay-liH*)

borrow (to)   ausleihen (hat ausgeliehen) (*ous-lay-uhn*)

bottle   Flasche (*flah-shuh*) f.

bowl   Schüssel (*shü-suhl*) f.

box   Schachtel (*shACH-tuhl*) f.

boy   Junge (*yoon-guh*) m.

bra   Büstenhalter, BH (*bü-stuhn-hAl-tuhR*), (*bey-hah*) m.

brain   Gehirn (*guh-hiRn*) n.

brave   mutig (*mew-tiH*)

bread   Brot (*bRoht*) n.

break (to)   brechen (bricht, hat gebrochen) (*bRe-Huhn*)

bright   bunt (*boont*)

bring (to)   bringen (hat gebracht) (*bRin-guhn*)

broccoli   Brokkoli (*bRo-koh-lee*) m.

brother   Bruder (*bRew-duhR*) m.

brown   braun (*bRoun*)

burn (to)   brennen (hat gebrannt) (*bRe-nuhn*)

bus   Bus (*boos*) m.

busy   beschäftigt (*buh-shäf-tiH*)

butcher   Metzger/Metzgerin (*mets-guhR/in*) m./f.

butcher shop   Metzgerei (*mets-guh-Ray*) f.

butter   Butter (*boo-tuhR*) f.

button   Knopf (*knopf*) m.

buy (to)   kaufen (*kou-fuhn*)

C

cabbage   Kohl (*kohl*) m.

cake   Kuchen (*kew-CHuhn*) m.

call (to)   rufen (hat gerufen) (*Ruh-fuhn*)

calm   ruhig (*Rew-iH*)

camera   Kamera (*kah-me-Rah*) f., Fotoapparat (*foh-toh-ah-pah-Rat*) m.

can   Dose (*doh-zuh*) f.

can (to be able to)   können (kann) (*kö-nuhn*)

candies   Süßigkeiten (*süh-siH-kay-tuhn*) pl.

cap   Mütze (*mü-tsuh*) f.

car   Auto (*ou-toh*) n.

carpet   Teppich (*te-piH*) m.

carrot   Karotte (*kah-Ro-tuh*) f.

carry (to)   tragen (trägt, hat getragen) (*trah-guhn*)

carry-on luggage   Handgepäck (*hAnt-guh-päk*) n.

cash   Bargeld (*bahR-gelt*) n.

cat   Katze (*kA-tsuh*) f.

catch a cold (to) sich erkälten (*ziH eR-käl-tuhn*)

catch (to) fangen (fängt, hat gefangen) (*fAn-guhn*)

cathedral Kathedrale (*kah-tey-drah-luh*) f.

cauliflower Blumenkohl (*blew-muhn-kohl*) m.

celery Sellerie (*ze-luh-Ree*) m.

cell phone Handy, Mobiltelefon (*hahn-dee, moh-beel-tey-ley-fohn*) n.

chair Stuhl (*shtewl*) m.

change (coins) Wechselgeld, Kleingeld (*vek-suhl-gelt, klayn-gelt*) n.

change one's clothes (to) sich um.ziehen (hat sich umgezogen) (*ziH ewm-tsee-uhn*)

changeable wechselhaft (*vek-suhl-hAft*)

cheap billig (*bi-liH*)

cheese Käse (*käh-zuh*) m.

cherries Kirschen (*keeR-shuhn*) pl.

chest Brust (*bRoost*) f.

chicken Huhn (*hewn*) n.

chicken breast Hühnerbrust (*hüh-nuhR-broost*) f.

chicken salad Geflügelsalat (*guh-flüh-guhl-zah-lAt*) m.

child Kind (*kint*) n.

chocolate Schokolade (*shoh-koh-lah-duh*) f.

church Kirche (*keeR-Huh*) f.

cinema Kino (*kee-noh*) n.

city Stadt (*shtAt*) f.

city map Stadtplan (*shtAt-plAn*) m.

clean sauber (*zou-buhR*)

clean (to) reinigen (*ray-ni-guhn*), putzen (*poo-tsuhn*)

clearly klar (*klahR*)

climb (to) steigen (ist gestiegen) (*shtay-guhn*)

clock Uhr (*ewR*) f.

close (to) schließen (hat geschlossen) (*shlee-suhn*)

closet Schrank (*shrAnk*) m.

clothes Bekleidung (*buh-klay-doong*) f.

clothing store Bekleidungsgeschäft (*buh-klay-doongz-guh-shäft*) n.

cloudy bewölkt (*buh-völkt*)

coat Mantel (*mAn-tuhl*) m.

cod Kabeljau (*kah-buhl-you*) m.

coffee Kaffee (*kA-fey*) m.

coffee table Couchtisch (*kouch-tish*) m.

coins Münzen (*mün-tsuhn*) pl.

coke Cola (*ko-lA*) f.

cold kalt (*kalt*)

cold (illness) Erkältung (*eR-käl-toong*) f.

comb Kamm (*kAm*) m.

comb one's hair (to) sich kämmen (*ziH kä-muhn*)

computer Computer (*kom-pyew-tuhR*) m.

come (to) kommen (ist gekommen) (*ko-muhn*)

come back (to) zurück.kommen (ist zurückgekommen) (*tsuh-Rük-ko-muhn*)

comfortable bequem (*buh-kveym*)

command (to) befehlen (befiehlt, hat befohlen) (*buh-fey-luhn*)

commuter train S-Bahn (*es-bahn*) f.

concierge Pförtner/Pförtnerin (*pföRt-nuhR/in*) m./f.

conditioner (hair) Pflegespülung (*pfley-guh-shpüh-loong*) f.

cook (to) kochen (*kO-CHuhn*)

cookie Plätzchen (*pläts-Huhn*), Keks (*keks*) n.

corduroy Kord (*koRt*) m.

corn Mais (*mays*) m.

cost (to) kosten (*kos-tuhn*)

cotton (Baumwolle) (*boum-vo-luh*) f.

cough Husten (*hew-stuhn*) m.

country Land (*lAnt*) n.

courtyard Innenhof (*i-nuhn-hohf*) m.

cousin cousin/cousine (*koo-zin/kou-zinuh*) m./f.

crab Krebs (*kreyps*) m.

cream Crème (*kReym*) f.

cross Kreuz (*kRoyts*) m.

cry (to) weinen (*vay-nuhn*)

cucumber Gurke (*gooR-kuh*) f.

cup Tasse (*tA-suh*) f.

curly lockig (*lo-kiH*)

currants Johannisbeeren (*yoh-hA-nis-bey-Ruhn*) pl.

cutlery Besteck (*buh-shtek*) n.

cutlet Schnitzel (*shni-tsuhl*) n.

D

daily täglich (*tähk-liH*)

dance (to) tanzen (*tAn-tsuhn*)

dark dunkel (*doon-kuhl*)

daughter Tochter (*toCH-tuhR*) f.

day Tag (*tahk*) m.

day after tomorrow übermorgen (*üh-buhR-moR-guhn*)

day before yesterday vorgestern (*foR-ges-tuhRn*)

debt Schulden (*shool-duhn*) pl.

December Dezember (*dey-tsem-buhR*) m.

delicious lecker (*le-kuhR*)

dentist Zahnarzt/Zahnärztin (*tsahn-ARtst/tsahn-äRtst-in*) m./f.

depart (to) ab.fahren (fährt ab, ist abge-fahren) (*ap-fah-Ruhn*)

dessert Nachtisch (*nahCH-tish*) m., Nach-speise (*nahCH-shpay-zuh*) f.

develop (to) entwickeln (*ent-vi-kuhln*)

dial a phone (to) wählen (*väh-luhn*)

diarrhea Durchfall (*dooRCH-fAl*) m.

die (to) sterben (stirbt, ist gestorben) (*shteR-buhn*)

dining room Esszimmer (*es-tsi-muhR*) n.

dinner plate   Teller (*te-luhR*) m.

dirty   dreckig (*dRe-kiH*), schmutzig (*shmoo-tsiH*)

discover (to)   entdecken (*ent-de-kuhn*)

dish (of food)   Gericht (*guh-RiHt*) n.

dishes   Geschirr (*guh-sheeR*) n.

dishwasher   Spülmaschine (*shpül-mA-shee-nuh*) f.

do (to)   tun (hat getan) (*tuhn*)

doctor   Arzt/Ärztin (*aRtst/äRtst-in*) m./f.

door   Tür (*tühR*) f.

double room   Doppelzimmer (*do-puhl-tsi-muhR*) n.

download   herunter.laden (*heR-un-tuhR-lah-duhn*)

draw (to)   zeichnen (*tsayH-nuhn*)

dream   träumen (*tRoy-muhn*)

dress   Kleid (*klayt*) n.

dress oneself (to)   sich anziehen (hat sich angezogen) (*ziH An-zee-uhn*)

dresser   Kommode (*ko-moh-duh*) f.

drink (to)   trinken (hat getrunken) (*tRin-kuhn*)

drinks   Getränke (*guh-tRän-kuh*) pl.

drive (to)   fahren (färt, ist gefahren) (*fah-Ruhn*)

drizzle   Sprühregen (*shpRüh-Rey-guhn*) m.

drug store   Drogerie (*dRoh-guh-Ree*) f.

dry   trocken (*tRo-kuhn*)

dryer   Trockner (*tRok-nuhR*) m.

E

ear   Ohr (*ohR*) n.

early   früh (*fRüh*)

eat (to)   essen (isst, hat gegessen) (*es-uhn*)

easy   leicht (*layHt*)

egg   Ei (*ay*) n.

eggplant   Aubergine (*oh-beR-jee-nuh*) f.

elevator   Aufzug (*ouf-tsewk*) m.

email   Email (*ee-meyl*) f.

employee   Angestellte (*An-guh-shtel-tuh*) m./f.

empty   leer (*leyR*)

enjoy (to)   genießen (hat genossen) (*guh-nee-suhn*)

enough   genug (*guh-newk*)

envelope   Briefumschlag (*bReef-oom-shlahk*) m.

error   Irrtum (*iR-tewm*) m.

evening   Abend (*ah-buhnd*) m.

event   Ereignis (*eR-ayk-nis*) n.

every day   jeden Tag (*yey-duhn tahk*) m.

examine (to)   untersuchen (*oon-tuhR-zew-Huhn*)

excellent   ausgezeichnet (*ous-guh-tsayH-net*)

exchange rate   Wechselkurs (*vek-suhl-kooRs*) m.

exit   Ausgang (*ous-gAng*) m.

expensive   teuer (*toy-uhR*)

eye   Auge (*ou-guh*) n.

F

face Gesicht (*guh-ziHt*) n.

fall (to) fallen (fällt, ist gefallen) (*fA-luhn*)

false falsch (*fAlsh*)

false alarm blinder Alarm (*blin-duhR A-lARm*) m.

farmer Bauer/Bäurin (*bou-uhR/boy-Rin*) m./f.

fashion Mode (*moh-duh*) f.

fashionable modisch (*moh-dish*)

fast schnell (*shnel*)

fat dick (*dik*)

father Vater (*fah-tuhR*) m.

father-in-law Schwiegervater (*shvee-guhR-fah-tuhR*) m.

fear Angst (*Angst*) f.

February Februar (*feb-Rew-ahR*) m.

feel (to) sich fühlen (*ziH füh-luhn*)

fever Fieber (*fee-buhR*) n.

fill out (to) aus.füllen (*ous-fü-luhn*)

find (to) finden (hat gefunden) (*fin-duhn*)

fingernail Fingernagel (*fin-guR-nah-guhl*) m.

finished fertig (*feR-tiH*)

fireplace Kamin (*kah-meen*) m.

fish Fisch (*fish*) m.

fish (to) angeln (*An-geln*)

fitness center Fitnesscenter (*fit-nes-sen-tuhR*) n.

flight Flug (*flewk*) m.

flight number Flugnummer (*flewk-noo-muhR*) f.

floor Fußboden (*fews-boh-duhn*) m.

floor (story) Stock (*shtok*) m.

florist Blumengeschäft (*blew-muhn-guh-schäft*) n.

flounder Flunder/Rochen (*floon-duhR/Ro-CHuhn*) f.

flower Blume (*blew-muh*) f.

flu Grippe (*gRi-puh*) f.

fly (to) fliegen (ist geflogen) (*flee-guhn*)

fog Nebel (*ney-buhl*) m.

foggy neblig (*ney-buh-liH*)

follow (to) folgen (*fol-guhn*)

food Essen (*e-suhn*) n.

foot Fuß (*fews*) m.

for für (*fühR*)

foreign country Ausland (*ous-lAnt*) n.

forget (to) vergessen (vergisst, hat vergessen) (*feR-ge-suhn*)

fork Gabel (*gah-buhl*) f.

French fries Pommes frites (*po-muhs*) pl.

Friday Freitag (*fRay-tahk*) m.

fried eggs Spiegelei (*shpee-guh-lay*) n.

friend Freund/Freundin (*fRoynt/fRoyn-din*) m./f.

from von (*fon*)

from where woher (*voh-heR*)

fruit Obst (*opst*) n.

full voll (*fol*)

funny   lustig (*loos-tiH*)

furnished   möbliert (*möh-bleeRt*)

furniture   Möbel (*möh-buhl*) pl.

G

game   Spiel (*shpeel*) n.

garden   Garten (*gAR-tuhn*) m.

garlic   Knoblauch (*knohp-louCH*) m.

gas tank   Benzintank (*ben-tseen-tAnk*) m.

Germany   Deutschland (*doytch-lAnt*) n.

get oneself ready (to)   sich fertig machen (*ziH feR-tiH mA-CHuhn*)

ghost   Geist (*gayst*) m.

gift   Geschenk (*guh-shenk*) n.

gift shop   Geschenkartikelladen (*guh-shenk-AR-tee-kuhl-lah-duhn*) m.

give (to)   geben (gibt, hat gegeben) (*gey-buhn*)

glass   Glas (*glAs*) n.

glasses   Brille (*bri-luh*) f.

gloves   Handschuhe (*hAnt-shew-uh*) pl.

go (to)   gehen (ist gegangen) (*gey-uhn*)

go on (to)   weiter.gehen (ist weitergegangen) (*vay-tuhR-gey-uhn*)

good   gut (*gewt*)

good day   Guten Tag (*gew-tuhn tahk*) m.

good evening   Guten Abend (*gew-tuhn ah-bent*) m.

good morning   Guten Morgen (*gew-tuhn moR-guhn*) m.

good-bye   auf Wiedersehen (*ouf vee-duhR zey-uhn*)

grandfather   Opa (*oh-pah*) m.

grandmother   Oma (*oh-mah*) f.

gray   grau (*gRou*)

green   grün (*gRün*)

grocery store   Lebensmittelgeschäft (*ley-buhnz-mi-tuhl-guh-shäft*) n.

group   Gruppe (*gRoo-puh*) f.

grow (to)   wachsen (wächst, ist gewachsen) (*vak-suhn*)

H

hail   Hagel (*hah-guhl*) m.

hair   Haar (*hahR*) n.

hair dryer   Fön (*föhn*) m.

hairbrush   Haarbürste (*hahR-büR-stuh*) f.

haircut   Haarschnitt (*hahR-shnit*) m.

ham   Schinken (*shin-kuhn*) m.

hand   Hand (*hAnT*) f.

hang (to)   hängen (hängt, hat gehangen) (*hän-guhn*)

hanger   Kleiderbügel (*klay-duhR-büh-guhl*) m.

happen (to)   geschehen (geschieht, ist geschehen) (*guh-shey-uhn*)

happy   froh, (*fRöh-liH*), glücklich (*glük-liH*)

hard   schwer (*shveR*), hart (*hARt*)

hat   Hut (*hewt*) m.

have (to)   haben (hat, hat gehabt) (*hah-buhn*)

hazelnuts   Haselnüsse (*hah-zuhl-nü-suh*) pl.

head   Kopf (*kopf*) m.

headache   Kopfschmerzen (*kopf-shmeR-tsuhn*) pl.

healthy   gesund (*guh-zoont*)

hear   hören (*höh-Ruhn*)

heart   Herz (*heRts*) n.

hello   hallo (*hA-loh*)

help (to)   helfen (hilft, hat geholfen) (*hel-fuhn*)

herbs   Kräuter (*kroy-tuhR*) pl.

here   hier (*heeR*)

hers   ihr (*eeR*)

high   hoch (*hoCH*)

hike (to)   wandern (*vAn-duhRn*)

his   sein (*zayn*)

history   Geschichte (*guh-shiH-tuh*) f.

hit (to)   schlagen (schlägt, hat geschlagen) (*shlah-guhn*)

hold (to)   halten (hält, hat gehalten) (*hAl-tuhn*)

horrible   schrecklich (*shRek-liH*)

horse   Pferd (*pfeRt*) n.

horseradish   Meerrettich (*mey-Re-tiH*) m.

hot   heiß (*hays*)

hotel   Hotel (*hoh-tel*) n.

hour   Stunde (*shtoon-duh*) f.

hourly   stündlich (*shtünt-liH*)

house   Haus (*hous*) n.

how   wie (*vee*)

human being   Mensch (*mensh*) m.

humid   feucht (*foyHt*)

hunger   Hunger (*hoon-guhR*) m.

hungry   hungrig (*hoon-gRiH*)

I

ice cream   Eis (*ays*) n.

immediately   sofort (*zoh-foRt*)

important   wichtig (*viH-tiH*)

in front of   vor (*fohR*)

in the mornings   morgens (*moR-guhnz*)

in-laws   Schwiegereltern (*shvee-guhR-el-tuhRn*) pl.

industrious   fleißig (*flay-siH*)

injure oneself (to)   sich verletzen (*ziH feR-le-tsuhn*)

inspect (to)   kontrollieren (*kon-tRo-lee-Ruhn*)

interesting   interessant (*in-te-Re-sAnt*)

internet access   Internetzugang (*in-tuhR-net-tsew-grif*) m.

internet connection   Internetanschluss (*in-tuhR-net-An-schloos*) m.

iron   Bügeleisen (*büh-guhl-ay-zuhn*) n.

iron (to)   bügeln (*büh-guhln*)

J

jacket   Jacke (*yA-kuh*) f.

jam   Marmelade (*mAR-muh-lah-duh*) f.

January   Januar (*yah-new-ahR*) m.

jewelry   Schmuck (*shmook*) m.

juice   Saft (*zAft*) m.

K

key   Schlüssel (*shlü-suhl*) m.

kingdom   Reich (*RayCH*) n.

kiss (to)   küssen (*kü-suhn*)

kitchen   Küche (*kü-Huh*) f.

knee   Knie (*knee*) n.

knife   Messer (*me-suhR*) n.

know a fact (to)   wissen (weiß, hat gewusst) (*vi-suhn*)

know, be familiar with (to)   kennen (hat gekannt) (*ke-nuhn*)

knowledge   Erkenntnis (*eR-kent-nis*) f.

L

lady   Dame (*dah-muh*) f.

lake   See (*zey*) m.

lamb   Lamm (*lAm*) n.

late   spät (*shpäht*) late

later   später (*shpäh-tuhR*)

lay (to)   legen (*ley-guhn*)

lazy   faul (*foul*)

learn (to)   lernen (*leR-nuhn*)

leather   Leder (*ley-duhR*) n.

leave (to)   lassen (lässt, hat gelassen) (*lA-suhn*)

left   links (*links*)

leg   Bein (*bayn*) n.

lemon   Zitrone (*tsi-troh-nuh*) f.

lend (to)   leihen (hat geliehen) (*lay-uhn*)

less   weniger (*ve-nee-guhR*)

letter   Brief (*bReef*) m.

lettuce   Kopfsalat (*kopf-zA-laht*) m.

library   Bibliothek (*bib-lee-oh-tek*) f.

lie (to), be situated   liegen (hat gelegen) (*lee-guhn*)

lift (to)   heben (hat gehoben) (*hey-buhn*)

light   Licht (*liHt*) n.

light   hell (*hel*)

lightning   Blitz (*blits*) m.

like (to)   mögen (mag) (*möh-guhn*)

linen   Leinen (*lay-nuhn*) n.

lip   Lippe (*li-puh*) f.

little/not much   wenig (*vey-niH*)

living room   Wohnzimmer (*vohn-tsi-muhr*) n.

load (to)   laden (lädt, hat geladen) (*lah-duhn*)

long   lang (*lang*)

look (to)   blicken (*bli-kuhn*)

look (to look for)   suchen (*zew-Huhn*)

lose (to)   verlieren (hat verloren) (*feR-lee-Ruhn*)

love   Liebe (*lee-buh*) f.

love (to)   lieben (*lee-buhn*)

low   tief (*teef*)

M

magazine   Zeitschrift (*tsayt-shRift*) f.

main course   Hauptgericht (*houpt-guh-RiHt*) n.

make (to)   machen (*mA-CHuhn*)

man   Mann/Männer (*mAn/mä-nuhR*) m./pl.

March   März (*mäRts*) m.

market   Markt (*mARkt*) m.

marry (to)   heiraten (*hay-rA-tuhn*)

matches   Streichhölzer (*shtRayH-höl-tsuhR*) pl.

May   Mai (*may*) m.

maybe   vielleicht (*fee-layHt*)

meat   Fleisch (*flaysh*) n.

meet (to)   treffen (trifft, hat getroffen) (*tRe-fuhn*)

melon   Melone (*me-loh-nuh*) f.

menu   Speisekarte (*shpay-zuh-kAR-tuh*) f.

midnight   Mitternacht (*mi-tuhR-nACHt*) f.

milk   Milch (*milH*) f.

minute   Minute (*mi-new-tuh*) f.

mirror   Spiegel (*shpee-guhl*) m.

mister   Herr (*heR*) m

misunderstand (to)   missverstehen (hat misverstanden) (*mis-feR-shtey-uhn*)

Monday   Montag (*mohn-tahk*) m.

month   Monat (*moh-nAt*) m.

monthly   monatlich (*moh-nAt-liH*)

more   mehr (*meyR*)

morning   Morgen (*moR-guhn*) m.

mother   Mutter (*moo-tuhR*) f.

mother-in-law   Schwiegermutter (*shvee-guhR-moo-tuhR*) f.

motorcycle   Motorrad (*moh-toh-Rat*) n.

mouth   Mund (*moont*) m.

movie   Film (*film*) m.

much   viel (*feel*)

mushrooms   Pilze (*pil-tsuh*) pl.

music store   Musikgeschäft (*mew-zeek-guh-shäft*) n.

must   müssen (muss) (*mü-suhn*)

mustard   Senf (*zenf*) m.

my   mein (*mayn*)

N

name   Name (*nah-muh*) m.

napkin   Serviette (*zeR-vee-e-tuh*) f.

narrow   eng (*eng*)

neck   Hals (*halz*) m.

necktie   Schlips (*shlips*) m., Krawatte (*kRah-VA-tuh*) f.

need (to)   brauchen (*bRou-CHuhn*)

nervous   nervös (*neR-vöhs*)

never   nie (*nee*)

new   neu (*noy*)

news   Nachrichten (*nACH-RiH-tuhn*) pl.

newspaper   Zeitung (*tsay-toong*) f.

newsstand   Kiosk (*kee-osk*) m.

night   Nacht (*nACHt*) f.

night club   Nachtclub (*nACHt-kloob*) m.

nonsense   Quatsch (*kvatsch*) m.

nose   Nase (*nah-zuh*) f.

novel   Roman (*roh-mahn*) m.

now   jetzt (*yetst*)

nurse   Krankenpfleger/Krankenpflegerin (*kRan-kuhn-pfley-guhR/in*) m./f.

nuts   Nüsse (*nü-suh*) pl.

O

occasionally   gelegentlich (*guh-ley-gunt-liH*)

October   Oktober (*ok-toh-buhR*) m.

of course   selbstverständlich (*zelpst-feR-shtänt-liH*)

offer (to)   bieten (hat geboten) (*bee-tuhn*)

often   oft (*oft*)

oil   Öl (*öhl*) n.

old   alt (*Alt*)

older   älter (*äl-tuhR*)

onion   Zwiebel (*tsvee-buhl*) f.

only   nur (*nooR*)

open (to)   öffnen (*öf-nuhn*)

operator   Vermittlung (*feR-mit-loong*) f.

opposite   gegenüber (*gey-guhn-üh-buhR*)

order (to)   bestellen (*buh-shte-luhn*)

our   unser (*oon-zuhR*)

outdoors   draußen (*dRou-suhn*)

over   über (*üh-buhR*)

P

pack (to)   packen (*pA-kuhn*)

package   Paket (*pah-ket*) n.

painting   Bild (*bilt*) n.

pair of pants   Hose (*hoh-zuh*) f.

pajamas   Schlafanzug (*shlahf-An-tsook*) m.

parents   Eltern (*el-tuhRn*) pl.

park (to)   parken (*pAR-kuhn*)

parking lot   Parkplatz (*pARk-plAts*) m.

passport   Pass (*pAs*) m.

pastry shop   Konditorei (*kon-dee-toR-ay*) f.

patterned   gemustert (*guh-moos-tuRt*)

peaches   Pfirsiche (*pfeeR-ziH-uh*) pl.

pears   Birnen (*beeR-nuhn*) pl.

peas   Erbsen (*eRp-suhn*) pl.

pepper mill   Pfeffermühle (*pfe-fuhR-müh-luh*) f.

perfume   Parfüm (*paR-füm*) n.

permission   Erlaubnis (*eR-loup-nis*) f.

pharmacy   Apotheke (*ah-poh-tey-kuh*) f.

pickles   eingelegte Gurken (*ayn-guh-leyg-tuh gooR-kuhn*) pl.

piece   Stück (*shtük*) n.

pillow Kopfkissen (*kopf-ki-suhn*) n.

pineapple Ananas (*ah-nah-nAs*) f.

pink rosa (*Roh-zah*)

pizza Pizza (*pi-tsuh*) f.

plaid kariert (*kah-ReeRt*)

plan (to) planen (*plah-nuhn*)

play (to) spielen (*shpee-luhn*)

please bitte (*bi-tuh*)

podcast Podcast (*pod-kAst*) m.

poison Gift (*gift*) n.

police officer Polizist/Polizistin (*poh-lee-tsist/in*) m./f.

police station Polizeiamt (*poh-lee-tsay-Amt*) n.

polka-dotted gepunktet (*guh-poonk-tuht*)

poor arm (*Arm*) m.

pork Schweinefleisch (*shvayn-flaysh*) n.

possess (to) besitzen (hat besessen) (*buh-zi-tsuhn*)

postcard Ansichtskarte (*An-ziHts-kAR-tuh*) f.

post office Post (*post*) f.

potato Kartoffel (*kAR-to-fuhl*) f.

praise (to) loben (*loh-buhn*)

produce shop Obst- und Gemüsehandlung (*opst-oot-guh-müh-zuh-hAnt-loong*) f.

promise (to) versprechen (verspricht, hat versprochen) (*feR-shpRe-Huhn*)

property Eigentum (*ay-guhn-tewm*) n.

proud stolz (*shtolts*)

prove (to) beweisen (*buh-vay-zuhn*)

pull (to) ziehen (hat gezogen) (*tsee-uhn*)

punctually pünktlich (*pünkt-liH*)

purple lila (lee-*lah*)

purse Handtasche (*hAnt-tA-shuh*) f.

Q

quite ziemlich (*tseem-lih*)

R

rain Regen (*Rey-guhn*) m.

raincoat Regenmantel (*Rey-guhn-mAn-tuhl*) m.

rainy regnerisch (*Reyg-nuh-Rish*)

read (to) lesen (liest, hat gelesen) (*ley-zuhn*)

receipt Quittung (*kvi-toong*) f.

receive (to) bekommen (hat bekommen) (*buh-ko-muhn*)

recommend (to) empfehlen (empfiehlt, hat empfohlen) (*em-pfey-luhn*)

recuperate (to) sich erholen (*ziH eR-hoh-luhn*)

red rot (*Rot*)

regularly regelmäßig (*rey-guhl-mäh-siH*)

relax (to) sich entspannen (*ziH ent-shpA-nuhn*)

remain (to) bleiben (ist geblieben) (*blay-buhn*)

rent (to) mieten (*mee-tuhn*)

reserve (to) reservieren (*Re-zeR-vee-Ruhn*)

reside (to)   wohnen (*voh-nuhn*)

result   Ergebnis (*eR-gep-nis*) n.

ride (to)   reiten (ist geritten) (*Ray-tuhn*)

right   rechts (*ReHts*)

river   Fluss (*floos*) m.

roll   Brötchen (*bRöt-chuhn*) n.

roll (to)   rollen (*Ro-luhn*)

room   Zimmer (*tsi-muhR*) n.

roughly   etwa (*et-vah*)

run (to)   laufen (läuft, ist gelaufen) (*lou-fuhn*)

rye bread   Roggenbrot (*Ro-guhn-bRoht*) n.

S

sad   traurig (*tRou-RiH*)

sail (to)   segeln (*zey-guhln*)

sailboat   Segelboot (*zey-guhl-boht*) n.

salmon   Lachs (*lAks*) m.

salt shaker   Salzstreuer (*zAlts-shtRoy-uhR*) m.

Saturday   Samstag (*zAms-tahk*) m.

saucer   Untertasse (*oon-teR-tA-suh*) f.

sausage   Wurst (*vooRst*) f.

save money (to)   Geld sparen (*gelt shpah-Ruhn*)

say (to)   sagen (*zah-guhn*)

scarf   Schal (*shahl*) m.

scratch (to)   kratzen (*krA-tsuhn*)

seafood   Meeresfrüchte (*mey-Ruhs-fRüH-tuh*) pl.

season   Jahreszeit (*yah-Ruhs-tsayt*) f.

second   Sekunde (*ze-koon-duh*) f.

see (to)   sehen (sieht, hat gesehen) (*zey-uhn*)

sell (to)   verkaufen (*feR-kou-fuhn*)

send (to)   schicken (*shi-kuhn*)

send (to)   senden (*zen-duhn*)

serious   ernst (*eRnst*)

set (to)   setzen (*ze-tsuhn*)

shadow   Schatten (*shA-tuhn*) m.

shampoo   Haarshampoo (*hahR-shAm-pew*) n.

shave oneself (to)   sich rasieren (*ziH rah-zee-Ruhn*)

shine (to)   scheinen (ist geschienen) (*shee-nuhn*)

ship   Schiff (*shif*) n.

shirt   Hemd (*hemt*) n.

shoes   Schuhe (*shew-uh*) pl.

shopping center   Einkaufszentrum (*ayn-koufs-tsen-tRoom*) n.

short   kurz (*kooRts*)

shoulder   Schulter (*shool-tuhR*) f.

show (to)   zeigen (*tsay-guhn*)

shower   Dusche (*dew-shuh*) f.

shrimp   Garnele (*gahR-ney-luh*) f.

sick   krank (*kRAnk*)

side dish Beilage (*bay-lah-guh*) f.

sign Schild (*shilt*) n.

signature die Unterschrift (*oon-tuhR-shRift*) f.

silk Seide (*zay-duh*) f.

since seit (*zayt*)

sing (to) singen (hat gesungen) (*zin-guhn*)

single room Einzelzimmer (*ayn-tsel-tsi-muhR*) n.

sink (to) sinken (hat gesunken) (*zin-kuhn*)

sister Schwester (*shves-tuhR*) f.

sit (to) sitzen (hat gesessen) (*zi-tsuhn*)

skin Haut (*hout*) f.

skirt Rock (*Rok*) m.

sky Himmel (*hi-muhl*) m.

sleep (to) schlafen (schläft, hat geschlafen) (*shlah-fuhn*)

slice Scheibe (*shay-buh*) f.

slow langsam (*lAng-zAm*)

small klein (*klayn*)

smart klug (*klewk*)

smoke (to) rauchen (*rou-CHuhn*)

snake Schlange (*shlanuh*) f.

snow Schnee (*shney*) m.

socks Socken (*zo-kuhn*) pl.

soap Seife (*zay-fuh*) f.

society Gesellschaft (*guh-zel-shAft*) f.

sometimes manchmal (*mAnH-mahl*)

son Sohn (*zohn*) m.

song Lied (*leed*) n.

soon bald (*bAlt*)

soup dish Suppenteller (*zoo-puhn-te-luhR*) m.

sour sauer (*zou-uhR*)

speak (to) sprechen (spricht, hat gesprochen) (*shpRe-Huhn*)

spin (to) spinnen (hat gesponnen) (*shpi-nuhn*)

spinach Spinat (*shpi-naht*) m.

spine Wirbelsäule (*viR-buhl-zoy-luh*) f.

spoon Löffel (*lö-fuhl*) m.

sport shop Sportgeschäft (*shpoRt-guh-shäft*) n.

spring Frühling (*fRüh-ling*) m.

stand (to) stehen (hat gestanden) (*shtey-uhn*)

stationery Schreibwaren (*shRayp-vah-Ruhn*) pl.

still noch (*noCH*)

stink (to) stinken (hat gestunken) (*shtin-kuhn*)

stomach Magen (*mah-guhn*) m., Bauch (*bouCH*) m.

store Geschäft (*guh-shäft*) n., Laden (*lah-duhn*) m.

storm Sturm (*shtooRm*) m.

straight ahead geradeaus (*guh-Rah-duh-ous*)

strawberries Erdbeeren (*eRt-bey-Ruhn*) pl.

street Straße (*shtRah-suh*) f.

streetcar Straßenbahn, S-bahn (*shtRah-suhn-bahn, es-bahn*) f.

strength Stärke (*shtäR-kuh*) f.

striped gestreift (*guh-shtRayft*)

strong stark (*shtARk*)

study (to) studieren (*shtew-dee-Ruhn*)

stupid blöd (*blöd*)

suckle (to) lutschen (*loo-tchun*)

suddenly plötzlich (*plöts-liH*)

suede Wildleder (*vilt-ley-duhR*) n.

suffer (to) leiden (hat gelitten) (*lay-duhn*)

sugar Zucker (*tsoo-kuhR*) m.

suit Anzug (*An-tsewk*) m.

suitcase Koffer (*ko-fuhR*) m.

summer Sommer (*zo-muhR*) m.

sun Sonne (*zo-nuh*) f.

Sunday Sonntag (*zon-tahk*) m.

sunny sonnig (*zo-niH*)

supermarket Supermarkt (*zew-puhR-mARkt*) m.

suspenseful spannend (*shpA-nuhnt*)

sweet süß (*zühs*)

swim (to) schwimmen (ist geschwommen) (*shvi-muhn*)

swimming pool Schwimmbad (*shvim-baht*) n.

T

table Tisch (*tish*) m.

tablecloth Tischdecke (*tish-de-kuh*) f.

take (to) nehmen (nimmt, hat genommen) (*ney-muhn*)

tea Tee (*tey*) m.

teach lehren (*ley-Ruhn*)

teacher Lehrer (*ley-RuhR*) m., die Lehrerin (*ley-Ruh-Rin*) f.

teaspoon Teelöffel (*tey-lö-fuhl*) m.

telephone Telefon (*te-le-fon*) n.

telephone number
Telefonnummer (*tey-ley-foh-noo-muhR*) f.

telephone (to) telefonieren (*te-le-foh-nee-Ruhn*)

television set Fernseher (*feRn-zey-uhR*) m.

tennis shoes Tennisschuhe (*te-nis-shew-uh*) pl.

text message SMS (*es-em-es*) f.

texting Simsen (*zim-suhn*) n.

thank (to) danken (*dAn-kuhn*)

thanks danke (*dAn-kuh*)

that dass (*dAs*)

their ihr (*eeR*)

then danach (*dA-nahCH*)

there da, dort (*dA*), (*doRt*)

therefore also (*Al-zoh*)

thin dünn (*dün*)

thing Zeug (*tsoyk*) n.

think (to) denken (hat gedacht) (*den-kuhn*)

thirst Durst (*dooRst*) m.

thirsty durstig (*dooRs-tiH*)

throat Kehle (*key-luh*) f.

thunder Donner (*do-nuhR*) m.

Thursday Donnerstag (*do-nuhRz-tahk*) m.

time Zeit (*tsayt*) f.

tired müde (*müh-duh*)

to zu, (*tsew*) nach (*nahCH*)

today heute (*hoy-tuh*)

toe Zeh (*tsey*) m.

together zusammen (*tsew-zA-muhn*)

tomato Tomate (*toh-mah-tuh*) f.

tomorrow morgen (*moR-guhn*)

tongue Zunge (*tsoon-guh*) f.

too little zu wenig (*tsew vey-niH*)

too much zu viel (*tsew feel*)

tooth Zahn (*tsahn*) m.

toothbrush Zahnbürste (*tsahn-büR-stuh*) f.

torment Qual (*kvahl*) f.

towel Handtuch (*hAn-tewCH*) n.

traffic Verkehr (*feR-keyR*) n.

train Zug (*tsewk*) m.

train station Bahnhof (*bahn-hof*) m.

transfer in travel (to) um.steigen (ist umgestiegen) (*oom-shtay-guhn*)

transfer money (to) Geld überweisen (*gelt üh-buhR-vay-zuhn*)

travel (to) reisen (*Ray-suhn*); fahren (fährt, ist gefahren) (*fah-Ruhn*)

tree Baum (*boum*) m.

trout Forelle (*foh-Re-luh*) f.

true wahr (*vahR*)

try (to) versuchen (*feR-zew-Huhn*), probieren (*pRo-bee-Ruhn*)

Tuesday Dienstag (*deenz-tahk*) m.

tuna Thunfisch (*tewn-fish*) m.

turkey Truthahn (*tRewt-hahn*) m.

turn (to) ab.biegen (ist abgebogen) (*ap-bee-guhn*)

U

ugly hässlich (*häs-liH*)

umbrella Regenschirm (*rey-guhn-shiRm*) m.

unbelievable unglaublich (*oon-gloup-liH*)

uncle Onkel (*on-kuhl*) m.

under unter (*oon-tuhR*)

underpants Unterhose (*oon-tuhR-hoh-zuh*) f.

understand (to) verstehen (hat verstanden) (*feR-shtey-uhn*)

underwear Unterwäsche (*oon-tuhR-väh-shuh*) f.

unfortunately leider (*lay-duhR*)

until bis (*bis*)

upload auf.laden (*ouf-lah-duhn*)

use (to) benutzen (*buh-noot-suhn*)

V

veal Kalbfleisch (*kAlp-flaysh*) n.

vegetables Gemüse (*guh-müh-zuh*) n.

vegetarian vegetarisch (*vey-gey-tah-Rish*)

very sehr (*zeyR*)

vinegar Essig (*e-siH*) m.

W

wait (to) warten (*vAR-tuhn*)

waiter Kellner (*kel-nuhR*) m.

waitress Kellnerin (*kel-nuh-Rin*) f.

wall Wand (*vAnt*) f.

wallet Portemonnaie (*poRt-moh-ney*) n.

want (to) wollen (will) (*vo-luhn*)

warm warm (*vahRm*)

warning Warnung (*vAR-noong*) f.

wash (to) waschen (wäscht, hat gewaschen) (*vah-shuhn*)

watch TV (to) fern.sehen (sieht fern, hat ferngesehen) (*feRn-zey-uhn*)

water Wasser (*va-suhR*) n.

weak schwach (*shvACH*)

wear (to) tragen (trägt, hat getragen) (*trah-guhn*)

weather Wetter (*ve-tuhR*) n.

Wednesday Mittwoch (*mit-voCH*) m.

week Woche (*vo-CHuh*) f.

weekly wöchentlich (*vö-Hent-liH*)

well done gut durchgebraten (*gewt dooRch-guh-bRa-tuhn*)

wet nass (*nahs*)

what was (*vAs*)

when wann (*vAn*)

where wo (*voh*)

where (to) wohin (*voh-hin*)

which welch (*velCH*)

whipped cream Schlagsahne (*shlAk-zah-nuh*) f.

whistle Pfeife (*pfay-fuh*) f.

white weiß (*vays*)

white bread Weißbrot (*vays-bRoht*) n.

who wer (*veyR*)

whole-grain bread Vollkornbrot (*fol-koRn-bRoht*) n.

why warum (*va-Room*)

wide breit (*brayt*)

wife Frau (*fRou*) f.

win (to) gewinnen (hat gewonnen) (*guh-vi-nuhn*)

wind Wind (*vint*) m.

window Fenster (*fen-stuhR*) n.

wine Wein (*vayn*) m.

winter Winter (*vin-tuhR*) m.

wish (to) wünschen (*vün-shuhn*)

without ohne (*oh-nuh*)

woman Frau (*fRou*) f.

wonderful herrlich/wunderbar (*heR-liH/voon-duhR-bAR*)

wool Wolle (*vo-luh*) f.

work (to) arbeiten (*AR-bay-tuhn*)

wrist Handgelenk (*hAnt-guh-lenk*) n.

write (to) schreiben (hat geschrieben) (*shray-buhn*)

wrong falsch (*fAlsh*)

X–Y

year Jahr (*yahR*) n.

yearly jährlich (*yähR-liH*)

yellow gelb (*gelp*)

yesterday gestern (*ges-tuhRn*)

yogurt Jog(h)urt (*yoh-gooRt*) m./n.

young jung (*yoong*)

younger jünger (*yoön-guhR*)

your dein (informal), Ihr (formal) (*dayn, eeR*)

Z

zigzag Zickzack (*tsik-tsAk*) m.

ZIP code Postleitzahl (*post-layt-tsahl*) f.

German to English

A

ab.biegen (*ap-bee-guhn*) to turn

Abend (*ah-buhnd*) m. evening

ab.fahren (*ap-fah-Ruhn*) to depart

Adresse (*A-dre-suh*) f. address

alle (*A-luh*) all

allergisch (*A-leR-gish*) allergic

also (*Al-zoh*) therefore

alt (*Alt*) old, aged

Ananas (*A-nah-nAs*) f. pineapple

angeln (*An-guhln*) to fish

Angestellte (*An-guh-shtel-tuh*) m./f. employee

Angst (*Angst*) f. fear

Anhang (*An-hAng*) m. attachment

an.kommen (*An-ko-muhn*) to arrive

Anruf (*An-Rewf*) m. call

Anrufbeantworter (*An-Rewf-buh-Ant-voR-tuhR*) m. answering machine

an.rufen (*An-Rew-fuhn*) to call

anschließend (*An-shlee-suhnt*) then, afterward

Ansichtskarte (*An-ziHts-kAr-tuh*) f. postcard

antworten (*Ant-voR-tuhn*) to answer

an.ziehen (sich) (*ziH An-tsee-uhn*) to dress oneself

Anzug (*An-tsewk*) m. suit

Apfel (*Ap-fuhl*) m. apple

Apfelsine (*Ap-fuhl-zee-nuh*) f. orange

Apotheke (*A-po-tey-kuh*) f. pharmacy

App (*Ap*) m. app

Aprikose (*ah-pRee-koh-zuh*) f. apricot

April (*ah-pReel*) m. April

arbeiten (*AR-bay-tuhn*) to work

ärgerlich (*äR-guhR-liH*) angry

arm (*Arm*) poor

Arzt/Ärztin (*aRtst/in*) m./f. doctor

Aschenbecher (*A-shun-be-HuhR*) m. ashtray

Aubergine (*oh-beR-jee-nuh*) f. eggplant

auf.laden (*ouf-lah-duhn*) to upload

auf Wiedersehen (*ouf vee-duhR-zey-uhn*) good-bye

Aufzug (*ouf-tsook*) m. elevator

Auge (*ou-guh*) n. eye

August (*ou-goost*) m. August

aus.füllen (*ous-fü-luhn*) to fill out

Ausgang (*ous-gAng*) m. exit

ausgezeichnet (*ous-guh-tsayH-net*) excellent

Ausland (*ous-lAnt*) n. foreign country

außer Betrieb (*ou-suhR buh-treep*) out of order

aus.steigen (*ous-shtay-guhn*) to climb off

aus.ziehen (sich) (*ziH ous-tsee-uhn*) to take off one's clothes

Auto (*ou-to*) n. car

B

backen (*bA-kuhn*) to bake

Bäcker/Bäckerin (*bä-kuhR/in*) m./f. baker

Bäckerei (*bä-kuh-Ray*) f. bakery

Badeanzug (*bah-duh-An-tsewk*) m. bathing suit

baden (*bah-duhn*) to bathe

Badezimmer (*bah-duh-tsi-muhR*) n. bathroom

Bahnhof (*bahn-hof*) m. train station

bald (*bAlt*) soon

Balkon (*bAl-kon*) m. balcony

Bankautomat (*bank-ou-toh-mAt*) m. ATM

Bargeld (*bahR-gelt*) n. cash

Basilikum (*bah-zee-lee-koom*) n. basil

Bauch (*bouCH*) m. stomach

Bauer/Bäurin (*bou-uhR/boy-Rin*) m./f. farmer

Baum (*boum*) m. tree

Baumwolle (*boum-vo-luh*) f. cotton

befehlen (*buh-fey-luhn*) to command

beginnen (*buh-gi-nuhn*) to begin

Bekleidung (*buh-klay-doong*) f. clothes

Bekleidungsgeschäft (*buh-klay-doongz-guh-schäft*) n. clothing store

bekommen (*buh-ko-muhn*) to receive

bei (*bay*) at, near

beige (*beyj*) beige

Beilage (*bay-lah-guh*) f. side dish

Bein (*bayn*) n. leg

benutzen (*buh-noot-suhn*) to use

Benzintank (*ben-tseen-tAnk*) m. gas tank

bequem (*buh-kveym*) comfortable

beschäftigt (*buh-shäf-tiH*) busy

besitzen (*buh-zi-tsuhn*) to possess

besser (*be-suhR*) better

Besteck (*buh-shtek*) n. cutlery

bestellen (*buh-shte-luhn*) to order

Bett   (*bet*) n. bed

Bettdecke   (*bet-de-kuh*) f. blanket

beweisen   (*buh-vay-zuhn*) prove

bewölkt   (*buh-völkt*) cloudy

Bibliothek   (*bib-lee-oh-tek*) f. library

Bier   (*beeR*) n. beer

bieten   (*bee-tuhn*) to offer

Bild   (*bilt*) n. painting

billig   (*bi-liH*) cheap

binden   (*bin-duhn*) to bind

Birnen   (*beeR-nuhn*) pl. pears

bitte   (*bi-tuh*) please

bis   (*bis*) until

blasen   (*blah-zuhn*) to blow

blau   (*blou*) blue

Blaubeeren   (*blou-bey-Ruhn*) pl. blueberries

bleiben   (*blay-bun*) to remain

blicken   (*bli-kuhn*) to look, glance

Blitz   (*blits*) m. lightning

blöd   (*blöd*) stupid

Blume   (*blew-muh*) f. flower

Blumengeschäft   (*blew-muhn-guh-schäft*) n. florist

Blumenkohl   (*blew-muhn-kohl*) m. cauliflower

Bluse   (*blew-zuh*) f. blouse

Bohnen   (*boh-nuhn*) pl. beans

Bohnensuppe   (*boh-nuhn-zoo-puh*) f. bean soup

Boot   (*boht*) n. boat

brauchen   (*bRou-CHuhn*) to need

braun   (*bRoun*) brown

brechen   (*bRe-Huhn*) to break

breit   (*brayt*) wide

brennen   (*bRe-nuhn*) to burn

Brief   (*bReef*) m. letter

Briefumschlag   (*bReef-oom-shlahk*) m. envelope

Brille   (*bri-luh*) f. glasses

bringen   (*bRin-guhn*) to bring

Brokkoli   (*bRoh-koh-lee*) m. broccoli

Brot   (*bRoht*) n. bread

Brötchen   (*bRöt-chuhn*) n. roll

Bruder   (*bRew-duhR*) m. brother

Brust   (*bRoost*) f. chest, breast

Buch   (*bü-HuhR*) n. book

Bücherregal   (*büh-HuhR-Rey-gal*) n. bookshelf

Buchhandlung   (*bewCH-hAnt-loong*) f. bookstore

Bügeleisen   (*büh-guhl-ay-zuhn*) n. iron

bügeln   (*büh-guhln*) to iron

bunt   (*boont*) bright

Bus   (*boos*) m. bus

Bustenhalter   (*boo-stuhn-hAl-tuhR*) m. bra

Butter   (*boo-tuhR*) f. butter

C

circa (*tseeR-kuh*) about

Couchtisch (*kouch-tish*) m. coffee table

cousin/cousine (*koo-zin/kou-zinuh*) m./f. cousin

Crème (*kReym*) f. cream

D

da (*dAh*) there

Dame (*dah-muh*) f. lady

danach (*dA-nACH*) then

danke (*dAn-kuh*) thanks

danken (*dAn-kuhn*) to thank

dass (*dAs*) that

denken (*den-kuhn*) to think

Deutschland (*doytch-lAnt*) n. Germany

Dezember (*dey-tsem-buhR*) m. December

dick (*dik*) fat

Dienstag (*deenz-tahk*) m. Tuesday

Donner (*do-nuhR*) m. thunder

Donnerstag (*do-nuhRz-tahk*) m. Thursday

Doppelzimmer (*do-puhl-tsi-muhR*) n. double room

dort (*doRt*) there

Dose (*doh-zuh*) f. can

draußen (*dRou-suhn*) outdoors

dreckig (*dRe-kiH*) dirty

Drogerie (*dRoh-guh-Ree*) f. drug store

dunkel (*doon-kuhl*) dark

dünn (*dün*) thin

durch (*dooRCH*) through

dürfen (*dür-fuhn*) to be allowed to

Durst (*dooRst*) m. thirst

durstig (*dooRs-tiH*) thirsty

Dusche (*dew-shuh*) f. shower

E

Ei (*ay*) n. egg

Eigentum (*ay-guhn-tewm*) n. property

Einkaufszentrum (*ayn-koufs-tsen-tRoom*) n. shopping center

ein.steigen (*ayn-shtay-guhn*) to climb on/into

Einzelzimmer (*ayn-tsel-tsi-muhR*) n. single room

Eis (*ays*) n. ice cream

Eltern (*el-tuhRn*) pl. parents

Email (*ee-meyl*) f. email

empfangen (*em-pfAn-guhn*) to receive

empfehlen (*em-pfey-luhn*) to recommend

endlich (*ent-liH*) at last

eng (*eng*) narrow

entdecken (*ent-de-kuhn*) to discover

entlang (*ent-lAng*) along

entspannen (sich) (*ziH ent-shpA-nuhn*) to relax

entwickeln (*ent-vi-kuhln*) to develop

Erdbeeren (*eRt-bey-Ruhn*) pl. strawberries

Ereinmis (*eR-ayk-nis*) n. event

Ergebnis (*eR-gep-nis*) n. result

Erkenntnis (*eR-kent-nis*) f. knowledge

Erlaubnis (*eR-loup-nis*) f. permission

Erbsen (*eRp-suhn*) pl. peas

erholen (sich) (*ziH eR-hoh-luhn*) to recuperate

erkälten (sich) (*ziH eR-käl-tuhn*) to catch a cold

Erkältung (*eR-käl-toong*) f. cold

ernst (*eRnst*) serious

etwa (*et-vah*) roughly, about

etwas (*et-vAs*) some

essen (*es-uhn*) to eat

Essen (*es-uhn*) n. meal

Essig (*e-siH*) m. vinegar

Esszimmer (*es-tsi-muhR*) n. dining room

F

fahren (*fah-Ruhn*) to drive

Fahrrad (*fah-Rat*) n. bicycle

fallen (*fA-luhn*) to fall

falsch (*fAlsh*) wrong

fangen (*fAn-guhn*) to catch

fast (*fAst*) almost

faul (*foul*) lazy

Februar (*fey-bRew-ahR*) m. February

Fenster (*fen-stuhR*) n. window

fern.sehen (*feRn-zey-uhn*) to watch TV

Fernseher (*feRn-zey-uhR*) m. television set

fertig (*feR-tiH*) finished

fertig machen (sich) (*ziH feR-tiH mA-CHuhn*) get oneself ready

feucht (*foyHt*) humid

Fieber (*fee-buhR*) n. fever

Film (*film*) m. movie

finden (*fin-duhn*) to find

Fingernagel (*fin-guR-nah-guhl*) m. fingernail

Fisch (*fish*) m. fish

Fitnesscenter (*fit-nes-sen-tuhR*) n. fitness center

Flasche (*flah-shuh*) f. bottle

Fleisch (*flaysh*) n. meat

fleißig (*flay-siH*) industrious

fliegen (*flee-guhn*) to fly

Flug (*flewk*) m. flight

Fluggesellschaft (*flewk-guh-zel-shAft*) f. airline

Flughafen (*flewk-hah-fuhn*) m. airport

Flugnummer (*flewk-noo-muhR*) f. flight number

Flugsteig (*flewk-shtayk*) m. gate

Flugzeug (*flewk-tsoyk*) n. airplane

Flunder (*floon-duhR*) f. flounder

Fluss (*floos*) m. river

folgen (*fol-guhn*) to follow

Fön   (*föhn*) m. hair dryer

Forelle   (*foh-Re-luh*) f. trout

fragen   (*fRah-guhn*) to ask

Frau   (*fRou*) f. woman, wife

Freitag   (*fRay-tahk*) m. Friday

Freund/Freundin   (*fRoynt/fRoyn-din*) m./f. friend

froh   (*fRoh*) happy

früh   (*fRüh*) early

Frühling   (*fRüh-ling*) m. spring

furchtbar   (*fooRHt-bahR*) awful

Fuß   (*fews*) m. foot

Fußboden   (*fews-boh-duhn*) m. floor

Fußknöchel   (*fews-knö-Huhl*) m. ankle

fühlen (sich)   (*ziH füh-luhn*) to feel

für   (*fühR*) for

G

Gabel   (*gah-buhl*) f. fork

ganz   (*gAnts*) quite, entirely

Garnele   (*gahR-ney-luh*) f. shrimp

Garten   (*gAR-tuhn*) m. garden

geben   (*gey-buhn*) to give

Geburtstag   (*guh-booRts-tahk*) m. birthday

Geflügelsalat   (*guh-flüh-guhl-zA-laht*) m. chicken salad

gegenüber   (*ge-guhn-ü-buhR*) opposite, facing

gehen   (*gey-uhn*) to go

Gehirn   (*guh-hiRn*) n. brain

Geist   (*gayst*) m. ghost

gelb   (*gelp*) yellow

gelegentlich   (*guh-ley-gent-liH*) occasionally

gemustert   (*guh-moos-tuhRt*) patterned

Gemüse   (*guh-müh-zuh*) n. vegetables

Gemüsehandlung   (*guh-müh-zuh-hAnt-loong*) f. vegetable stand

genießen   (*guh-nee-suhn*) to enjoy

genug   (*guh-newk*) enough

gepunktet   (*guh-poonk-tuht*) polka-dotted

geradeaus   (*guh-Rah-duh-ous*) straight ahead

Gericht   (*guh-RiHt*) n. dish (of food)

Geschäft   (*guh-shäft*) n. store

geschehen   (*guh-shey-uhn*) to happen

Geschenk   (*guh-shenk*) n. gift

Geschenkartikelladen   (*guh-shenk-AR-tee-kuh-lah-duhn*) m. gift shop

Geschichte   (*guh-shiH-tuh*) f. history, story

Geschirr   (*guh-sheeR*) n. dishes

Gesellschaft   (*guh-zel-shAft*) f. society, company

Gesicht   (*guh-ziHt*) n. face

gestern   (*ges-tuhRn*) yesterday

gestreift   (*guh-shtRayft*) striped

gesund   (*guh-zoont*) healthy

Getränke   (*guh-tRän-kuh*) pl. drinks

gewinnen   (*guh-vi-nuhn*) to win

Gift   (*gift*) n. poison

Glas   (*glAs*) n. glass

glauben   (*glou-buhn*) to believe

glücklich   (*glük-liH*) happy

grau   (*gRou*) gray

Grippe   (*gRi-puh*) f. flu

groß   (*gRohs*) big

grün   (*gRün*) green

Gruppe   (*gRoo-puh*) f. group

Gurke   (*gooR-kuh*) f. cucumber

Gürtel   (*güR-tuhl*) m. belt

gut   (*gewt*) good, well

Guten Abend   (*gew-tuhn ah-bent*) m. good evening

Guten Morgen   (*gew-tuhn moR-guhn*) m. good morning

Guten Tag   (*gew-tuhn tahk*) m. good day

H

Haar   (*hahR*) n. hair

Haarbürste   (*hahR-büR-stuh*) f. hairbrush

Haarschnitt   (*hahR-shnit*) m. haircut

Haarshampoo   (*hahR-shAm-pew*) n. shampoo

haben   (*hah-buhn*) to have

Hagel   (*hah-guhl*) m. hail

hallo   (*hA-loh*) hello

Hals   (*halz*) m. neck

halten   (*hAhl-tuhn*) to hold

Hand   (*hAnT*) f. hand

Handgelenk   (*hAnt-guh-lenk*) n. wrist

Handgepäck   (*hAnt-guh-päk*) n. carry-on luggage

Handschuhe   (*hAnt-schew-uh*) pl. gloves

Handtasche   (*hAnt-tA-shuh*) f. purse

Handtuch   (*hAn-tewCH*) n. towel

Handy   (*hahn-dee*) n. cell phone

Handynummer   (*hahn-dee-noo-muhR*) f. cell phone number

hängen   (*hän-guhn*) to hang

hart   (*hArt*) hard

Haselnüsse   (*hah-zuhl-nü-suh*) pl. hazelnuts

hässlich   (*häs-liH*) ugly

Hauptgericht   (*houpt-guh-RiHt*) n. main course

Haus   (*hous*) n. house

Haut   (*hout*) f. skin

heben   (*hey-buhn*) to lift

heiraten   (*hay-RA-tuhn*) to marry

heiß   (*hays*) hot

helfen   (*hel-fuhn*) to help

hell   (*hel*) light

Hemd   (*hemt*) n. shirt

Herbst   (*heRpst*) m. autumn, fall

Herr   (*heR*) m. mister

herrlich   (*heR-liH*) wonderful

herunter.laden   (*heR-un-tuhR-lah-duhn*) to download

Herz   (*heRts*) n. heart

heute   (*hoy-tuh*) today

hier   (*heeR*) here

Himmel   (*hi-muhl*) m. sky

hinter   (*hin-tuhR*) behind

Hinterhof   (*hin-tuhR-hohf*) m. backyard

hoch   (*hohCH*) high

hören   (*höh-Ruhn*) to hear

Hose   (*hoh-zuh*) f. pair of pants

Hotel   (*hoh-tel*) n. hotel

Huhn   (*hewn*) n. chicken

Hühnerbrust   (*hüh-nuhR-broost*) f. chicken breast

Hunger   (*hoon-guhR*) m. hunger

hungrig   (*hoon-gRiH*) hungry

Husten   (*hew-stuhn*) m. cough

Hut   (*hewt*) m. hat

I

immer   (*i-muhR*) always

Innenhof   (*i-nuhn-hohf*) m. courtyard

interessant   (*in-tey-Re-sAnt*) interesting

Internetanschluss   (*in-teR-net-An-shloos*) m. internet connection

Internetzugang   (*in-tuhR-net-tsew-grif*) m. internet access

Irrtum   (*iR-tewm*) m. error

J

Jacke   (*yA-kuh*) f. jacket

Jahr   (*yahR*) n. year

Jahreszeit   (*yah-Ruhs-tsayt*) f. season

jährlich   (*yähR-liH*) yearly

Januar   (*yah-new-ahR*) m. January

jeden Tag   (*yey-duhn tahk*) every day

jetzt   (*yetst*) now

Jog(h)urt   (*yoh-gooRt*) m./n. yogurt

Johannisbeeren   (*yoh-hA-nis-bey-Ruhn*) pl. currants

jung   (*yoong*) young

Junge   (*yoon-guh*) m. boy

K

Kabeljau   (*kah-buhl-you*) m. cod

Kaffee   (*kA-fey*) m. coffee

Kalbfleisch   (*kAlp-flaysh*) n. veal

kalt   (*kalt*) cold

Kamin   (*kah-meen*) m. fireplace

Kamm   (*kAm*) m. comb

kämmen (sich)   (*ziH kä-muhn*) to comb one's hair

kariert   (*kah-ReeRt*) plaid

Karotte   (*kah-Ro-tuh*) f. carrot

Kartoffel   (*kAR-to-fuhl*) f. potato

Käse   (*käh-zuh*) m. cheese

Kathedrale   (*kah-tey-drah-luh*) f. cathedral

Katze   (*kA-tsuh*) f. cat

kaufen   (*kou-fuhn*) to buy

Kehle   (*key-luh*) f. throat

Kellner   (*kel-nuhR*) m. waiter

Kellnerin   (*kel-nuh-Rin*) f. waitress

kennen   (*ke-nuhn*) to know, be familiar with

Kind   (*kint*) n. child

Kino   (*kee-noh*) n. cinema

Kiosk   (*kee-osk*) m. newsstand

Kirche   (*KeeR-Huh*) f. church

Kirschen   (*keeR-shuhn*) pl. cherries

klar   (*klahR*) clear, clearly

Kleid   (*klayt*) n. dress

Kleider   (*klay-duhR*) pl. clothes

Kleiderbügel   (*klay-duhR-büh-guhl*) m. hanger

klein   (*klayn*) small

Kleingeld   (*klayn-gelt*) n. change (coins)

Klimaanlage   (*klee-mah-An-lah-guh*) f. air-conditioning

klug   (*klewk*) smart

Kneipe   (*knay-puh*) f. bar (pub)

Knie   (*knee*) n. knee

Knoblauch   (*knohb-louCH*) m. garlic

Knopf   (*knopf*) m. button

kochen   (*ko-CHuhn*) to cook

Koffer   (*ko-fuhR*) m. suitcase

Kohl   (*kohl*) m. cabbage

kommen   (*ko-muhn*) to come

Kommode   (*ko-moh-duh*) f. dresser

Konditorei   (*kon-dee-toR-ay*) f. pastry shop

können   (*kö-nuhn*) can, to be able to

kontrollieren   (*kon-tRo-lee-Ruhn*) to inspect

Kopf   (*kopf*) m. head

Kopfkissen   (*kopf-ki-suhn*) n. pillow

Kopfsalat   (*kopf-zA-laht*) m. lettuce

Kopfschmerzen   (*kopf-shmeR-tsuhn*) pl. headache

Kord   (*koRt*) m. corduroy

Körper   (*köR-puhR*) m. body

kosten   (*kos-tuhn*) to cost

kostenlos   (*kos-tuhn-los*) free of charge

Kraftbrühe   (*krAft-bRüh-uh*) f. beef broth

krank   (*kRAnk*) sick

Krankenpfleger/Krankenpflegerin   (*kRan-kuhn-pfley-guhR/in*) m./f. nurse

kratzen   (*krA-tsuhn*) scratch

Kräuter   (*kroy-tuhR*) pl. herbs

Krawatte   (*kRah-vA-tuh*) f. necktie

Krebs   (*kreyps*) m. crab

Kreuz   (*kRoyts*) n. cross

Küche   (*kü-Huh*) f. kitchen

Kuchen   (*kew-CHuhn*) m. cake

Kunst   (*koonst*) f. art

kurz   (*kooRts*) short

küssen   (*kü-suhn*) to kiss

L

Lachs   (*lAks*) m. salmon

laden   (*lah-duhn*) to load

Laden   (*lah-duhn*) m. store

Lamm   (*lAm*) n. lamb

Land   (*lAnt*) n. country

lang   (*lAng*) long

langsam   (*lAng-zAm*) slow

langweilig   (*lAng-vay-liH*) boring

lassen   (*lA-suhn*) to leave, to let

laufen   (*lou-fuhn*) to run

Lebensmittelgeschäft   (*ley-buhnz-mi-tuhl-guh-shäft*) n. grocery store

lecker   (*le-kuhR*) delicious

Leder   (*ley-duhR*) n. leather

leer   (*leyR*) empty

legen   (*ley-guhn*) to lay

lehren   (*ley-Ruhn*) teach

Lehrer   (*ley-Ruhr*) m. teacher

Lehrerin   (*ley-Ruhr-in*) f. female teacher

leicht   (*layHt*) light

leiden   (*lay-duhn*) to suffer

leider   (*lay-duhR*) unfortunately

leihen   (*lay-uhn*) to lend

Leinen   (*lay-nuhn*) n. linen

lernen   (*leR-nuhn*) to learn, to study

lesen   (*ley-zuhn*) to read

Licht   (*liHt*) n. light

lieben   (*lee-buhn*) to love

Lied   (*leed*) n. song

liegen   (*lee-guhn*) to lie, be situated

lila   (*lee-lah*) n. purple

links   (*links*) left

Lippe   (*li-puh*) f. lip

loben   (*loh-buhn*) to praise

lockig   (*lo-kiH*) curly

Löffel   (*lö-fuhl*) m. spoon

Luft   (*looft*) f. air

lustig   (*loos-tiH*) funny

lutschen   (*loo-tchun*) to suckle

M

machen   (*mA-CHuhn*) to make

Magen   (*mah-guhn*) m. stomach

Mai   (*may*) m. May

Mais   (*mays*) m. corn

manchmal   (*mAnH-mahl*) sometimes

Mandel   (*mAn-duhl*) f. almond

Mann/Männer   (*mAn*) m./pl. man

Mantel   (*mAn-tuhl*) m. coat

Markt   (*mARkt*) m. market

Marmelade   (*mAR-muh-lah-duh*) f. jam

März   (*mäRts*) m. March

Meeresfrüchte   (*mee-Ruhs-fRüH-tuh*) pl. seafood

Meerrettich   (*meyR-Re-tiH*) m. horseradish

mehr   (*meyR*) more

Melone   (*me-loh-nuh*) f. melon

Mensch   (*mensh*) m. human being

Messer   (*me-suhR*) n. knife

Metzger/Metzgerin   (*mets-guhR/in*) m./f. butcher

Metzgerei   (*mets-guh-ray*) f. butcher shop

mieten   (*mee-tuhn*) to rent

Milch   (*milH*) f. milk

Minute   (*mi-new-tuh*) f. minute

missverstehen   (*mis-feR-shtey-uhn*) to misunderstand

Mitternacht   (*mi-tuhR-nACHt*) f. midnight

Mittwoch   (*mit-voCH*) m. Wednesday

Möbel   (*möh-buhl*) pl. furniture

Mobiltelefon   (*moh-beel-tey-ley-fohn*) n. cell phone

möbliert   (*möh-bleeRt*) furnished

Mode   (*moh-duh*) f. fashion

modisch   (*moh-dish*) fashionable

mögen   (*möh-guhn*) to like

Monat   (*moh-nAt*) m. month

monatlich   (*moh-nAt-liH*) monthly

Montag   (*mohn-tahk*) m. Monday

morgen   (*moR-guhn*) tomorrow

Morgen   (*moR-guhn*) m. morning

morgens   (*moR-guhnz*) in the mornings

Motorrad   (*moh-toh-Rat*) n. motorcycle

müde   (*müh-duh*) tired

Mund   (*moont*) m. mouth

munter   (*moon-tuhR*) awake

Münzen   (*mün-tsuhn*) pl. coins

Musikgeschäft   (*mew-zeek-guh-shäft*) n. music store

müssen   (*mü-suhn*) must

mutig   (*mew-tiH*) brave

Mutter   (*moo-tuhR*) f. mother

Mütze   (*mü-tsuh*) f. cap

N

nach   (*nahCH*) after

Nachmittag   (*nahCH-mi-tahk*) m. afternoon

Nachrichten   (*nahCH-RiH-tuhn*) pl. news

Nachspeise   (*nahCH-shpay-zuh*) f. dessert

Nacht   (*nACHt*) f. night

Nachtclub   (*nACHt-kloob*) m. night club

Nachtisch   (*nahCH-tish*) m. dessert

Name   (*nah-muh*) m. name

Nase   (*nah-zuh*) f. nose

nass   (*nahs*) wet

Nebel   (*ney-buhl*) m. fog

neblig   (*ney-buh-liH*) foggy

neben   (*ney-buhn*) beside

nehmen   (*ney-muhn*) to take

nervös   (*neR-vöhs*) nervous

neu   (*noy*) new

nie   (*nee*) never

noch   (*noCH*) still

Null   (*nool*) f. zero

nur   (*nooR*) only

Nüsse   (*nü-suh*) pl. nuts

O

Obst   (*opst*) n. fruit

öffnen   (*öf-nuhn*) to open

oft   (*oft*) often

ohne   (*oh-nuh*) without

Ohr   (*ohR*) n. ear

Oktober   (*ok-toh-buhR*) m. October

Öl   (*öhl*) n. oil

Oma   (*oh-mah*) f. grandmother

Onkel   (*on-kuhl*) m. uncle

Opa   (*oh-pah*) m. grandfather

P

packen   (*pA-kuhn*) to pack

Paket   (*pah-ket*) n. package

Parfüm   (*pAR-füm*) n. perfume

parken   (*pAR-kuhn*) to park

Parkplatz   (*pARk-plAts*) m. parking lot

Pass   (*pAs*) m. passport

Pfeffermühle   (*pfe-fuhR-müh-luh*) f. pepper mill

Pferd   (*pfeRt*) n. horse

Pfirsiche   (*pfeeR-ziH-uh*) pl. peaches

Pflegespülung   (*pfley-guh-shpüh-loong*) f. conditioner

Pfeife   (*pfay-fuh*) f. whistle

Pförtner/Pförtnerin   (*pföRt-nuhR/in*) m./f. concierge

Pilze   (*pil-tsuh*) pl. mushrooms

planen   (*plah-nuhn*) to plan

Plätzchen   (*pläts-Huhn*) n. cookie

plötzlich   (*plöts-liH*) suddenly

Podcast   (*pod-kAst*) m. podcast

Polizeiamt   (*poh-li-tsay-Amt*) n. police station

Polizist/Polizistin   (*poh-lee-tsist/in*) m./f. police officer

Pommes frites   (*po-muhs*) pl. French fries

Portemonnaie   (*poRt-moh-ney*) n. wallet

Post   (*post*) f. post office

Postkarte   (*post-kAR-tuh*) f. postcard

Postleitzahl   (*post-layt-tsahl*) f. ZIP code

probieren   (*pRo-bee-Ruhn*) to try

pünktlich   (*pünkt-liH*) punctually

putzen   (*poo-tsuhn*) to clean

Q

Qual   (*kvahl*) f. torment

Quatsch   (*kvatsch*) m. nonsense

Quittung   (*kvi-toong*) f. receipt

R

rasieren (sich)   (*ziH Rah-zee-Ruhn*) to shave oneself

raten   (*Rah-tuhn*) to advise

rauchen   (*Rou-CHuhn*) to smoke

rechts   (*ReHts*) right

regelmäßig   (*Rey-guhl-mäh-siH*) regularly

Regen   (*Rey-guhn*) m. rain

Regenmantel   (*Rey-guhn-mAn-tuhl*) m. raincoat

Regenschirm   (*Rey-guhn-sheeRm*) m. umbrella

regnerisch   (*Reyg-nuh-Rish*) rainy

Reich   (*RayCH*) n. kingdom

reinigen   (*Ray-ni-guhn*) to clean

reisen   (*Ray-zuhn*) to travel

reiten   (*Ray-tuhn*) to ride

reservieren   (*Re-zeR-vee-Ruhn*) to reserve

Rindfleisch   (*Rint-flaysh*) n. beef

Rochen   (*Ro-CHuhn*) f. flounder

Rock   (*Rok*) m. skirt

Roggenbrot   (*Ro-guhn-bRoht*) n. rye bread

rollen   (*Ro-luhn*) to roll

Roman   (*Roh-mahn*) m. novel

rosa   (*Roh-zah*) pink

rot   (*Rot*) red

Rücken   (*Rü-kuhn*) m. back

rufen   (*Rew-fuhn*) to call

ruhig   (*Rew-iH*) calm

rund   (*Roont*) around

S

S-Bahn   (*es-bahn*) f. commuter train

Saft   (*zAft*) m. juice

sagen   (*zah-guhn*) to say, to tell

Sahne   (*zah-nuh*) f. cream

Salzstreuer   (*zAlts-shtRoy-uhR*) m. salt shaker

Samstag   (*zAmz-tahk*) m. Saturday

sauber   (*zou-buhR*) clean

sauer   (*zou-uhR*) sour

Schachtel   (*shACH-tuhl*) f. box

Schal   (*shahl*) m. scarf

Schatten   (*shA-tuhn*) m. shadow

Schauspieler/Schauspielerin   (*shou-shpee-luhR/in*) m./f. actor/actress

Scheibe   (*shay-buh*) f. slice

scheinen   (*shay-nuhn*) to shine

schicken   (*shi-kuhn*) to send

Schiff   (*shif*) n. ship

Schild   (*shilt*) n. sign

Schinken   (*shin-kuhn*) m. ham

Schlafanzug   (*shlahf-An-tsook*) m. pajamas

schlafen   (*shlah-fuhn*) to sleep

Schlafzimmer   (*shlahf-tsi-muhr*) n. bedroom

schlagen (*shlah-guhn*) to hit

Schlagsahne (*shlahk-zah-nuh*) f. whipped cream

Schlange (*shlanuh*) f. snake

schlecht (*shleCHt*) bad

schließen (*shlee-suhn*) to close

Schlinge (*shlin-guh*) f. snake

Schlips (*schlips*) m. necktie

Schlüssel (*shlü-suhl*) m. key

Schmuck (*shmook*) m. jewelry

Schnee (*shney*) m. snow

schnell (*shnel*) fast, quick

Schnitzel (*shni-tsuhl*) n. cutlet

Schokolade (*shoh-koh-lah-duh*) f. chocolate

schön (*shöhn*) beautiful

Schrank (*shRAnk*) m. closet

schrecklich (*shRek-liH*) horrible

schreiben (*shray-buhn*) to write

Schreibwaren (*shRayp-vah-Ruhn*) pl. pens, stationery

Schuhe (*shew-uh*) pl. shoes

Schulden (*shool-duhn*) pl. debt

Schulter (*shool-tuhR*) f. shoulder

Schüssel (*shü-suhl*) f. bowl

schwach (*shvACH*) weak

schwarz (*shvARts*) black

Schweinefleisch (*shvayn-flaysh*) n. pork

schwer (*shveR*) hard

Schwester (*shves-tuhR*) f. sister

Schwiegereltern (*shvee-guhR-el-tuhRn*) pl. in-laws

Schwiegermutter (*shvee-guhR-moo-tuhR*) f. mother-in-law

Schwiegervater (*shvee-guhR-fah-tuhR*) m. father-in-law

Schwimmbad (*shvim-baht*) n. swimming pool

schwimmen (*shvi-muhn*) to swim

See (*zey*) m. lake

Segelboot (*zey-guhl-boht*) n. sailboat

segeln (*zey-guhln*) to sail

sehen (*zey-uhn*) to see

sehr (*zeyR*) very

Seide (*zay-duh*) f. silk

Seife (*zay-fuh*) f. soap

seit (*zayt*) since

seitlich (*zayt-liH*) at the side

Sekunde (*ze-koon-duh*) f. second

selbstverständlich (*zelpst-feR-shtänt-liH*) of course

Sellerie (*ze-luh-Ree*) m. celery

senden (*zen-duhn*) to send

Senf (*zenf*) m. mustard

Serviette (*zeR-vee-e-tuh*) f. napkin

Sessel (*ze-suhl*) m. armchair

setzen (*ze-tsuhn*) to sit

Simsen (*zim-suhn*) n. texting

singen (*zin-guhn*) to sing

sinken (*zin-kuhn*) to sink

sitzen (*zi-tsuhn*) to sit

SMS (*es-em-es*) f. text message

Socken (*zo-kuhn*) pl. socks

sofort (*zoh-foRt*) immediately

Sohn (*zohn*) m. son

Sommer (*zo-muhR*) m. summer

Sonne (*zo-nuh*) f. sun

Sonntag (*zon-tahk*) m. Sunday

spannend (*shpA-nuhnt*) suspenseful

sparen (*shpah-Ruhn*) save

Spargel (*shpahR-guhl*) m. asparagus

spät (*shpäht*) late

Speck (*shpek*) m. bacon

Speisekarte (*shpay-zuh-kAR-tuh*) f. menu

Spiegel (*shpee-guhl*) m. mirror

Spiegelei (*shpee-guh-lay*) n. fried egg

Spiel (*shpeel*) n. game

spielen (*shpee-luhn*) to play

Spinat (*shpi-naht*) m. spinach

spinnen (*shpi-nuhn*) to spin

Sportgeschäft (*shpoRt-guh-shäft*) n. sport shop

sprechen (*shpRe-Huhn*) to speak

Sprühregen (*shpRüh-Rey-guhn*) m. drizzle

Spülmaschine (*shpül-mA-shee-nuh*) f. dishwasher

Stadt (*shtAt*) f. city

Stadtplan (*shtAt-plAn*) m. city map

stark (*shtARk*) strong

Stärke (*shtäR-kuh*) f. strength

stehen (*shtey-uhn*) to stand

steigen (*shtay-guhn*) to climb

sterben (*shteR-buhn*) to die

Stiefel (*shtee-fuhl*) pl. boots

stinken (*shtin-kuhn*) to stink

Stock (*shtok*) m. floor

stolz (*shtolts*) proud

Straße (*shtRah-suh*) f. street

Straßenbahn (*shtRah-suhn-bahn*) f. streetcar

Streichhölzer (*shtRayH-höl-tsuhR*) pl. matches

Stück (*shtük*) n. piece

studieren (*shtew-dee-Ruhn*) to study, to look over

Stuhl (*shtewl*) m. chair

stumpf (*shtoompf*) blunt

Stunde (*shtoon-duh*) f. hour

stündlich (*shtünt-liH*) hourly

Sturm (*shtooRm*) m. storm

suchen (*zew-Huhn*) to look for

Supermarkt (*zew-puhR-mARkt*) m. supermarket

Suppenteller (*zoo-puhn-te-luhR*) m. soup dish

süß   (*zühs*) sweet

Süßigkeiten   (*züh-siH-kay-tuhn*) pl. sweets, candies

T

Tag   (*tahk*) m. day

täglich   (*tähk-liH*) daily

Tante   (*tAn-tuh*) f. aunt

tanzen   (*tAn-tsuhn*) to dance

Tasse   (*tA-suh*) f. cup

Tee   (*tey*) m. tea

Teelöffel   (*tey-lö-fuhl*) m. teaspoon

Telefon   (*te-le-fon*) n. telephone

telefonieren   (*te-le-foh-nee-Ruhn*) to telephone

Telefonnummer   (*te-le-foh-noo-muhR*) f. telephone number

Teller   (*te-luhR*) m. dinner plate

Tennisschuhe   (*te-nis-shew-uh*) pl. tennis shoes

Teppich   (*te-pish*) m. carpet

teuer   (*toy-uhR*) expensive

Thunfisch   (*tewn-fish*) m. tuna

tief   (*teef*) low

Tiergarten   (*teeR-gAR-tuhn*) m. zoo

Tierpark   (*teeR-pARk*) m. zoo

Tisch   (*tish*) m. table

Tischdecke   (*tish-de-kuh*) f. tablecloth

Tochter   (*toCH-tuhR*) f. daughter

Toilette   (*toy-le-tuh*) f. bathroom

Tomate   (*toh-mah-tuh*) f. tomato

tragen   (*trah-guhn*) to wear, to carry

träumen   (*tRoy-muhn*) to dream

traurig   (*tRou-RiH*) sad

treffen   (*tRe-fuhn*) to meet

trinken   (*tRin-kuhn*) to drink

trocken   (*tRo-kuhn*) dry

Trockner   (*tRok-nuhR*) m. dryer

Truthahn   (*tRewt-hahn*) m. turkey

tun   (*tuhn*) to do

Tür   (*tühR*) f. door

Tüte   (*tüh-tuh*) f. bag

U

über   (*üh-buhR*) over, across

übermorgen   (*üh-buhR-moR-guhn*) day after tomorrow

überweisen   (*üh-buhR-vay-zuhn*) to transfer money

Uhr   (*ewR*) f. clock

um.steigen   (*oom-shtay-guhn*) to transfer (en route)

um.ziehen (sich)   (*ziH oom-tsee-uhn*) to change one's clothes

ungefähr   (*oon-guh-fähR*) approximately

unglaublich   (*oon-gloup-liH*) unbelievable

unter (*oon-tuhR*) beneath, below, under

Unterhose (*oon-tuhR-hoh-zuh*) f. underpants

unterschreiben (*oon-tuhR-shRay-buhn*) to sign

Unterschrift (*oon-tuhR-shRift*) f. signature

untersuchen (*oon-tuhR-zew-Huhn*) to examine

Untertasse (*oon-tuhR-tA-suh*) f. saucer

Unterwäsche (*oon-tuhR-väh-shuh*) f. underwear

V

Vater (*fah-tuhR*) m. father

vergessen (*feR-ge-suhn*) to forget

verkaufen (*feR-kou-fuhn*) to sell

Verkehr{em}(*feR-keyR*) m. traffic

verletzen (sich) (*ziH feyR-le-tsuhn*) to injure oneself

verlieren (*feR-lee-Ruhn*) to lose

Vermittlung (*feR-mit-loong*) f. operator

versprechen (*feR-shpRe-Huhn*) to promise

verstehen (*feR-shtey-uhn*) to understand

versuchen (*feR-zew-Huhn*) to try

viel (*feel*) a lot of

vielleicht (*fee-layHt*) maybe

voll (*fol*) full

Vollkornbrot (*fol-koRn-bRoht*) n. wholegrain bread

von (*fon*) from

vor (*fohR*) in front of

vorgestern (*foR-ges-tuhRn*) day before yesterday

Vorspeise (*foR-shpay-zuh*) f. appetizer

W–X–Y

wachsen (*vak-suhn*) to grow

wählen (*väh-luhn*) to dial a phone, to choose

wahr (*vahR*) true

wann (*vAn*) when

Wand (*vAnt*) f. wall

wandern (*vAn-duhRn*) to hike

warm (*vahRm*) warm

Warnung (*vAR-noong*) f. warning

warten (*vAR-tuhn*) to wait

warum (*vah-Rum*) why

was (*vAs*) what

waschen (*vah-shuhn*) to wash

Wasser (*va-suhR*) n. water

Wechselgeld (*vek-suhl-gelt*) n. change (coins)

wechselhaft (*vek-sel-hAft*) changeable

Wechselkurs (*vek-suhl-kooRs*) m. exchange rate

Wecker (*ve-kuhR*) m. alarm clock

Wein (*vayn*) m. wine

weinen (*vay-nuhn*) to cry

weiß (*vays*) white

Weißbrot (*vays-bRoht*) n. white bread

weiter.gehen (*vay-tuhR-gey-uhn*) to go on

welch- (*vel-HuhR*) which

wenig (*vey-niH*) little/not much

weniger (*vey-nee-guhR*) less/fewer

wer (*veyR*) who

werden (*veR-duhn*) to become

Wetter (*ve-tuhR*) n. weather

wichtig (*viH-tiH*) important

wie (*vee*) how

wie lange (*vee lAn-guh*) how long

wie viel (*vee feel*) how much

Wildleder (*vilt-ley-duhR*) n. suede

Wind (*vint*) m. wind

Winter (*vin-tuhR*) m. winter

Wirbelsäule (*viR-buhl-zoy-luh*) f. spine

wissen (*vi-suhn*) to know a fact

wo (*voh*) where

Woche (*vo-CHuh*) f. week

wöchentlich (*vö-Hent-liH*) weekly

woher (*voh-heR*) from where

wohin (*voh-hin*) where (to)

wohnen (*voh-nuhn*) to reside

Wohnung (*voh-noong*) f. apartment

Wohnzimmer (*vohn-tsi-muhr*) n. living room

Wolle (*vo-luh*) f. wool

wollen (*vo-luhn*) to want, desire

Wurst (*vooRst*) f. sausage

wüschen (*vün-shuhn*) to wish

Z

Zahn (*tsahn*) m. tooth

Zahnarzt/Zahnärztin (*tsahn-ARtst/tsahn-äRtst-in*) m./f. dentist

Zahnbürste (*tsahn-büR-stuh*) f. toothbrush

Zeh (*tsey*) m. toe

zeichnen (*tsayH-nuhn*) to draw

zeigen (*tsay-guhn*) to show, to indicate

Zeit (*tsayt*) f. time

Zeitschrift (*tsayt-shRift*) f. magazine

Zeitung (*tsay-toong*) f. newspaper

Zeug (*tsoyk*) n. thing

Zickzack (*tsik-tsAk*) m. zigzag

ziehen (*tsee-uhn*) to pull

ziemlich (*tseem-liH*) quite

Zimmer (*tsi-muhR*) n. room

Zitrone (*tsi-troh-nuh*) f. lemon

zu (*tsew*) to

zu viel (*tsew feel*) too much

zu wenig (*tsew vey-niH*) too little

Zucker (*tsoo-kuhR*) m. sugar

Zug (*tsewk*) m. train

Zunge (*tsoon-guh*) f. tongue

zusammen   (*tsew-zA-muhn*) together

Zwiebel   (*tsvee-buhl*) f. onion

zwischen   (*tsvi-shuhn*) between

Index

U–V

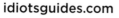

WARRANTY LIMITS

READ THE ENCLOSED AGREEMENT
AND THIS LABEL BEFORE OPENING
AUDIO PACKAGE.